International studies in t
series editor *J. A. Mangan*

Sport and the English middle classes

1870–1914

Sport and the English middle classes 1870–1914

John Lowerson

MANCHESTER UNIVERSITY PRESS
Manchester and New York

Distributed exclusively in the USA and Canada by St. Martin's Press

Copyright © John Lowerson 1993, 1995

Published by Manchester University Press
Oxford Road, Manchester M13 9NR, UK
and Room 400, 175 Fifth Avenue, New York, NY 10010, USA

Distributed exclusively in the USA and Canada
by St. Martin's Press, Inc., 175 Fifth Avenue, New York,
NY 10010, USA

British Library Cataloguing-in-Publication Data
A catalogue record for this book is available from the British Library

Library of Congress Cataloging-in-Publication Data applied for

ISBN 0 7190 4651 3 *paperback*

Paperback edition published 1995

Printed in Great Britain
by Biddles Ltd, Guildford and King's Lynn

Contents

Tables

Series Editor's foreword

John Lowerson brings a sharp mind and a graceful style to that most important of English late Victorian and Edwardian activities – recreation.

The period from 1870 to 1914, he suggests in a delightful phrase, was characterised by the Scramble for Sport.

Lowerson smoothly weaves five thematic threads, highly significant to the future social evolution of the English, indeed the international, community, into a tightly knit interpretative cloth: 'active recreation' as a significant criterion for social demarcation, the emergence of athletic entrepreneurship on a large scale, the development of new notions of disposable assets (notably time, space and income), the creation of the habit of voluntaryism and finally the establishment of a new breadth and depth of social involvement.

In another striking expression Lowerson describes the period as that of the Great Sports Craze. And while he carefully notes continuities and discontinuities, he sees the 'Craze', in my view quite rightly, as representing a sharp historical disjunction. Only now are social historians beginning to recognise the full ideological, political, economic and cultural implications of this recreational disjunction for the modern world in the second half of the twentieth century – the Age of the Second Recreational Revolution.

Patterns for the future throughout the entire technological world were spun out of the five English late Victorian and Edwardian social threads Lowerson traces so well. In describing and analysing these threads, both painstakingly and subtly, he fills a social historical vacuum and makes a notable contribution to the major purposes of this series: the incorporation of sport within conventional historical debate about *inter alia* ideologies, social control, social structures, stratification and mobility, and the setting of sport in its full cultural context.

J. A. Mangan

Preface

This book began with my exasperation at finding virtually no second-ary works on the development of golf as an activity for the inhabitants of the growing resorts of the late Victorian decades. I soon came to realise that there were parallel phenomena which both explained the boom in golfing and opened up new lines for investigation. So the work widened rapidly into a more general study of the active recreations of the middle classes of a relatively raw industrial and urban society. As my research progressed I found some similar works appearing on working-class sports and rather rarer monographs on particular aspects of middle-class life. Most notable among the latter was Dr Mangan's study of public school athleticism. It is given its due credit in the text.

In this work I focus on a social class (or classes) and its members and the extent to which sport became an agent of their development and an instrument of their self-definition. It does not aim to be a 'Making of the English Middle Classes'; rather it examines a significant part of that making. With rare exceptions it concentrates on the *English* rather than the *British*. This results from no misplaced sense of patriotism. To have included the so-called Celts would have lengthened it considerably. It is also very masculine in its subject, and not all feminist historians are likely to approve of the place I have given to women's sport (see Chapter 7). But they offer their own special pleading elsewhere. There is much regional material in this book; there is much more yet to be exploited by scholars. This is a summary and a pointer rather than a last word – such are the joys of relativity in modern historical scholarship.

I could not have written the book without a considerable amount of support and help. If someone is missed in the list which follows, my deepest apologies. I owe a great deal to my colleagues in History and Continuing Education at the University of Sussex, who have given me time and advice without limit. I am grateful to the university for two periods of paid leave which allowed fieldwork and the bulk of the writing to be done. The British Academy, the Twenty-Seven Foundation and the university gave generous financial help with travel and accommodation.

The archivists of East and West Sussex, Bristol, Devon, Leeds, Lincolnshire, Northamptonshire, Reading, Walthamstow and Warwickshire, and the PRO were all more than helpful. I am especially grateful to the secretary of Leeds Golf Club for his help and advice and to the officials of the Cruising Association, the Humber Yawl Club, the Alpine Club and the Salmon and Trout Association for theirs. The staffs of the libraries of Brighton, Bristol, Exeter, Hull, Leamington Spa, Leeds, Lincoln, Newcastle-upon-Tyne, Northampton, Reading, Sheffield and Worthing did much fetching, carrying and copying, as did those of the Registrar of Companies and the various branches of the British Library. Without the London Library it is difficult to see how great parts of the work could have been done – so much of the sports stock of the British Library seems to have been lost through bomb damage. John Jaques & Co. and Hardy's of Alnwick gave advice on records and their lack.

Anyone working in this field now would be lost without the help of the British Society for Sports History. To Tony Mangan, Richard Cox, Richard Holt, Tony Mason, Russell Potts, Wray Vamplew, Jack Williams, Gareth Williams, Beryl Furlong and others I owe a great deal. The same applies to Jean Lindsay, Helen Walker, Ruth Richardson, Carol Dyhouse, Norman Vance, Alun Howkins, Chris Wrigley, Fred Gray and all those others who have sent me references, titbits and sound advice. Jinny and Simon Briant coped remarkably with my appalling handwriting. But is to my family that I owe most, and this book is dedicated to them as an apology for those many lost hours and absences which they have supported so well.

Note

Except where stated, throughout the notes at the end of each chapter, the place of publication of all printed works is London.

Chapter 1
A class at play

Half a century ago the travel entrepreneur Arnold Lunn claimed that 'Sport has to mature like old brandy before the academic historian will condescend to note its existence.'[1] If sport is still maturing historians are catching it up rapidly. The growth in leisure studies in the early 1970s focused strongly on the apparent discontinuity between industrial society and its predecessors; central were the rise of social sensibilities, ordered and rational recreations, and the bureaucratisation and commercialisation of facilities. Leisure seemed to offer a convenient battleground for an assumed conflict between economic puritanism and earthy folkways, with the former's eventual victory. A swing away from this view was perhaps inevitable, with a reiteration of continuity. But the historians' search for heroic survivals has now threatened to smoothe the face of social history into one great plain, throwing away the sharp disjunctures.[2]

One such break occupied the last third of Victoria's reign and the decade of her son's. In the forty-four years after 1870 the English middle classes discovered sport and surprised themselves with their enthusiasms. Sport became embroiled in the sophistication of a class society anxious to define its own position in a world of very raw newness. In late Victorian society the idea of 'elite' sports acquired a breadth of meaning unknown either in its rural antecedents or to the industrial middle classes of mid-century. Some older recreations grew, but their scale was generally modest by comparison with the invention and diffusion of new ways of filling spare time with physical activity. Most obvious for the latter, especially lawn tennis and golf, was the formalisation of rules and the provision of organising structures common to almost all sports in the period. We are currently passing through the decades of centenary celebrations which produce so many tantalising, frustrating and banal catalogues of achievement for each body founded in those years.[3]

1

Late Vic sports booms
Overlapping

① Sport marks Social closure
② Running of venue
③ Re-thinking of time, space + income
④ Voluntaryism
⑤ Increased choice

Sport and the English middle classes

To call this a boom is justified, although it was actually a series of overlapping booms with some considerable fluctuations in popularity between different activities. We shall examine those in detail in later chapters; the main thrust here is to provide some understanding of why it happened at all. A century later what comes across most strongly is the sense of a vacuum's existing, or being created, and then being filled with a haphazard jumble of responses. Yet there were common strands of experience and demand. Pleasure was eventually as suffused with fervour as the moral earnestness conventionally ascribed to the Victorian Social Gospel. On to the great mid-century virtues of Work, Punctuality, Thrift and Respectability was grafted a sports ethic, although it often comes across as rather specious pleading provoked by a sense of guilt at not being either at work, study or prayer, let alone being at home. There are times when it seems as if, having created the workshop of the world with great effort, the middle classes felt a collective need for a rest and turned with typical earnestness to modes of filling time which often had all the charm of monastic self-mortification.[4]

Through this book five themes in particular will run and interweave, as the keys to this scramble for sport. Firstly, it was a society in which social differentiation had become sufficiently complex and mature to allow active recreations to become significant criteria of demarcation. Secondly, the establishment of sports in wholesale *popular* but not *mass* terms made them an arena for entrepreneurship in the shift towards a service economy which has attracted argument ever since. In turn this was a response to redeveloped or new notions about disposable assets, principally time, space and income, among certain social groups. Although it offered opportunities for venture capitalism, sport's fourth asset was that it encouraged extensive voluntaryism in its participants. Self-initiation, self-control and so on were alternatives not so much to any state intervention, that traditional bogey of Victorian individualism, as paradoxically to the commercialism which generated so much of the disposable income.

Finally, the late Victorian sports boom provided comprehensiveness and variety for a wider range of ages and physical capacities than had previously been possible. It also catered for all weathers and seasons and, perhaps most important, for a very wide spectrum of incomes. Even at the bottom levels these could be marked off from the tastes and opportunities of the working classes whilst still providing a number of targets for aspirations.

2

It would be crudely deterministic to assume that any of the participants, with the possible exception of the entrepreneurs, actually sat down and articulated these considerations before deciding which activity to pursue and when. But we shall see that such issues permeated the whole period, accentuating a pattern of change where the overt consumption of active leisure pursuits made paradoxically for the strengthening of implicit, often shadily sketched, codes of values.

Continuities

Of discontinuity there was plenty. But there was also considerable continuity, of building on earlier periods of expansion offering, particularly in the 'manly sports', an ethical framework. This often had to be bent in some peculiar ways to fit the activities of the late Victorian decades, offering a ready target for lampoon. The beginning of the great sports craze, marked perhaps by the invention of lawn tennis in 1874, matched the peaking of the cult of public school athleticism so brilliantly described by Dr Mangan.[5] 'Peaking', with its sense of imminent decline, is perhaps the wrong word; if a gently rising plateau is possible, it had been reached by the 1870s. The Eton wall game and the far more important spread of rugby football, albeit with many in-school variations, occupied a fairly narrow central area which was rapidly taken up in the new schools outside the great nine of the Clarendon Commission, the Marlboroughs, Wellingtons and so on. The calculated ease with which E. M. Forster's unpleasant schoolmaster, Herbert Pembroke, in *The Longest Journey* (1907) added to his burgeoning 'public' school the paraphernalia of athleticism aroused a later liberal cynicism which few similar academic entrepreneurs could have felt.

Dr Mangan has gone on to identify the process of diffusion in post-Taunton Commission grammar schools and the slow emergence of physical education training. This encouraged Kipling's 'muddied oafs and flannelled fools' to move with some effort but limited thought through a sporting life which began on school rugger fields in the 1860s, continued in a Cambridge or Oxford college after the days of Leslie Stephen and returned, if not to their own school, at least to a not-too-pale imitation. There, wrapped in blues or college colours, they could roar exhortations at their successors.[6] But this cult appealed largely to a restricted age group. It was offset partly by the annual

3

bursts of nostalgia and identifying with sides to which most people could never actually have belonged that have continued to accompany the Boat Race and the Oxford–Cambridge match at Twickenham.

More deep-rooted but still adopted as tools of educational reform were the semi-rural games, cricket pre-eminently, encouraging local patriotism and an appeal to quintessential (i.e. rural) values as disenchantment with some of the nastier features of urban society grew. Reforming parsons of the 1850s from such different segments of the Church as John Keble and Charles Kingsley had used a reformed cricket to bond their parishes and narrow the gateways to disorder.[7] The pan-class, deferential nature of much village cricket survived unabated or was often introduced where it had not existed before. But it also offered, through elite associative groups like I Zingari (founded 1845), an avenue to exclusive play overlapping with school and collegiate structures. Newbolt's classical hymn to manly sport, *Vitai Lampada*, in which duty overcomes failure in a final desperate effort, was hardly a suitable model for any form of planned development. Yet from its setting in a cricket match in an aspiring public school it offered just as much a dislocation with the sporting past as did many of the newer games.[8]

Greater continuities could be found in the field sports, most noticeably fox-hunting, which had allowed some access to gentrihood and whose maintenance demanded an increasing flexibility of membership to allow the activities to be maintained at all. Anthony Trollope observed a 'democratisation' of the hunting field by 1867:

> The non-hunting world is apt to think that hunting is confined to country gentlemen, farmers, and rich strangers: but anyone who will make himself acquainted with the business and life of the men whom he sees around himself in an average hunting field will find that there are in the crowd attorneys, country bankers, doctors, apothecaries – the profession of medicine has a special aptitude for fox-hunting – maltsters, millers, butchers, bakers, innkeepers, auctioneers, graziers, builders, retired officers, judges home from India, barristers who take weekly holidays, stockbrokers, newspaper editors, artists and sailors.[9]

These were, however, groups which had existed across the fringes of rural hierarchies since the Tudor period. The 'new' middle classes – manufacturers, new professionals and all who manned the superstructures of the new Victorian cities, Manchester, Birmingham and so on – were conscious of building a new society until well past mid-century. Committed sabbatarians, they worked as many hours on weekdays as possible. The dictum of the elder Edward Baines, founder of the *Leeds Mercury* dynasty (the 'Bainesocracy'), that one should live on half one's income and save the rest, scarcely allowed of disposable income's being used for expensive pleasure. Nonetheless he rounded off his namesake son's dissenting academy education with a Grand Tour that allowed young Edward to walk over Alpine passes. [10] But Edward Baines Junior's contemporaries (he lived 1800–90) and his own sons grew up in a world where, although running and other physical games were available, they were largely unstructured and 'sports' were very much versions of northern village athletics, modified to take out the rougher elements of drink and violence. Their early manhood was more likely to be devoted to the burgeoning opportunities for 'self-improvement' and 'rational' recreation, Literary and Philosophical Societies and Mechanics' Institutes, which rarely ever reached those for whom they were intended.[11]

In the more prosperous reaches of this expanding urban middle class the emphasis was on conformity and social leadership by example rather than by inherited authority; at the lower aspirant levels it inspired the groups for which Smiles produced *Self Help* in 1859. It was a stratum of society suspicious of much of the older elite and fearful of its employees, the working classes. Wray Vamplew has reminded us firmly that the growth of horse-racing, attractive to both those groups, was virtually without middle-class support.[12] When the new groups turned belatedly to sport it was to those games in which ethical purity could be most happily maintained or the inner self tested, such as golf.

By the mid-1860s the point had been reached when the middle classes were responsive to a further change. The cult of athleticism came together with other factors to allow for the first of the interlocking booms. What began as an instrument for containing the potentially disruptive powers of youth was extended as a means of training for future roles. Through emphasising collective responsibility it provided social bonding which supported younger men as they moved towards positions of influence. When an emphasis on relaxation emerged it offered an escape route from its serious antecedents. The core of the new society had been created; sport allowed the fringes to be polished.

New men

The key problem at this point is how this new clientele can be identified, and with how much precision. Whilst various estimates are possible of the overall size of the middle classes and their component groups at different late Victorian points, these only indicate the widest possible constituencies for take-up. It is virtually impossible to give any reasonably accurate estimate of the total number involved in the sports boom. There are broad indicators of the growth patterns of particular sports, to be covered in later chapters, but the likelihood of overlapping individual enthusiasms, either seasonal or in serial participation as life progressed, makes an overall estimate hazardous. Sports have never owed very much of their development, at least before the days of the Central Council for Physical Recreation (founded 1935) and the Sports Council (founded 1972) to forward projections of participation as a percentage of a given market.

Harold Perkin has placed some 1,500,000 families in the broad 'middle classes' by 1867. Guy Routh has offered a possible 2,500,000 families in the same general categories by 1914. Musgrove has offered a wider constituency, from 1,699,000 families in 1881 to 2,869,000 in 1911. W. J. Reader has estimated a 50 per cent growth in middle-class numbers during a period when general population growth was 39 per cent.[13] Estimates like this identify or group, but only in the grossest possible terms. A 'rising middle class' *in toto* only offers us a vacuum into which activities and ascriptions can be pumped; evenly distributed, they would be spread far too thinly to have any real impact.

So far we have used the structural concept 'classes' rather than ascribing any sense of identity in terms that E. P. Thompson might favour.[14] The very nature of occupational definition causes problems in establishing middle-class roles as either innovators or consumers of sports. Clearly there were large areas of class concentration, particularly in the new suburbs of late Victorian cities, most obviously in London. Mitcham and Croydon had their Midland and northern equivalents in Birmingham's Edgbaston or Leeds's Headingley. But many members of the new middle classes were not packaged with quite such geographical neatness; their role lay in the upper social reaches of smaller and established country towns. This in itself offers a sharp warning about identifying

6

the sports craze of a maturing industrial society with its cities alone. Many market towns had lawn tennis and golf clubs well before the larger settlements, and there is little to be gained by assuming or attempting to reconstruct any progressive diffusion into zones outside the metropolitan centres. As Dr Bale has shown, regional variations in growth must modify considerably any crude attempt at linking sports with simple class/occupational urban patterns.[15]

Yet we have to come back to the key role of certain parts of the middle classes. Either as leaders of fashions or because of broadly common professional and commercial bonds or similarities in life styles and aspirations they exercised a central importance in the spread of sport. In contemporary literature or in club records they appear too frequently to be lumped into an amorphous catch-all of class. We shall now examine some of those groups briefly.

Although the fashion for certain sports was not based solely on a model of downward diffusion through social/income brackets, such diffusion did sometimes take place. Wealthy individuals, largely with 'new' money, enjoyed an ambivalent place in the strengthening of older sports and the popularisation of newer pursuits because of their place at an awkward hinge point, between the upper middle classes and the older landed ones. Lawrence Stone's recent attempt to suggest

Table 1 **Selected professional occupations, England and Wales, 1891–1911**

Profession	Actual numbers (male)		± %
	1891	1911	
Accountants	7,930	9,480	+19.5
Actors	3,625	9,076	+150
Architects	7,825	8,914	+13
Auctioneers and house agents	11,740	17,623	+50
Authors, editors, journalists	5,111	12,030	+135
Barristers, solicitors	19,978	21,380	+7
Civil engineers	9,605	7,208	−24
Clergy (Anglican)	24,232	23,918	−1.3
Dentists	4,628	7,424	+60
Medicine (surgeons, GPs)	18,936	22,922	+21
Total	113,610	139,975	+23

that the English landed elite was less open to newcomers than has usually been argued finishes just as our period of boom is taking off but there is more than adequate evidence to suggest an enhanced role for a semi-landed plutocracy around the turn of the century. Dr Rubinstein has shown in a number of studies how the bulk of the late nineteenth-century wealthy, in his rather limited terms, came either from established landed families or from financial rather than manufacturing roots. But he missed a large group whose role in spreading new forms of consumption was probably seminal.[16]

Given the English talent for understatement, this group is perhaps better described as the 'new comfortable' rather than the 'new rich'. Its members are best seen in the thirty-two volumes published by Pike of Brighton, picture profiles of 'county society' reinforced by a smattering of this new elite; it was, understandably, strongest in the Home Counties.[17] Although a number of these people had bought landed estates, most purchased only a house and pleasure gardens, often building in a derived vernacular style. Within this group of several thousand in the counties surrounding London was a wide mix. Some were undoubtedly *rentiers* but many combined some continued professional activity, in the City or the law, with a semi-gentry life style. Their social reference point was that of the gentry but their landed pattern was often closer to a suitably modified yeomanry.

On the lines of such fictional models as the Forsytes, Wilcoxes or the anthropomorphised Mr Badger in *The Wind in the Willows* their aim was escape from the city towards a carefully synthesised rural innocence:

> Since he has possessed it, the house has been greatly improved and has been made exceedingly comfortable, while the grounds possess a beauty which suggest Arcadia. Amid these ideal surroundings Sir Henry [Harben] finds that rest and peace so necessary to a mind and body occupied with great business affairs, for is not the owner of Warnham Lodge President of that stupendous concern the Prudential Assurance Company?[18]

Harben was a major reviver of Sussex cricket. Elsewhere his contemporaries resuscitated flagging hunts or formalised boating on Windermere. Some, like Harben, moved rapidly into landed society, acquiring the commission of the peace and deputy lieutenantships, but many lesser men and their wives needed to create social bonding at a relatively new level and, for them, lawn tennis, golf and yachting with their social peripheries offered major attractions. Because their

8

semi-rural life came with the prosperity of middle age the men were a natural market for sports which were less strenuous than some of the classical forms.

Included in this group but with a wider social base were those 'of independent means', the *rentiers*. In theory a society moving towards a major investment role should have produced a major *rentier* sector but a number of *caveats* need to be entered. The fall in prices after the 1880s and general low levels of interest, with 5 per cent as quite high, meant that only those with very large share or property holdings would have much disposable income. The number in this group fluctuated. In 1871 some 25,510 men were returned as of 'independent means'. The figure rose to 97,466 by 1891 but had fallen back sharply to 52,432 by 1911.[19] The other major problem is quite simple, viz. the lack of clear information about actual levels of wealth within this group. Probably far more important in yielding capital for sports entrepreneurship and increasing levels of disposable income was the spread of shareholding which supplemented earned income.

One group benefiting particularly from this trend was that of stockbrokers and jobbers. Despite the relatively strict conditions of Stock Exchange membership, concerned largely with financial probity, there was a huge expansion during the key twenty years of the sporting boom, 1891–1911; the censuses show a rise in the number of male bill discounters and brokers from 990 to 3,183 over the two decades. Notwithstanding the London Exchange's working a six-day week for much of the period its members managed to achieve key roles in the popularisation of sport. The extent of this becomes apparent with even the most cursory glance at the volumes of *The House on Sport*, published in aid of charity by various brokers.[20]

This wealthy group was hardly large enough to sustain anything but the most exclusive and expensive of elite sports such as game-shooting and yachting. It was to professional men that the key demand may be traced. They provided a body of moderately prosperous young middle-aged men whose social ambiguity and need to extend bonding with actual and potential clients made the organisation of sports clubs a potent factor in most communities. The very nature of their work often allowed some of it to be conducted in relatively informal surroundings. Some, such as Anglican clergymen (generally with declining incomes) had fairly well established boundaries at the beginning of the booms. Others showed quite remarkable shifts, as table 1 shows, using a fairly loose definition of 'professional'.[21]

Although the overall increase is hardly staggering, it should be set against the increase in the male population for the period – some 8 per cent. The key lies less in aggregates, however, than in the social influence these groups could wield locally, particularly where there were large groups of commuters. As important in terms of the regional bias of certain elite sports is the residential weighting towards the south-east. Of the above occupations 44.5 per cent lived or worked in London or its surrounding counties of Berkshire, Buckinghamshire, Essex, Hertfordshire, Kent, London, Middlesex, Surrey and Sussex, all containing Edwardian commuter zones. If the Anglican clergy are discounted because of the relative evenness of parochial distribution the figure rises to 47.8 per cent. Since the proportion of the occupied male population in the same counties was only 28 per cent of the national total, the balance in favour of the professional groups is obvious. The highest proportions, 56 per cent of authors and 51 per cent of engineers, were matched by our earlier group, discounters, some 55 per cent. Although the overall group in the south-east, 59,419 (excluding Anglican clergy and discounters) was small compared with the overall regional population of 10,355,422 (0.5 per cent of the total, or 1.2 per cent of the area's male population) it was its concentration of wealth and interest that mattered.

We have had to use 'profession' relatively loosely to establish this pattern. Within its members a growing core had experienced a minor public school and university education, with its infusion of athleticism, continued through into societies attached to the Inns of Court and so on. In the provinces the groupings were often less formal, and many aspirants to the newer professions probably relied more on local clubs as their own compensators. The more expensively trained percolated into local life through their occupational roles – muscular curates, for instance, were by no means confined to running clubs and teams for the lower orders, and they did much to popularise cricket. Doctors, from a wider range of professional training, appeared frequently as leaders in local sporting organisations, not least because of a growing emphasis on recuperative and preventive treatment for which they needed to provide models themselves. Well before Rotary International was founded in Chicago in 1905 sport was one area where overlapping professional and commercial interests in local hierarchies were cemented, demonstrated and exploited.

elite m/c leaders
but also
l/m/c

But this group, however influential as leaders, could not have sustained the level of the sports craze even if a majority of its members had been highly committed. Beyond the elite lay a much larger target for growth, a mass in relative terms, rarely innovators but containing many aspirants and consumers. This is that problematic body, the 'lower middle class'. Dr Crossick's major work has established its general social parameters.[22] Our concern here is with two of its components, the men most likely to 'play the game' in wider social terms. Firstly, the army of commercial and professional expansion had as its main troops a vast body of *clerks* clerks; their numbers expanded by 62 per cent between 1891 and 1911, from 319,721 to 519,289. Matching them largely in terms of *Teachers* income and life style if not in numbers were male teachers, who increased by 35 per cent in the same period, to a total of 68,670. Clearly, both groups contained a considerable range of experience if only because of the vagueness of the job description. But all were targets for the means of establishing the minor differentials so important because they could rarely afford the geographical distancing which suburban sprawl made possible for the higher reaches of the middle classes. C. F. G. Masterman's dictum of 1909, 'The rich despise the Working People, the Middle Classes fear them,' was exaggerated, and certainly one which some 'respectable' sports clubs in bowls and fishing would go far to modify, yet it revealed the urgent general need to erect and strengthen social barriers where possible.[23]

Petty snobbery and timid hopes linked by a social code of unsubtle restriction are images traditionally associated with the Edwardian lower middle class. Literature has done a great deal to furnish this caricature. The quintessential desperation of Forster's Leonard Bast welded to the hinted insecurity of Mr Pooter and the comically heroic banalities of Well's Hoopdriver ('how little he was noticeable') emerged from the writers' frustration with the apparent simplicity of their subjects' world pictures.[24] In more serious, if less effective, terms the clerk could be portrayed as seething with a barely suppressed impatience at his imprisonment:

> Four grey walls and a dusky ceiling,
> And over my head the tired flies wheeling,
> A window grimed by a hundred winters,
> An ink-smudged desk with the ledge in splinters;
> And the scratch-scratch-scratch of the nibs is madding,

And I'm sick and shamed of this cursed adding;
I! to be chained to this office dreary
With the blood of my veins of sea and prairie . . .

[Harold Begbie[25]]

Arcadianism marched hand-in-hand with a desperate need for adventure. The gymnastic, bowls and cycling societies, the home practising with Indian clubs, appear as incongruous and inadequate surrogates for these urges but they probably provided a more realistic appreciation of what was possible for such dreamers. Aspiring to greater middle-class heights had to be tempered by a hard realization of what was socially and economically feasible. Although social differentiation received through this group its most acute polishing and delineation, there was a very real sense in which, in the common late Victorian division of 'the classes and the masses', it fell into the latter.

Linking these poles of the new society, bonding them, offering both a 'solid middle class' and a penumbra for it, was a group that saw equally rapid growth – that of 'tradesmen', dealers and shopkeepers. These increased by 38 per cent in the twenty years before 1911, from 27,984 to 38,697. By taking the male figures only we can exclude to a considerable extent the host of small corner shops whose owner/managers were often the wives of artisans. The range is tremendous, from Selfridge's and Harrod's to the general emporia and drapers of market towns, a range far too great to allow an easy assumption of overwhelmingly common experiences and interest. There are too few local studies to provide any very firm ground for assessing interaction. Yet, as Michael Winstanley has shown, they provided a filling for all the bastions of late Victorian respectability: churches and chapels, choral societies, chambers of commerce, political parties and, eventually, sports organisations.[26] The more prestigious often enjoyed a significant role as innovators, particularly as the Early Closing movement after the 1870s posed the problem of finding socially acceptable leisure behaviour for the released shop assistants, order boys and so on. In Hull it led belatedly to the founding of the Hull Tradesmen's Athletic Association in 1908, dominated by the town's large grocers.[27]

Cost and clients

Membership of a class in itself was a base for identifying with new activities. But disposable income also played a major part in their uptake. Within the possible clientele for sports we have identified the actual range of income was far greater than that of the much larger working classes. Using either Routh's or Crossick's estimates for the lower middle class as a base line, gross personal income ranged from just over £100 to several thousands. Both Stamp and Hamish Fraser have demonstrated that the number of income tax payers (i.e. those earning over £160 per annum) rose from 280,000 in 1860 to 1,190,000 by 1913, with an inevitable catchment of a lower social range.[28] Yet the average annual income of the latter cohort was as high as £838, and that at a point when Routh puts an average solicitor's income at £568, a general practitioner's at £395, a teacher's at £154 and a business clerk's at £96. With low housing costs, generally reckoned at about 12 per cent of gross income, and falling real food prices boosted by imperial resources, the level of disposable income for even the lowest middle-class groups allowed a wide range of leisure choice.

Household budgets at different levels are notoriously difficult to establish. Such patterns as might be culled from Mrs Beeton and similar writers are more valuable as models for aspirants than as indicators of overall patterns. It is almost impossible to determine the actual levels of middle-class income devoted to sport, although we shall examine in chapter 8 the significance of some Edwardian calculations of percentages of the gross national product, as well as of annual aggregates of sporting expenditure. Except in the most affluent of bachelor households or the most ruthlessly patriarchal of the married, the male head's personal outgoings on sport must have been modified by the demands both for family holidays and for piano lessons.[29] Sport must always have been in tension with other forms of domestic leisure. For instance, burgeoning suburbia was strongly identified with gardening; its most committed form, membership of the Royal Horticultural Society, rose from 2,500 in 1894 to 14,500 in 1914.[30]

One way in which the choice of sport was clearly determined was by cost. Most men probably came to a sport through relatives or friends but it became possible for the as yet uncommitted searcher to work out what it would cost him. As the boom matured it produced a literature of calculation, a shopping list for activities, although many basic manuals for individual sports were surprisingly coy about expenditure. The key work in this genre was F. G. Aflalo's *The Cost of Sport*, published in 1899.[31] Aflalo collected a team of experts to cover a number of activities. Because of the demands of different

13

sports and the very varied interpretation of their brief the work did not produce a gradation equating social desirability with cost. Some sports which boomed subsequently, such as bowls, were not included. Nonetheless, it is possible to establish some likely annual costs for a moderately active sportsman, excluding equipment and clothing purchase (table 2).

The implications for individual sports will be dealt with elsewhere in this book but, cycling and yachting apart, many of the costs were kept down to these levels by the operation of clubs or syndicates. To take the most popular of the boom sports by the time Aflalo's book appeared, golf, anyone with £300 or less a year would be spending close to 10 per cent of his income, a hefty budgetary commitment. Whilst other considerations for sports such as rowing continued to reinforce the notion of elites it was hard cash which created boundaries beyond which some hopefuls could not go. Diffusion did eventually reduce some costs, most noticeably where municipalities became involved with lawn tennis and golf; one Edwardian commentator estimated that an artisan could play golf for £5 a year.[32] That peculiar English middle-class euphemism 'modest means' made frequent appearances in the two decades before 1914 as a number of writers attempted to prove rather heroically that even hunting could become a middle middle-class pursuit.

Table 2 **Annual cost of sporting activity** c. 1899 (£)

Activity	Annual cost
Shooting preserved game	500–600
Angling:	
Salmon	30–1,000
Trout	20+
Coarse	10+
Hunting	100+
Rowing	10+
Yacht racing	200+
'Modest' yachting	50+
Norfolk Broads sailing	7–8 a fortnight
Golf	20–30
Lawn tennis	10
Cycling	5–10
Alpine mountaineering	50

What is important is the extent to which participation in some form of 'sport' became possible for a widening middle-class constituency around 1900. Even at this restrained level, let alone with the wide range possible in such a cover-all game as golf, expenditure on sport had the major value of being conspicuous, a symbol of arrival and acceptance. Although it was predominantly male, and women experienced considerable difficulty in participating in many sports (see chapter 7), there was an undoubted boost to social tone where they did win acceptance, not least because sport provided an area outside home and church where a husband's or father's relative prosperity could be demonstrated vicariously.

Time and space

Money was only one component of class identity in sport. It was effectively inseparable from another major item of consumption, disposable time. This proved a thorny issue where sport-dedicated time clashed with other expectations of middle-class behaviour. The most significant problem was its demands on potential working hours as sport spread outside annual holiday periods into regular seasonal and weekly enjoyment. Participation usually involved travelling as well as the time needed for play; a round of golf could take three hours, most field sports needed a whole day, coastal cruising at least two. The traditional gentry sports overlapped seasonally throughout the year, allowing shifts in participation compatible with the productive needs of a rural society. Many of the newer late Victorian sports such as lawn tennis or dinghy racing had clear seasonal limits but some provided an overlap (lawn tennis in summer, badminton in winter). Others, especially golf, became virtually all-season, most-weather pursuits. This process had to be accommodated with a middle-class working week that in many cases at the beginning of our period was actually little shorter than that of working-class employees. Whilst the liberal professions had traditionally enjoyed a flexible working week many commercial concerns were geared to a six-day week using all the daylight hours.

The much-vaunted and by no means universal manual workers' Saturday half-day of the 1870s did see some white-collar emulation over the next thirty years. Many market town firms adopted a seasonal weekday early closure to allow their male staff to go cycling or play cricket until the peak was reached in such groups as that organised by the Hull Grocers. Further up the social hierarchy by the 1890s many new professional or commercial men were clearly adopting a more flexible approach to their own working hours. For them the role of partnerships and the employment of competent juniors and office managers allowed absences an earlier generation of entrepreneurs would have regarded as unthinkable, often with a not entirely specious justification for business negotiations taking place on a golf course. For the less well placed the extension of sports which could occupy an early summer evening, such as cycling or bowls, marked them out from the working classes, even if only by an hour.

The new sports were land and water-hungry as never before. Hunting and shooting both shared land used primarily for other purposes but the late Victorian pioneers moved relatively quickly towards dedicating space to single purposes. In many areas agricultural depression and farmers' withdrawal from marginal land made this easy and cheap but there were many places in and around the cities where sportsmen came into direct conflict with other, more traditional, users or with competing developers. We shall return to this issue; the key here is the way in which some middle-class bodies established a spatial hegemony, increasing significantly the number of places from which the non-select were excluded.

The sharpest expression of this was in the London suburbs. Contemporary writers of fiction and journalism as well as subsequent historians have drawn attention to the importance of class gradation in late Victorian suburbia, Twickenham, Edgware, Croydon and so on. But, as contributors to F. M. L. Thompson's study of suburbia have shown, class boundaries could never have been too sharply drawn within most such settlements because of their close relationship with speculative returns.[33] Yet some estates prided themselves on their exclusiveness; the development of the St George's Hill estate, combining high-cost housing with lawn tennis and golf facilities, outside Weybridge in Surrey, was probably the most successful of a series of ventures which were prone to over-ambition and failure.

Closer into the cities suburbanites tended to colonise and attempted to monopolise common land, often with resulting legal or physical battles which forced either compromise or a retreat into the ownership of their own controlled territory. The movement towards public parks often recognised the need to cater for the socially marginal groups, the lower middle classes, who could afford neither a legal nor a

proprietorial response to conflict. A variation on this was the deliberate exploitation of sporting demand by the corporations of resorts who
recognised early the importance to general commercial developments
of leisure magnets. Both Roberts and Walton have documented this,
dealing with the pioneering role of Bournemouth, which provided
a golf course in 1894, to be followed by Brighton in 1908.[34] Such
interventionism was, however, rare before the First World War,
although the corporations of both Sheffield and Manchester, hardly
resorts, moved towards recognising artisan aspirants by providing
municipal golf courses.

On the whole, however, it was the inevitable tense interaction
between social exclusiveness and the need for enough width of access
to sustain profit which characterised private enterprise as the main
provider of socially separated space.

Values

The availability and exploitation of money, time and space are not
enough, however, to explain the upsurge in sport. To do this, it
is necessary to identify the values ascribed to it by enthusiasts,
including those less consciously articulated. Their most obvious
worth was to offer non-passive recreation. Late Victorian England
saw a partial transference to selected physical activities of the earnest
values associated a few decades earlier with the more cerebral forms
of rational recreation. Providing a much-needed adjunct to work,
they were initially still defined in terms of it. This utilitarian concern
spread not only to the lower middle classes but into upper groups
seeking to justify their adoption of traditional gentry occupations in
terms other than those of social emulation, tinged with a growing
aestheticism:

> ... in otter hunting, the hounds, the invigorating air of the early
> morning, and the superb beauty of England's valleys and dales constitute
> the chief attractions, and ... the quarry itself is quite a secondary
> consideration.[35]

Apart from the arcadian Englishness the key word in this passage is
'invigorating'. Sport acquired a double value: physical refreshment
was augmented by mental demands which could prove relaxing. As
we saw in Begbie's speaking for the office-bound clerk, brain work,
the keynote of the new professions and their ancillaries in particular,

was increasingly identified with stress. By 1887 in his *Life and Labour* Samuel Smiles claimed:

> Overwork has unfortunately become one of the vices of our age, especially in cities. In business, in learning, in law, in politics, in literature, the pace is somewhat tremendous, and the wear and tear of life becomes excessive. The strain of excitement bears largely on the delicate part of our system.[36]

The growing popular press offered repeated articles on sport's value as therapy. The increased frequency of such claims after 1900 suggests strong guilt at repeated over-indulgence in play and a frantic attempt to fend off growing criticisms that it was less overtly valuable than had been claimed.

As we shall see again in chapter 9, the picture moves into the world of Wiener's challenging thesis on the decline of the English industrial spirit.[37] He argues persuasively, largely from literary sources, that this period saw the deliberate rejection of the urban and industrial culture created by those who depended on its functioning for their life styles and aspirations. The rider which Wiener does not really explore is that these people do not seem to have viewed themselves, with the exception of fringe socialist groups, as agents of entropy. Rather they claimed to operate the system more efficiently by moderating its less humane demands upon their peers. There is one area of this which can be mentioned only briefly. For males sport at all ages offered a refuge not only from work pressures but also from domestic demands and tensions. Little enough is known about domestic gender relations to evaluate this aspect properly here, but it might reasonably be claimed that a significant portion of the more prosperous male population by 1900 no longer found home life a sufficiently adequate complement to the world of work. The idea of the golf or angling 'widow', quite widely current in wittier Edwardian fringe writing on sport, concealed some harsh realities about the ways in which adult men learned to cope with the stresses of marriage by temporary escape routes.[38] Sporting clubs, not necessarily associated with heavy drinking, provided for many middle-class men the *cameraderie* which codes of respectability prevented their finding in the pubs favoured by the working classes.

The main emphasis, however, remained on physical health. Mangan's study of public school athleticism reminds us that sport had a basic instrumental role in reducing the likely spread of infectious disease to which all semi-enclosed institutes are prone.[39] The same applied to Leslie Stephen's efforts as part of the professionalisation of Victorian dons that both Rothblatt and Engel have catalogued, undergraduates being protected from the excesses of study and carousing apparently still inseparable from university life.[40] Outside those seminaries the notion of *in corpore sano* had a hard edge in the conditions of city living. Despite late Victorian sanitary conquests typhoid and consumption could still erupt; the eugenic values of sport attached particularly to female participation will be examined later. Greater importance probably lay in extending a moderated athleticism through the whole age ranges of adulthood and with a growing concern with the physical well-being of the middle-aged, the elderly and the predominantly sedentary. Mocking claims that bowls and its ilk were 'old men's games' concealed their social value, their ascribed properties of life extension. A health-obsessed middle class was offered a general assurance of the desirability of modest exercise, if only to encourage productivity:

> Indeed, to have a hobby of some kind is a necessity of life, and should form quite an incentive to increased industry, in order to have the necessary time and means to indulge in one's fancy.[41]

Occasional warnings of the risks of over-exertion, such as heart disease induced by enthusiastic cycling, only served to reinforce this.[42] General practitioners usually sought more than their own well-being when they became key figures in local sports clubs, and they were well supported by strings of articles on physiology in sports journals. The looser claims that athletic pressures reduced sexual tension or over-indulgence, particularly among bachelors obliged to defer marriage, are less easy to establish, although there were frequent overtones of what some recent writers have tended to dismiss as sexual repression. It is probably beyond historical reconstruction to gauge the extent to which the costs of sport for the married man contributed to the well catalogued decline in late nineteenth-century middle-class family size.[43]

Those who were born found from their preparatory school days that sport assumed a major role as preparation for and carriage through life. Mangan's work has covered this so well that any other historian now runs the serious risk of merely rehashing his ideas. Moral virtues were reinforced by religious teaching, at least for those touched by the Anglicanism of most public schools and their lesser imitators. There is little enough indication as to how far the Dissenting academies went, except where upward mobility in the case of a Congregational foundation like Mill Hill demanded it. Life became a game, not with any frivolous overtones, but in deadly seriousness. Slogans such as 'playing the game' and 'sporting behaviour' were trumpeted loudest and codified most where the British were losing.

For this the sports heroes, Grace, Fry and so on, were essential, to be adored and copied where an earlier age had promoted military leaders such as Wolfe, Nelson and Wellington. The essential selectivity with which these rules were applied can be seen in the Social Darwinism with which lower orders, either English working classes or non-white imperial subjects, were regarded. Dilemmas could occur; Ranjitsinjhi, the cricketing hero of the 1890s, enjoyed the adulation of polite society in England yet belonged to a group, the Indian princes, which was frequently snubbed and ignored by the British rulers of his homeland.[44] But problems like this could be overlooked in the urge to participate in life's games – 'playing the game' meant literally that, often in near-hysterical terms at some points of the imperial adventure. Whilst Lord Lugard and others could disregard the rules with relative impunity when slaughtering Africans they were never more clearly stated than in the fulsome obituaries of those English heroes who died because their own blind adherence to rules was ignored by enemies playing by a different code to secure victory.[45]

The Social Darwinian game was at its most complex, however, on home ground. The peaking of the language of manly virtue coincided roughly with the growth from the 1880s of radical questioning of the simplistic assumptions of utilitarian progress. Despite the role of men like Leslie Stephen, the cult of sport on the whole expressed suspicion of middle-class intellectual interests as well as of the demands of an emerging labour consciousness. Even those who noticed the victims of social injustice tended to offer manly sport as an absolute panacea. C. B. Fry became increasingly involved in the training ship *Mercury* and the Hon. and Revd. Edward Lyttelton, cricketer, headmaster and sports propagandist, wrote of an Eton tailor:

> At one of the windows, about 3 o'clock in the afternoon, may be seen a pale, sad face, which belongs to one of the workmen . . . Now, gentlemen, there are many people who, nowadays, are full of ideas for the amelioration of the condition of a working man like this one. Some would give him higher wages: others seem to propose a transfer to him of his master's

property: others, again, are very anxious that his wife should have a vote. I would give him, if I could, something which would lighten his spirits and lift his own view of life; and that is a good sweat in the open air once a day.[46]

Views like this reiterated sport's place in defining and supporting a class society and reinforcing attitudes which, no doubt, would have shocked the relatively benevolent Lyttelton. It would be wrong to express this solely in terms of inter-class conflict, although restrictive land use, selective club membership and amateur–professional clashes demonstrated it frequently. The prime role was to define boundaries between the broad middle class and its inferiors, and occasionally superiors, and between different status levels within the middle classes. Here the subsequently applied categorisation of 'elite' sports is particularly important, for this was partly a demarcation *within* elites. Some of the sports were broadly shared – athletics and early Association Football in particular – whilst others were more clearly distinguished, often fiercely so, such as polo and lawn tennis. It was a world of border disputes. Participation became an aid to social ascent, a means of providing *stasis* or a very tense equilibrium and, occasionally, of staving off the risk of social descent.

Clubs and symbols

Organisations could be as important as the activities. Clubs in particular provided exclusiveness and a protective role for their members. Here they drew strongly on extant models of voluntaryism such as the rational recreation societies and religious denominations. Studies of power in Victorian cities have often suffered from the expressed utilitarianism of their subjects, council memberships and so on being investigated in terms of party or religious affiliation; sport, it would seem, has been too frivolous for the earnest students of the Victorian city.[47] Yet sport must have reinforced bonds such as these; it would be naive to assume an absolute internal middle-class division between the solemn and the frivolous. The number of councillors on club committees should kill such a view stone-dead. Yet the tightly defined studies of power groups continue to offer far too much compartmentalisation.

There is a considerable place for studies of local networks. One area of major significance to all studies of male Victorian middle-class organisations is Freemasonry, then far more openly recognised than has been the general case since. Yet very few historians have enquired into or penetrated it. In the period 1870–1912 2,329 lodges were founded, bringing the total to 3,630, with the highest annual rates during the Edwardian years. Their memberships must have overlapped with other bodies, and their arcane rituals found many sporting club echoes.[48]

This gave sporting bodies a familiar mode of inception. For the provincial or suburban middle classes in particular the sports club provided that peculiar mixture of oligarchy with apparent democracy which was so strongly defended as an issue of class freedom in urban politics. For the newer sports in the newer areas there was often a very simple model of formation. A few enthusiasts would see the game on holiday or read about it, acquire a few of the necessary implements and a list of rules or a handbook, play it informally until joined by their friends, then hold a 'public' meeting to form a club. This was usually reported in the local press in that classical Victorian euphemism, 'a number of influential gentlemen'; a committee, largely self-appointed, would emerge, premises and ground be leased and a membership list (frequently limited) opened. There would be an entrance fee and subscription, largely determined by estimated running costs.

It was not the actual level of subscription which made for social desirability, since some quite prestigious bodies often imposed modest demands; it was the selection process, of nominating and voting, which was the key. Most club rules contained a blackballing clause. The historian's real difficulty is establishing the extent of its use, since almost all club records list only those who were admitted. Certainly the need to meet costs meant that many of the more popular games had to pursue a relatively open policy; nevertheless, some clubs, like the Hove Select Lawn Tennis Club, cloaked such needs with a very clear assumption of exclusiveness in their name.

Within suburbs and provincial cities there emerged clear hierarchies of clubs, rarely documented but forming an essential reinforcement of the pecking order of an area. Class differentiation was often a matter of local perceptions and of verbal or physical symbolism rather than of the written word. Occasionally, within a broadly similar class grouping, other elements of discrimination could occur. The most powerful was antisemitism. A number of late Victorian large towns had substantial and prosperous Jewish groups whose social integration, whatever the similarity of life styles, remained doubtful. It is rare, however, for the historian to find a letter such as the following, written to the secretary of a provincial golf club just before the First World War: 'We the undersigned [seventeen members] object to any further members of the *Jewish* fraternity being elected to the club.'[49] It is hardly surprising that, as a result of such blatant selectivity, some clubs now have a local reputation for being 'Jewish'.

Whatever the level of membership, social or numerical, the established sports club provided much more than playing facilities for its members. We shall examine later the pressures for sophistication which popularity brought to some games; the concern here is with semi-ritualised behaviour and a secular calendar. Despite the predominantly seasonal nature of most activities, clubs soon came to operate on an annual cycle, seeking social reinforcement with entertainment. Male life was enhanced by the sustained banality of smokers, concerts and dinners. Within themselves the clubs sought particularly to create 'tradition' in the fruitful sense outlined by Ranger, Hobsbawm and Cannadine.[50] Ceremonial conduct, titles, insignia and chains for officers, the opening of the first match of the season, uniforms and badges were wrapped in specialised language. Whether casting a 'Dunkeld', 'luffing', selecting a 'mashie' or rolling a 'jack', the new sportsman moved into a world distinguished by arcane and dedicated terms offering him separateness and a bond with the elect, even in humour. The sense of participating in a craft was reinforced by the glossaries which accompanied the burgeoning number of handbooks.

Money, time and space were surrounded and barricaded with sporting slang and revetted with visual images. The design of a club uniform or badge and membership and event cards created an iconography which then passed further into team and club photographs. Their display in the press was probably less powerful than their presence in the office, drawing room or study where clients, neighbours, pupils and parishioners could reflect on the worth of their holder. Minor trophies, creating an industrial form of their own to be latched on to the production of other commemoratives, hinted at a prowess and skill assumed to be matched in business or profession.

Membership's advantages could bring pressures for further display. Beyond subscriptions sophistication brought demands for self-capitalisation. The shareholder and debenture lists of clubs have been remarkably neglected by social historians, yet appearance on them, a readiness to provide money at less than current market rates, brought a recognition of place in local oligarchies; over-anxiety to do it could ensure ostracism. The late Victorian upper and middle-middle classes found perhaps the apotheosis of this when sport was linked with charity, for which athletics were particularly suitable; good works could be seen to be done.

The urge to organisation and the social advantages of self-advertisement reflected some of the more formal and potentially restrictive features of social hierarchy lampooned by the Grossmiths and H. G. Wells. Yet a major paradox emerged. Much of the drive towards sport occurred because it offered an area of relative infor-mality away from work or the public face of the home and church. Popularisation and acceptance by some higher social groups, and the intervention of some women, induced tensions, a move towards order which saddened many pioneers who felt that it diverted effort from the game itself. In golf, for instance, some Scots castigated the English for not taking the game seriously.[51] Whilst a few socially prestigious bodies such as the East Brighton Golf Club, which had royal members (the Duke and Duchess of Fife), pursued a relaxed atmosphere, and the 'old clothes' of Norfolk jacket and knickerbockers remained acceptable, the trend was towards a restrictive formality seen at its peak at Henley or Cowes. Social tone triumphed most where the accompanying display mattered more than the activity itself.

Sport served the social needs of the leaders and noncommissioned officers of a maturing capitalist society, promising both recreation before further battles and a reinforcement of necessary social and eco-nomic competition. But many popular sports stressed the individual rather than the group. The key in many of the games which appealed to older men was the testing of self, either against a theoretical standard of performance – 'bogey' in golf, for instance – or against one's own previous best. It became an ideal tool for extending the charactistics of Riesman's 'inner-directed' man.[52] Of course, this is to oversimplify drastically. An equal value was to provide some areas of regulation in an apparently increasingly unregulated and uncertain world. Sport, with its sense of gentlemanly conduct, could become a real haven.

Downwards and outwards

Having seen some of the values sport could offer at different points of life and social experience, some attempt must be made to assess

its diffusion. It is highly unlikely that a simple model of downward
and outward dispersal from the upper middle classes will suffice. As
we shall see, the downward extent of some, such as fox-hunting, was
limited, whilst others, like bowls, operated within a broadly lower
band with limited upwards appeal. The 1895/96 cycling boom certainly attracted Guards officers and their ladies to practise cycling but
the breadth of its appeal could hardly be ascribed in any major part to
their wobblings in Battersea Park. Yet some contemporary observers
of the 'classes and masses' claimed as much. David Rubinstein's work
and the fluctuations in Cyclists' Touring Club membership suggest a
far wider range of influences.[53]

In many games the spread was lateral rather than downwards, golf's
being by far the best example. For many it was peer groups that
mattered. The lawn tennis boom of the 1870s and its revival in the
1890s owed a great deal to informal networks. Publicity in journals
aimed at the aspiring – Country Life (founded 1897) and The Tatler
(founded 1901), for instance – could help, but identification with the
higher elites could prove sharply counterproductive. When ping-pong
or table tennis was promoted rapidly in 1902 the lids of boxed sets
often depicted men and women in full evening dress playing, obviously after a substantial country house meal.[54] It failed to attract this
group, more likely to play billiards, and was too energetic and noisy
to find favour in most smaller middle-class homes. The craze flopped,
only to be revived in the changed circumstances of the 1920s.

The final point in this discussion must be the nature of the 'craze'
for sport and the contemporary assumption of its unique Englishness.
There are obvious limits, not least because Somers and Hardy have
shown a parallel growth in the United States.[55] But while the English
claimed it as a national trait a great deal of its diffusion overseas owed
just as much to emigrant Scotsmen.[56]

The empire and British trading networks contributed considerably
to the spread of an athletic ideal outside England. Dunae has examined the role of expatriate gentlemen in Canada, Holt has shown the
singular influence of the English wine trade on the growth of rugby
around Bordeaux.[57] Early in our century a French observer, already
aware of England's declining economic performance, could still see
sport, coupled with Protestant morality, as the basis of imperial
expansion: 'Thanks to it, they accomplished the most magnificent
task of the nineteenth-century . . . in penetrating the world's savage
countries and founding centres of civilisation there.'[58] By that time

many of the more perceptive English commentators were not so convinced.

Sport became one model of the potential of English society around 1900 for growth and for expressing its internal crises, paradoxically turning its back on its antecedents whilst reiterating them. Even with its role in reinforcing divisiveness, however, it avoided much of the obloquy poured on another craze, for playing bridge: '. . . it is breaking up Society, making it less pleasant and easy'. [59] The addicts of sport preferred to claim that they were strengthening social bonds. They were, but not as widely as they hoped.

Notes

1 A. Lunn, *Switzerland and the English* (1944), 2.
2 For the older pattern see: P. Bailey, *Leisure and Class in Victorian England* (1978); J. Lowerson and J. Myerscough, *Time to Spare in Victorian England* (Hassocks, 1977); K. A. P. Sandiford, 'The Victorians at play: problems in historical methodology', *Journal of Social History*, 15 (1984); W. J. Baker, 'The state of British sports history', *Journal of Sport History*, 10 (1983), 53 ff. For the new approach see R. Holt, *Sport and the British* (Oxford, 1989); D. Brailsford, *Sport, Time and Society: the British at Play* (1991).
3 For instance, B. Butler, *The Official Illustrated History of the Football League* (1987) and *The Official History of the Football Association* (1991).
4 L. Davidoff and C. Hall, *Family Fortunes: Men and Women of the English Middle Class, 1780–1850* (1987); P. Earle, *The Making of the English Middle Class, 1660–1730* (1989).
5 J. A. Mangan, *Athleticism in the Victorian and Edwardian Public School* (Cambridge, 1981).
6 J. A. Mangan, 'Imitating their betters and disassociating from their inferiors: grammar schools and the games ethic in the late nineteenth and early twentieth centuries', *Proceedings of the 1982 Annual History of Education Society Conference* (1983).
7 J. Lowerson, 'Sport and the Victorian Sunday: the beginnings of middle-class apostasy', *British Journal for Sports History*, 1 (1984), 202 ff.
8 H. Newbolt, *Collected Poems* (1910).
9 A. Trollope, *British Sports and Pastimes* (1967), 75.
10 E. Baines Junior, *The Life of Edward Baines* (1851), 35, 136; J. Lowerson, 'The Political Career of Sir Edward Baines, 1800–90', unpublished University of Leeds M. A. thesis, 1965.
11 J. F. C. Harrison, *Learning and Living* (1961); G. Kitson Clark,' The Leeds elite', *University of Leeds Review*, 17 (1974), 252 ff.; R. J. Morris, 'Middle-class culture, 1700–1914', in D. Fraser (ed.), *A History of Modern Leeds* (Manchester, 1980).
12 W. Vamplew, *The Turf* (1976).
13 H. J. Perkin, *The Origins of Modern English Society, 1780–1800*(1969), 420; G. Routh, *Occupation and Pay in Great Britain, 1906–1960* (Cambridge, 1965), 104; F. Musgrove,' Middle-class education and employment in the

nineteenth century', *Economic History Review*, 12 (1959), 104; W. J. Reader, *Professional Men* (1966), 211.

14 E. P. Thompson, *The Making of the English Working Class* (1963), 1968 edition, 10 ff.

15 J. Bale, *Sport and Place: a Geography of Sport in England, Scotland and Wales* (1982).

16 L. Stone, *An Open Elite: England, 1540–1880* (Oxford, 1984); W. D. Rubinstein, 'The man of wealth and the purchase of land in nineteenth-century England', *Past and Present*, 92 (1981), 125 ff., and *Men of Property* (1981); R. J. Morris, 'The middle class and the property cycle during the industrial revolution', in T. C. Smout (ed.), *The Search for Wealth and Stability* (1979).

17 J. Lowerson, 'Breakdown or reinforcement? The social and political role of the late Victorian gentry in the south-east', in M. D. G. Wanklyn (ed.), *Landownership and Power in the Regions* (Wolverhampton Polytechnic, 1979).

18 *Sussex, Historical, Biographical and Pictorial* (1907), n. p.

19 See the occupational listings, decennial census returns.

20 W. A. Morgan (ed.), *The House on Sport* (1898).

21 A. Russell, *The Clerical Profession* (1980); A. Haig, *The Victorian Clergy* (1984); H. J. Perkin, *The Rise of a Professional Society: England since 1880* (1989).

22 G. Crossick (ed.), *The Lower Middle Class in Britain* (1977); see also C. Booth, *Life and Labour of the People of London*, third series, 'Religious Influences', vol. 7: 'Summary' (1902), 397, 399.

23 C. F. G. Masterman, *The Condition of England* (1909), 1960 edition, 58.

24 E. M. Forster, *Howards End* (1910); G. and W. Grossmith, *The Diary of a Nobody* (1892); H. G. Wells, *The Wheels of Chance* (1896).

25 H. Begbie, 'The clerk', *C. B. Fry's Magazine* (June 1904), 525 ff.

26 M. Winstanley, *The Shopkeeper's World, 1830–1914* (Manchester, 1983).

27 Hull Reference Library, Hull Tradesmen's Athletic Association, Annual Reports (1910–13).

28 J. C. Stamp, *British Incomes and Property* (1916); W. H. Fraser, *The Coming of the Mass Market, 1850–1914* (1981).

29 J. Burnett, *Plenty and Want: a Social History of Diet in England* (1966); J. A. R. Pimlott, *The Englishman's Holiday* (1947); C. Ehrlich, *The Piano: a History* (1976).

30 The membership figures of the Royal Horticultural Society were provided by that body, for which I am deeply grateful.

31 F. G. Aflalo, *The Cost of Sport* (1899).

32 Mary E. L. Height, 'The expenses of golf', in H. Seton-Karr *et al.*, *Golf* (1970), 58.

33 F. M. L. Thompson (ed.), *The Rise of Suburbia* (Leicester, 1982).

34 R. Roberts, 'The corporation as impresario', in J. Walton and J. Walvin, *Leisure in Britain, 1780–1939* (Manchester, 1983); J. K. Walton, *The English Seaside Resort: a Social History, 1750–1914* (Leicester, 1983).

35 See East Sussex Record Office, AMS 5788/3/1–3, Crowhurst Otter Hounds.

36 S. Smiles, *Life and Labour* (1887), 308; see also *Hull Daily Mail*, 12 April 1901, advertisement for Dr Williams's Pink Pills.

37 M. Wiener, *English Culture and the Decline of the Industrial Spirit, 1850–1980* (Cambridge, 1981).

38 E.g. Mrs E. Kennard, *The Sorrows of a Golfer's Wife* (1896).
39 Mangan, *Athleticism*.
40 S. Rothblatt, *The Revolution of the Dons: Cambridge and Society in Victorian England* (Cambridge, 1968); A. J. Engel, *From Clergyman to Don: the Rise of the Academic Profession in Nineteenth-century Oxford* (Oxford, 1983).
41 A. Morris, *The Romance and Realm of Commerce: a Book for Parents and Sons* (1904), 118.
42 G. Herschell, *Cycling as a Cause of Heart Disease* (1896).
43 A. Comfort, *The Anxiety Makers* (1967); J. A. Banks, *Prosperity and Parenthood: a Study of Family Planning* (1954).
44 A. Ross, *Ranji, Prince of Cricketers* (1983).
45 J. A. Mangan, *The Games Ethic and Imperialism* (1986); J. M. MacKenzie, 'The imperial pioneer and hunter and the British masculine stereotype in late Victorian and Edwardian times', in J. A. Mangan and J. Walvin (eds.), *Manliness and Morality: Middle-class Masculinity in Britain and America, 1800–1940* (Manchester, 1987); T. Pakenham, *The Scramble for Africa* (1991), 425–7.
46 *Recreation*, August 1886, 9.
47 E. P. Hennock, *Fit and Proper Persons: Ideal and Reality in Nineteenth-century Urban Government* (1973); D. Fraser, *Municipal Reform and the Industrial City* (1982); *Power and Authority in the Victorian City* (Oxford, 1978).
48 *Masonic Yearbook, 1913.*
49 The author uncovered this in records still held by the club. It is quoted on the understanding that the location would be withheld because the issue is still a sensitive one in the area.
50 E. Hobsbawm, 'Mass-producing traditions: Europe, 1870–1914', in E. Hobsbawm and T. Ranger (eds.), *The Invention of Tradition* (Cambridge, 1983). See especially the papers by Cannadine and Hobsbawm.
51 W. Park junior, *The Game of Golf* (1901), 160.
52 D. Riesman *et al.*, *The Lonely Crowd* (New Haven, 1950).
53 D. Rubinstein, 'Cycling in the 1890s', *Victorian Studies* (1977), 47 ff.
54 One such set is held in Worthing Museum.
55 D. A. Somers, 'The leisure revolution: recreation in the American City, 1820–1920', *Journal of Popular Culture*, V (1971); *The Rise of Sport in New Orleans, 1850–1900* (Baton Rouge, 1972); S. Hardy, *How Boston Played* (Boston, Mass., 1982).
56 G. Redmond, *The Sporting Scots of Nineteenth-century Canada* (1982).
57 P. A. Dunae, *Gentlemen Emigrants* (Vancouver, 1981); R. Holt, *Sport and Society in Modern France* (1981).
58 Translated from P. Adam, *La Morale des sports* (Paris, 1907), 14: 'Grace à elle . . .'.
59 *Fortnightly Review*, LXX (1901), 158.

Chapter 2

Land and water

Romance and style

The introduction of the journal *Land and Water* in 1866 reflected one major area of sporting growth. Traditionally, 'sport' was interpreted as a contest between man and Nature, more precisely seen as animals, birds and fish. The broad delineation of seasons for each 'field' sport (a term coined eventually when other pursuits forced a more generic description) allowed their meshing in with other activities, economic and social, and alleviated the possible boredom of country living. The development of widely accepted socially rather than legally enforced sporting etiquettes helped the survival and expansion of activities which might otherwise have been loosely branded as the brutishly cruel habits of upper-class 'roughs'. Indeed, the idea of 'traditional country sports', employed in their defence in the later nineteenth century, demonstrated their attractions to a wider clientele. Field sports grew rapidly because the connotations of participation were just as significant as their intrinsic merits. They reflected the tensions in land-use compatibility of land-hungry upper middle-class sportsmen encountering a sectoral and regional 'depression' in agriculture. At the simplest level they offered a new financial significance for much agriculturally marginal territory.

The impetus for this was complex. What had become identified as an acceptable pattern of social mobility (at least for a rather limited group) was clarified into an urban–rural momentum, sometimes for settlement, often for specialised exploitation. Certain sports allowed social mingling, if not cohesion, and added a range of degrees to the process of male acceptance in 'Society'. The limited codes of etiquette were expressed not just as models of social and financial acceptability but also in terms of the acquisition of some physical skills and technical prowess.

These codes were overlaid with, and often justified by, a new sub-Romantic appreciation of Nature, fostered in literature and painting. Its central focus was the 'countryside', not the rural England of High Farming or economic depression but a tamed wilderness which became an object of consumption, a general sporting arena.

C. F. Dowsett's *Land: its Attraction and Riches* of 1892 was a compendium of short articles largely devoted to fostering amenity values. The country heritage provided a base for national and imperial greatness. In a book designed for urban middle-class readers, perhaps the greatest irony came when a barrister, E. A. Armstrong, pleaded virtually for a rural middle class, 'men of more moderate incomes', clearly well differentiated from the much older rural middle classes of yeomanry and tenant farmers. In Armstrong's eyes the most suitable country sport for this group would be golf.[1] Following country sports, another writer observed, would renew 'The natural man', strengthen 'The oakwood character'.[2]

This hoped-for rejuvenation was less commonly sought, however, than relaxation and some personal reconstitution. The second Westley Richards (1816–99), a baron in the Birmingham armaments firm of the same name and an almost classically work-addicted industrialist, provided an ideal model for this for his biographer: 'he loved the countryside, the open air, the sunshine, the wind-swept moor, and all things pertaining to the countryside.' Running his factories was still compatible with being High Sheriff of Rutland and the banality of this pseudo-romanticism.[3] Activity was central to the field sportsman; mild risk, particularly in riding, opened the body and mind to the benefits of weather: Begbie's clerk only condensed the views of many hunting men, however rarely they may have articulated them personally.

This fitted easiest into an extension of the established patterns of gentrification of the more economically successful urban middle classes, particularly as they moved to live in the countryside. It was most conspicuous in the south-east and the Home Counties but it was well established elsewhere. Walton has shown the importance of Windermere as a gathering point for north Lancashire's more prosperous men after the mid-Victorian years; Leeds had a similar bolt hole in Ilkley, twenty miles up the Wharfe valley. The development of secondary and tertiary railway networks from the 1860s was crucial for this; the growth of weekend or seasonal commuting to a city work base, the leasing or purchase of 'retreats' in the country, encouraged a drift from the passive attractions of seaside resorts.[4]

One attraction of most of these developing 'natural' sports (perhaps more comprehensive than the relatively limited delineation of 'field' sports) was their general lack of formal competition, although personal aggression on the hunting field and the virtually unmeasurable level of betting compensated for this. 'Form' mattered, so did 'style', even where the activities were essentially isolated and individual rather than 'social' in a group sense. When 'democratisation' took place it was rarely in an overtly pejorative sense – even the 'democratic' horde noted on the hunting field of the 1860s by Trollope had well defined limits. The democracy of late Victorian middle-class sport was Athenian rather than industrial, although to take the illustration to the extreme sense of its being founded on a slave society is perhaps far-fetched outside the Marxian corpus.[5]

Horses and hounds

The greatest prestige was attached to a sporting instrument the railway and the internal combustion engine were slowly combining to render anachronistic. It is, nonetheless, a paradox that, in Theo Barker's phrase, 'the horse-drawn world [was] at its zenith' in the last Victorian years. Vamplew has noted the minimal importance of the race track for the respectable middle classes, although more recent work has stressed their role as investors in turf facilities. The number of horses in Great Britain rose sharply from 277,000 in 1851 to 600,000 by 1901, about a sixth of them devoted apparently to pleasure. That was not always for strenuous sport, however: 'The City clerk on his hired hack enjoying Saturday afternoon' may have cantered for style, but it was not cheap; the client was possibly closer to one of Trollope's civil servants than to a stockholder's pen pusher. T. W. Dale, the literary populariser of polo, hoped that the impact of cars and cycles would bring horse prices down 'within the reach of many who have hitherto regarded it as prohibitive'; in the long term he was right, as the boom in riding schools in the 1920s and 1930s demonstrated, but the gentle canter was very much the prerogative of the upper middle classes before 1914.[6]

The most conspicuous place where the stockjobber on horseback could find sport was on the hunting field. Despite vicissitudes, hunting boomed. T. H. S. Escott, writing in 1897, calculated that the number of English fox-hunting packs had risen from twenty-eight to sixty-one during Victoria's sixty years on the throne. It proved a remarkable underestimate: despite the disappearence or amalgamation of some hunts there were actually 164 packs of foxhounds by the 1890s and 178 by 1911, fifty-three of them founded since 1850. Fox-hunting was, however, by no means universal in England and Wales, since both terrain and local ecologies were often unsuitable. More specialised, and rather lowlier, variations were to be found, actually providing for a far wider range of both prestigious and native rural sport than the over-concentration of attention on fox-hunting would suggest.[7] The figures in table 3 are the totals of those still extant in 1912; they do not include packs which folded. The growth of almost a fifth in foxhounds is remarkable, but even more so is that of over 300 per cent in the key foot hunts, ideal for the socially ambitious but less well heeled.

By 1893, the American observer Caspar Whitney reckoned, some 48,825 people followed hounds every week of the season; at an average field of 120, it would seem that he was including foot watchers as well, the clear division in fox-hunting at least between the mounted and the pedestrian being blurred.[8] Watching was one thing; it was being on horseback that mattered. 'The community at large' in the countryside, as the *Field* put it, comprised two-thirds businessmen and the rest *rentiers*.[9] In the 'shires' (the Midland focus of the most prestigious hunts, the Quorn, Belvoir and so on) Whitney reiterated the essential pan-class nature of foxhunting, but 'democracy' was a singularly inadequate description for a sport whose great value was its symbolic reiteration of hierarchy, one with which to be positively identified. Total integration probably mattered less for most of the

Table 3   **Hunts in England and Wales, 1912**

Type	Total	Founded 1870–1912
Foxhounds	178	37
Harriers	88	27
Staghounds	16	8
Foot harriers and beagles	91	71
Otter hounds	19	11
Draghounds	12	6
Total	404	160

Source: Baily's Hunting Directory, 1912–13

aspirants than being tolerated and seen by outsiders to be part of a glamorous social world.

Raymond Carr has shown that justification of this growth was covered with more than elitist tinsel, that skill on the hunting field would stiffen the sinews of the business classes to create a new imperial guardianship. Rather more functionally, he portrayed them as a significant source of hunt secretaries, the adjutants of landed prestige.[10] Whatever the ambiguities of social interaction, this middle-class passion for the hunting field had a strict utilitarianism for the rural upper classes; the influx of wealth kept a sport alive, effectively reducing some of the aristocracy's leisure costs during the agricultural depression. Itzkowitz's work has shown that many hunts were in severe financial difficulty by the 1870s.[11] The answer was to replace broad guarantees of meeting masters' exceptional costs with individual subscriptions and 'capping' fees for visitors: these were often irregular but unavoidable and, paradoxically, gave some hunts more of the appearance of a middle-class club with a facade of landed recreation. Many hunts were surprisingly coy in admitting that they did this, *Baily's Hunting Directory* of 1912–13 listing only about two-thirds specifically. One estimate put the cost of each day's meet at £700; the Quorn reacted by charging a £2 fee for each visitor, particularly the 'lack land' hunters, the bulk of what older addicts regarded as 'evil' large fields. Claims that the new middle classes got their sport far too cheaply were voiced, the paradox being that without them much of the sport would probably have folded.[12]

Riding to hounds, with only one horse, on one day a week, could cost a minimum of £70 per annum, although the 'modest means' school claimed that judicious living could reduce this to £37: the reality was probably closer to £150.[13] Yet even at this rate the demand for facilities led to growth in some bizarre places. In 1891 one of the most respectably sedentary of the new Victorian seaside resorts, Eastbourne, acquired its own hunt. It was founded at the behest of leading residents by the town's principal developer, the Duke of Devonshire, both to cope with the influx of early-retired *rentiers* and local professional men and to add to the resort's autumn and winter attractions for visitors. It took its country from the adjoining Southdown and East Sussex hunts and ran on subscriptions; the joint master in 1908–10 was a retired master builder, T. K. Stapley. Attractive though it proved to visitors, the subscriptions were insufficient to meet its costs and the duke stepped in to take over the running in 1910, hunting it out of his own funds for two days a week; the committee agreed to cover any remaining costs. A similar pattern affected the neighbouring Bexhill Harriers, who were negotiating with the financially inept Earl de la Warr, that town's developer, for a similar arrangement when the First World War broke out. The symbiosis of aristocracy and middle classes was rarely more clearly demonstrated.[14]

That some of the latter were not always personally as welcome as their subscriptions surfaced occasionally when the transmission of field codes by example proved inadequate. *Baily's* offered 'Hints to beginners', arising out of alarm that the over-enthusiasm of crowded fields of horsemen led to bad form. 'Always give way to the huntsman or any other Hunt servants; it is their duty to be with hounds, whereas it is your pleasure.' Horses should be treated kindly. And so on. When the hunt secretaries formed a central association in 1904 one of their first assumed tasks was the compilation of a 'private black list'; like the blackballing of London clubs, it is virtually impossible to assess its extent and power but it marked a formalisation in associational terms of the social ostracism which the pressure of the sport's popularity had made increasingly difficult to apply by the older forms of obloquy.[15]

Fox-hunting appealed strongly to those able to manage horses, but an equally significant growth was apparent in its slightly less glamorous relations, foot harriers, beagles and otter hounds. These offered many of the attributed recreational advantages, and a rather modified social cachet with the distinct advantage of lower costs. Proper dress still mattered, subscriptions were usually lower and there were no horse costs. Suburban and commuter settlements proved particularly attractive centres for new packs, and they fitted more easily into many middle-class employment patterns than the traditional mid-week foxhunting meets. The Berkhamstead Beagles, in Hertfordshire, were formed in 1883 as a subscription pack to hunt on Saturdays. In 1891 the Airedale Beagles emerged to hunt out of Bingley, the small West Riding moorside industrial town, on Saturday afternoons. For a minimum subscription of 10s 6d it was possible to follow a meandering walk across the moors in suitably garbed company. By the Edwardian period the notion of conspicuously disposable time had had its impact: the Airedale also hunted on Tuesdays.

For north-east Londoners the Forest Drag Hounds, chasing an

artificially laid scent, were formed in 1895, meeting on Saturdays and on alternate Tuesdays at 3.00 p.m., covering fifteen miles or so a day. It actually used horses, replacing the Forest Mounted Paper Chase Club (a distinctly up-market shift), formed in 1892; in turn it changed its name to the Essex in 1905. Income was maintained by a ten-guinea subscription. In the Sussex–Kent borders a similar demand for sport among both established and 'pseudo' gentry led to the founding in 1902 of the Crowhurst Otter Hounds. Walter Cheesman bought the Culmstock pack from Somerset for £60, adapting his out-buildings for them; they accounted for five brace of otters in their first season. Perhaps the Crowhurst's most original contribution was that its master from 1904–06 was Mrs Cheesman. Subscriptions in 1904 reached £297 7s, with a further £34 19s in capping fees: of these the Cheesmans received £175 for expenses. Members wore red coats, blue caps, white knickerbockers with blue stockings, and distinctive buttons. Using local railways to transport the pack, they assumed a right to hunt the area's rivers which was not always welcome, particularly to those riparian owners who liked otters. One such, E. C. Lister-Kay, of Godmersham Park, Canterbury, used two keepers to ward them off, despite the claims of this four-year-old pack to be exercising 'ancient custom'. It was by no means the only instance when a land-use-hungry middle class demanded 'traditions' in the face of established territorial practice.[16]

Hunting eventually generated growing but diffuse and usually ineffective opposition. Its claims to develop the sinews of leadership provoked scepticism:

> A vicarious sport in which all the brain and muscle work is delegated to the dogs and horse: whilst to all the social functions attached to these hunts, these ladies and gentlemen are very careful to keep to themselves and to their friends: in fact they are most exclusive.[17]

This diatribe revealed the prime reason why the sport grew: it was the social mixing at the appendages of hunting, the point-to-points and the hunt balls, which proved so attractive, particularly where the female etiquette networks were grafted on to predominantly male activities. But not all the ex-urban or rural middle classes welcomed hunts. One major threat to the sport's future was identified in the 1890s as coming from:

> the man who has become suddenly rich, who has been reared in towns and cares little for the accounts and interests and traditions of

the countryside, and especially that of foxhunting ... He is too old, too soft, or has too little nerve to acquire the difficult art of riding to hounds; but he can and does acquire a certain amount of skill in shooting.

It was pheasant-shooting syndicates of 'new men' who often viewed the hunts with most distaste, but the established rural middle class, of small and tenant farmers, was also proving less amenable, less deferential in a world where tenants had more choice. The Quorn was ordered by a court to pay £51 for damage done to a farm in 1893. One observer saw this as a major threat to the sport's future, the tenants often being upset by the bad manners of 'urban sportsmen, or so-called sportsmen, totally ignorant of country life'. But it also, in his view, arose out of the 'unmistakable tendency among the lower classes to look with envy and jealousy at the sports and pastimes of their betters' instead of seeing sport as a social bond.[18]

It was not class envy, however, which prompted the most outspoken attacks on hunting: these came from other middle-class groups with a very different view of the values of Nature, the 'Humanitarians'. E. H. Freeman's onslaught 'The morality of field sports' in the *Fortnightly Review* in 1869 was the reflective beginning of a campaign that still continues. Trollope's answer that God had created foxes to be hunted perhaps carried less weight than his claims for the economic value of hunting for rural employment, the actual base on which most of its defence has since rested. The reformers eventually formed the Humanitarian League in 1891, as a radical departure from the RSPCA, in response to the creation in 1884 of the National Sports Protection and Defence Association, retitled the Field Sports Protection and Encouragement Association.

During the 1890s controversy focused on a specific issue, the Royal Buckhounds, who hunted a stag carted to the field for the purpose, and their disbandment was a minor victory. Field sports' defenders early applied a domino theory, in which all would eventually fall if not protected against 'the mawkish, intolerant, and un-English method of damning the pursuits of your neighbour because they are not your own'. In this mode, reformers could be accused of a lack of Englishness, an absence of patriotic virtues and class envy. The Humanitarians found considerable ecclesiastical support, not least from the Revd. Edward Lyttelton, and the Deans of Ely and Durham. Within the attack were expressed hierarchies of sport's virtues, and the 'traditional' sports came low in these, not least because they were 'adopted by men who seldom do any useful work'. But Lyttelton's support proved ambiguous. When he was translated from Haileybury to Eton he refused to ban the latter's beagles, despite a petition from Thomas Hardy, Arthur Conan Doyle, the Dean of Llandaff and Canon Barnett. Fishing, the largest of all field sports, was rarely attacked, if only because, unlike hunting, it could be adapted to fit the hegemonic work codes of the new industrial society.[19]

In fact many of the defence arguments for field sports revealed a woolly anthropomorphising of animal life, one which Aflalo pointed out was even more likely to increase opposition. His views were more robust; hunting was good training for cavalry officers, prolonged fit and active lives, and tended 'to prevent the demoralisation of luxury and over-civilisation, the growth of effeminacy and sloth, and to the maintenance of a little manhood in an age the leading characteristics of which are fanaticism, cant and hypocrisy'. The debate kept a steady pace through the Edwardian literary journals. Its value for sportsmen was the fact that it led to a sharper definition of codes of etiquette and the curtailing of some over-enthusiastic actions, at least where publicly visible.

In one area the Humanitarians could claim success, the ending of competitive live pigeon shooting. This sport had a pan-class following; it was popular with Sheffield steelworkers, who shot in matches organised by local publicans, but its most prestigious form was at the expensive and exclusive Hurlingham Club, formed in 1867 specifically for the purpose. As the club prospered, adding golf and polo, the membership, and its ladies in particular, proved less prepared to defend it. After a Chancery lawsuit between polo and shooting members the club voted to abolish live pigeonshooting by 504 votes to 175 in December 1905: 'since 1868, times and manners have changed, people are more humane'. The respectable triumphed over the upper-class 'roughs', despite repeated claims that Humanitarians actually embodied national decadence. But the core of field sports remained untouched.[20]

Big guns

By comparison with hunting's flamboyance, shooting was more private. In its most developed and socially prestigious form, the *battue* (shooting in a line at driven game), this was substantially true, because it took place in the relative privacy of a single estate.

The role of the *battue* in late Victorian and Edwardian society has attracted considerable subsequent attention, not least because of its combination of an apparently reckless opulence with the ruralism of a world obsessed with the behaviour of the landed upper classes.[21] As a mode of shooting, driving game had steadily replaced its being stalked, or 'walked up', by small groups or individuals with dogs since mid-century. The keepered shoot, breeding pheasants, grouse or partridges solely for the sport of house guests, because a major adjunct of country house life, invited access to which made for even great mysteries of etiquette and acceptance in a highly ritualised sport. By 1900 the royal estate at Sandringham was raising 12,000 birds a year – it needed to, since George V and a peer between them accounted for 4,000 pheasants on one day in 1913.

There was a steady growth in the number of licences issued to shoot game between 1870 and 1914, from 45,914 to 54,701, with an intermediate low point of 38,324 in 1890 and an overall peak of 62,501 in 1902. But this 19 per cent growth was far exceeded by the licensing of guns in general, a rise of 148 per cent, from 83,046 to 206,189. Since these licences were issued for individuals rather than guns, the spread is far more significant.[22] As we shall see in chapter 9, some of these represented a harnessing of sport to national fears, but it meant a far wider constituency of people in search of sport – 120,000 more represented considerable pressure in English terms, although shooting never acquired the popularity with middle-middle and lower middle-class groups to be seen in neighbouring France.

The greatest pressure for *battue* shooting came clearly from the new plutocracy, for whom a few days' shooting a year could be used in social and business bargaining as an adjunct to a distinctly urban-based work style. For them, country sports were there to be vigorously exploited; they were usually far less reticent in publishing their guest lists than those established gentry who could still afford to shoot. This drew bitter criticism: '. . . the sportsman of today lives more as a gunner than a hunter of game', since field skills were rarely cultivated by these ex-urban artillery men.[23] The 'new men' were also widely blamed for exacerbating class tension in the countryside by insisting on protecting birds on land previously used for leisure by local people. Against this came the repeated utilitarian rejoinder that they found work for locals who would otherwise be unemployed. For keepers, at least, this was true, since their number rose from 12,431 in 1871 to 17,148 in 1911, but the rest, beaters and so on, represented the continued casualisation of an already poorly paid labour force.

At this level, sport was expensive. Round London in particular the pressure pushed land values up, usually where landowners were able to exploit the rents of marginal land severely affected by agricultural depression. The best land could command a rent of £4–£5 per acre, although farther out the prices could be 1s 6d an acre; 2,100 acres in north Hertfordshire were available for £550 in 1909. To this had to be added wage costs, say £100, and breeding costs. The total cost of rearing a pheasant was about 18s; its market value as game was about 2s. Economical returns were impossible on this type of shooting and, as with hunting, middle-class pressure to participate led to a growth of rental syndicates, so that costs per person could go down to £200–£300 a year, particularly where the game was sold. For the rare occasional shot, a good day out on a rented shoot cost £20–£30 a day, and ten days a year was about enough.

Almost inevitably, some writers tried to prove it could be done for less, and some managed. The don A. C. Benson found a 700 acre isolated fenland estate, with shooting as well as the house, for £70 per annum. But syndicating was decried as turning sport and its etiquette into a matter of the business world; the paradox is that this mode of shooting, 'the promiscuous slaughter of pheasants', could not have survived without it.[24]

'Rough shooting', walking game up on heaths and farms, could be got much cheaper but the less affluent of the late Victorian middle classes anxious to shoot turned to, and developed rapidly, two alternatives of gunmanship, and gave them a national form quite distinct from that of the sporting estate. Driven game had acquired by mid-century an equally static parallel: shooting live pigeons released from traps in competitions. In a sense this was a truly pan-class activity, not because of the range of participants in any given match but because it was followed by both aristocracy and manual workers, albeit as a distinct minority. Like horse-racing, it did not initially attract the urban middle classes, and was reinforced by considerable entrepreneurial and betting input. Eventually a distinctive 'respectable reform' was foisted on it, and it turned into a minority middle-class pursuit until the later twentieth century widened its class base very rapidly.

The first spurt of growth in London came with the founding of the Notting Hill Gun Club in 1861, by Sir George East, and the institution of the Hurlingham Club in 1869. At the latter several hundred members fired at the helpless birds to the accompaniment of Guards bands. Eventually the Humanitarian lobby drove Hurlingham to give it up, although the Notting Hill Club defiantly shot them until the eve of the First World War, releasing 100 birds at a time, with extensive side-betting. After experiments with feathers in glass balls as an alternative, other clubs began to adopt the American system of shooting at clay 'pigeons', hardened discs. Hurlingham had tried these 'clay saucers' in 1883, but continued with live birds until 1905. It is difficult to establish just how many alternative gun clubs were formed, both literature and archives being very sparse. The Inanimate Bird Shooting Association was founded in 1893, changing into the Clay Bird Shooting Association in 1903; it lasted till war broke out, offering an annual challenge. A. H. Gale, the manager of Westley Richards's Bond Street gun shop, founded the Middlesex Clay Bird Shooting Club in 1895, and acted as hon. secretary until 1913. The advantage of these clubs was relatively low costs, shooting on Saturdays within the time and distance limitations of busy city men, but clay-pigeon shooting remained esoteric, unable to offer the contact with 'wild' Nature that fostered the other field sports, and it was still associated with the prize mentality that risked 'professionalism'.[25] 'True Sport' could be found by those willing to take to the country both in relative isolation and some personal danger in wildfowling.

Although 'it is considered by the majority as being a game that is hardly worth the candle', wildfowling revealed a particular strand in middle-class sporting attitudes that we shall see paralleled again.[26] It was long established in coastal and marshland waters as a tradable food source by hardy professional gunners devoted virtually to wholesale slaughter for a booming market expanded even further by the railways. The same railways made relatively wild shoreland accessible to town sportsmen with a taste for isolation, fieldcraft and natural history, and for the danger inherent in tidal areas. This danger made it attractive, not for the foolhardy, but to men prepared to take calculated risks and to the solitary-minded. Until some local authorities fell in belatedly with sabbatarianism wildfowling did not share game shooting's disadvantage of being illegal on Sundays.

It also appealed, through an 'international freemasonry' to a deep-felt ruralism:

> To him the secrets of nature are disclosed. On the far saltings on the lonely marshes of the sea he has wonderful moments. Downs that are august in their splendour rise for him in his lonely eagerness.[27]

There was also the advantage that the bulk of such shooting was free, although access could be bought to the 15,000 acres of Barnard Castle marshes for a mere £15, or the rabbit warrens of Brandon, Suffolk, for £1 a day or £5 a week. For the cost of a day's boat hire, sea birds could be shot off Flamborough Head or Beachy Head.[28]

It remained largely the pursuit of an eccentric fringe, rising before dawn, heavily clothed and prepared to shoot in horrendous weather. Inevitably there were tensions. The professional gunners, frequently idolised in shooting literature for their earthy folk ways, regarded the newcomers with ambivalence; the latter offered guiding fees but wanted to conserve stocks, supporting the 1869 Sea Birds Preservation Act and the 1872 Wild Birds Protection Act with an enthusiasm that threatened to undermine local incomes. The deferred gratification offered by shooting over decades had little appeal to men needing immediate earnings. The professionals usually shot from punts with virtual cannons able to kill 100 birds with one shot, in sharp contrast with the amateur shore gunner's satisfaction with a brace of geese.[29]

There was another paradox. The compulsively isolated 'loners', the amateur wildfowlers, produced a systematic national organisation devoted to their sport. In this the key figure was a forty-year-old Hull railway engineer, 'Stanley' Duncan, who founded the Wildfowlers' Association of Great Britain at a meeting at the Imperial Hotel, Hull, in April 1908. Duncan was on that middle-class fringe of fowlers who paid for their sport by selling some of the bag, yet his favourite fowling companion was a local doctor, and he was friendly with the *doyen* of late Victorian shots, Sir Ralph Payne-Gallwey, Bart. Clad in old clothes, wildfowling's deliberate and utilitarian rejection of the elite uniforms of more select field sports, Duncan used a pair of guns he had bought for £26 4s from a London firm. He was in the tradition of self-taught Victorian naturalists, a compulsive diarist, using notebooks from his railway employer; he was also a photographer and artist, and he wrote what has long been regarded as the sport's standard text, *The Complete Wildfowler*, in 1911. His association grew slowly, even with a 10s subscription, to reach

220 by 1914. (Renamed the British Association for Shooting and Conservation, it now has over 60,000 members.) It was the tip of the sport, the beginnings of an information and defensive network that avoided the obsessive bureacracy of many other sporting associations, and Duncan remained honorary secretary until 1948.[30]

Rod and line

The most popular means of escaping urban congestion was fishing. When the late Victorians celebrated the tercentenary of Izaak Walton's birth in 1893 they attached tremendous value to his dictum 'Study to be quiet'.[31] Angling offered the sportsman calm, and 'that dreamy contemplative repose, broken by just enough amusement to keep his body active, while his mind is quickly taking in every sight and sound of nature'.[32] Charles Kingsley offered a distinctly utilitarian justification:

> Fishing is the sport of sports for overworked business men and professional men, for barristers and statesmen and merchants, who seek mental relaxation after a term or session of overstrain.[33]

Certainly it had appealed for a long time to the crisis-ridden; Kingsley used it as a tranquilliser during busy pastoral work in his fever-ridden rural parish. It continued to offer this appeal to clergy and dons. The embittered Oxford reformer Mark Pattison escaped the savagery of college politics in the 1850s by spending April to July each year fishing in the north, taking also 'a well-selected box of books and a large store of tobacco'. Professor Philip Ransome, of the Yorkshire College (later the University of Leeds), kept his family by wholesale popular publishing but 'he did not waste good fishing-weather on writing history books'. Even William Morris found time in his overcrowded life to fish. When on a visit to the Cobden family in 1889 he caught thirty-four fish; the best were stolen. His hosts 'agreed that, as a Socialist, he should have rejoiced that others had enjoyed his fish at their evening repast', whereupon he lost his temper.[34]

Relatively few fishermen had their own waters. During the Victorian period considerable pressure developed as water rights became a tradable commodity and the sport itself became increasingly socially differentiated in terms of both space and quarry. In broad terms, the middle classes took to 'game' fishing (for salmon, trout and grayling), leaving 'coarse' fish (all the other freshwater species) for a mass working-class following. In fact this division was never absolute. There were very few working-class game fishermen but many of the middle classes angled for coarse fish. London clerks shared the banks of the Thames with artisan clubs, and the Norfolk Broads owed a considerable part of their tourist development to the more prosperous in search of large pike. The clear, pure waters essential for game fish were, however, rapidly annexed by middle-class groups who used collective purchasing or rental power selectively and sometimes ruthlessly.

It began in the 1830s when Henry Wix, a London bookseller, founded the Amwell Magna Fishing Club on the river Lea in Hertfordshire in 1831, staying as honorary secretary until 1874, for a membership of the City's upper middle class and gentry. Initially aimed at pike, it gradually shifted to trout by fly fishing only.[35] In Sheffield the Derwent Flyfishers' Club began in the 1830s to fish the Peak District's best waters: with an annual subscription of ten guineas it was limited to twenty of 'the wealthiest and most notable of Sheffield's citizens'.[36] Most of the Midland and northern industrial cities had relatively clear game waters near by which were similarly annexed, but their main rivers were too polluted for ordinary fish life and working-class anglers were often forced to travel considerable distances to find their quarry. Whilst Sheffield boasted only a few hundred trout fishermen with access to nearby Derbyshire by 1900, it had over 20,000 working-class anglers who travelled regularly ninety miles or more into Lincolnshire.[37]

Birmingham, Manchester and Bolton produced similar small middle-class clubs, as did Newcastle.[38] The latter's Northumberland Angling Club was founded in 1881; when it lost its waters some years later it remained as a social club for 'numbers of professional and Conservative gentlemen', with its own club songs, written in a Northumberland dialect none of its members spoke regularly, as a bonding agent.[39] Smaller towns responded too. In Whitby, Yorkshire, local professionals and superior tradesmen banded together in 1864 to protect the local river Esk's salmon and trout for their own fishing against two enemies. The first, commercial offshore netsmen, have remained a thorn in the side of sport fishermen. More easily dealt with were local iron miners who had long assumed a customary right to take fish from the river. The new association allotted them a small area to continue this but closed it in 1868 when it found out that the miners were following another custom, selling their catches to augment income. The Esk Fishery Association attracted rich weekenders from the Yorkshire textile trade as well as locals. It became necessary to limit the membership to fifty, and balloting for newcomers was introduced by the turn of the century, with a clear assumption that friends of existing members would receive preference.[40]

Many market towns produced similar small bodies, such as the Darley Dale club in Derbyshire with a long waiting list for its balloting.[41] The opera singer Henry Plunket Greene moved out to a Berkshire village in 1902 to find fishing on the river Bourne, in an informal local club of Lord Portsmouth's tenants.[42] By far the most prestigious of these clubs was the Piscatorial Society, established at the Marquess of Granby inn in South Audley Street, London. Its subscription was low, initially 5s, but membership was coveted. Until the 1870s it was basically a dining club, organising occasional matches on open waters, but it moved then into renting its own waters and was clearly identified as at odds with the broad run of London's working-class clubs, which were:

> Exclusive, or select (you can choose which you like) in the extreme, never striving to carry out the law of good fellowship or Angling Freemasonry, so eloquently preached by honest old Izaak Walton.[43]

The Piscatorials ignored this, acquiring waters in Hertfordshire and Berkshire. If it had freemasonry it was in a later, exclusive sense, away from the collective values of working-class angling. Such overt statements of class feeling as that just quoted were comparatively rare, but they were a constant undercurrent to the assumption that angling was non-divisive.

Pan-class it may have been but the classes were usually clearly separated. In 1884 the Wilkinson Angling Association, of Hull, split when some members tried to ban all working-class members from the club.[44] The clearest statement of the class issue came in an ill considered attempt to impose a shilling rod licence on coarse fishing in 1896. It was defeated after wholesale northern anglers' meetings, but not before some harsh condemnation of game fisherman, 'those who toil not, neither do they spin otherwise', by 'the more democratic army of coarse-fishers'.[45]

By contrast there was little resistance to the imposition of licensing for trout fishermen in the 1870s (except in Scotland, where it has not yet succeeded), so that, unlike coarse fishing, which escaped generally until the 1960s, it is at least possible to plot the sport's growth. In 1879, the first year of licensing, 9,109 anglers were listed: there was a rapid rise to 46,757 in 1900 and a steady increase to 59,655 in 1910.[46] The most obvious result was huge pressure on waters and a soaring cost for good rivers when landowners affected by agricultural depression recognised a new source of income. On the chalk lands of the south annual rents doubled or more in the 1880s; the Hampshire Itchen, a prime trout location, was fetching £100 a mile by the 1890s; some salmon stretches reached £1,000. Few individuals could afford this, so clubs and syndicates spread widely throughout the south, the more exclusive costing £50 or more per rod annually, with £20 regarded as a reasonable minimum. In more than one case this led to fierce intra-middle-class rivalry for desirable stretches, in which the ruthless practices of some City men were used to underpin their Waltonian idylls. Perhaps the harshest of these conflicts took place over the Stockbridge stretch of the Hampshire Avon.[47]

This prime trout chalk stream had been fished since 1822 by the Houghton Club, a loose group of London gentry and professionals. When the surrounding land changed hands in 1874 the new owner wanted more rent than the club thought reasonable and a group of twenty other men took it over, calling themselves the Houghton Fly Fishing Club. Beneath the relatively ordered accounts in Edwardian club histories, however, lurked considerable acrimony and personal animosity. The new group included F. M. Halford, the self-appointed apostle of dry-fly purism (see below), conspicuous for his 'pugnacity of spirit, an intolerance of outlook, and an inflexibility of doctrine'. He and the others were prepared to pay £400 between them (£500 after 1882) for the stretch, rather more than the old club.

The old club, now calling itself the Stockbridge Fishing Club, looked round for fresh waters. After various individual members had purchased waters at their own expense it formed itself into a limited company, the Stockbridge Fishery Association, in 1883, eventually raising £18,900 in share capital. Subscriptions rose from £30 a year for its sixteen members in pre-company days to £60 in 1893. In that year its old water came on the market and it moved in rapidly to buy what it regarded as the usurper out, setting about major improvements, with its own hatcheries. Halford was clearly annoyed at the success of this 'simple business proposition'. 'They were wise in their generation, and the members of our Club were much wanting in foresight.' He and his friends shifted to the Berkshire Kennet, the three others leasing a five-mile stretch. They rejected being called a 'syndicate'; 'those among us who had business experience were not greatly impressed by this title, which we had too often found synonymous with "Swindle"' (a dig at the old Houghton club) and settled for becoming the whimsical 'quadrilateral'.[48]

It was business, however, which met the urgent middle-class need for trout-fishing in some areas. When the Bellagio Bungalow Estate was developed in Surrey in the 1880s, one of its attractions for residents was a stocked trout pool. At Baldock, Hertfordshire, the Northern Fisheries breeding farm stocked its local river for a developer-led club, annual membership of which cost thirty-five guineas.[49] But by far the greatest response was a by-product of the industrial cities' own health needs, the opening up of large reservoirs. Liverpool led, with the leasing of its Lake Vyrnwy in Wales to an hotel which used the fishery as a major attraction. The biggest spurt came when Bristol opened its Blagdon reservoir, having stocked it, for bank fishing at 10s a day. Birmingham followed with its Welsh waters in 1904, another step in what has long been regarded in Wales as English imperialism. By 1909 forty authorities allowed it; Manchester did not because of a supposed risk to water purity. Although this was a moderate form of municipal socialism, the daily costs usually limited fishing to the more prosperous; in some cases, such as Bolton, management of the fishery was handed over to a local middle-class club. The Manchester Anglers' Association (by no means as comprehensive as its name suggests) took over part of Ribblesdale and opened golf links for its members as well. For Yorkshiremen there was an alternative to both club and corporation, buying a day ticket from the large estates bordering the river Wharfe for 5s. This spread of day-ticketing allowed many to escape clubs for solitude.[50]

Late Victorian trout fishing offered its own peculiar variant of the search for ethical purity in sport. For several centuries, particularly in the rougher and darker streams of the north, the artificial flies used had been 'wet', fished below the surface to imitate either emergent insect forms or as flashy lures. With the colonisation of the expensive, clear south-country chalk streams, emphasis shifted to 'dry' flies, dropped lightly on to the surface in front of a rising fish, a method which appeared to demand greater precision in casting; 'the greater the difficulties to be overcome the greater the sport'. What had been largely a regional variation, a minor version of the north–south divide so pervasive in English society, became a furious argument when the dogmatic and combative Halford published a series of books, particularly his *Dry Fly Fishing*.

He became the self-appointed priest of a dry-fly cult, loathed particularly by northerners, whom he regarded as poachers. The new clubs in the south turned to the dry fly wholesale, not least because they combined Halford's vision of ethical purity with a pragmatic belief that the use of the wet fly would make catching easier, increasing their costs, as more restocking was required. The debate lasted until well after the First World War, but a significant counterblast appeared with the publication in 1910 of G. E. M Skues's *Minor Tactics of the Chalk Stream*, a plea for the limited use of imitative wet-fly forms in the south. It was typical of Halford that he abused Skues personally, not least, one suspects, because Skues appeared to claim that the old and northern method could be just as ethically correct as his own cult. The north had need to be defensive, since some of the Sheffield middle classes had gone over to the new faith on their Derbyshire streams by 1906.[51]

Halford and his followers had an easy forum for their views. In 1884 R. B. Marston, the proprietor of the influential *Fishing Gazette*, founded the Fly Fishers' Club, a purely social organisation based on established West End models, its motto *Piscator non solum piscator*, 'It is not all of fishing to fish'. It used rented rooms in the Adelphi at first, with dining and card nights for its emphatically professional memberships: clergy, lawyers and writers in particular. Although it claimed to support harmony, Halford was a leading member, and it demonstrated only too clearly the distinctions exercised so often in sport within upper middle-class groups. In 1894 the club banned any fishing tackle manufacturer or dealer from membership; tradesmen were clearly not acceptable, despite the fact that a number of the club's 400 members made some part of their income from angling writing or editing.

Although most of the club were practising fishermen, with access to the better streams, there was also a strongly developed late Victorian collectors' and exhibitionist element. The club acquired stuffed fish, a superb library and standard displays of tackle and fly-tying, and published its own journal from 1911. Some members acquired rather more. Dr Goulland, who died in 1896, had spent £30,000 in the previous decade on sporting tackle, include 367 rods. It is not recorded how much his fishing cost, or how successful he was.[52]

Game fishing faced pressures other than that of numbers, not least commercial netting and a growing risk of pollution. In 1903 a small but active group formed the Salmon and Trout Association, a pressure group for collecting information and lobbying the authorities. Like the WAGBI it grew slowly – game fishermen were, for once, far less concerned than their working-class brethren with maintaining powerful defensive bodies – so that it reached only 250 members before 1915. Its concentration on salmon limited its appeal to the majority of trout fishermen, not least when its most overt claim was to have asked successfully for the Salmon and Freshwater Fishermen Act (England and Wales), 1907. Its council, comprising a fourth of its total pre-war membership, included landed gentry, peers and a journalists' group, F. G. Aflalo, R. B. Marston and William Senior.

The latter two also became vice-presidents of a new fly and bait-casting club, founded in 1910 to provide tournaments in distance casting; Lord Desborough, the Grenfell of Olympic fame, was its president. Although it soon numbered 100 members, its introduction to English field sports of a European model, patterned on the Casting Club de France, was probably anathema to the majority of fly fishermen, who turned to the sport precisely because it offered relative solitude and an escape from the stresses of a competitive working life.[53]

There was one other form of angling where, as with wildfowling, middle-class newcomers took a traditional occupation based on meeting market needs and turned it into a 'sport': sea fishing. It grew alongside the great Victorian boom in seaside resorts, a suitable male activity whilst female family members engaged in gentler pursuits. It also met the needs of men seeking group activities, and was gradually adopted also by professional and businessmen settling permanently in the burgeoning seaside towns. Its leading proponent was the ubiquitous F. G. Aflalo, who founded the British Sea Anglers' Society in 1893 as a body for publishing information on good fishing and negotiating favourable terms with local boatmen for the society's members. As in fowling, the professionals found themselves in the uneasy position of becoming the virtual servants of prosperous amateurs. The latter frequently let the class base of their sporting ethics show openly, dismissing the effective crudity of professional methods as unworthy of sport:

> The worthy fellows are very apt to form rough and ready conclusions which a scientific observer with a quarter of their experience could say with certainty were inaccurate. The members of the British Sea Anglers' Society, on the other hand, come of a class consisting mainly of intelligent,

educated men, and their observations on baits, the migration of fish and kindred matters are likely to be of considerable value. Certainly in obtaining general conclusions, the educated, practical, amateur sea fisherman is less likely to go astray than the uneducated professional fisherman and the unpractical scientist.[54]

This ambivalence towards professional skills in a group owing much of its social and economic position to its own increased professionalism ran throughout the fabric of late nineteenth-century sport. What rarely surface are the ways in which this arrogance was reciprocated by its victims. At the lower end of the middle-class scale, sea fishing shared with coarse angling the risk of losing ethical purity because it was open to competition. It helped bond together resident groups within the resorts, who clearly used competition to foster this. The Bexhill Sea Angling Club, made up of middling shopkeepers, butchers, grocers and so on, used their Wednesday half-days to fish matches from the beach for prizes up to 10s in value. Its members could hire a boat for 15s a day; cost and occupation clearly delineated the club's social role.

On the water

Killing was not the only attraction of open space; other activities fostered isolation and conspicuousness as well. It is singularly unfortunate that late twentieth-century nostalgia has isolated one of these, yachting, within an ambience of rigid formality, inevitably portrayed by photographs of aristocratic visitors in blazers and white flannels at Cowes. Certainly this grew with the onset of wealth: Walton has identified the role of yachting as 'one of the most exclusive activities of all in promoting the social tone of particular resorts', Cowes and Torquay being the most obvious.[55] There was a certain pathos in the attempts of lesser towns, such as Seaford, to boost their flagging development with summer regattas which never succeeded. There were individuals – Sir Alfred Lipton is always the most quoted – who used commercially based wealth to move into the restrictive world of racing large, professionally crewed yachts, the 12 m and above. The descendant of the railway contractor turned landowner Thomas Brassey sailed round the world in his large yacht *Sunbeam*.[56]

This followed a familiar pattern of limited downward diffusion with the growth of increasingly exclusive yacht clubs. By 1914 *Lloyd's Register* listed 120 in England and Wales, thirty-two of which had acquired the prefix 'Royal'. They ranged from the Royal Yacht Squadron, founded in 1815, to much more recent but ambitious bodies.[57] The Royal Yorkshire Yacht Club started with landed patronage in 1847, as did the Royal Welsh Yacht Club, based on Caernarvon. Membership of the latter was by ballot, one black ball in five being sufficient for exclusion. Politics and religion were banned from club meetings. As it developed it increased in formality, the later club rules demanding club 'dress, undress, and dinner dress', each with a slightly different blue jacket. The majority of its 164 members were nominally resident in Wales, although often actually based in Liverpool, with sixty-five boats between them; any boat used for trade or charter was banned.

The role of socially ambitious outsiders in colonising such clubs could provoke tensions which were perceived more in local than in specifically class terms. The Royal Cornwall Yacht Club, founded in 1871, had a turbulent period after 1890, when the local members felt obliged to form a rival body, the short-lived Falmouth Sailing Club. When that failed and they came back to the mother body they forced out the 'hucksters who gained membership after 1900'. As in a number of other cases, club membership had been used to boost wider social status. Yacht clubs were one of the multiple organisations where *bona fide* membership, for participation in the sport actively, posed considerable difficulties for club control and development.[58]

The absolute *raison d'être* of most of these clubs was racing, and there was a considerable range of regional variants of the Cowes model. Much of this deliberately avoided the professional crewing of the grander clubs and emphasised the amateurism of 'Corinthian' yachting. Because of local pride and differing water conditions, many of the clubs produced specialist racing boats for their own needs: 'one-designers'. In the case of the Royal Yorkshire Yacht Club, it was a three-quarter-decked, lug-rigged craft some 25 ft 6 in. long.[59] Many more clubs compromised with the realities of their members' ownership, particularly those founded for the proverbial 'man of moderate means'.[60] By the late 1890s the Solent had thirteen such clubs, including the appropriately named Minima, for which subscriptions were a deceptive 10s 6d a year, a twentieth of the Royal Yacht Squadron's.[61]

The greatest pressure came on those waters within easier reach of London, with clubs catering essentially for Saturday afternoon sailors. Although convention forbade Sunday racing, these clubs increasingly attracted 'pleasure' as well as competitive sailors. Southend, at the mouth of the Thames, boasted five clubs by 1913, with a total of 1,150 members. In addition, there were at least 350 independent sailors drawn to the local facilities but not to club life.

By far the greatest pressure of this period led to the remarkable development of the river Crouch in Essex, with Burnham as its focus. What had been a quiet village dependent on the oyster trade was transformed by a late Victorian railway line into bustling chaos. By 1910 estimates put 300 yachts at Burnham, with a further 500 regularly moored near by, and waiting lists for moorings were growing. The local watermen found a new addition to their seasonal work, charging a shilling a week for each boat they watched over and $9^{1}/_{2}d$ an hour for maintenance work. A club network developed. The London Sailing Club renamed itself the Eastern Yacht Club, and the Royal Corinthian Yacht club, epitome of amateur purism, based itself there. The Burnham Yacht Club was founded in 1895, to provide a boat house and club room for 'amateur sailors'. It began with fifty-one members, forty of them London residents who included eighteen gentlemen, seven stockbrokers, two barristers, two solicitors, one medical doctor and four oyster merchants. By 1900 membership had increased to 125, and by 1910 to 217, after which the club could not really cope with further growth. As with so many similar clubs in boom sports the need to increase membership to provide communal faculties for those of moderate means clashed with the face-to-face importance of social interaction in the club.[62]

Saturday afternoon sailing was justified as ideal for men without 'sufficient time to indulge in games of manual dexterity that require much practice'. The sport demanded considerable skill, however, and involved no small element of danger. Although this seemed most apparent in the structured world of seasonal racing, dominated by the increasingly tight rules of the Yacht Racing Association, formed in 1875, it was far greater in the branch of the sport which developed most appeal, cruising.[63] Cruising combined relative isolation with the Romantic themes we have noted before: 'the solitude of Nature and the presence of the immeasurable'.[64] Here the physical and mental challenge was mixed into a conscious bohemianism, the sense of camping out on the water, and apparent rejection of many of the values which provided, paradoxically, the means to pursue the sport.

Of all the outdoor sports, cruising produced a literary model which reinforced the sense of scruffy adventure and a defensive patriotism.

An Anglo-Irish lawyer based in London, Erskine Childers, took a seven-ton craft (30 ft x 7 ft), the *Vixen*, to the Baltic in 1897, across the mudflats of Heligoland and through German canals. A fairly bland summary of the journey was published in *Yachting Monthly* in 1898, but Childers went on to build it into one of the better Edwardian tales of espionage, *The Riddle of the Sands*. Dismissed by the *Times Literary Supplement* as 'a bewildering romance', the work became one of the great inspirations of Edwardian cruising, together with the American Joshua Slocum's *Sailing alone around the World*,[65] It was in the wake of such adventures that London's professionals and literary men took to lone sailing in virtual droves. They included the journalist and politician Hilaire Belloc, who bought a thirty-year-old cutter, the *Nona*, in 1901 with Arthur Stanley, who sold his share later to Belloc for £50. The hyper-energetic Belloc explored the Welsh and English coasts in stages in the months before the First World War, escaping grief at his wife's death: 'The sea has taken me to itself whenever I sought it and has given me relief from men.'[66]

Cruising became popular in the 1880s and grew rapidly thereafter. Even the man pottering around the Essex estuaries on a fine Saturday afternoon could imagine that he was 'free and untravelled as the winds, reckless as a Viking, adventurous as a Columbus'. [67] Helped by guides such as that written by the London ophthalmic surgeon Claud Worth, he would usually buy a small second-hand boat for £20 or so and expect to spend about the same amount each year on his sport. [68] Inevitably, perhaps, it acquired a 'respectable' end, the Royal Cruising Club, founded in 1880 and made 'Royal' in 1901. Its first commodore, the Revd. A. J. van Straubenzee, bought his boat with a cheque from his parishioners. In effect it was an adventurous, rather practical version of a West End dining club.[69] Much closer to the needs of sailing individualists who still needed an association to provide advice and information was the Cruising Association, whose monthly bulletin, first published in 1910, provided a mix of solid advice and accounts of cruises. These ranged from coastal crawls in 15 ft dinghies upwards. Even cruising could not avoid competition; the Cruising Association awarded its first challenge cup for the best cruise in March 1912, for a voyage by four men in a 32 ft yawl, the *Winnie*, to Spain and back, some 1,115 miles.[70]

Cruising's appeal was often as much to young married couples as to bachelors or escapist husbands.[71] The provinces exercised a considerable influence, despite London's numerical dominance. In

1883 the Humber Yawl Club was formed, to take over the sailing pastimes of a declining local sailing–canoe club some twenty years old. Its early thirty or so members were largely Hull solicitors, merchants and other commercial men; although it grew slowly until an Edwardian spurt took it to 123 members in 1913, its social composition and Hull-based focus did not shift. It emphasised its informality by replacing the customary club hierarchy, led by a commodore, with a captain and mate. Although it did some sailing on Hornsea Mere and manageable East Riding rivers, its main emphasis was on the Humber itself, the eastern coastal waters and, increasingly, the other side of the North Sea. The prime movers were George Holmes, from a local tanning family, who sailed with the club until the 1930s, and Albert Strange, the principal of Scarborough School of Art. Both of them designed their own boats, Strange in particular developing a very strong line in work for other members. His plans are still classics, small boats manageable by individuals, designed for living in as well as sailing, and suited particularly to lying flat on the mud left by tides in shallow waters.

Both men took a simple local racing or day-sailing design, the canoe yawl, and turned it into craft capable of sustained voyages in rough conditions. For longer overseas cruises both Holmes's *Eel* and Strange's *Cherub* could be shipped as deck cargo on a tramp steamer. In 1897 Holmes took *Eel* to the Baltic by this means, and to Holland the following year. A similar one-month trip in 1898 cost Albert Strange a total of £15. The Yawl Club's main role was to provide a place for chatting in bad weather, a journal where the cruises were logged, and an annual round of smoking concerts, dinners and festivities to foster out-of-season spirits. In style it was almost as far from that of the Royal Yacht Squadron as it is possible to imagine: if nothing else, it fostered carefully a stern image of Viking northerners with little time for the soft living of the south.[72]

The fascination of water produced a much milder variant of the flirting with danger which was an essential part of sailing's appeal, in which some of the outward form of yachting's informality could be linked with family holiday needs. There appeared a lower penumbra in which the participants could at least imagine themselves as 'sporting', even if the strictest criteria of risk and exertion were not met. The Humber Yawl Club developed a flotilla of 'houseboats', shallow draft craft with heavy topsides for accommodation, restricted to the local rivers and canals.

These were matched elsewhere in England with the development of inland sailing. The Norfolk Broads, offering 200 miles of waterways, developed rapidly between 1850 and 1870 as a sailing centre after the building of local railways, offering a sheltered playground for small craft. Alongside dinghies and canoe yawls there emerged a sporting modification of local commercial vessels. In 1880 the Press brothers of North Walsham converted a Broads wherry for cruising, letting it with a crew of two men for ten to twenty guineas a week, according to season. If such craft were suited to genteel meanderings, the spread of smaller boats and the participation of the local urban middle classes led to the familiar pattern of club formation. The Great Yarmouth Yacht Club, for ninety local people 'of importance', was formed in 1883, to be followed by the rather larger Lowestoft Club in 1887. Bordering the local waters and the sea was the Norfolk and Suffolk Club, 'exclusive and expensive'.[73]

Other rivers produced milder forms (rowing, with its athletic demands, will be more properly discussed in chapter 3). Inevitably dominant were the Thames and its tributaries, where some 10,482 pleasure boats were registered by 1898.[74] On these waters style and etiquette probably mattered more than prowess, but it was essentially an area where London clerks who flexed their muscles with Indian clubs during the winter could display modest physical co-ordination; rowing on summer weekends or on summer holidays like Jerome K. Jerome's *Three Men in a Boat* (1889). A similar duality applied to the punt. Developed from moored fishing vessels in the 1860s, it was popularised in the 1890s for sport. The great thrust came with the foundation in 1885 of the Thames Punting Club, with its Amateur Rowing Association-derived rules and a steady series of annual racing regattas.[75]

This sporting earnestness had to work hard to overcome the common assumption that punting represented leisured indolence, an escape from the necessity to work best associated with the older universities in springtime. One individual gave it both moral purpose and social acceptability: W. H. Grenfell, the pan-athlete, later Lord Desborough.[76] Other rivers produced their own variations, some club-based, many distinctly individual. On the Midland Avon the Warwick Boat Club fluctuated repeatedly between emphasising sporting rowing and bowing to its members' urge for gentle meanderings on summer evenings. The spread, in Edwardian England, of motor yachts along the coast had its inland imitators. One of the most

complete insights into this is to be found in the log book kept by
J. R. Halkes, a Lincoln architect and surveyor, of his voyages in the
Asp on local waters, dogged by repeated engine failure. All told, in
1907, he travelled 240 miles, the longest trip being ninety, but more
usually short ones of some five to twelve miles. In 1908 he covered
410 miles; in 1913, 339. All these voyages were written up in a style
which indicated only too clearly his debt to Jerome K. Jerome, a
combination of humorous meanderings with earnest combating of
navigational and mechanical problems which very clearly stemmed
from his devout Wesleyanism.[77]

On top of the land

The English middle classes (or at least a very small group of them) were
widely credited with inventing a sport which combined Romanticism
and risk with demanding athleticism: mountaineering. Although the
discovery of hills was deeply rooted in the aesthetic aftermath of the
Grand Tour, it was the mid-Victorian generation which turned it into a
climbing challenge rather than distant appreciation. Convention puts
the 'golden age' of this effort in the years 1854–65, beginning when a
young barrister, Alfred Wills, climbed the Wetterhorn in the Bernese
Oberland during a few days off from his honeymoon and finishing
with the disastrous first ascent of the Matterhorn, led by a professional
artist, Edward Whymper.[78] In those eleven years forty major Alpine
peaks were ascended for the first time by English amateurs, with the
help of local guides as porters. The focus was the relatively limited
territory of the Swiss Alps, ranged over during the extended summer
vacations of the upper professional classes.

Alpine mountaineering fitted the needs of relatively wealthy
bachelors, lawyers, clergy and dons in particular, who found in
Switzerland both an individualistic or small-group physical outlet
and a moderately wild informality which allowed a brief escape
from their highly structured and eminently respectable home-based
lives. By the very nature of Victorian mountaineering, it also offered
a singular asceticism, a rediscovery of the wilderness which some
were prepared to see in biblical terms. For many it was literally an
expression of muscular Christianity; for those like Leslie Stephen who
lost their faith the mountains became a source of secular mysticism,
despite Ruskin's oft trumpeted denunciations that they had turned
the majesty of Nature into a race track.[79]

Yet, with the exception of some personal rivalries, and the particular demon which drove Whymper, this was not a competitive sport. Rising out of the clubable world of the universities, the Inns of Court and St James's there was an early move to form a specialist body, the Alpine Club. Founded in 1857, over half its early members were barristers, clergy, solicitors, dons and schoolmasters. This 'aristocracy of intellect' limited its numbers to those who not only performed similar feats but were also likely to fit easily into the common-room nature of its gatherings. The club provided a meeting place for information and for the didacticism virtually inseparable from such high-minded endeavours, with lectures, publications and a superb library.

Its membership, 323 by 1870, rose slowly to over 700 by 1914, a growth far slower than the sport's overall increase. And it ossified, laying down patterns of climbing practice and etiquette which came to be seen by many climbers of the later Victorian generation as restrictive, emphasising style rather than new directions.[80] As Geoffrey Winthrop Young, a turn-of-the-century Young Turk among climbers, remarked, 'Inevitably, and with the precision of the senior boys in a school, they established the rule of how Alpine climbing was to be done. All else became not done.'[81] The habits of the public school appeared inescapable. To climb properly meant with a local guide, going out from one centre, avoiding wandering freely; and for many the only mountains a true gentleman could climb were the Alps.

Despite the enormous possibilities of the British Empire, it was left to later generations, or the less socially acceptable to try the Rockies, the Himalayas and New Zealand. The Alpine Club's members included John Hopkins (1849–98), a Fellow of Trinity, Cambridge, who went on to design lighthouses and Manchester's lighting system; Harold Ward Topham, a non-practising barrister and Florida orange planter who eventually retired to live on his investments, to climb and sail; and Edward Broome, whose avocation as a Worcestershire carpet manufacturer was compensated by his being 'an artist by temperament, with the appearance and the appetite of a conquistador'. Charles Wollaston, a bank director, cricketer and footballer, took up Alpine climbing aged forty in 1849 and spent every summer in Zermatt; despite severe mountain sickness, his 'indomitable perseverance' made him a very good mountain all-rounder. For all his prominence, he was virtually never photographed, nor spoke in public.[82] Class issues alone do not always explain the powerful personal drive which took these men to the peaks. Some, such as Edward Lyttelton, frightened themselves out of climbing: as a young master he was nearly killed in 1880 as he 'dabbled in Swiss mountaineering'. With his usual depressive earnestness he warned, 'Beware of exhilaration of spirits in the champagne air.'[83]

The love of high snows and summer climbing prompted a further extension of the season, a more conspicuous display of wealth and another essentially British invention, winter sports. These took the aesthetic challenge of mountaineering and combined it with the strongly developed hypochondria which drove the more affluent Victorians to take a winter cure in centres like Davos, St Moritz and Grindelwald. Unlike members of the Alpine Club, these people dressed for dinner on a Swiss evening. Ice-skating and tobogganing grew in popularity, particularly with younger men who had not yet developed the skills of winter climbing.

The growth, inchoate at first, became far more highly organised than climbing when Dr Henry Lunn co-operated with a Harrow master, John Stogdon, to arrange 'package' tours. By 1900 Lunn was sending 5,000 people a year on such tours, under the separate arrangements of Alpine Sports Ltd, a company he formed so that its clients would avoid the embarrassment of having the label of his other concern, Lunn's Tours, on their luggage. Alpine Sports Ltd became the booking agency for the Public Schools Sports Club, whose Eton and Harrow domination meant that the resorts patronised were as exclusive as clubland. The Public Schools Alpine Sports Club, founded as the Winter Sports Club in 1905, published its own *Who's Who*, and had no subscription, yet provided 'all the elective advantage of an English Club . . . for a Continental holiday'. For a 10s 6d entrance fee, open only to public school, university and service families, and presided over by the ubiquitous Edward Lyttelton, its 5,000 members could be sure, booking through Lunn, that they would meet only their own sort in the Alps. There the more strenuous could take up skiing, a distinct Edwardian vogue, fostered yet again by the enterprising Lunn family, whose younger member, Arnold Lunn, made a ski-climbing traverse of the Oberland in January 1908 and founded the Alpine Ski-Club in March. The Lunns combined athletics with commercial acumen and a sharp eye for the social foibles of their clientele. Any one of their clients risked, however, being caricatured by serious climbers as likely to spend 'half his time in dancing and the other half in winter-sports carnivals'.[84]

The London–Alpine axis and its social restrictions grated increasingly on many middle-class men just below its social circles, especially those in the provinces. For them the native wildernesses of North Wales and the Lake District provided a more convenient outlet for spirits little different from the mid-Victorian pioneers and allowed the development of a sport, rock-climbing, which was both risky and demanding of high athletic ability.

Snowdonia had drawn tourists since the early nineteenth century but from the 1870s it became increasingly attractive to vacation reading parties from the universities and public schools. With the ingenuousness of their class they prided themselves on their informality, openness and lack of exclusiveness; in real face-to-face terms they were inevitably little different from their Alpine counterparts. Based on the hotels at Pen y Gwryd and Pen y Pass, they eventually formed the Climbers' Club in 1897. Their leaders were schoolmasters such as J. M. Archer Thompson, the Head of Llandudno School, and scientists like the Huxleys. Sport and sociability ran close together, but a claim by their apologist, Winthrop Young, that 'Position in the forgotten outside world, titles, even the claims of seniority seemed faintly ludicrous' must be treated carefully: their very presence and pursuits belied it. Looking back from the more crowded inter-war years of this century, Young hankered after 'the days when only the literary, the learned and the artistic element thought [the club's] remote simplicity worthwhile'.[85]

A similar, sometimes overlapping world was created in the Lake District, centred on Wasdale Head, when an Oxford undergraduate, Walter Perry Haskett Smith, began climbing there in 1883. The movement's modern historian sees the years 1882–1903 as English rock-climbing's 'golden age'. Its participants sought small but difficult challenges, in which a few hundred yards of a rock face meant more than an Alpine peak. Dismissed as 'chimney sweeps' by many members of the Alpine Club, they climbed cracks as a form of sprint and gymnastics. Some Alpinists, such as Hopkinson, joined them but most came as scientists, or schoolmasters, from a grade just below their Alpine equivalents. The key personnel came from the Liverpool, north Cheshire and Manchester areas; they were often far more prosaic in style and approach than men like Stephen but they showed a similar background.

In 1886 Haskett Smith climbed Napes Needle solo and the efforts of his followers exploded. Dominated by Smith, the chemist and polymath J. N. Collie and O. G. ('the only genuine') Jones, a London schoolmaster, they tackled crag after crag, often with little sense of danger and with minimal equipment. They stare out still from club photographs in ancient tweeds and heavy boots. The movement waned sharply in 1903 when four experienced climbers died together on Scafell pinnacle, and the dangers were taken up for an apprehensive public with press sensationalism.[86]

In 1907 the next generation formed the Fell and Rock Climbing Club, to provide both publications and safety rules.[87] The Leeds men who climbed formed the Yorkshire Rambling Club in 1899, with both physical and social tests of membership.[88] In Manchester those who climbed the Peak's gritstone formed the Rucksack Club in 1902.[89] These provincial clubs marked a new stage, the movement of wildness into respectability. Club huts gradually replaced the hotels which earlier climbers had colonised with remarkable *insouciance* towards the feelings of other visitors, sleeping on the billiard tables and practising handholds around the dining rooms. They became bastions of amateurism, bolstered by club dinners, songs and doggerel. But when the Fell and Rock Climbing Club, two-thirds of whose 170 members lived north of the Trent, claimed, 'It is rock-climbing that has helped to make mountaineering universal and democratic,' they were not using the latter word in the sense it had come to acquire in Edwardian England.[90]

All these bodies remained quintessentially for the professional classes, often living out schoolboy dreams, such as when members (all over twenty-one) of the Rucksack Club played 'a great game' on Scafell Pike at Easter 1906. They divided themselves into 'scouts' and 'outposts' to attack the mountain as a pretend castle.[91] It fitted the growing militarism of their world and, however much they decried 'pot hunting' in the mountains, they were justifying Ruskin's outburst.

Notes

1 C. F. Dowsett (ed.), *Land: its Attraction and Riches* (1892), 163 ff.

2 G. A. B. Dewar, *Life and Sport in Hampshire* (1908), 244 ff.

3 L. B. Taylor, *A Brief History of the Westley Richards Firm, 1812–1913* (Stratford upon Avon, 1913), 29.

4 J. Lowerson, 'Breakdown or reinforcement?'; J. K. Walton, 'The Windermere tourist trade', in O. Westall (ed.), *Windermere in the Nineteenth Century* (Lancaster, 1976).

5 T. S. Hendricks, 'The democratisation of sport in eighteenth-century England', *Journal of Popular Culture*, 18 (1984), 3 ff.

6 T. C. Barker, 'The delayed decline of the horse in the twentieth century', in F. M. L. Thompson (ed.), *Horses in European Economic History: a Preliminary*

Canter (Reading, 1983), 101 ff.; K. Chivas, 'The supply of horses in Great Britain in the nineteenth century', in Thompson, *op. cit.*, 33; T. F. Dale, *Riding, Driving and Kindred Sports* (1899), xii.

7 T. H. S. Escott, *Social Transformations of the Victorian Age* (1897), 413; *Baily's Hunting Directory, 1912–13, passim.*

8 C. Whitney, *A Sporting Pilgrimage* (1895), 26.

9 R. Carr, *English Foxhunting* (1986), 154.

10 Carr, *English Foxhunting*, 157.

11 D. C. Itzkowitz, *Peculiar Privilege: a Social History of English Foxhunting, 1753–1885* (Hassocks, 1977), 157 ff.

12 *Baily's, 1912–13, passim;* 'Capping in the hunting field', *Fortnightly Review,* LXXV (1904).

13 'Is hunting a rich man's luxury?', *Baily's Magazine* (November 1905).

14 Walton, *English Seaside Resort,* 184; *Baily's Hunting Directory, 1912–13,* 63–4; *The Times,* 23 April 1910.

15 *Baily's Hunting Directory, 1912–13,* 359–60; *Baily's Magazine,* 82 (1904), 48 ff.

16 *Baily's Hunting Directory, 1912–13,* 270–1, 269, 265; East Sussex Record Office, AMS 5788/3/1–3.

17 H. C. Donovan, *The Brain Side of Games* (1909), 121.

18 'Hunting and its future', *Fortnightly Review,* LXIII (1898); Hon. F. Lawley, 'How long will fox-hunting live?', *Baily's Magazine,* September 1894, 148 ff.

19 Carr, *English Foxhunting,* 195 ff.; Itzkowitz, *Peculiar Privilege,* 143 ff; *Horse and Hound,* 5 April 1884; *Sporting Mirror,* 7 (1884), 35; H. R. Sargent, *Thoughts upon Sport* (1895), xiv ff.; Humanitarian League, *Humanity, passim.*

20 F. G. Aflalo, 'The morals of sport', *C. B. Fry's Magazine,* 13, 242 ff.; 'A sportsman on cruelty to animals', *Fortnightly Review,* LXX (1901); B. Tozer, 'The abuse of sport', *Fortnightly Review,* LXXX (1906); 'What is cruelty in sport?', *Baily's Magazine,* 77 (1902), 209–30; C. Graves, *Leather Armchairs* (1963), 103 ff.; T. Dorling, *The Hurlingham Club* (1954), 13; J. Galsworthy, 'Reverie of a sportsman', *Fortnightly Review,* XLVII (1915), 685 ff.

21 J. G. Ruffer, *The Big Shots* (1977).

22 The figures are extracted from the annual Excise Returns in *Parliamentary Papers.*

23 H. Sharp, *The Gun: Afield and Afloat* (1904), xiv–xv; see also Sportsman (ed.), *British Sports and Sportsmen, Past and Present* (1908); G. W. E. Russell, *For Better? For Worse? Notes on Social Changes* (1903), 40.

24 *Golf Illustrated,* 30 July 1909; *The Times,* 10 November 1908; *Baily's Magazine,* 71 (1899), 200; C. E. Walker, *Shooting on a Small Income* (1900); D. Newsome, *On the Edge of Paradise: A. C. Benson the Diarist* (1980), 184–5; W. Bromley-Davenport, 'Covert shooting', *Nineteenth Century,* December 1883; Spartan, 'The decadence of sport', *Baily's Magazine,* March 1905, 199.

25 W. W. Greener, *The Gun and its Development* (1881), 1910 edition, 470; Dorling, *Hurlingham Club, passim;* Dicken's Dictionary of the Thames (1894), 112; Tom Quinn, 'The history of the British Open', *Shooting Times,* 17–23 May 1984; Taylor, *Westley Richards,* 72 ff.; G. T. Teasdale-Buckell, *Experts on Guns and Shooting* (1902), 21, 120 ff.

26 E. Harrison, *A Dissertation upon Guns and Shooting* (1906), 210.
27 S. Duncan and G. Thorne, *The Complete Wildfowler* (1911), 17.
28 Wildfowler, *Public Shooting Quarters* (1881), *passim*.
29 J. Marchington, *The History of Wildfowling* (1980); H. G. Hutchinson (ed.), *Shooting*, 2 (1902).
30 J. Humphreys, *Stanley Duncan – Wildfowler* (Rossett, Clwyd, 1983); Marchington, *Wildfowling*, 229 ff.
31 A. Lang, *The Tercentenary of Izaak Walton* (1893); *The Times*, 31 July 1893; J. Lowerson, 'Izaak Walton: father of a dream', *History Today*, December 1983.
32 C. Kingsley, 'Chalk stream studies', *Miscellanies*, I (1859), 166.
33 F. G. Aflalo, 'The infinite variety of sports', *Baily's Magazine*, 94 (1910), 28–9.
34 S. Chitty, *The Beast and the Monk* (1974), 195; B. Colloms, *Charles Kingsley* (1975), 119; M. Pattison, *Memoirs* (1885), 299 ff.; H. Shelley, *Arthur Ransome* (1960); A. Ransome, *The Autobiography of Arthur Ransome* (1976), 24, 30; West Sussex Record Office, Cobden–Unwin Papers 966.
35 K. Robson, 'Izaak's other river', *Trout Fisherman*, January 1985, 62–3.
36 Sheffield Reference Library, *Cuttings*, 12, 127.
37 J. Lowerson, 'Brothers of the angle: coarse fishing and working-class culture', in J. A. Mangan (ed.), *Pleasure, Profit, Proselytism: British Culture and Sport at Home and Abroad, 1700–1914* (1988), 105 ff.
38 *Fishing Gazette*, 24 March 1900; Victoria County History, *Yorkshire*, 2 (1912), 529; *Northern Angler*, 18 February 1893; *Fishing Gazette*, 7 October 1893; 12 December 1877, 6 January 1878.
39 J. Harbottle, *A Fisherman's Garland* (Leeds, 1904), 75.
40 T. H. English, *A Memoir of the Yorkshire Esk Fishery Association* (Whitby, 1925).
41 W. M. Gallichan, *Fishing in Derbyshire and Around* (1905), 117.
42 H. Plunket Greene, *Where the Bright Waters Meet* (1924), 12.
43 *The Book of the Piscatorial Society, 1836–1936* (1936), 28.
44 *Hull News*, 26 April 1884.
45 *Sheffield Independent*, 11 May 1896; P. Bartrip, 'Food for the body and food for the mind: the regulation of freshwater fisheries in the 1870s', *Victorian Studies*, 28 (1985), 285 ff.
46 *Parliamentary Papers*, 1907, XI, 72–3; 1913–14, XXVI, 766; 1914–16, XXII, 250.
47 *Fortnightly Review*, LV (1894), 503; *Badminton Magazine*, III (1896), 486; G. A. B. Dewar, *The South Country Trout Streams* (1899), 26; *Fishing Gazette*, 2 December 1905; W. M. Gallichan, *The Trout Waters of England* (1908), 16 ff.
48 F. M. Halford, *An Angler's Autobiography* (1903); Sir H. Maxwell, *Chronicles of the Houghton Fishery Club, 1822–1908* (1908).
49 *Fishing Gazette*, 11 March 1905.
50 J. P. Taylor, 'Trout fishing in reservoirs', *C. B. Fry's Magazine*, 9 (1908), 127 ff.; E. Phillips, 'Trout fishing in reservoirs', *Baily's Magazine* XCI (1909), 481 ff.; E. Phillips, *Trout in Lakes and Reservoirs* (1914).
51 J. H. R. Taylor, 'The land of the wet fly', *C. B. Fry's Magazine*, 9 (1908), 455 ff.; A. K., 'What is sport?', *Fishing Gazette*, 4 October 1878; W. E. Hodgson, 'Fly fishing', *Nineteenth Century*, May 1908; *Fishing Gazette*, 12 March 1910;

W. Carter Platts, 'The spread of the dry-fly cult', *Baily's Magazine*, 86 (1906), 194 ff.; F. M. Halford, *Dry Fly Fishing in Theory and Practice* (1889); G. E. M. Skues, *Minor Tactics of the Chalk Stream* (1910).

52 Graves, *Leather Armchairs*, 112 ff.; *The Book of the Flyfishers' Club, 1884–1934* (1934), 19; Fly Fishers' Club, *Journal*, 1911.

53 Salmon and Trout Association, *Journals*.

54 J. Bickerdyke, *Sea Fishing* (1895), 7–8; F. G. Aflalo, *Sea Fishing on the English Coast* (1891); P. L. Haslope, *Practical Sea Fishing* (1905); F. G. Aflalo, 'The rise and progress of sea angling', *C. B. Fry's Magazine*, II, 165 ff.

55 Walton, *Seaside Resort*, 184.

56 T. Brassey, *Voyages and Travels of Lord Brassey from 1868 to 1894*, Captain S. Eardley-Wilmot (1895).

57 *Lloyd's Register of Yachts*, 1914.

58 *The Royal Yorkshire Yacht Club, 1847–1947* (Hull, 1947); Caernarfon Record Office, XM/923/59, 63, 56, Royal Welsh Yacht Club, 'Laws and Regulations'; C. J. H. Mead, *History of the Royal Cornwall Yacht Club, 1871–1949* (Plymouth, 1951), 193.

59 *Royal Yorkshire Yacht Club*, 33.

60 *Yachting Monthly*, 7 (1909), 178 ff.

61 Thalassa (ed.), *Yacht Racing in the Solent Classes* (1892).

62 W. E. Wigfull, 'The yacht clubs of the Southend district', *Yachting Monthly*, 15 (1913), 398; Homeland Association, Handy Guides 14, *Burnham on Crouch* (1909); Public Record Office (hereafter PRO), BT 31/15466, Co. 43622, Burnham Yacht Club Co. Ltd; Cruising Association . . . *Bulletin*, November 1910, May 1911, July 1911.

63 F. B. Cooke, *Yacht Racing for Amateurs* (1911).

64 *Yachting Monthly*, 1 (1906), 78.

65 E. Childers, 'How we drifted to the Baltic in a seven-tonner', *Yachting Monthly*, 1 (1898), 267 ff.; *The Riddle of the Sands* (1903): *Times Literary Supplement*, 14 August 1903; Joshua Slocum, *Sailing alone around the World* (1900).

66 A. N. Wilson, *Hilaire Belloc* (1984), 213.

67 F. Cowper, *Sailing Tours* (1892), 5.

68 C. Worth, *Yacht Cruising* (1910).

69 *A Short History of the Royal Cruising Club, 1880–1930* (1930).

70 *Cruising Association Bulletin*, March 1912.

71 M. Speed, *A Yachtswoman's Cruises* (1911).

72 Humber Yawl Club, *Centenary Year Book 1983* (Hull, 1984); Humber Yawl Club, *Yearbooks*, 1889 onwards; A. V. Watts, *The Humber*, 33 ff.; Cruising Association Bulletin, November 1913; *Hull Daily Mail*, 8 September 1978.

73 N. Everett, *Broadland Sport* (1902), 238 ff, 276 ff, 289; *The Builder*, July – December 1903, 75.

74 S. Crossland, *Pleasure and Leisure Boating: a Practical Handbook* (1899).

75 R. T. Rivington, *Punting: its History and Techniques* (Oxford, 1982), *passim*.

76 R. T. Rivington, *Punts and Punting* (1982), 9.

77 Lincolnshire Record Office, J. R. Halkes of Lincoln, 'Log Book of the Motor Boat *Asp*'.

78 A. Hankinson, *The First Tigers* (1972), 5.

79 Lunn, *Switzerland*, *passim*.

80 A. Lunn, *A Century of Mountaineering, 1857–1957* (1957); Alpine Club, *List of Members* (1870 onwards).
81 G. Winthrop Young, 'Club and climbers, 1880–1900', *Alpine Journal*, 62 (1957), 52 ff.
82 A. L. Munn, *The Alpine Club Register, 1877–90* (1928); C. Schuster, *Men, Women and Mountains* (1931), 47 ff., 63 ff.; *Rucksack Club Journal*, II (1911–14), 161.
83 E. Lyttelton, *Memories and Hopes* (1925), 121.
84 *Who was Who, 1929–40*, 'Henry Lunn'; *Who was Who, 1971–80*,' 'Arnold Lunn'; Lunn, *Switzerland*, 178 ff.; A. Lunn, *Come what May* (1940), 99; A. Lunn, *Memory to Memory* (1956), 25 ff.; *The Public Schools Winter Sports Club Who's Who, 1909* (1908); *Public Schools Alpine Sports Club Year Book* (1910 onwards); Lunn, *Switzerland*, 200 ff.; *Fell and Rock Climbing Club Journal*, III (1915), 143.
85 H. R. C. Carr (ed.), *The Mountains of Snowdonia* (1925), 1948 edition, *passim*.
86 Hankinson, *Tigers*; Climber's Club, *Journal* (1898 onwards).
87 *Fell and Rock Climbing Club Journal* (1907 onwards), I, 92.
88 *Yorkshire Ramblers' Club Journal*, I (1899–1902), 3.
89 *Rucksack Club Journal*, I (Manchester, 1907).
90 *Fell and Rock Climbing Club Journal*, I, 125.
91 *Rucksack Club Journal*, I, 33.

Chapter 3
Manly games

Virtues

Most studies of organised Victorian sport have concentrated on a few athletic and team activities, especially cricket and the various forms of football. Their high visibility has made then attractive symbols of the industrialisation of 'mass' leisure activities and supposed ethical enlightenment. This is very well trodden ground where it is virtually impossible to avoid heavy dependence on some major recent works. Especially influential, perhaps even satisfying to a conservative English sense of hierarchical order, has been a model of downward diffusion. In it, activities virtually created, or at least transmogrified, for the benefit of a new upper middle-class public school clientele were adapted through emulation or as a direct result of social mission. The stock figures of the muscular curate and university settlement worker have featured large. The wide currency of a sub-Newboldian language of 'playing the game' has lent credence to this idea but the beneficiaries often gave it different values.

Generally the emphasis was on purity in the development of the individual, physically, mentally and, hopefully, spiritually. This lent itself readily to a secular Christian model for a society obsessed with liberal individualism. The language of conditioning seemed at first sight to offer the best basis for growth in later life. Many of the activities to which it was attached were so physically demanding that they could be played only by the relatively young, but the moral benefits were supposed to yield their greatest value when actual participation had ceased. But individualism needed to be moderated by social realities; *stasis* or equipoise had to be provided if the aggressive forces released were not to become socially destructive. Even in track athletics compromise had to be reached so that the team's performance could be rated higher than any one athlete's records. Running for the school, the college, the club was of greater import than running for oneself. The pattern that emerged of awarding 'colours' (most notoriously the Oxford and Cambridge 'Blues') for the most successful athletes embodied a collective reward system in which group honour was seen as the highest attainable individual goal and which imprisoned personal pride in whatever conventionality the group chose. Wearing the appropriately decorated blazer marked off membership of a self-proclaimed elite but contained the individual within it.

What this ethical overboost did was to allow the rapid development and eventual fixation in the later nineteenth century of a range of activities which had long existed in the localised and unco-ordinated form of traditional games. 'Game' was elevated to the more serious and absorbing status of 'sport'. The bureaucratisation of sports in this period is well covered ground; the tendency towards officialdom was in itself a measure of the new ethical seriousness. I shall deal elsewhere with the concomitant obsession with purity; it is worth attempting here a brief assessment of the religio-cultural impetus to this spurt.

'Muscular Christianity' has been blamed for a great deal, and it offered victims for caricature: the cricketing parson, muscular curate, ex-rowing bishop and so on were based on real figures such as Winnington-Ingram, the Bishop of London (1898–1939). As models within the Church they slotted relatively easily into a later Victorian context of professional persons committed to new forms of evangelising and maintaining the allegiance of their congregations. They featured in Anglicanism of the post-Kingsley generation but by the Edwardian period there were not a few Dissenting ministers, at least among the more obviously middle-class and theologically flex-ible Wesleyans and Congregationalists, who used sport as a defence against and an inevitable compromise with the changing *mores* of their flock. Church and chapel-based football, cricket and running clubs were to be found almost as much in the newer suburban areas as surrounding those outposts in the slums, the university and public school settlements. The paradox of this becomes obvious in organised religion's attaching itself to the new agencies of voluntary secular organisation during the years of its own continued relative decline. It found itself lending weight to the development of an extra-ecclesiastical folk religion, the late Victorian sentimentalisation of ethics only occasionally buttressed by active participation in religious worship.

This Christian absorption into athletics had surprisingly thin roots to bear the Victorian weight put upon it. Its scriptural justification is minute, two brief lines in the Pauline Epistles: I Corinthians 9: 24, 'Know ye not that they which run in a race run all, but one receiveth the prize? So run that ye may obtain' and Hebrews 12: 1, '. . . let us lay aside every weight and the sin which doth so easily beset us. And let us run with patience the race that is set before us' (Authorised Version). Both these passages are illustrative exhortations rather than any justification for athleticism – hardly surprising, given St Paul's general distaste for the delights of the body, especially his own. In actual fact, however, the context of Paul's *dicta* fitted their nineteenth-century extension singularly well; the development in hermeneutics which caused lively Victorian theological controversy demonstrated how important was the apostle's synthesis of the apparent inhibitory Judaic culture with the cosmic pictures and cultural expectations of Hellenism. Athletics, at least, offered rather more of a synthesis than the bleak portrayal of cultural conflict which suffuses Matthew Arnold's *Culture and Anarchy* of 1869. Old Testament Hebraic eugenics mingled with a much modified physical and aesthetic hedonism derived from Greek models, particularly those whose idealised 'democracy', could be taken easily into the self-justification of late Victorian elites.

The surprise which still often surrounds that distinctly unathletic aesthetic paragon Walter Pater's fellowship of a notably hearty college, Brasenose, is much less paradoxical when one considers the ways in which philosophical justification was developed for sport. Pater escaped from his surroundings into the classics, taking Victorian conceptions of physique with him; others imported Greek, especially Homeric, models wholesale into their contemporary concerns. When Warre, the headmaster of Eton, lectured his boys on Athenian oarsmanship he was reinforcing what Richard Jenkyns has called a 'Graeco-Britannic ideal' from the top.[1]

The tensions in the Pauline model were enlarged when the university and public school enthusiasm for the Hellenic was distorted. It was a much older and sadder Edward Lyttelton who saw the Etonian emphasis on cricket as producing less than rounded beings but who could still let slip, 'we unconsciously conceived of beauty almost entirely in terms of physical motion and physical skill', with its destruction of a childhood love of nature.[2] This emphasis was male and enclosed, at the least latently homosexual, although hardly fitting the subsequent educational progressives' contention that it helped to manufacture that state of being. The crucial problem lay in the contrast between the sweaty movements of individuals and the idealised physical abstractions which desexualised bodies in a cold, semi-sculptural form.

Cleanliness, purity and maleness became the essence of 'manly' activities which proved valuable for channelling the pubescent masculinity of public school boys to avoid a potentially destructive assertiveness. It was certainly closer to the aesthetic tendency of 'decadence' than most of its proponents were prepared to admit; we have seen Pater's flirting with it through the medium of scholarship but it was several decades before Evelyn Waugh's character Anthony Blanch (in *Brideshead Revisited*) could be allowed to point out to his undergraduate tormenters just how close they were in mutual appeal, how fragile the apparently firm hearty/aesthete divide was.[3]

Concern with athletic and team sports focused essentially on the young, almost in cultic forms. Control was accompanied by optimism for the future. In many senses Victorian England was the first major society – certainly the first industrial and urban one – to develop a relative consensus as to how its future citizens should be formed, its expected leaders most of all. Public, grammar school and university games were supposed to provide alike the physical well-being to cope with stressful competition in maturity and the sense both of striving and of decency to ensure success. The irony was that, as Wiener has shown, much of what the cult was intended to produce in later life was undermined precisely because of addiction to, and the ramifications of, the values it sought to inculcate.[4]

The physical demands were most suited to the under-thirties. A few notably went on through another decade of their lives, but that was exceptional. As the standards of performance had grown by 1900 so had the barriers to continued personal participation. Age-related sports fitted a world in which the male companionship of school or university continued for middle-class youths until a relatively late age of marriage was supposed to remove them from it. Whilst working-class male culture, at least below the white-collar stratum, continued to demand participation in erstwhile bachelor activities alongside marriage, many middle-class men had to develop new forms of gender-specific recreation to avoid giving up their erstwhile contacts more or less altogether. They could do this in part through contact with and management of the next generation of participants.

The press, and club and school magazines, bolstered memory, reinforced acquired status (especially in the cult of the Blue) and provided a continued vicarious experience. Not perhaps since knightly circles were militarily important had prolonging a youth focus been so important, and Girouard rightly treats of sport in his discussion of Victorian Camelots.[5] For the less privileged many athletic bodies offered similar significance to the separate folk memories of army regiments:

> The grand lesson of sport, more particularly indeed of games, is the subordination of self for the good of the side. The cricket field is not the House of Commons, wherein every individual makes a party unto himself. If it were, there would be no cricket.[6]

In writing that F. G. Aflalo was not running down the value of democracy but rather making a claim for discipline and collective style as the quintessence of games.

C. B. Fry was very doubtful, much later in his life (was there something about the inter-war experience of philathletic heroes which made them cast off the models for which they had been largely responsible?) about the public schools' emphasis 'on the greater ball games which had little or no connection with the classical tradition' and their neglect of field events, at which the ancients had been masters.[7] But it is revealing that he criticised the decline of an art form rather than performance levels; once again the extrapolation from the impact of the statuesque was probably more influential than the physical reality. The usual appeal was more banal but it did have the value of removing sport from the simple role of being merely a convenient time-filler towards providing a major bond between the individual, the local and the national, even when the activity fulfilled something basic; 'the boy runs because he thinks it is good to run'.[8] What the elaborated ethic proffered was a justification when he asked *why* it was good.

One obvious value offered was that of sacrifice, not least in the disciplining of self. Throughout the period there was a strong debate as to just how demanding this should be, how time-consuming? Whilst public school conditions could be made deliberately spartan by magisterial control, the fleshier possibilities of university or working life needed a more obvious counterpoint. The clerk or young teacher, for instance, clearly needed more of such exhortations than his more privileged counterpart conditioned by his school. A large part of many of the cheaper games-boosting pamphlets of the century's end was devoted to this. There were relatively few variations on the model typified by H. L. Curtis is his shilling paperback *Principles of Training for Amateur Athletics*. Early rising, 7.00 a.m. in summer, should be followed by a cold bath and a quarter of an hour's exercise 'with the dumb-bells or Indian clubs', followed by a brisk twenty-minute walk before a substantial, slowly eaten breakfast at 8.00. After coffee – not tea, to avoid flatulence – one should walk to work (rarely practicable in expanding suburbia) and a substantial plain dinner should be eaten at one o'clock. A cold supper should be followed by evening exercise on the morning model. Tobacco should be avoided as a poison, but moderate drinking of alcohol was allowed.[9]

In view of the overemphasis on games often ascribed to these pioneers, it is perhaps rather surprising to find repeated warnings that over-training should be sedulously avoided. At the height of the mid-1890s cycling craze a pamphlet, *Cycling as a Cause of Heart Disease*, uttered the sort of dire prophecy which has accompanied later crazes such as marathons or jogging.[10] The importance was that the young should keep fit for their present concerns, declining slowly towards a middle age for which they were physically prepared. Few expected the relatively elderly over-thirties to become actively involved *de novo* in team games or track events.

Heroes

The mainstream emphasis on corporate activity produced tensions when individual performers, winners above all, were made into heroes. Greek culture, typified by the Spartan Leonidas at Thermopylae, offered individual models for emulation as well as abstract conceptions of formal performance. In the school and university context, where the strongest performer of the First Eleven or Fifteen could be seen easily in the essentially face-to-face world of a small-scale society and passed on through spoken legend and the pages of institutional magazines, this was easily comprehensible.

The key figures of the late Victorian athletics boom acquired a significance far beyond this. They personified ideal social types far outside the institutional mode, and their reputations were often deliberately manipulated as such. Despite the rapid growth of spectatorship at games, only a small constituency could ever have seen them perform at their peak. When still photography of action became possible after the turn of the century the better endowed magazines showed pictures of an elderly W. G. Grace's batting, with some shade of his skills at his prime showing through. It was, however, the printed word which created the aura of heroism. Scores and records could be given matter-of-fact, but it was the ascription of moral values by the mediators which was of most importance.

Four men in particular received this 'star' treatment over the four decades before the First World War, and not one was 'typical' of the middle classes whose sporting virtues they were said to encapsulate. As an 'aristocracy' of sport (and, in two cases, of society) they allowed for the deference and emulation which has marked and confused so much of the English *bourgeois* identity.

The most obvious figure, rightly described as 'legendary', was W. G. Grace. This West Country doctor, who did not depend for his livelihood on the medical skills he rarely practised, was actually a thinly veiled professional. Because of his country background Grace fitted easily into a distinctive model of continuity in cricket, an embodiment of a particular form of 'Englishness', a John Bull figure at the crease. His *Who's Who* entries disarmingly described as one of his 'recreations' the cricket which was the undoubted source of his income and wealth. Only rarely in the vast hagiography which surrounds him does his less than pleasant nature peep through. Born in 1848, Grace played continually for Gloucestershire from 1870 until he was fifty-two in 1900, the one great example of active involvement in a first-class game long after most others would have recognised their physical decline.[11]

Grace also beagled, shot and played bowls but lacked the range of pan-athletic skills which characterised the inmates of the Edwardian pantheon. Only just younger but guaranteed socially a much more managerial role in sporting government was William Henry Grenfell, created first Baron Desborough in 1905. He played cricket for Harrow, ran for Oxford (he was a Balliol man), rowed in the Oxford–Cambridge Boat Race in 1877 and 1878, stroked a rowing eight across the English Channel, was a champion fencer in his late forties, climbed in the Alps, hunted big game and was a Thames punting champion. In between he ran a 12,000 acre estate in Hertfordshire and sat for over twenty years in the House of Commons, the *doyen* of a singularly gilded family. With such credentials he was a powerful figure in English Olympic organisation and other sports, where his stance eventually produced a purist middle-class backlash. What mattered to his followers, however, was the apparently effortless ease with which he moved from one activity to another, a living refutation of the growing criticism of flannelled fools, the sportsmen of one skill and few thoughts.[12]

A similar glorious ease was ascribed to a man who had to work much harder for a living, C. B. Fry. 'As cricketer, footballer and athlete combined he has not his equal, and those who lament the physical decadence of the age might perhaps be challenged to find his rival, outside the realm of myth, in any other period.' Aflalo's encomium of 1904 reveals just how close such portraits ran to their mythological precursors. Fry was a distinguished cricketer at his relatively minor public school, captain of both cricket and football at Oxford when an undergraduate of a minor college, Wadham, and holder of the record long jump of 23 ft 6$^{1/2}$ in. He played cricket for Surrey in 1891, toured with Lord Hawke's team in South Africa in 1895–96, played for Sussex after 1897 and repeatedly in Test matches. He also hunted, shot and fished, a life style maintained by his income from journalism and his marriage to a wealthy man's cast-off mistress (not to be found in the autobiography). Even where he did not express his attraction to Hellenic models, it was done for him: 'Fry's is the healthy mind in the healthy body; the beautiful balance of action and thought which means as much in the game of life as in the game of cricket.'[13] Like all the best heroes, he was the willing source of enthusiasm and anecdote.

Such qualities were also ascribed to a man who, at first sight, was far less suitable: Fry's close friend and cricketing colleague, Prince Kumar Shri Ranjitsinhji. 'Ranji', born in 1872, and eventually the Maharajah Jamsahb of Nawanagar, was at Trinity College, Cambridge, and played cricket for Sussex after 1895. Unlike Fry and Grace, cricket had not the same economic function for him, particularly in view of his life style of generosity and lavish consumerism, more suited to a plutocratic playboy than an earnestly self-denying sportsman. Yet his style and skill at the wicket allowed commentators to construct around him a framework of desperate moral earnestness – 'he is essentially the patient and dogged student of whatever he takes up' – all the more striking in a society singularly committed to xenophobia and a racial sub-Darwinism. Ranji was certainly happier in the intermediate world of middle-class sportsmen and aristocratic patrons he found in Sussex and national cricket than in the viceregal snobberies of his homeland. Despite his *penchant* for big game shooting and pig-sticking it was the absorbed Englishness of his virtues that made him popular with commentators; 'his untiring application and constant practice', even where they could be praised slightly snidely: 'careful coaching by the best professionals and assiduous practice whenever opportunity offers have much to say to his success'. It came almost as relief to Aflalo to note that the prince could not swim, row or hunt: 'Perhaps in our winters it makes his feet cold.' Only of someone quite so racially distinctive could such flaws be openly stated.[14]

Collegiality

Beyond these heroes there were many to whom similar, if not quite so wide-ranging, virtues were ascribed in the potted biographies of the local and specialist press. They appeared for a constituency whose creation has been well charted, at least in terms of its core, the burgeoning schools and colleges of the late Victorian middle classes. This has produced a diffusionist model which it is difficult not to accept, one in which the spread is downward and outward from the reformed public schools and their imitators. Whilst the chronology of wholesale dispersal is impossible to establish, the course of growth seems reasonably clear: public, then grammar, schools; older, then newer, universities, followed by the metropolitan and provincial clubs in which former public schoolboys played an organisationally if not necessarily numerically dominant role until the ethos was so well established that imitation could run of its own accord.

G. W. E. Russell identified, in 1902, a further religious core within this. 'The Universities send their best athletes and social favourites to curacies in the slums or martyrdom in the mission-field.'[15] The two were apparently virtually indistinguishable, although the spread of secular athleticism probably had more self-interest than religious service at its core. Yet they were not opposites, as, neither, were the athletic and the intellectual. The greatest period of collegiate and urban athletic formation coincided both with the most remarkable spurt in Victorian missionary effort and with the toughening up of intellectual standards in schools and universities.[16]

The agents of this trend could be clearly identified: the muscular curate perhaps, but far more so the public schoolboy turned university student, then master in any one of a growing number of institutions: the cycle spiralled, inexorably, outwards. Mangan has charted brilliantly the progress of this movement within the schools in the mid-century, driven on by such men as Thring of Uppingham.[17] Beginning as a disciplinary tool, it was taken over in many schools by the boys themselves, perpetuating and extending the cult with little magisterial aid, often making it a much distorted monster. When a letter appeared in *The Times* in 1889 decrying this, and the fact that the obsession with games now left Eton boys with no time for relaxation, a host of critics rounded angrily, pointing out that boys played cricket only fourteen times a week in summer and that any parents could allow their son 'to become a legalised loafer'. The critics showed little awareness of the agonising pressures which would blackmail anyone who sought to do so. Games were held to prevent the deterioration of the school's tone, likely to be brought about by 'a pasty-faced, sunken-eyed, weak-chested, "corseted", empty-headed noodle, whose one care is what his friends will think of his dress'.[18]

This spectre of an aesthete plunged into secret vices reached well outside the public schools and obsessed the local grammar schools, reformed after the report of the Taunton Commission, and the new ones founded on public school models. Schools such as Bristol Grammar School or Aireborough Grammar School, founded in 1910 for the sons of Yorkshire tradesmen who would never have reached even the newer public schools, still offered the whole house/team/games package as a *sine qua non* of middle-class training, despite the fact that they did not have to cope with pupils who actually lived on the premises.[19]

The spread of imitative games was even more obvious in higher education, if only because the numbers both of institutions and of students involved were much smaller. Oxford and Cambridge, which had begun to compete in cricket in 1827 and on the river in 1829, increased the range of contests steadily after mid-century, each sport's adoption marking a major signpost in its general acceptability.[20] Sheldon Rothblatt has rightly seen this as part of a process of professional modernisation within Oxford and Cambridge, adjusting to social hierarchies which were competitive rather than inherited, a picture usually more accurate in outline than in implementation.[21]

The process was more clearly visible in Cambridge reforms than in Oxford, not least because its ascribed pioneer was Leslie Stephen, a young clerical don at Trinity Hall in the 1850s. Recent biographers have been rather more critical in probing the roots of this in Stephen's psychological make-up than was Maitland in 1906: 'He was the personification of the "muscular Christian" of that date.'[22] Lord Annan has seen him more as trying to overcome his own nervous sensibilities, ill health and lack of social ease through a dominance of sporting men, seeking comradeship in rowing, at which he was indifferent, and leadership in coaching, at which he was better.[23] Others have pointed to Stephen's growing agnosticism as leading him to outdo more obviously Christian musculars such as Kingsley.[24]

If Stephen, with his long walks and eccentric coaching garb, managed to cut down loafing among a brief Cambridge generation, he found many followers for their successors, such as Reginald Mckenna, who coached the Hall crew until it won the Henley Ladies' Plate in 1887.[25] Colleges in Cambridge were, and often still are, distinctively aggressive towards each other, and the older universities differed from the public schools in one prime factor vital for athletic growth, namely that there were so many rival bodies close at hand. The house cult of the public schools was readily expanded into the collegiate loyalties of the two universities. Jesus, Cambridge, had at one time in the 1890s eighteen Blues in residence, turning its attention to the field after its glories on the river in the 1870s had departed.[26] Despite the attempts of some heads of houses, such as Hastings Rashdall of New College, Oxford, to curb over-athleticism, the younger dons and, even more, the undergraduates translated into university life the high degree of sporting self-government they had acquired at school.[27]

It was not an all-embracing phenomenon. Sporting men in the universities were less able to maintain the hegemony school had allowed them, because many undergraduates sedulously avoided the disciplinary hierarchy which post-Arnoldian schools had chosen to impose. M. R. James, by a singular irony later to be Provost both of King's, Cambridge, and of Eton, welcomed entering Cambridge in 1882 as an opportunity to throw off team sports, especially rowing: 'the feelings of repulsion for the Cam and its surroundings which had long been festering within me broke out', so he took to cycling around the Fens in search of antiquities.[28] A. C. Benson, eventually Master of Magdalene, having played football at Eton with 'a certain distinction' because of his bulk, found himself rowing for King's until his natural preference for thoughtful relaxation triumphed.[29] But there were others who revelled in it, such as Edward Lyttelton, who at Trinity, Cambridge, in the mid-1870s saw sport as an essential part of daily life:

In the afternoon, after playing a very stiff game or match at football, the finest I have ever played – we would come in at 4.45, wash and sit down to the best two-hours' work in the day, and then dinner at seven.[30]

Strenuous leisure of this type appealed also to the poor scholars training largely for ordination at the newly founded Keble College, Oxford, who despite a reputation for post-Tractarian ritualism frequently linked with limp-wristed mincing took to rigorous games with enthusiasm, 'a couple o' hundred 'ardy young chaps a-livin' on the cheap', surviving without the steak dinners of other undergraduates.[31] The establishment of the Rhodes scholarships, monuments to imperial eugenics with their fifth of marks given for athletics, was seen by *Truth* as the absolute vindication of this trend: 'Verily the muddied oafs and flannelled fools have been avenged.'[32]

Elsewhere in Victorian higher education games had a much more utilitarian role, deliberately bonding a fledgling elite, marginally more uncertain in its role than the established upper middle class on which it was modelled. The religious and social exclusiveness of the older universities carried on in more subtle ways beyond the mid-Victorian reforms; for an increasingly ambitious group just below the established gentry and professionals new institutions were created, adapted in both organisation and curriculum to the perceived needs and pockets of an industrial urban middle middle class. For their students these new university colleges were far more than the emporia of stale and second-hand goods which D. H. Lawrence portrayed in *The Rainbow*.[33]

Following the first London college of 1825 and Durham in the 1830s, the 1870s marked the beginning of a jerky growth of provincial university institutions, the pseudo-Gothic 'redbricks' of Manchester, Leeds, Liverpool, Bristol and so on. With the notable exception of Durham, which made an important contribution to rowing, they were largely non-residential and faced an early need to promote a collegiate consciousness amongst home-based students. The 1880s were a key decade in this process, when both students and authorities modified the pedagogic utilitarianism which had marked the foundations. Student debates and literary societies were usually the first fruit of this, but were eventually reinforced by sport. King's College, London, the Anglican reaction to University College's 'godlessness', developed an athletic club in the late 1860s; its fortunes were uncertain until Arthur Headlam, subsequently Bishop of Gloucester, became principal in 1904 and fostered athleticism deliberately to give his scattered charges a sense of 'university life'.[34] University College, closer to the grim purposes of its founder, Jeremy Bentham, tried athletics in the 1860s but was able to give them no real foundation until 1886 when its Athletics Association was formed, offering cricket, football, lawn tennis and racquets. A major problem for these bodies was space; University College played cricket in Regent's Park and football on Primrose Hill until it acquired its own grounds in 1897. By this time athletics had been absorbed as part of the newly founded union.[35]

In the assertive north the council of Owens College, later the University of Manchester, leased grounds in the suburbs in 1880 and gave a grant to the various societies which had emerged more or less spontaneously. In 1885 its Athletic Union was formed and the next great step forward came in 1897 when the Whitworth trustees gave ten acres of their Firs estate as an athletics ground. It cost £7,000 to level and furnish, paid for by a £3,000 gift and the proceeds of a local bazaar.[36] Owens's sister college in the federal Victoria University, Yorkshire College, Leeds, formed football and cricket clubs in 1885 and an Athletics Union in 1889. With five acres of poor grounds at Kirkstall it staged a 'medieval fayre', where one professor ran a shooting gallery to raise £2,000 for a new gymnasium. The sports club became part of the wider students' union and, after the granting of a university charter in 1904, spent £275 of the union's £350 annual income. But until it acquired twenty acres of grounds in 1914 Leeds's sporting facilities were inadequate, and it was very difficult to construct the hoped-for corporate sense.[37]

Liverpool faced similar problems, with an athletics club founded in 1885 playing on a rented ten-acre field at Wavertree and changing in a local hotel beyond even the reach of the local horse-drawn buses. Its fortunes changed markedly in 1908 with the acquisition of new grounds at Calderstones Park and the opening of a majestic pavilion, balconied, with two stories. Around it, and a room converted to a gymnasium in the city and the use of public baths, there built up a considerable range of student athletic activities. In this case local students brought their growing perception of the role of sport in their own home lives to the patronage of the new university's Professor of Latin, H. A. Strong, who dominated collegiate athletic management for thirty years before the First World War.[38]

Firth College, Sheffield, later the university, owed its athletic spread to a similarly dedicated academic, Dr George Young, lecturer in organic chemistry, a sprinter, a skater, fencer and boxer. The Athletic Club's eighty members, paying a 5s subscription in the 1890s, had the perennial difficulties in finding grounds common to all the five colleges. They owed their first field to Sheffield's dominant landlord, the Duke of Norfolk, but lost it to an expanding railway company in 1899 and followed a nomadic course of lettings for the next decade.[39]

All these new bodies faced a major problem not shared by Oxford and Cambridge – their home-based students were closely tied in to local networks. Most of the sporting undergraduates were already committed to local clubs, so that the college bodies had major recruitment difficulties. Yet this factor allowed the academic clubs to slot into local fixture patterns much more easily than their older counterparts, whose sporting links tended to be inter-collegiate or with their former schools. It helped bond the local concerns of professional men, especially the burgeoning provincial medical schools, and teachers as agents of urban sporting development. One issue which most of them faced, but whose complexities the evidence makes it difficult to establish, is what happened in local elite circles when those who had been detached to attend the older universities came back to assume inherited roles in their base communities. The Blue and collegiate champion presumably helped to reassert the finer patterns of deference within local associations.

Leather on willow

It has become a truism that the games in which these men functioned as leaders were industrialised, bureaucratised and 'democratised' rapidly after the mid-nineteenth century. The quintessential activity in this transition and, paradoxically, the most difficult to come to local grips with was cricket. The game enjoys a deceptive sense of timelessness, if only because of the apparent eternal slowness of pace, at least to the less enthusiastic observer, and an arcadian paradigm of social cohesion rising out of its village roots and its older south-eastern emphasis. Reformed in the south-east as nineteenth-century sensibilities tried to reduce rural carousing, it combined a sense of the bucolic increasingly sought after by a distinctly anti-urban industrial culture with a model of social control of various levels of sophistication. In particular it helped generate a sense of county identity after the 1860s, with the focus of what were often regarded as pastoral entities shifting to industrial centres: the Yorkshire club at Headingley in Leeds, Lancashire at Old Trafford in Manchester, Nottinghamshire at Trent Bridge, and Warwickshire at Edgbaston in Birmingham. The majority of county clubs had been formed by 1875; a few more came in the next two decades, with only Worcestershire, Northamptonshire and Glamorgan lagging behind.[40]

Control and justification of these higher reaches stayed largely in the hands of the landed gentry and their *arriviste* fringe, not least through the agency of the Marylebone Cricket Club, which managed to maintain its leadership despite repeated suggestions that regional and national councils akin to developing patterns of local government might be more appropriate. Despite the game's suitability as a marker of urban progress, cricket's 'fit and proper persons' remained less easily defined than their political counterparts, although the honorary vice-presidential structures of the larger urban clubs did feature aldermen and other civic leaders and were another means of identifying urban oligarchies.[41] The power of these groups was openly admitted to continue behind and through the vaunted egalitarianism of the cricket field, which 'served to soften local asperities between classes', although 'social distinctions are resumed directly stumps are drawn, but they are far less irksome because of the sporting interlude to the business of life'.[42]

Sir Home Gordon's sense of the intermission was deceptive, since it was precisely the business of life management which the cricket field encapsulated. This was most obvious in the repeated emphasis given to the need to accept umpires' decisions, not always easy when team members regarded themselves as coming from the order-giving classes: 'it is from them' (claimed A. G. Steel) 'that the standard or tone of morality in the game is given'.[43] Just how crucial this was in terms of the importance of upper middle-class exemplars appeared in Steel's disarmingly frank query as to 'what will happen on smaller matches, when there is not the same publicity and notoriety to restrain the rowdiness which has before now been the result of wordy warfare?' It was an issue which became even more imperative as the game's popularity drove it into spectator demonstration of local loyalties.

In his book on cricket W. G. Grace noted the influence of gentlemen amateurs in turning a regional into a national game after the 1840s and the continued influence of members 'mostly in good positions . . . usually elected by ballot'.[44] Alongside the emerging county teams, and of major importance as ambassadors of the model style, were the wandering amateur clubs without fixed grounds or premises which brought first-class university and ex-public school players to play local sides of their near social equals. The Knickerbockers, Irrepressibles, Perambulators, Hic et Ubique, I Vagabondis and, most prestigious of all, I Zingari (The Gypsies) were seen both as missionaries to northern parts and, equally important, as far preferable to teams of travelling professionals, on which many country clubs in their early days had had to rely for outside competition. The amateurs provided a useful bridge between the Lords and Oval-dominated cricket of the MCC and Surrey clubs and the provincial bodies until the latter were sufficiently strong to develop county fixtures. But their leisure and wealth had to be modified substantially if the example they offered was to be adopted by others lower down the middle-class scale, for whom a slightly wider mix, but still within broad class limits, was necessary.

Grimsby, growing rapidly on its fishing trade in the wake of railway building, spawned a number of clubs in the 1860s, led by the Worsley Cricket Club, the elite of local tradesmen, whose team included clergy, doctors, lawyers and the owners of the larger shops. It lasted until the 1890s; many similar clubs had an equally limited life span before their key figures moved to other bodies or other sports.[45] On a wider level, the Lincolnshire County Cricket Club was re-formed in 1880 with Lord Yarborough as its president and marked its regional ambitions by choosing Lincoln rather than the expanding new seaside resort of Skegness as its headquarters.[46] Rather humbler, the Hull Railway Clerks' Cricket Club was formed in 1873 with a grant of £10 from the employers. It used a local field grazed by cattle in the winter and played entirely in the summer evenings until 1900, when clerks were given regular Saturday afternoon holidays for the first time: here, emphatically, very short matches had to be played to tailor the older village form to an industrial employment timetable.[47] These work-group-related clubs were much more closely mono-class in their make-up than the idealised pan-class rural model. Yet this older pattern continued, being adapted to the intermediate trading world of county and market towns. The Priory Cricket Club of Lewes, Sussex, organised a Cricket Week in August 1881 at which visiting teams from I Zingari and the Woodard Foundation public school, Hurst College, were expected. The event was bolstered with local balls and amateur dramatics and fitted easily into the town's annual work cycle.[48] Similarly the grocers of Tonbridge in Kent built an annual festival around the town's cricket week, allowing shop men either one day off to attend it, as spectators rather than players, or early evening closing without loss of pay.[49]

The game's growing popularity, as we have seen, allowed individuals to personify social virtues as well as playing proficiency. Fry wrote of the Hon. F. S. Jackson, the youngest son of Lord Allerton, an ennobled Leeds businessman, that he had 'broadminded, shrewd common sense, the power of seeing facts as they are, of being equal to the occasion, the only kind of equality worth consideration between man and man or men and things', still widely regarded as the hallmarks of Yorkshiremen.[50] Cricket also enabled increasingly professional clergymen to justify their sport as part of their mission.[51] When the Revd. F. H. Gillingham, an Essex vicar and county player, was criticised by some parishioners for the amount of time he spent on the field, he rejoindered in his parish magazine that he was always home on Sundays, his sportsmanship lured people to his services, and that it had enabled him to raise some £300 without which he could not have afforded to serve the parish. He seems to have silenced further criticism but it is not clear whether he did so on grounds of financial utility or because he provided an alternative to the popular image of clergymen as 'emaciated pale-faced weaklings, who are incapable of doing anything robust'.[52]

The game offered other virtues, too. It has been claimed that cricket was a more effective agent of imperialism than Christianity because it allowed competition with other Indian castes without body contact. In the English context it enabled a similar competition or co-operation between widely distributed class participants because collaboration ceased off the field.[53] Middle and upper-class-dominated though it remained, it avoided the middle–working class split that characterised the other major field game, football, with its much greater possibilities of physical contact.

The increasing later Victorian emphasis on high-level spectator cricket, at county and Test level, produced a growing unease in the game's leading proponents who viewed the 1860s and early 1870s as a golden age of practice and values from which descent was inevitable. Edward Lyttelton claimed that it had become too perfect, too mechanical, too individualistic, that its value as the quintessential team activity was being lost. He felt that the increasing intellectual demands of the universities, in which sporting prowess had been a similar reforming agency, and the pressure for efficiency in professional men's working lives, added to the distaste widely felt for a game played by professionals masquerading as amateurs, were driving its real value underground. By 1890, as headmaster of Haileybury, he was postulating that it was 'stale', pervaded with a 'gloom of spirit'.[54] Home Gordon, some twenty-one years later, saw cricket as trapped in its own popularity, unable to adapt sufficiently to the social demands on a modern game.[55] For others the patriotic model appeared to be failing, sullied by its own success. What was more, its older characteristic of apparent timelessness was no longer a virtue – 'in first-class cricket there is a waste of time that would never be tolerated in any other pursuit'. It was no longer the perfect moral exemplar for youth.[56]

Nonetheless, there were many for whom cricket continued to provide just those virtues with little sense of taint. By 1911 there were at least 1,100 clubs in London alone. It will be a long time before sufficient regional studies are completed to allow an assessment of its spread.[57] Much cricket below county level remained almost anarchic in its organisation, until it could be drawn into other social purposes. In 1887 E. A. C. Thomson attempted to draw London clubs into a series of matches aimed at supporting urban charities. He failed, but a fresh effort in 1910 was more successful, at least among about 10 per cent of the clubs.[58] Yet his work revealed both the strength and the vulnerability of what were often quite ephemeral organisations. Outside the increasingly structured world of educational and county institutions, cricket's continued appeal rested on fluidity as much as permanence, in that it allowed for temporary associations of groups whose prime bonding lay elsewhere. All small clubs in large towns faced a constant threat which made them almost as nomadic as their mid-Victorian predessors, although on a smaller scale. 'The conquering builder' and the leapfrogging spread of new suburbs made it difficult to acquire permanent premises, and cricket clubs, except for the richest, rarely displayed the acquisitive land hunger (and its associated expense) of so many other boom games.[59] They veered between older common land, scruffy suburban fields and such public parkland as could be wheedled out of the London County Council and its provincial counterparts. Playing the game was one thing; the abstract sense of a cult reinforced by the published score tables of the newspaper press and *Wisden's* was probably just as important in maintaining its appeal as a fundamental sport in English life, and a barometer of national fortunes.

Chasing balls

The deceptively meditative rusticity of cricket contrasted sharply with the late Victorian boom in football-playing, which has attracted most attention because of its role as a mass working-class spectator activity. The latter has usually been seen as the reason for one of the most significant splits along class lines in modern sport – the division of middle-class Rugby Union from the working-class following of both Rugby League and Association Football. In fact the Association game was eventually rent within itself over the amateur–professional issue and questions of ethical purity.

Certainly football in all its variants fits more easily than cricket into the model framework of a socially downward diffusion: 'Football has always been a game better suited to the masses than cricket: more spectacular; less technically exciting; more concentrated on thrilling moments; more satisfying to the combative instincts of adolescents,' wrote the elderly Edward Lyttelton somewhat sniffily.[60] But it was precisely that sense of the combative which had accounted for its initial popularity in the 1860s and 1870s among the middle-class youths and their public school teachers, defended as an essential part of the racial nature and with a direct value for imperial greatness or, at least, the propensity to behave properly: 'The game is manly and fit for Englishmen: it puts a courage into their hearts to meet an enemy in the face.'[61] At this point it was an external rather than a class enemy that was foreseen, but the social divisions within the game did eventually indicate a considerable middle-class reluctance to face compatriots on the field.

Other values attached to football. With the development of the more fluid 'passing game' with its assumptions of planned tactics in the 1870s the team was stressed rather than the individual player. Combination rather than personal flair now mattered.[62] In a sense this reflected the maturity of soccer; the 'dribbling game' developed steadily since the 1850s. Despite the usual assumptions that sporting change was fostered by a London-based upper middle class, soccer owed as much to the recreational needs of a provincial urban elite, exemplified by the great Sheffield football boom that followed the foundation of Sheffield and Hallam football clubs in 1857. Its rapid adoption in the metropolis – Crystal Palace emerging in 1861, the Civil Service Club in 1862 and the founding of the Football Association in 1863 – was matched by similarly rapid developments in that 'mimic warfare', rugby football. If the latter could be portrayed as an 'English' game, soccer was more easily recognised as 'national' in the geographical sense with the institution of a London *v*. Sheffield match as an annual feature in 1871, until which it 'was rather a recreation and a means of exercise for a few old public-school boys than a really national sport'.[63] Yet it took another six years for rules to be agreed.

The middle-class ideal, having departed from Sheffield, rested with the Corinthians, founded in 1882, limited to fifty members and banned by their rules from competing in any competition for which a cup was awarded. Not only was there 'an unwritten law confining membership to Old Public School Boys or members of a University', it was made clear that the middle-class centre of gravity had shifted firmly to the south, where the dominant form was modelled on the travelling amateur cricket teams.[64] This produced the usual range of exotic titles such as that of the Crouch End Vampires, founded in 1883 as the Balmoral Football Club. Elsewhere the middle classes spectated too, but their presence dropped significantly as workers spread on to the terraces.[65]

One of their refuges, not necessarily as numerous as amateur soccer by the turn of the century, but certainly more acceptably visible in social terms, was Rugby Union. Dunning and Sheard have seen this game as a product of the general class system's ability to innovate until the mid-nineteenth century, slowly ossifying thereafter.[66] Codification of playing practice was matched by a less overtly specified index of membership, the essential extension of 'manly' into 'gentlemanly'. The Rugby Football Union's foundation in 1871 grew out of an increasingly negative reaction to 'unsportsmanlike' behaviour, 'hacking' on the field for unfair mastery. Paradoxically, the higher level of contact violence enshrined in the rugby codes may have meant that the values sought in this branch of middle-class leisure were out of step with the generally desirable shifts towards softer modes of activity. This has been ascribed to a backward-looking insecurity among the aspirant elites, in some senses easier in the south of England than in the north.

This was turned on its head in one area of rapid late Victorian industrial expansion, Wales. In the South Welsh urban centres old public school boys were augmented by new professional men and their clerks, anxious to conform to codes they were coming to after, rather than during, adolescence. But the Welsh took it further, to the fringes of the middle and working classes, and made a mass spectator sport out of an amateur game.[67] After the 1880s the only time at which the English could boast this was in the annual Oxford–Cambridge or public school matches at Twickenham, where the masses were furnished by the participation of the teams' social equals in an annual festival of reunion.

English rugby football depended essentially on its appeal to the participants, but had the advantage that it could be fitted more easily than cricket into the time and work requirements of their servicing an industrial and commercial society. Just occasionally a real class battle was fought out on the field, at least before the final Union–League division. The Oxford don G. B. Grundy played as a young housemaster with the Blackheath club in 1881, in the side it fielded on its first match against a northern club made up of miners. For once the much ascribed middle-class fear that they could never play against muscle-hardened manual workers proved groundless:

> Their idea evidently was, 'There's a team of southern amateurs, let's frighten them by playing rough.' And they *did* play rough! But they never made a greater mistake in their lives. At half-time Blackheath had thirteen men left and the others eleven. The rest had been taken in cabs to the nearest hospital.[68]

The referee stopped the match, but incidents like this provided the legends of middle-aged reminiscences. They also fostered a fluctuating debate as to whether young men should be allowed to play such a dangerous game; the literary signifying of this is the hearty Gerald's death on the field in Forster's *The Longest Journey*.[69]

The cult of manliness won, if only because it allowed the systematic venting of excess spirits which fitted so well into Victorian ideals of contained stress, although it could still produce conflict in local clubs. In Leeds the Headingley Hill Chapel Sunday class formed a club in 1885, dominated by Leeds Grammar School boys. After a shaky start it was reborn in 1881 under the aegis of Headingley Wesleyan Methodist Church, and amalgamated the following year with the Woodhouse Moor Methodist Society. But the chapel leaders rejected the game as 'degrading', so the players broke away to form their own independent club, which eventually joined the Yorkshire and national Rugby Football Unions.[70] In Cornwall the class issue became clear in the 1870s when strong local working-class participation in the game was ousted by public school men who used their committee expertise to forge stronger links with the English game and formed the

Cornwall Rugby Football Union in 1884. The miners and fishermen turned elsewhere.[71]

It has been suggested that rugby's appeal was weakest among Evangelicals, because of phobias about body contact.[72] Cricket provided some sporting outlet for them, but it was perhaps their need for year-round activity which fostered the rapid growth of a team game never touched by professionalism or mass considerations, men's hockey. The rider has to be added, however, that religious enthusiasms do not seem adequate explanations of its growth, rather more a support or recognition of an emerging phenomenon. The game has vague medieval origins, ascribed or at least invented by late nineteenth-century apologists, and was played, as were so many other embryonic Victorian sports, on Blackheath Common in the 1850s. Hockey traces its spread and codification to the 1870s. Its early growth was regional and idiosyncratic; the 'isolationist' Teddington club, formed in 1871, was matched by growth around Bristol, and Marlborough College developed its own game. This West Country game was codified into the Clifton-based National Hockey Union, whose short life stretched from 1887 to 1895. Its late Victorian historians, J. Richardson Smith and P. A. Robinson, disarmingly blamed its collapse on the limited appeal it found in small West Country towns – what they were effectively saying was that such centres had an insufficient middle-class base to sustain a game with no pan-class or mass appeal. It was the London suburban clubs which developed most strongly, forming the Hockey Association in 1886, a model for the Northern Counties Hockey Association of 1888, catering out of Manchester for every industrial county except Durham.[73]

The associations were dominated from the beginning by the Wimbledon club, founded in 1883, which built the national rules around eleven-man teams, amateurism and the rule of 1892 which banned the award of cups or prizes in any hockey competition. Despite the Manchester efforts, and the first north–south match at London's Queens Club, the sport made only limited headway outside the south, and only twenty of the 200 clubs affiliated to the Hockey Association by 1900 were to be found in the north. But when a rapid spurt began around 1907 the regional imbalance changed somewhat, so that by 1914, out of 518 affiliated clubs, 201 were 'southern', 110 'northern', ninety-six from the Midlands and sixty from Lincolnshire and East Anglia; the rest were scattered across the west.

This growth was attributed to two factors, desertion of an increasingly corrupt soccer after 1907 and the visibility afforded by the game's inclusion in the 1908 Olympics in London.[74] Its appeal to the 'genteel' was reported in Edwardian accounts of its growing popularity, offering 'a certain cachet of social distinction' akin to bridge. When it was played alongside other team games in Preston Park, Brighton, virtually annexed for middle-class pleasures, 'Mostly crowds assembled to watch the several football matches down in the park itself. But carriages and motor cars inevitably line the hockey ground.'[75] An outburst by the vice-captain of the Devon Hockey Club, Mr Gardiner, drew the fierce rebuke from *Truth* that he had far overstepped the self-control necessary in a game for gentlemen and that his resignation would be the only honourable course.[76] Hockey's chivalric models were reinforced powerfully in such terms, and any other viewpoint was rarely expressed. One, reported in such a way as to reinforce the teller's own sense of class difference, was heard by the Revd. A. W. Hopkinson, a young Nottingham curate, at the turn of the century. Injured on the field, he appeared bandaged in a Sunday procession to hear a working-class parishioner murmur, 'You can see he's a married man.'[77] It was this self-depreciation that made hockey and its fledgling sister, lacrosse, much more popular as low-key amateur activies for some men than the football variants.[78]

Grace in the body and soul

If ethics and pressure for playing space determined hockey's appeal, class models and abstractions of physical ethics and team ideals underpinned the most select of all the manly sports, rowing. Although organised round competition, most famously the Oxford–Cambridge race and the Henley Regatta, its fundamental emphasis was on the role and operation of the crew itself, as exemplar of both moral tone and physical style. Rowing gave purpose, defeated slackness, produced calm self-discipline and provided 'the type of a Race on the River of Life, not indeed a child of Christianity, but akin to its idea, and a faithful ally in the role of life'.[79] The Bishop of Truro's encomium and other praise of rowing's effectiveness against Satan were asserted also in more Hellenic terms 'as an art which requires on the part of its votaries a sense of rhythm, a perfect balance and symmetry of bodily effort, and the graceful control and repose which lend an appearance of ease to the application of the highest muscular energy', coupled with 'silence, prompt obedience, absolute subordination of the individual self to the collective good of the crew'.[80]

Rowing was undoubtedly the most ascetic of all sports in its demands on its participants in terms of diet and discipline during the brief annual season; a merged unison was the desired end, and its great appeal to middle-class oarsmen was in the crew of eight. Individual sculling, with rare exceptions, was thought more suitable to muscular professional watermen. Perhaps its greatest advantage was the concealment of individual physical mediocrity in the polished performance of a crew rowing essentially for itself rather than to win. When the later decades of the century saw repeatedly poor English performances against American crews rowing with ruthless efficiency but abominable style, the emphasis on grace of body (and, therefore, of soul) provided a compensatory fallback. The combination of excellence with mediocrity offered another rationale for rowing, particularly as a preparation for life. At Oxford the unscholarly Tom Brown apparently found the river's demands of more value than his reading, and the acerbic Leslie Stephen justified his enthusiastic coaching of undergraduates on the grounds that 'Their sphere of thought is somewhat limited; but they are very good fellows, and are excellent raw material for country parsons, or for any other profession where much thinking power is not required.'[81]

Sport was, after all, a preparation for an aggressive entrepreneurial life, even if its organisation did much to moderate that aggression into the 'clockwork regularity' of rowing, the one sport where mechanical analogies were regularly employed; the marriage of Hellenism with industrialisation.[82] Unlike cricket, the pan-class exemplar, the river attracted few aristocrats and, when the working classes tried to join in, they were shunted off to separate organisations and, in the London area, segregated waters: the Lea, away from the Thames, with its dominant middle-class rowers.

Along the latter river some thirty clubs emerged, dominating the Amateur Rowing Association and centring on the old university oarsman's haven, Leander, founded in 1825.[83] As former Blues and college oars filtered into a number of the City clubs the social tone of metropolitan rowing was forced up and erstwhile white-collar bodies were pushed towards links with working-class clubs in an ethical split to be discussed in chapter 6. Whilst the London Rowing Club was formed in 1854 specifically for 'gentlemen' members, the

Thames Rowing Club began in 1861 as a pleasure boat club, the City of London, for clerks and salesmen in the 'rag trade' around St Paul's churchyard. Its members caught the 6.35 'rowing train' from Paddington each weekday evening in season to practise at Putney. Gradually, though, an influx of new members, City professional people and ex-university men, pushed out the 'rag trade'. 'The social status (conventionally speaking) is, I suppose, higher, but we are still, happily, a "mixed lot".'[84]

For university and City oarsmen the season peaked with Henley, begun in 1839.[85] Run for the members of a carefully selected number of clubs, thirty-six of the 167 in England by the 1890s, with a few socially acceptable overseas visitors, it eventually became more of a social than a sporting event, old oarsmen shaking their heads at the spread of prize giving and an 'entertainment costly beyond the means of the middle-class income'.[86] But this was another sport where the distinctive regionalism of English middle-class life was able to assert itself. The industrial north-west produced thriving amateur clubs.[87] Sussex, Warwickshire and Lincolnshire had small local clubs in which the very difficulty of finding waters wide enough to allow competitive rowing meant that the members had often to row as a single team for the sheer exertion of it. They faced an issue which their London counterparts did not, a tendency to opt for leisurely pleasure rowing to impress their lady friends rather than ascetic self-discipline.[88]

A miniature version of the older university model appeared in the north-east when the Durham colleges began to found clubs in the 1830s and 1840s, amalgamating in 1877 into the Durham University Boat Club.[89] Apart from internal fixtures on the Wear, it had to travel to find competition from the Yorkshire Ouse to the Tyne and the Aln. A minor variation, eventually providing twenty-one clubs, grew round the seaports and new resorts – sea rowing. Here there were problems, because the only opposition was usually the crews put up by professional watermen, rowing against whom effectively barred clubs from meeting other middle-class agencies. In Whitby the Friendship Club, founded in 1879, attracted fishermen at first, then a growing component of clerks, until a former Oxford cox joined in 1905, signalling its severance from its crude roots.[90] Other clubs such as Worthing Amateur Boat Club followed the pattern of isolated freshwater bodies, where a small group of oarsmen provided the focus for a penumbra of pleasure-takers for whom the social cachet of membership proved a lure but whose subscriptions were needed to meet the costs of boat and boathouse purchase and maintenance.[91]

Track and bedroom

A much greater growth but one with which middle-class agents had a much more ambivalent relationship was in athletics. It is a paradox that the emphasis on 'athletic' sports as manly was applied increasingly to all team games as well as field track sports at a time when the latter raised issues of ethics and participation. Much centred around distrust of the distinctly commercial and frequently rigged pedestrianism of mid-century infiltrating into 'pure' events, together with the mass appeal, the relationship of gate money to facilities, and the risk of the sport's ascetic requirements being merged into unacceptable social demands. When cycling was introduced as a track event it appealed less to the practitioners of traditional elite athletic events such as sprinting or long-jumping than to a borderline working-class group. In athletics the diffusionist model faces perhaps its most difficult test. Activity grew rapidly after mid-century in a university and public-school context, although always as the poorer relation of team games. Athletic events were staged literally on the periphery of team playing space, on tracks round cricket and football grounds. In the collegiate institutions participation could be restricted; the sport's functions could be related to other corporate needs, but it was difficult to enforce this outside. Fry observed that most university athletes dropped it after graduation, because of the stress on individual performance in London and the provinces and because of the functionalism without social support that characterised the outside clubs.[92] It was only in the Olympics that the university-trained athlete seemed happy away from his institution, because the sense of nation could augment the house/college ideal.

Field and track events owed their growth in amateur sport to two factors – individual performance was matched against ideal achievements, either personal or in records, and they were justified as fitting the recreational needs of young men in offices. As the Duke of Norfolk told the *conversazione* of the Electric Athlete Association of the Central Telegraph Office in 1895, there was, 'in view of the sedentary character of the Post Office officials, no better means of retaining or promoting their health'.[93]

The *Badminton* series' author on athletics dated the growth of the amateur sport from 1864, the first meeting of the Mincing Lane (from 1866 the London) Athletic Club, but he also pointed out that there was a distinct regional split by the 1880s.[94] Whereas London-based athletics were dominated by the professional classes, the midland and northern events included middle and working-class participants, and the extra-metropolitan events were usually dependent on other activities for their base. When the northerners dominated the Stamford Bridge championship of 1886, it signified the withdrawal of southern runners from serious activity outside the universities. Where growth came after that it was largely in the spread of cross-country running and paper-chasing among London clerks, eager to run but also anxious about costly facilities and the threat to minor social snobberies implicit in gate-money crowds. For them the day's highlight was 'The tea, which is usually followed by a formal meeting and a "sing-song", used to close the evening very pleasantly.'[95]

Moral value and the stern Englishness of manly sports were also attached to activities which paralleled a similar class-based separation, boxing, gymnastics and physical training. It has been claimed that the middle classes just could not compete physically or gracefully with burgeoning working-class bodies. Although the Amateur Boxing Association comprised fifty-one clubs by 1910, only a few depended on substantial middle-class support. Whilst the Honourable Artillery Club could grow naturally out of class-delimited volunteer militancy, it is difficult to imagine how much real meeting could ever be arranged between the Cambridge University Boxing Club and the Hairdressers' Athletic and Cycling Club.[96] The relatively rare upper middle-class sportsman who entered the ring against an artisan or labouring opponent was only too clearly 'slumming', as was his swimming equivalent.[97] Debarred both by status from select sports clubs and by physique from tougher working-class associations, the humble clerk sought other outlets. His great contribution to the late Victorian athletics boom was in gymnastics and physical fitness. In the latter the training became an end in itself. Whether using Sandow's or Eustace Miles's system, the clerk tended to do it alone.[98] His athleticism could be privatised rather than institutionalised, in a 'work-out' in the bedroom. This offered the illusion of athleticism and preparation for a strenuous life in the countless thousands of weedy young men swinging Indian clubs:

Aye for the joy – the glory, the passionate burst
of life,
The pride and the strength and the power that
thrills to the tramp of strife,
Aye, for the leap of the pulses, for the spring
where the muscles rise,
For the clean red mouth, cold temples, and the
wide, glad, vivid eyes.

That was part of an Edwardian hymn to Christ in *C. B. Fry's Magazine*, 'Lord of the clean and strong'; muscular Christianity lived on in surburbia.[99]

Notes

1 R. Jenkyns, *The Victorians and Ancient Greece* (Oxford, 1980), 217.
2 Lyttelton, *Memories and Hopes*, 5–6.
3 E. Waugh, *Brideshead Revisited* (1945), 1962 edition, 49–51.
4 Wiener, *English Culture*.
5 M. Girouard, *The Return to Camelot* (New Haven, 1981).
6 F. G. Aflalo, 'The sportsman', *Fortnightly Review*, LXXX (1907), 166–7.
7 C. B. Fry, *Life worth Living* (1939), 61.
8 H. Graham, *Athletics of Today* (1901), 148.
9 H. L. Curtis, *Principles of Training for Amateur Athletics: its Advantages and Evils, with Special Regard to Bicyclists* (1892).
10 Herschell, *Cycling as a Cause of Heart Disease*.
11 E. Midwinter, *W. G. Grace* (1981).
12 R. T. Rivington, *Punting* (Oxford, 1986), 46–7.
13 A. W. Myers, *C. B. Fry: the Man and his Methods* (Bristol, 1912); Fry, *Life Worth Living*.
14 M. Ross, *Ranji*.
15 Russell, *For Better?*, 186.
16 C. J. Wright, 'Before Tom Brown: education and the sporting ethos in the early nineteenth century', *Journal of Educational Administration and History*, LX (1977), 14.
17 Mangan, *Athleticism*.
18 *The Times*, 20, 23, 24, 25 September 1889.
19 See chapter 1, n. 24.
20 Mangan, *Athleticism*, 125; *Oxford University Sports Register* (Oxford, 1909); A. M. Croome (ed.), *Fifty Years of Sport at Oxford, Cambridge and the Great Public Schools* (1913).
21 Rothblatt, *Revolution of the Dons*.
22 F. W. Maitland, *The Life and Letters of Leslie Stephen* (1906), 58.
23 N. Annan, *Leslie Stephen* (1951), 29.
24 N. Vance, *Sinews of the Spirit* (Cambridge, 1985), 104.
25 C. Crawley, *Trinity Hall: the History of a Cambridge College* (Cambridge, 1976), 171.
26 A. Gray and F. Brittain, *A History of Jesus College, Cambridge* (1979), 187.

27 J. Buxton and P. Williams (eds), *New College, Oxford, 1379– 1979* (Oxford, 1979), 99.
28 M. Cox, *M. R. James: an Informal Portrait* (Oxford, 1983), 155.
29 Newsome, *Edge of Paradise*, 29, 34.
30 Lyttelton, *Memories*, 48–9.
31 Lyttelton, *Memories*, 97–8.
32 *Truth*, 10 April 1902.
33 D. H. Lawrence, *The Rainbow* (1915), 1958 edition, 434–6.
34 C. H. Driver, 'The Union Society', in F. J. C. Hearnshaw, *The Centenary History of King's College, London, 1828–1928* (1929), 530 ff.; R. Jasper, *Arthur Cayley Headlam: Life and Letters of a Bishop* (1960), 92.
35 H. Hale Bellot, *University College, London, 1826–1926* (1929), 398–9.
36 E. Fiddes, *Chapters on the History of Owens College and Manchester University, 1851–1914* (Manchester, 1937), 121.
37 A. N. Shimmin, *The University of Leeds: the First Half-century* (Leeds, 1954), 84; P. H. J. H. Gosden and A. J. Taylor, *Studies in the History of a University, 1874–1974* (Leeds, 1975), 70 ff.
38 T. Kelly, *For Advancement of Learning: the University of Liverpool, 1881–1981* (Liverpool, 1981), 94–5, 164–7.
39 A. W. Chapman, *The Story of a Modern University: a History of the University of Sheffield* (Oxford, 1955), 88, 166–7.
40 Bale, *Sport and Place*, 76.
41 Hennock, *Fit and Proper Persons*, 304.
42 H. Gordon, 'Cricket and the country gentleman', *Badminton Magazine*, XXXII (1911), 558–9.
43 A. G. Steel and R. H. Lyttelton, *Cricket* (1888), 223.
44 W. G. Grace, *Cricket* (Bristol, 1891), 35.
45 B. Lincoln, *Reminiscences of Sport in Grimsby* (Grimsby, 1912), 89 ff.
46 L. Tasker, *Lincolnshire in 1880* (Lincoln, 1980), 16.
47 M. Ulyatt, *Hull Railway Clerks' Cricket Club Centenary, 1873–1973* (Hull, 1973).
48 *Sussex Express*, 16 April 1881.
49 Winstanley, *Shopkeeper's World*, 136.
50 P. C. Standing, *The Hon. F. S. Jackson* (1906), 119–20.
51 *The Times*, 10 June 1912.
52 *The Times*, 6 June 1912.
53 R. Cashman, 'The phenomenon of Indian cricket', in R. Cashman and N. McKernan, *Sport in History* (Queensland, 1979), 190, 195.
54 *Who was Who, 1941–1950*,' 'A. E. Lyttelton'; Lyttelton, *Memories*; 'Cricket', in E. Bell, *Handbook of Athletic Sports* (1890), 87.
55 Home Gordon, 'Problems of contemporary cricket', *Fortnightly Review*, CX (1911), 175 ff.
56 Home Gordon, 'Cricket and crowds', *Badminton Magazine*, 29 (1909), 197; P. Trevor, 'The future of cricket', *Fortnightly Review*, LXXX (1906), 526 ff.; Home Gordon, 'Youth in cricket', *Fortnightly Review*, LXXXVIII (1910), 985 ff.
57 Club Cricketers' Charity Fund, *Official Handbook* (1911), 107 ff.; J. Williams, 'Cricket', in T. Mason (ed.), *Sport in Britain: a Social History* (Cambridge, 1989), 116 ff.
58 Club Cricketers' Charity Fund, *Official Handbook* (1911).

59 Club Cricketers' Charity Fund, *Official Handbook* (1913), 57 ff.
60 Lyttelton, *Memories*, 42.
61 M Shearman, *Athletics and Football* (1889), 370.
62 Shearman, *Athletics and Football*, 355.
63 Shearman, *Athletics and Football*, 336; T. Mason, *Association Football and English Society, 1863–1915* (Brighton, 1980).
64 Amateur Football Association, *Annual* (1907–08), 38.
65 Mason, *Football*, 152.
66 E. Dunning and K. Sheard, *Barbarians, Gentlemen and Players: a Sociological Study of the Development of Rugby Football* (1979), 8. Much of the following paragraph is based on this important work.
67 D. Smith and G. Williams, *Fields of Praise: the Official History of the Welsh Rugby Union, 1881–1981* (Cardiff, 1980).
68 G. B. Grundy, *Fifty-five Years at Oxford* (1945), 165.
69 E. M. Forster, *The Longest Journey* (1907), 1960 edition, 56.
70 Headingley Football Club, *Centenary Souvenir Brochure, 1878–1978* (Headingley, 1978).
71 K. Pelmear, *Rugby in the Duchy* (Falmouth, 1960), 11–12.
72 D. Newsome, 'Pumping moral muscle', *Times Literary Supplement*, 8 August 1986, 856.
73 J. N. Smith and P. A. Robinson (eds), *Hockey, Historical and Practical* (1899); M. K. Howells, *A Century of Modern Hockey* (1971).
74 *Truth*, 6 November 1902; *Hockey and Amateur Football Monthly*, May 1910.
75 *Brighton Season*, 1905–06, 1908–09.
76 *Truth*, 13 February 1907.
77 A. W. Hopkinson, *Pastor's Progress* (1942), 142.
78 *Baily's Magazine*, November 1907; J. H. C. Fagan *et al.*, *Football, Hockey and Lacrosse* (1900).
79 Bishop of Truro, 'The ethic of boat races', *The Barge* (Oxford, 1905).
80 R. C. Lehmann *et al.*, *Rowing* (1897), 1, 124.
81 Vance, *Sinews*, 156; L. Stephen, *Sketches from Cambridge by a Don* (1865), 20.
82 W. G. East, *Rowing and Sculling* (1904), 30.
83 *Dickens's Dictionary of the Thames* (1894).
84 R. C. Lehmann *et al.*, *The Complete Oarsman* (1908), 179 ff.; H. Cleaver, *A History of Rowing* (1957), 62.
85 C. Dodd, *Henley Royal Regatta* (1981).
86 M. Cobbett, *Sporting Notions of Present Days and Past* (1908), 270; A. E. T. Watson, *English Sports* (1903), 160 ff.
87 N. Wigglesworth, 'A history of rowing in the north-east of England', *British Journal of Sports History*, 3(1986), 145 ff.
88 East Sussex Record Office, AMS 5730, Lewes Rowing Club, Subscription Book; Warwickshire Record Office, CR 1798/3, Warwick Boat Club, Minutes; F. Henthorn, *History of the Ancholme Rowing Club, 1868–1976* (Humberside, 1980).
89 A. A. Macfarlane-Grieve, *A History of Durham Rowing* (1922).
90 W. J. Walker, *Friendship, 1879–1951* (Whitby, 1954).
91 Cleaver, *History*, 178.
92 Fry, *Life Worth living*, 94.

93 *Sheffield Telegraph*, 16 November 1895.
94 Shearman, *Athletics and Football, passim*; Graham, *Athletics*.
95 W. Rye, 'Paper-chasing and cross-country running', in Shearman, *Athletics and Football*, 382; R. R. Conway, 'Cross-country running', *Badminton Magazine*, VI(1898), 561.
96 A. J. Newton, *Boxing* (1907); *Health and Strength Annual* (1910), 109; S. Shipley, 'Boxing', in Mason, *Sport in Britain*, 78.
97 *Dickens's Dictionary of the Thames* (1894), 'Swimming clubs'; Amateur Swimming Association, *Handbooks*, 1899–1914.
98 *Physical Education*, February 1904; G. M. Adams (ed.), *Sandow's System of Physical Training* (1894); E. Miles, *The Eustace Miles System of Physical Culture* (1907); *Fitness for Play and Work* (1912); F. G. Aflalo, 'The sportsman's library', *Fortnightly Review*, LXXIX (1906), 173; *Baily's Magazine*, October 1897, 300 ff.; *Health and Strength Annual* (1910).
99 H. Begbie, 'Strength', *C. B. Fry's Magazine*, April 1904.

Chapter 4
Clubability

Lawns, private and public

Manly sports had one major defect for a leisure-hungry middle class;
the requirement of physical fitness made them unsuitable for most
over-thirty-fives and the sedentary. Yet their raised profile and the
wider social currency of sports language meant that the terms were
tailored, or often considerably distorted, to fit activities which could
be seen as 'sporting' only by a singular stretch of the imagination.
With the possible exception of cricket, it was well outside the accepted
coda of public-school-derived sports that the greatest shift of the
spectrum of athletic demands occurred.

Activities that began, and kept their most effective social base, as
'pastimes' soon acquired much of the language and organisational
paraphernalia of 'sports'. In addition there was a wide band of gender
confusion, where women not only took to the games but actually
played with and against men. A claimed athletic legitimacy was
weakened in other ways, not least in patterns of social organisation
that were often seen as being at actual odds with raising levels of
performance. In many senses they reversed C. B. Fry's explanation for
many university men's dropping track and field athletics after graduation, because they provided for sociable activities as an intrinsic part
of their growth. That explained much of their popularity with many
who joined, although some objected to such apparently unfettered
intimacy:

> The root of much difficulty in all pastimes under modern conditions is
> the circumstance that a number of people entirely unknown to each other
> are suddenly brought together in a peculiarly familiar way.[1]

This objection grew out of a worry that organising games such as
croquet and lawn tennis into leagues and tournaments would weaken

the more easily controlled local networks. Such links had to be forged or reinforced in fluid urban and suburban surroundings where sports clubs played a major role in delineating status and social achievement. They also provided a forum for male interaction and, frequently, some sort of escape from the domestic environment. Many of the games around which they were constructed were themselves typical of the ambivalent private/public interplay of middle-class non-working lives in that they could be pursued in the private gardens of the more affluent as well as in the clubs which grew to cater for the less wealthy.

It is difficult in many cases to reconstruct the local patterns of sideways and downward diffusion but the spread of some games enabled a formal oligarchic control to replace the personal and familial exclusivity of the private grounds. The greatest tensions in this process appeared when the 'democratisation' of a game reached such a level that even private clubs could not cope and a providing role was assumed by a municipal authority, usually in association with a self-regulatory local group. The final major problem faced by the participants in this growth was the fluctuation in popularity of particular games, especially when a pursuit was 'hyped', either by a commercial investor, such as happened in the ping-pong craze of 1902–03, or by social emulation, as in the Edwardian badminton boom.

Sporting clubs were not invented by the later Victorian middle classes but developed rapidly from the 1870s. Two models already existed but the end result differed substantially from both. The London gentlemen's club which offered the gentry and upper professionals a combination of a self-regulated hotel and an alternative to domestic provision for the unmarried spawned a small number of provincial copies, such as the Leeds or Hove clubs. On the other hand were the widespread pub-based working-class bodies, based on informal friendly societies which burgeoned into the huge angling network of the later century, in which drink and work-related bonding played a major role. The organisation of all these was similar, with a parallel committee structure, election patterns and, usually, entry dependent on some mode of control by existing members. The middle-class contribution was to spread club organisation outside town centres and pubs to an extensive suburban base.

Few of these new bodies could afford to state their exclusiveness as narrowly as did the Isthmian:

a club for those who play games; the qualification is educational, and candidates must have belonged to the best public schools, or have been admitted to Oxford or Cambridge.[2]

The Queen's Club in West Kensington boasted eighteen peers and four knights on its committee; the Prince's Racquet and Tennis Club forbade gambling.[3] Bodies like this had already been exported to the new resorts, such as Leamington Spa, where the Leamington [Real] Tennis Club had been formed in the 1840s to provide essentially for a genteel membership. Hurlingham, already noted for its role in pigeon-shooting, expanded rapidly into polo, tennis and golf as a suburban centre for London's aristocracy and plutocracy, but the English middle classes produced very few examples of this type of the North American model growing rapidly in the 1880s, the country club with a wide range of activities for a select membership on a large estate.

With the exception of golf, to be dealt with later, the hallmark of most of these new English clubs was their spatial modesty: for all their rapid growth in popularity, the new games were often distinctly understated. Some faced proliferating demands from a growing membership with a wider range of sex and age for an extension of activities both in type and in seasonal availability, and many accepted these as a means of financing their basic enthusiasms. Those clubs which diversified often experienced conflicts between different interest groups within their membership, so that many bodies preferred to stay as single-pursuit entities, bonding together for other activities reluctantly. Just occasionally there were catch-all bodies, attempting comprehensive provision for the elite of one suburb. In 1889 a Leeds businessman, W. J. Howell, bought a small estate in Headingley and founded the Hyde Park Recreation Club: a limited liability company in which he was the largest shareholder, it provided lawn tennis, bowls and cycling for both men and women members.[4] On the Thames the Phyllis Court Club House was developed at Henley in 1907 to provide tennis, croquet and bowls as well as pleasure boating on the river.[5] But such proprietary clubs, however much they disguised ownership by passing formal responsibility for management and selection to an elected club committee, proved far less popular than bodies which grew out of a local urban oligarchy, reflecting in range and scale the opportunity for participation across the board. They were able both to organise their own capital formation and to act, occasionally, as non-party political pressure groups.

Their ostensible purpose was a particular sport. But often far more significant and far less easily reconstructed by historians was their role as instruments of relatively fine social differentiation and arbiters of public custom. For their core of dedicated members they offered a way of life, and additional layers of recognition, occasionally as alternatives to those provided by economic roles in status reinforcement. They frequently became the prime means of this outside the home, particularly where the roles ascribed to males in work and living places were significantly separate. For many, especially members of those nominally affiliated to the established Church, they provided a complement, or an alternative, to the local parish church as a meeting place. Unlike even the relatively overt Freemasonry of the later nineteenth century, they also offered a public sense of identity. Membership could reflect wealth, although the actual subscriptions of quite prestigious bodies were surprisingly small, in terms of disposable income.

What often mattered was the fact of membership itself as much as the activity, the game itself offering a focus for the minor snobberies which were intrinsic to establishing relationships in comparatively raw environments. This was often most acute where women were involved – the mixed clubs probably had far greater importance in determining local social codes than single-sex bodies. The management, especially in lawn tennis, might be effectively male but the real arbitrating force was often female. Style, etiquette and petty nuances were especially important where club life became the centre or part of a wider social calendar, with public and private circles overlapping. Winifred Holtby's experience in Hull before the First World War, recounted in her novel *The Crowded Street*, offers one of the sharpest accounts of the formalisation of social intercourse around sport, particularly in the use of lawn tennis clubs as acceptable marriage marts.[6]

For men in particular clubs provided a new secular ritual calendar. The seasonality of most games was always a problem in the maintenance of club dynamics, so intermediate high points emerged. These developments paralleled working-class lines of seasonal rituals and traditions – in some activities, such as bowls or cycling, there would have been little to identify the class basis of many clubs apart from refinements of speech and clothing. The peak was usually an annual dinner held out of season, often round Christmas:

... over the festive board many a lasting friendship is formed and good comradeship made. After justice is done to the good things provided, jokes and tales of prowess on the green are recited over the glass and pipe, and music is called upon to further enlighten the proceedings. Nothing 'goes down' so well as the song with a merry chorus . . .[7]

Usually held in a local hotel with strong links with sports clubs, the form was banal, the content even more so. But the very predictability of the meals, toasts, speeches and songs emphasised their value. Club songs, badges and ties were reinforced by mementoes of each event. When the Brondesbury Bowling Club in north London held its annual feast at New Year 1910, it produced a presentation card, seven inches of double circular rimmed in the club colours of yellow and green; on the reverse was 'a pretty little sketch of the green . . . Whilst the inner portion contained the menu with a few sketches of bowlers in the act of play, as also the programme for the toasts and music.'[8] On such little things much suburban self-esteem was built, particularly when this male-centred world explored the fringes of the *risqué*. If middle-class society largely excluded the 'rough' from its pleasures, many clubs liked to play on the edges of decorum at a few annual events. The *Hull and East Riding Athlete* was only one of a number of late Victorian papers which occasionally called for 'the purification of smoking concerts' from the *double entendre*.[9] Mild naughtiness managed to survive, however, although it was kept from the pages of the little club journals which proliferated as sporting parish magazines, like the Warwick Boat Club's *Arc Light*: jokes, hints and tips and fixture lists provided for many clubs the services that public school magazines offered to the more privileged.[10]

Arcane language was essential for a game's appeal to be successful. The terms of lawn tennis, 'sets', 'doubles' and the precise regulation of the game's playing space, had all to be learned and regurgitated, not only to make it playable but also to build up its mystique for the outsider and the aspirant. Sporting etiquette reflected both a need to play properly and a specific extension of genteel behaviour – paradoxically, the frequent reiteration of codes in sporting journals and club meetings suggests a healthy tension between socially acceptable conduct and the urge to win in some players. It was underpinned by nationally agreed practices and the local decisions of club officers. Rarely do the lines of power become observable, and the interplay of status and formality in any club's affairs remain largely outside documentary reconstruction. For most of our period power lay in the hands of founding members, if only because of the key financial role some of them played in club life, with loans to help in acquiring grounds. They admitted new members, and dissension is a rare sight in club minutes and annual meetings: where it occurred anonymity of recording suggests a careful keeping of control, an assumed solidarity. Clubs seem to have shared the late Victorian middle-class phobia of domestic scandals becoming open knowledge. Club uniforms, however modest, engendered identity even if dress codes were not as developed as in other sports, and some of these quintessentially suburban bodies actually increased in informality (and presumably self-assurance) the higher they appeared in the status pecking order. Bowlers playing in their shirtsleeves could be found in manual working-class and upper professional areas – they rarely appeared in the stolider suburbs.

The high level of social emphasis put upon croquet, lawn tennis and badminton reflected a barrier to wider acceptance which was never entirely resolved before 1914. Their major value, apart from providing social meeting grounds, lay in the extent to which they were relatively undemanding physically, able to operate at a lowest common denominator, lacking real danger, apart from the occasional heart attack, suitable to their preferred age groups and mixed gender activities.

Most of these games were 'pastimes', conceived originally as innocuous ways of filling up free time in a modestly frivolous fashion and they were frequently marketed as such, as incidental accompaniments to social graces, until growing numbers of their participants invested them with an awful solemnity. The fact that the lawn-based games used small balls detracted even further from the claims made for them; they were snidely dismissed as 'pat ball'. Yet in this respect they differed only marginally from cricket, and they often required greater immediate involvement by all players and a wide range of co-ordinated physical and mental skills. If claims for the latter's importance were frequently exaggerated they accounted, nonetheless, for some of the games' staying power in the face of criticism. What they could do but rarely, however, was penetrate the bastions of manliness, the public schools, although they did become a minor part of the university spectrum of recreation.

The bulk of upper middle-class male youth could play the new games only in the holidays and it was hardly surprising that many schools regarded them as contaminants against which vulnerable boys had to be protected in term time. But the appeal in many areas lay in the way in which some middle-class men affected by the public school sporting cult could find some sense of joining an elite when they had neither the opportunity nor the contacts for an apprenticeship in athletics. They were usually at a point in life when they could relax slightly in terms of achievement and seek wider recognition in local terms of having 'made their mark'. Yet it is also noticeable in just how many grander lawn tennis clubs public school and university athletes were able to expand their hegemony by dominating an increasingly competitive tournament structure.

The lawn or court-based games proved extremely susceptible to shifts in fashion. Underlying them all, but never popular, was the most consistent of the older gentry lawn sports, archery. The amount of space needed, as well as its fashionable links with hosting expensive garden parties, limited its downward spread among the urban middle classes; few gardens in Bedford Park, London, or Headingley, Leeds, would offer an area large enough for even a small archery contest. It served a limited purpose in bonding many counties' minor gentry and clergy together, or at least their womenfolk, who shot as well as providing tea and chat. But numbers were rarely large; the Northamptonshire Archery Association boasted fewer than twenty-four active members in the 1860s, and its successor, the Archers of the Nene, counted fourteen clergy, two army officers and five ladies among its twenty-three members in 1893.[11] Yet there was a mild, localised revival at the turn of the century, if only because it seemed suited to the ambitions of the new plutocracy, bent on ostentatious parallels to a gentry world they envied.[12] In Brighton it took the form of using the cricket ground at Preston Park, another colonisation of what was theoretically municipal public space. There the Brighton and Hove Archers, some forty women and seventy men, shot on four mornings a week and Friday afternoons during the short autumn season. 'Assuming you happen to secure the privilege of entrée to the charmed circle of this exclusive little archery coterie,' said a favourable reviewer, then the sport was open and relatively cheap.[13]

Patting balls

The game most commonly stereotyped as Victorian middle-class leisure is croquet, an over-expansion of a distinctly minority pursuit into a representative type. Typical it may not have been, but it demonstrated the singular impact of fashion and also the fudging of the boundaries between a totally private and a semi-public activity which even limited popularity could bring. Most late Victorian commentators ascribed its beginnings to the 1850s, an early product of the first major wave of affluent suburbanisation. It proved a useful tool for effecting introductions and determining the extent of social intercourse, an extension outdoors of complex visiting etiquettes. Its spread beyond the garden fence led to a rapid growth in clubs and national recognition with the tournaments held at Evesham in 1867 and Moreton in the Marsh in 1868. It moved rapidly from this provincial springboard to a metropolitan organisation, based on the All England Croquet Club at Wimbledon from 1870. Thereafter it collapsed extremely rapidly, weakened by the sudden popularity of lawn tennis and by the difficulties of transferring a country house sport to a London base. Intellectually too demanding though it may have been, other reasons were given for its decline in the late 1870s:

> Croquet was all very well in its way, but it gave no exercise; its social advantages are equally shared by lawn tennis; and it fostered (and for this reason principally it fell) the ascendancy of the curate.[14]

Ironically, the absolute model of muscular Christianity could degenerate into limp-wristed effeminacy.

The collapse lasted twenty years, although the game was kept alive in the minor country house world, where, around Petworth in Sussex at least, it managed a mild later 1880s revival.[15] In 1896 the ageing W. H. Peel, victor of the 1868 Moreton in the Marsh tournament, resurrected it by founding the All England Croquet Association, recognising that Wimbledon had finally succumbed to lawn tennis. He emphasised the 'scientific' game, based on rules and desperate to avoid garden party informality.[16] By 1900 it had 508 members, strongly linked with clubs based in provincial centres, Clifton, Bath, Cheltenham, Budleigh Salterton and Charnwood Forest.[17] What prompted Peel was a resurgence of tournament playing at Maidstone in 1894 and a widely expressed wish to spread the game in a structure of regulated competition, 'Compared with the old garden-party conditions, it is as the atmosphere of the busiest city in contrast to some quiet old-world town, sleepy, if you will, but without the disturbing competition of commercialism.'[18]

Organisation, culminating in an annual Eastbourne tournament, followed rapidly. Although Peel died in 1897 there was no shortage of people willing to take on the game's management, even when it was played as frivolously as was apparently the norm at Hurlingham, which it penetrated in 1900.[19] The bustle of the game's new-found 'commercialism' stood in sharp contrast with its centres of pursuit, the social tone-conscious resorts of the affluent retired, yet it grew there precisely because it increased the attractiveness of such towns for both visitors and ideal residents. Deliberate self-interest fostered its rapid Edwardian expansion; the Croquet Association claimed nearly 3,000 members by 1913. In Sussex the County Club was formed in 1901, taking five acres of land at Southwick, near Brighton and Hove, with 250 members, dominated by retired military men who kept it 'animated, picturesque and socially distinguished'.[20] The new clubs flourished in an atmosphere of controlled intellectual aggression, minimal physical activity and considerable social convenience.

Croquet's vicissitudes were linked with the rapid growth of one of late Victorian England's major sports, lawn tennis. Its deliberate invention as a garden party game has long been attributed to Major W. C. Wingfield: in the early 1870s he patented *Sphairistike*, to be played on an hourglass-shaped court easily marked out on any reasonably-sized domestic lawn. Whether it was Wingfield or another major, Harry Gem, who claimed to have played a similar game (*pelota*) on a rectangular court since 1859, popularising it in Leamington Spa, is still a matter for sporting antiquarians to squabble unhappily over.[21] The mere invention of a pastime does not account for its considerable national popularity by the later 1870s, but the ease of clubability and social selectivity discussed earlier do. Its adoption and regulation by the MCC in 1875 and its elevation into a 'national' championship by the All England Croquet Club at Wimbledon after 1877 allowed it to cover a spectrum of participation and aspiration which suited both the needs of a part of the middle classes and the economic considerations of manufacturers producing implements for a game in which consistent marketing was desirable.

One major impetus to its adoption, not least in resorts, was the unsuitability of existing racquet games for extensive participation. Real tennis, played since the late Middle Ages, demanded considerable indoor facilities and limited player access. It enjoyed modest early Victorian growth in centres where the 'social convenience and daily intercourse of the nobility and gentry' were otherwise limited with the older pursuits of archery, hunting and dancing. In April 1844 a group of Leamington Spa men, dissatisfied with both the limits of available recreations and, presumably, the easy entry of women to them, founded a (Real) Tennis Club, with the appurtenances of a London gentlemen's club – billiards, smoking and reading rooms.[22] The capital cost of providing courts 108 ft long (some £4,000) meant that similar ventures were few, restricted on the whole to the gathering places of the recognisably genteel: the older universities, London and the grander resorts. There men like the young A. J. Balfour, who found 'aesthetic rapture' in the game, played with their social and political peers, often with the ambitious, competitive ruthlessness the late twentieth century associates with squash.[23] But the limits of its popularity were clear by the 1870s: 'it is too expensive for a democratic age'.[24] Despite later attempts to prove otherwise, that it could be played for less than £30 a year, there were only thirty-three courts in England by the turn of the century: one percipient observer saw as its major problem that it lacked *esprit de corps*.[25]

The paradoxical combination of elitist *esprit* with financial cheapness made lawn tennis particularly suitable to a 'democracy' which had not reached the near-universal male suffrage of the 1884 Reform Act. There is no clear downward or lateral explanation of its spread in the later 1870s, since the growth of tournaments and regulation may have added a sporting near-respectability but hardly accounted for the breadth of its take up. It was, however, the first game to allow for a hierarchy of formalisation and activity at a number of levels and ages in which, whilst participants might move up a ladder, they were under no obligation to do so. The growing complexity of its competitive structure matched that of cricket, with touring amateur teams, but also with the bureaucratising of county and national activity. Yet, as 'a game that has so majestically received the hallmark of suburban gentility', it never achieved the pan-class provision for entry and specatorship that cricket offered.[26] It also allowed the mingling of sexes and ages in a way that only croquet so far had, but, unlike croquet, its potential for really active athleticism soon became apparent.

This produced a tension never easily resolved, displaying the never far removed uncertainty about physical recreation which suffused the period. Repeated claims came from both detractors and supporters that 'it just occupies a free space of time pleasantly', and for men like Balfour, Alfred Lyttelton or Willie Grenfell (later Lord Desborough) it was just that, releasing them from the 'hard bondage' and 'forced labour' croquet had imposed on house party guests.[27] Its amenity to easy flirtation, its reliability rather than apparently excessive demands and its value for time-conscious and health-wary middle-aged men prompted both its growth and repeated criticism as it moved into the fully developed sporting canon of the Edwardian years.[28] It came to be seen as an essential threat to cricket, 'and the physical pluck [which] is one of the most valuable things a game can teach a boy', offering serious risks both if it were to be adopted in public schools and, more so, in the softening domestic environment to which boys were exposed in the summer months, the peak of the game's season.[29]

Not only would social flippancy be encouraged but the deep corruption of 'pot hunting' competitiveness would take hold:

> ... public competition lawn tennis does not attract the most desirable type of athlete at the present time, and ... to play in a succession of English tournaments in the holidays is not a particularly desirable occupation for a public schoolboy.[30]

Yet the game's spread indicates that schoolboys were well among those willing to be corrupted.

What is often portrayed as a domestic or suburban game had a much wider geographical, if not social, appeal. The small village of Binbrook in the north of the Lincolnshire Wolds had acquired a club by 1881, with a weekly set of matches attracting thirty to forty members, often playing against clubs from nearby towns such as Grimsby. Its largest problem seems to have been the seasonal uncertainty caused by locals' going off to agricultural fairs or archery contests, but young Fannie Rainey Fieldsend recorded faithfully in her diaries a round of weekly club activities which would otherwise have been lost to the historian.[31] In the wider rural areas it was probably the domestic rather than the club game which predominated, as when G. Heniage, of Wragby, also in Lincolnshire, arranged a Saturday match in 1884 with S. Wintringham, to last two hours before lunch and two hours after, ladies not playing in the second half.[32] They could purchase their implements easily enough from the small local manufacturer, Lunn of Horncastle, who expanded his cricket business to cope.[33]

In suburbia, as in Binbrook, it was outside the domestic boundaries that lawn tennis flourished most as the quintessential small-club game for the middle classes. Major Gem's pelota was played from 1872 in Leamington Spa on a club ground easily adapted to tennis in the mid-decade. The uncertain hold in the early years of the game's popularity meant that many clubs either adopted a limited seasonal existence or became nomadic, at least in the large towns, until both an established membership and reasonable certainty of survival encouraged taking out longer commitments. The Haulgh Lawn Tennis Club of Bolton, Lancashire, brought together solicitors, doctors, small businessmen and superior clerks (and presumably their womenfolk) during its twenty years of life after 1887.[34]

Experience across the Pennines demonstrated the vicissitudes clubs in one town could face, depending upon their precise suburban location and their role in the micro-networks of middle-class socialising. The Holderness club was dying by 1890 because lawn tennis 'never has been very enthusiastically followed in Hull. Its adherents have generally preferred to play upon their own private lawns, rather than make a public exhibition of their prowess.'[35] Yet, a short distance away, the Hull Lawn Tennis Club, founded about 1880, continued a steady growth which allowed it to lay out ten new courts and two croquet grounds when it had to move its site on the expiry of its lease in 1901.[36] Hull's most prestigious suburb, the older market town of Beverley, acquired a club in 1883. It rarely had more than thirty members, yet its annual August bank holiday tournament, held on its three grass courts, drew entries from all over Yorkshire.[37] Clearly there were elements far more significant to a club's viability than either its location or its size which are often beyond conventional historical reconstruction.

In Leeds lawn tennis at its most organised sheltered under other wings, as a branch of the cricket, football and athletic organisations founded at Headingley: the sixteen members of 1891 grew to 180 by 1907 but shared in a decline thereafter, although its numbers, ninety-eight by 1911, were never seriously small.[38] Some residents of Walthamstow, London suburbia at its most stolid, founded the Rectory Manor Club in 1896, with twenty-four men and twenty-four ladies, sharing their ground with bowls players. By 1899 it boasted 133 members, 110 by 1913, kept together by regular out-of-season dances which helped raise the funds for maintaining land it had wisely bought in 1897.[39]

The new game also infiltrated and often took over existing sports clubs as well as fostering new ones. The Warwick Boat Club, founded in 1861 for young local tradesmen to prove their rowing prowess, admitted lawn tennis in 1894, clearly in an attempt to revive the fortunes of what had largely become a pleasure boating association. The new 'games section' (it also included some bowls and croquet) rapidly absorbed the club's energies and it remained 'Boat' virtually only in name until a mild rowing revival in 1902, laying out courts, running town events and buying balls by the gross for its 168 members. This 'drifting into tennis' was presided over nominally by Lord Warwick, to whom due obeisance was paid, but was run essentially for and by the professional and superior businessmen of the local triangle of Warwick, Leamington and Coventry. For them the social amenities of a new game combined well with the attractions of a recreational base in a picturesque market town in a club quite spectacularly situated on a river bank opposite a romantic castle.[40] Chivalry, Camelot, mild exercise and social tone merged very smoothly into one in Warwick.

Others, less fortunate but more affluent, had to combine in London, facing both a certain urban unattractiveness with the need for year-round playing necessitated by high land costs and the possibilities of a restricted membership. The Maida Vale club was founded in 1880 but lost its ground when its lease expired in 1885; it moved, as the Hyde Park Lawn Tennis Club, to covered courts in Dorchester Square, meeting costs not dissimilar to real tennis.[41] By the turn of the century it had become possible for the *dévot* to play not only year round but day round, with the exploitation of electric light in covered courts. The Drive Club, 'the Queens' Club for the man of Modest Means', allowed play on its covered courts if the balloting process allowed one to penetrate to actually paying its two-guinea subscription.[42]

Club play moved almost inevitably to tournament organisation, whether at Wimbledon after 1877 or in Binbrook in the 1880s. Throughout its early experience the game saw considerable tensions as to how far this should go, the gentle older notions transferred from cricket combining very uneasily with the acquisitive competitiveness which had produced the finances for growth. Leamington Spa, that improbable centre for innovation, saw a tournament organised in 1881 to raise money for the Ladies' Home Mission Association and the Additional Curates' Society: jewellery was offered as the prize for both male and female competitors, who came over from Leicester as well as from around Warwickshire to play games surrounded by the stalls, refreshments and entertainments of what was really an open garden party.[43] Thereafter it was the town's business life rather than young clergymen who benefited, since the tournament became an annual event, run by the local club until 1888, when it was taken over by the Town Improvement Association, which passed it on to the Advertising Committee in 1904.

This commercial acumen, combined with a sense of the values of clearly identified social tone, fostered the spread of tournaments in other resorts. The most prestigious of all was Eastbourne's, offering 572 separate matches for 865 entries in Devonshire Park by 1902. An Edwardian boom in tournaments took the town's matches to 1,000 by 1904, putting the 'Empress of Watering Places' at the social peak of a round of over 100 tournaments each summer in England, despite Wimbledon's claims to be the greatest centre. It was made easier by the opportunist provision of cheap fares to tournaments by interested railway companies.[44]

The game's partial transference to sporting status grew with an emphasis on 'scientific play' and the annexation of a never fully determined central authority by the All England Lawn Tennis Club, which dropped 'Croquet' from its title in 1882.[45] For Wimbledon the money raised around the essentially amateur tournaments was ploughed back into grander facilities than could have been maintained by ordinary members' subscriptions alone. The 1880s saw a steady rise in dependence on this, but a sharp drop in tournament-playing in the 1890s demanded a readmittance of croquet merely to meet the bills. When an Edwardian revival began, the All England club found itself repeatedly at loggerheads with the Lawn Tennis Association, whose foundation in 1888 on the lines of the Football Association led to attempts to centralise the control of organised competitive tennis.[46] Wimbledon managed to stay just at the tournament peak, but the club never again held the moral sway that the MCC retained in cricket. The 'arrogant' LTA proposed an 'English' championship in 1906 (something the Wimbledon tournament was in effect but not in name) and the AELTC fell back on the ultimate defence of snobbery, its seniority and its dignity, rebutting repeated accusations that it was little better than a 'suburban' club.[47] Outranked in sheer match numbers by Eastbourne, it made a consistent appeal on the grounds of its quality and amateurism.[48]

In effect it was saved by its 'Henley factor', its nearness to London and a social cachet just ahead of the Sussex resort's. When Herbert Barrett, the singles winner of 1912, was forbidden to play in the tournament by his doctor, he went ahead 'only in realisation of his responsibilities to Wimbledon and the Public'.[49] This assumption of moral rectitude hid a fierce battle over ethical standards (see chapter

6) which underlay these mature years of lawn tennis. Its revived early twentieth-century popularity rested on a popular middle class base fostered by the performances of heroes. The game had verily become a sport but at those levels it had acquired some of the mystique and practical limits of first-class cricket. Wimbledon triumphed over the LTA, it was claimed, because:

> If an attempt is to be made to democratise it, something of the spirit that has hitherto pervaded it will probably be lost. It is not a game for the masses. Only the young man with ample means and leisure can hope to excel as an exponent of lawn tennis.[50]

The Edwardian successors of the Renshaw twins, who had turned it into a demanding physical sport in the 1880s, were far separated in assumptions about the game from the thousands who knocked balls around on new municipal courts, belonging to clubs on the outer fringes of the Lawn Tennis Association, and who continued to use it as a trysting point.[51] Its acceptability as a focus of social intercourse can be seen in the extent to which Nonconformist as well as Anglican churches added it to the the range of ancillary devices by which they sought to keep the allegiance of a younger middle-class membership they feared would drift away.

Lawn tennis's popularity was affected by seasonal limitations, confined to the finer weather of less than half the year. It was this which undoubtedly fostered the extremely rapid growth in badminton around the century's turn. Apparently developed by the British in India as a gentle outdoor game for whiling away the sojourn in the hill stations, and named nostalgically after the Duke of Beaufort's country seat, it was reintroduced into England by younger retiring Anglo-Indians in the 1880s as an antidote to the possible tedium of resort life.[52] The rules drawn up at Poonah in 1875 were used as a basis by J. H. E. Hart when he drafted the Bath Badminton Club's code in 1887.[53]

Growth among the indigenous middle classes was sufficiently strong to prompt the foundation of a Badminton Association in 1893, although it never reached anything like the popularity of lawn tennis. The association boasted twenty affiliated clubs in 1898, sixty-five in 1901, 190 by 1907 and 263 by 1912; it is virtually impossible to determine how broad was the penumbra of non-affiliated bodies, although one Edwardian estimate put it as equal to those within the association.[54] Seen by many participants as gentle winter training for lawn tennis, it nonetheless emerged as a 'scientific game', that near-universal accolade of late Victorian sporting respectability, with its own journal, the *Badminton Gazette*. With rare exceptions it grew as a parasite (in the nicest possible sense) on other middle-class public associations; being played indoors, it was ideally suited to partial use of the burgeoning number of church halls and of the drill halls which Edwardian volunteer militarism fostered. It also, very instrumentally in domestic terms, allowed the wives and daughters of the new part-time soldiers to share some of the facilities to which their males disappeared for part of the week. Strongest in the London suburbs of Ealing and Crystal Palace, it was usually dependent on the availability of such provided facilities. Only in the Kensington area, with its much higher levels of affluent commitment, did badminton acquire the dedicated premises common to many other games when a speculative developer, Boris Marishkine, built a special hall in 1908.[55]

No such lasting success attended one attempt to bridge the domestic and the associative and to provide the challenge of racquet games within a much smaller and affordable space: table tennis. The game had two parallel sources, which opened up into an organisational rivalry which did much to kill its popularity outside the home. Table tennis as such emerged loosely in the 1890s with amateur or craft-produced implements but developed rapidly in 1900 when the Nondescript Cricket Club, another wandering team, played it during the evenings of their tours. To keep it up they formed the Cavendish Club in London and it received the temporary fashionable accolade of being played by Grace and Stoddart.[56]

Its rival was marketed about the same time as a commercial experiment by Jaques & Co., the equipment manufacturers, under the name 'Gossima': it failed until John Jacques the third redesignated it 'ping-pong' and it fed a national boom in 1902.[57] There was a clear tension between the sporting associations of table tennis and the apparently frivolous ping-pong, of which the ever sceptical *Truth* said, 'We shall soon hear a lot of drivel talked about the science of the game.'[58] Yet such 'drivel' emerged very rapidly with the formation in December 1901 of the Table Tennis Association, 'to keep the control of the game in the hands of amateur players themselves, and independent of trade influence'. It soon acquired fifty affiliated clubs, including the 'All England' at the Royal Aquarium, Westminster: fifty-six of them were in Greater London.[59] Claiming 'quickness of eye, correct judgment [*sic*], prompt decision, and a fair amount of athletic skill and staying power', it drafted on to this modest pastime a moral load it was singularly unable to bear. Its rival, the Ping-Pong Association, tied to the Jacques rules, made similar claims but ironically the boxes in which sets came almost invariably showed it being played by ladies and gentlemen well encased in full Edwardian evening dress, with its inevitable restrictions on movement.[60]

The Ping-Pong Social Club Ltd, formed in March 1902 to 'promote the game in the London area', made up of twenty-four middling tradesmen, folded within a year, but there was still a drive to spread the 'sport'.[61] W. H. Grenfell became president of the High Wycombe Table Tennis Club, and the Marquess of Anglesea, harking back perhaps to the days of Livery and Maintenance, designed a uniform for the Anglesea Ping-Pong Club, 'a blazer of turquoise blue cloth, bound and lined with blue silk'.[62] The members seem to have paid for their own garb, however. The game was claimed to foster *esprit de corps* in other clubs, such as the Bristol Schoolmasters' Cricket Club.[63] The boom was as much commercial as participant – by 1902 there were forty-nine models of bat on the market. Social acceptance, as when the Preston Grocers' Association introduced it into their New Year celebrations as an alternative for non-dancers, was occasionally greeted with outrage; the Bishop of Manchester held that it led to the moral degeneration of women who played it, although he failed to produce evidence and recanted when challenged by the honorary secretary of the Table Tennis Association.[64] What later became one of the mainstays of moralising youth organisations was dropped almost as rapidly as it was taken up. In the higher social reaches the parallel bridge boom seemed a less exhausting after-dinner occupation, and the game was largely left until its revival in the 1920s as a domestic occupation for the more fortunate middle-class young, such as A. J. P. Taylor. His parents' sixteen-seater mahogany dining table in Southsea offered a useful court for his prowess.[65]

Rolling balls

Despite the social cachet of the successful racquet games, they proved too active and too time-demanding for many men. For them another boom sport appeared, bowls. Quintessentially sedentary (although not seated), associated with fine summer evenings, pipe smoke and the ruminations of age, it proved a major attraction to a whole range of turn-of-the-century men whose active involvement in work

left little time for sports more greedy of time and physique. The
Warwick Boat Club recognised this by letting its bowling members
play on lawn tennis courts, because they could not row or play
tennis when they were still at work until 7.00 p.m. It was also
predominantly male, singularly free of the female involvement of
lawn tennis. The constituency of players proved far wider than
the other clubable games and presents the historian with singular
difficulties: bowling was pan-class in the sense that it was played by
groups drawn on a line between professional men and respectable
artisans, sometimes within the same club. But it is clear that many
larger towns developed a spread of clubs which reinforced the class
patterns of neighbourhoods; in addition, there was a general divide
within the game, between the semi-professional crown green and
the totally amateur rink (or flat) green, which reinforced both a
class-ascriptive and a regional difference. In just over a decade,
beginning in the mid-1890s, it grew considerably in popularity and
shifted from being an essentially unregulated series of local happen-
ings towards some sense of national identity and bureaucratisation,
with an accompanying specialist press. Yet bowls retained the full
spectrum of activity, from meditative and convivial recreation to
earnest and ruthless competition.

Justified, as ever, by late Victorians as a paradigm for life, it
offered a gentle rather than strenuous manliness; 'undue or violent exercise is never necessary, such as in some games have a
dangerous tendency to result in severe chills, bring mischief, &
c.'.[66] It was a game for weekday and Saturday evenings, with a
major role in social bonding, 'a certain masonic feeling of unity',
such as attended the founding of the Sussex Bowling Association
in 1910.[67] The assumption that Freemasonry offered the strongest
form of association reveals, perhaps, less of a spread of lodges
into sport than a parallel with the strength of arcane rituals and
languages and the mutuality of closed business interests which are
popularly ascribed to Masonic life. 'Sober', despite its frequent links
with pubs, the ascription of 'a stateliness and gracefulness met in no
other sport' was perhaps a self-deluding justification for its popularity
with the comparatively elderly.[68] Decorum and after-work informality
survived in uneasy equipoise; social tone-conscious locals in Bath
expressed a deep objection in 1910 to 'the sight of the elderly
gentlemen in shirt-sleeves' playing in Henrietta Park.[69] Doggerel
verses and club songs, filling out the smokers and whist drives

which reinforced members' loyalties out of season, made great play of the game's 'democracy':

> Class differences 'twixt poor and rich
> When shown is driven to the ditch.[70]

Such hopefulness hardly fitted the contrast between 'South Country people, with their £600 bowling greens' and the pub-based facilities of many older villages and lesser suburbs, where 'the game of bowls is loved by many of the lower middle-class. Often enough these bowling greens are better than any of the lawns that are the pick of the more wealthy residents.'[71] Such untestable claims poke through contemporary writing with sufficient frequency to demonstrate the persistent social unease which accompanied the game's expansion and irritation at the widening opportunities for petty snobbery which it afforded, although there were genuine attempts to provide meeting grounds neutral to the barriers outside, clearly imported from a rosy idealising of cricket.

Bowls was played in England in the Middle Ages and lingered on very thinly after the seventeenth century in market towns such as Lewes in Sussex, played by local gentry and superior tradesmen. Late Victorian writers attributed its new growth to Scots exiles' refounding a game which had remained popular in their homeland as they trickled into English business life. The London and Southern Counties Bowling Association was founded in 1895 for 'rink players', together with the Midland Counties Bowling Association for the rival 'crown' code.[72] Scots influence flourished earlier in the north of England, where the crown game fitted more readily into working-class holiday and wager habits. This was fostered by the growth of semi-professional tournaments, peaking at the annual Blackpool event, which attracted 704 entries in 1903, at 5s a time, and offered £336 in prize money.[73] By the First World War there were estimated to be 600,000 crown green players in the north, a quarter of them dependent on greens provided in local parks by municipal authorities. By contrast, Surrey, the epitome of genteel southern play, could boast only 7,500 men playing the rink game in eighty clubs.[74]

Yet it was the rink game that set the public tone, and there was no clearer way of an aspirant northern group's reinforcing its self-identity than to form a rink club. Even then they tended to stay outside the south's domination of rule and tournament organisation: Yorkshire and Lancashire had not affiliated by 1914 to the English

Bowling Association, which represented and regulated 237 clubs in the rest of England, and probably set the standard for an equivalent number of the non-affiliated. Even that unity emerged with difficulty out of regional and personal rivalries. During the 1890s a visiting team from Australia played informally against various English clubs, and the Imperial Bowling Association was formed in 1898 to foster further ties, with Canada as well. Although it had some support it soon generated a rival, the English Bowling Association, which claimed a wider range of affiliates, dominated by W. G. Grace in his capacity as secretary of the London County Bowling Club.[75]

Such eminent patronage actually widened the split, since Grace had only been playing for a year and his self-assumed omniscience provoked considerable resentment at his 'thrusting good men aside'.[76] The two bodies amalgamated in 1905 and Grace's bullying subsided slightly; growth was steady, from ninety-five affiliations in 1907 to 237 in 1914, as well as twenty-three regional bowling associations.[77] But many preferred to remain outside what was seen as a southern preserve and there were repeated claims that the EBA did not impose regulations strongly enough or preserve the values of amateurism in 'an organised sport'. The game acquired some of the language and outlook of athleticism but localism and the recreational element survived, particularly in rural areas such as Norfolk and Suffolk, which 'still belong to the dark ages in respect of their greens and the laws of the game'.[78] At least in the still separate north the British Crown Green and County Amateur Bowling Association exercised firmer control over its members.

Most clubs were far more concerned with their own affairs, growth as well as survival. Most of this was unspectacular; the club records which survive reveal the welter of minor concerns which business demanded. The small tradesmen and artisans of north Leeds played at the Headingley club ('The Original Oaks') from the 1860s, dividing their members into 'Scotch' and 'English' for competitions.[79] Like the Chichester Quoit and Bowling Club, they were often socially little removed from the pub-based hundreds of working-class angling clubs.[80] Many such clubs deliberately avoided the drive towards more luxurious premises after 1900, on the grounds that they were 'unconsciously jeopardising the most cherished social attributes of Bowls', 'opening wide the door to class distinction and class sentiment', when the costs of membership would inevitably rise.[81] These tensions continued where many new municipal greens were virtually annexed by middle-class clubs unable to afford separate premises, virtually forcing working men's clubs into staying with their pub links. One such predator, belied by the apparent somnolent innocence of its photographs, was the Alexandra Bowling Club of Hastings, whose ninety members, 'mostly retired professional men', used the public green in a park.[82] Many recreational working-class players played without bothering to join a club, using municipal greens on a by-payment basis; London opened its first one in Battersea in 1895 and had seventy-six by 1907, on which 4,550 of the 24,749 games played were at the special cheap rate of a penny.[83]

Those clubs that did acquire their own green faced the usual pressures on space and the problems that conviviality brought for the game's efficiency. In Grimsby the 'leading townsmen' formed a club in 1887, teaching themselves to play; it was 1891 before they felt confident enough to play outside, against Hull. Initial popularity waned slightly until a 50 per cent cut in the guinea subscription brought in fifty new members in 1896, with the clear aim of reducing an accumulated £30 deficit. By 1903 they were 'more inclined to prosper from a social point of view than from a playing one'; perhaps it was this that encouraged the spate of emulation in the town, increasing the number of clubs to eight, with 1,000 members.[84] Some clubs were forced to acquired limited liability status to protect their grounds, thereby giving the historian lists of members in their role as shareholders. Retford, in Nottinghamshire, included a bank manager, two ironmongers, a boot and shoe merchant and a journalist on its committee of seven; neighbouring Worksop showed a similar range but also included teachers, bank clerks and pawnbrokers.[85] The Ranworth Bowling Club, of Bolton, Lancashire, numbered eight white-collar workers among its predominantly lower tradesman membership in the 1880s, collapsing in 1906.[86] The older Nether Edge Club of Sheffield catered more for the owners than the agents of industry; the Castleford club's membership consisted of six professionals, twenty-eight tradesmen and four white-collar workers, a pattern little different form that of Salford's Higher Broughton Bowling Club.[87] In some towns, such as Nottingham, bowling was publicly associated with the grocery trade, and it is perhaps no accident that a number of bowling associations gave considerable support to the 1911 Shops Act, with its guarantee of a weekly half-day holiday, vital to the sport.[88] In actual fact, of the eighty-seven playing members of the Nottingham Grocers' Bowling Club, many were not grocers at all but, as Dr Winstanley has shown in Blackburn, Preston, Southport and Darwin, it was the organised grocers who ran bowls leagues and their Manchester fellows offered a monthly trophy.[89] For some men clubs like this offered a new form of secular memorial, a monthly trophy a modest middle-class immortality, a self-advertisement either in the presentation of commemorative tournament trophies or in the gift of land, such as when Charles Milburn gave the Sunderland club a new ground in 1892.[90]

Despite occasional lapses into shirtsleeves, the game's new popularity brought social tone, so that bowls was added to the list of desirable accessories for burgeoning resorts and suburbs. In Weston-super-Mare the head postmaster, Mr P. Smith, founded the Victoria Bowling Club in 1900, which bought its freehold in 1904 'in the heart of one of the best residential districts', spending £300 on improving its greens and providing an open-air tea pavilion, because of the 'importance of the social functions of the season'.[91] Respectability and exclusiveness were frequently reinforced by association with other, more clearly elite, sports, as in Warwick. In suburban London the Ravenscroft Park Bowling Club was re-formed as the Chiswick and West London Bowling and Tennis Club in 1908, to offer year-round play in bowls, lawn tennis, badminton and croquet, concentrating facilities on one multi-purpose site. Playing all could cost one and a half guineas, any one a guinea for membership, with other costs on top.[92] It was this pattern which prompted protests, only really to bear fruit after the First World War, that north and west London clubs were too expensive or too distant for many lower middle-class locals to join: in the south the aspirant could be quite easily frustrated, and the social cachet was reinforced accordingly.[93]

Bowling away

By far the most widespread 'growing pleasure for the middle classes' relying on a club core with a wide periphery of individual pursuits and shifting over the whole pastime–athletic sport gamut whilst resisting historians' attempts to identify class-specific attributes was cycling.[94] Because of the visibility of the Clarion cycling clubs and their distinctive place in labour movements it is not uncommon to read claims that cycling was essentially a working-class recreation, and there can be little doubt that it was, at least by 1900, more distinctly pan-class as a participatory recreation than any other late

Victorian boom sport, with the exception of angling. The spread of the bicycle in the last thirty years of the nineteenth century was the athletic and functional equivalent of that of the piano. Unlike the piano, but like the horse, the use of sporting wheels overlapped with its eventual value as a mode of transport and it was supposed to keep young men fit as they travelled to work. But at this point it hovered on the fringes of respectability. By the 1890s some clubs were under suspicion because 'they fill themselves with liquor to the accompaniment of vulgar and often obscene songs', a timely reminder that sport was not automatically self-improving.[95]

Cycling's two periods of rapid growth, the 1870s and the 1890s, do appear to illustrate a middle-class-based diffusion pattern. Its early success was very largely linked with younger professional men, its great expansion around 1896 with a spread both temporarily into aristocratic fashion and rapidly downwards into the solid overlap of white-collar workers and prosperous artisans. In the latter period it provided for, and was reinforced by, a burst of humorous writing, cartoons and anecdotes best epitomised by the crazy amorous adventures of H. G. Wells's gullible fictional shop assistant, Hoopdriver, in *The Wheels of Chance*.[96]

Since it offered a very real sense of physical testing, with some adventure in the uneasy exploration of that still unknown territory, rural England, cycling in its early growth veered between attracting the 'bohemia-like band' of the Bristol Bicycle and Tricycle Club and the distinctive formality of the Northampton Cycling Club, whose members (largely doctors and accountants) out riding looked like superior postmen, in tight-fitting breeches, dark blue serge coats and gold-braided peaked caps. They opened their season on Good Friday with a thirty-mile run to Leamington Spa, warning other road users of their approach by blowing silver-plated bugles. The Bristol club cycled to Paris in 1878, but most clubs were less ambitious. The Walthamstow 'Eccentric Bicycle Club', which rarely had more than sixteen members, found a 'jolly spin' to nearby Broxbourne more typically to its taste. Conscious that it was trespassing on the fringes of respectability, it forbade its members to wear the club badge on Sundays unless they were touring.[97]

The sport's continued popularity through the 1880s reinforced its metropolitan role, and it was no longer seen as a threat to that other form of country transport, the horse, although, as *Horse and Hounds* observed in 1884, there were other dimensions of hostility:

... the only persons who in these enlighted days show animosities to the votaries of the 'iron steed' are the roughs, who resent every pastime in which they do not themselves participate as a direct affront to their own selfish motives.[98]

By the end of the 1880s Bristol boasted eight cycling clubs, including the Cycling Club, which seemed to be going the way of other activities, with seventy riding and thirty 'Club House members'.[99] What was clear by then was that cycling was spreading downwards. Whilst it could be linked still with an early didactic earnestness, represented by the Society of Cyclists, 'a learned society studying cycling as a scientific and historic pursuit', it appealed much more to the Hoopdrivers in terms almost of nature mysticism:

> Nothing is more delightful than, after a week's hard grind in the office and among the dry ledgers, day books etc. etc., to don your special garments, mount your glittering wheel, and then away to the green lanes, leafy woods, and rippling brooks, to the sweet country, there 'to mix your blood with sunshine, and to take the wind into your pulses'.[100]

A writer in *Baily's Magazine* in 1892, H. Hewitt Griffin, described it as a 'sport' throughout his article, claiming a national expenditure of up to £8 million on cycles alone, with a personal cost of from five guineas, depending on the degree of wealth and commitment.[101] Technical innovations, the 'safety' cycle and the inflatable Dunlop tyre, had reduced costs. The principal problem that he identified was a tension between the recreational and athletic values. The former were represented by club runs in the countryside, or the individual's meanderings, the latter by track and road racing. In the 1870s the latter had been identified as a sport of university men, but popularity meant that clubs had tended to be rather lower on the class scale, on the grounds that established professional and commercial men in their thirties 'cannot, without endangering their dignity, join a club composed of young clerks', particularly if they were their own employees.[102]

The racing clubs, avoiding as far as they could the taint of commercial pedestrianism which often touched the track cyclists, used main roads for timed events, by far the most popular venue being the Great North Road. On it in 1885 A. J. Wilson, editor of the *Bicycling Times*, formed a club for which applicants had to have ridden at least 100 miles in a day. Its thirty-seven members grew to 178 by 1895, and it took over a cottage in Roxton towards which each member paid 2s a week, and a further 3s 6d for each weekend's board and lodging. When it tried to branch out into track racing by forming a limited liability company in 1895 it soon hit trouble; its gentlemen amateurs just could not compete with top professionals, it could not attract enough gate money to cover its investment, so it returned to racing on the Great North Road.[103]

The bulk of cycling's appeal came more because 'the British householder mounted and rode away into fairyland. So did his wife' than because of any innate athleticism.[104] As with bowls, a physiological justification was found for this:

> . . . the athlete may enjoy vigorous health for the few years during which he is actively racing: *but this good health is no guarantee that degenerative changes are not slowly and surely taking place in the arteries.*[105]

Most local practice hovered between modestly strenuous and distinctly leisurely touring. The compulsive record-keeper from Lincoln J. R. Halkes logged his annual mileage between 1888 and 1914: 25,632, an average of 949.3 but with annual totals varying from 81½ in 1895 to 2,027 in 1903.[106] His firm Wesleyan catalogue of works was less likely to be taken up by the Guards officers who made cycling fashionable in Battersea Park in 1896, or by the visitors who hired bikes to wobble along the new cycle track built by Earl de la Warr in his speculative development of Bexhill on Sea.[107] The very level of its fashionable uptake gave mid-1890s cycling both advertising and a range of salutary warnings: in May–June 1896 the Countess of Warwick ran over her husband and both the Earl of Westmorland and Lord Calthorpe broke a leg whilst practising; a Dover woman collided with the big drum of a Volunteer regiment's marching band.[108]

Dinners and journals provided reinforcements for the cycling club world, anxious to exploit, as did the Bristol Bicycle and Tricycle Club, 'the many opportunities for sociability opened up by its runs, tea-table, gossip, picnic and excursion parties etc.'[109] The groups were usually small, at about the twenty mark, which made face-to-face contact manageable, a figure the Bristol Wheelers found acceptable, as did the Wood End 44 of Birmingham.[110] For the £10 or so a cycle cost by 1899 the choice was available between this sort of group activity and the solitude that David Rubinstein has described as so desirable.[111] It was one of the few sports which appears to have developed simultaneously among the middle classes of other industrialising countries, France and the United States.[112]

After the short-lived West End dabblings a number of social

exemplars remained. A. J. Balfour was a keen cyclist who actually went off on a spin during a Blenheim Palace house party in 1896 whilst the Prince of Wales and assorted Curzons and Grenfells shot the Duke of Marlborough's pheasants, a remarkable exercise in social self-confidence.[113] M. R. James, the antiquarian Provost of King's College, Cambridge, had taken to cycling instead of rowing as an undergraduate in the 1880s. Between 1895 and 1914 he made thirty cycling trips on the continent, riding from Dieppe to Regensberg, on the Danube, in 1895. More locally he cycled frequently in East Anglia, where he made major studies of church architecture.[114] In this context the bicycle served less as a sporting implement than as a healthy adjunct to the local studies of the informed or the autodidact, the church-crawler and the naturalist. As such G. W. E. Russell could claim that the cycle had become a major element in easing social intercourse, fostering an ease with other fellow travellers that the first-class railway carriage could never offer.[115]

The nature of cyling's boom and slow decline is illustrated by the fortunes of its attempts at national bureaucracy, particularly the Cyclists' Touring Club. Founded in 1878 with 148 members, it grew unevenly until it shot up from 16,343 in 1895 to 34,655 in 1896 and on to 60,449 by 1899. Then began a steady decline until 1914, when it touched 14,569. With this went a shift from an operating profit of £5,246 in 1897 to a deficit of £3,025 in 1907.[116] *Truth* saw much of this as linked with the personality of its 'honorary' secretary (paid £250 a year), E. R. Shipton, who ran the club as a costly personal fief. One of his outbursts cost the club £659 in libel damages.[117] After a bitter dispute among the members he was forced out in 1907, when his pension was cut from £150 to £78.[118]

Shipton's vision had been of the CTC as a major cyclists' pressure group, demanding legislative changes to prevent police harassment of 'scorchers', speeding members. But there were other problems. What had been *par excellence* the club for professional men' now attracted a residue only, 'a certain number of steady enthusiasts, who are gradually lessened by the natural causes of death, illness and infirmity, and the more accidental ones of marriage, poverty, and the rival attraction of golf'.[119] The use by artisans and others of the cycle as a primary means of work transport killed the sporting boom, and a national organisation which spent half its income on administration had little appeal to this market and less to many touring cyclists who felt they no longer needed an association to change the law, demand better roads and negotiate concessionary hotel rates. Shipton's reign ended in scandal, not least because he had hushed up the clandestine employment of his brother in the club. But the boom had gone anyway.

Notes

1 A. Lillie, *Croquet up to Date* (1900), 215.
2 A. Griffiths, *Clubs and Clubmen* (1907), 337.
3 Queen's Club, *Rules* (1888); Prince's Club, *Rules* (1891).
4 Leeds Reference Library, *The Hyde Park Recreation Club Chronicle*, September 1897.
5 *Builder*, 27 April 1907.
6 W. Holtby, *The Crowded Street* (1924).
7 *Bowling*, June 1908.
8 *Bowling*, January 1910.
9 *Hull and East Riding Athlete*, 11 December 1889.
10 Warwickshire Record Office, CR 1798/50, Warwick Boat Club, *The Arc Light*, May 1903.
11 Northampton Reference Library, 'Cuttings', 27 July 1861; Archers of the Nene, *Rules* (1893).
12 M. F. Drummond, 'How to become an archer', *Badminton Magazine*, 27 (1908), 294.
13 *Brighton Season*, 1905–06, 'Toxophilites of the twentieth century'.
14 H. W. W. Wilberforce, 'Lawn tennis', in E. Bell (ed.), *Handbook of Athletic Sports* (1890), 1.
15 Lillie, *Croquet*, 185.
16 J. D. Heath, *The Complete Croquet Player* (1904), 2–3.
17 Lillie, *Croquet*, xiii.
18 Lillie, *Croquet*, 214.
19 Dorling, *Hurlingham Club*, 31 ff.
20 E. Churchill, 'The revival of croquet', *Badminton Magazine*, III(1896), 219 ff.; *Croquet Annual* (1901–02); *Brighton Season* (1905–06), 'The croquet resurrection'; M. Towers, 'Croquet in Sussex', *Sussex Life*, June 1967, 32–3; A. Wallis Myers, *The Sportsman's Yearbook* (1905), 65 ff.
21 H. G. Clarke, *Royal Leamington Spa: a Century's Growth and Development* (Leamington Spa, 1947), 84; *Royal Leamington Spa, 1872–1972* (Leamington Spa, 1972), 3; J. G. Smyth, *Lawn Tennis* (1953), 16.
22 T. B. Dudley, *A Complete History of Royal Leamington Spa* (Leamington, 1901), 362–3; Clarke, *Leamington Spa*, 84.
23 A. J. Balfour, *Chapters of an Autobiography* (1930), 35–6.
24 S. S. Travers, *A Treatise on Tennis* (Hobart, 1875), 23.
25 E. Miles, *Racquets, Lawn Tennis and Squash* (1902); J. M. Heathcote *et al.*, *Tennis, Lawn Tennis, Rackets, Fives* (1890), 85.
26 *Baily's Magazine*, November 1907, 387.
27 *The All England Cricket and Football Journal and Athletic Review* (Sheffield), August 1877, article from *Daily News*; Balfour, *Chapters*, 226–7; R. D. Osborn, *Lawn Tennis: its Players and How to Play* (1880), 8.
28 *Lawn Tennis*, 9 September 1896; F. W. Payn, *Lifting the Veil* (1907), 11.

29 *Badminton Magazine*, 3 June 1913, 316.
30 *Badminton Magazine*, 3 June 1913, 317.
31 Lincolnshire Record Office, Misc. Dep. 265, Diaries of Fannie Rainey Fieldsend of Binbrook.
32 Lincs. RO, 2 HEN 5/11/62.
33 Tasker, *Lincolnshire*, 25.
34 PRO, BT 31/3861, Co. 24349, Haulgh Lawn Tennis Club Ltd.
35 *Hull and East Riding Athlete*, 16 April 1890.
36 *Hull News*, 23 November 1901.
37 *Beverley Bystander*, October 1968, 28.
38 Leeds Reference Library, Leeds Cricket, Football and Athletic Company Ltd, Annual Reports (1891–1911).
39 Walthamstow Record Office, W373884 RM8, Rectory Manor Lawn Tennis and Bowling Club, 1896–1919.
40 Warwicks. RO, CR1798, Warwick Boat Club records.
41 W. M. Brownlea, *Lawn Tennis* (Bristol, 1889), 16.
42 A. Wallis Myers (ed.), *Ayres' Lawn Tennis Almanack* (1910), 345.
43 *Leamington Courier*, 23, 29 July, 6 August 1881.
44 *Truth*, 25 September 1902, 2 June 1914; Myers, *Sportman's Yearbook*, 58 ff.
45 *Badminton Magazine*, 16 (1902), 365.
46 Bale, *Sport and Place*, 94; H. W. W. Wilberforce, 'The story of the All England Club', in G. W. Hillyard, *Forty Years of First Class Lawn Tennis* (1924), 25 ff.
47 *Truth*, 2 May, 6 June 1906.
48 J. P. Paret, *Lawn Tennis* (1904), 40.
49 *Gamages Lawn Tennis Annual* (1912), 11–12.
50 E.M., 'Lawn Tennis politics', *Baily's Magazine*, February 1907.
51 Hillyard, *Forty Years*, 5.
52 Bale, *Sport and Place*, 52.
53 S. M. Massey, 'Badminton', *Badminton Magazine*, 24 (1907), 136 ff.
54 Badminton Association, *Laws of Badminton and Rules of the Badminton Association*, 1898–1912.
55 *Badminton Gazette*, March 1908.
56 M. J. G. Ritchie and W. Harrison, *Table Tennis and how to Play it* (1902), 21.
57 *Jaques: 150th Anniversary, 1795–1945*, souvenir published by the company, 14.
58 *Truth*, 19 December 1901.
59 A. Binstead and G. Fitzgibbon (eds), *The Sporting Annual Illustrated* (1903), 214, 219–20.
60 *Cassell's Book of Sports and Pastimes* (1907), 226.
61 PRO, BT 31/9827, Co. 73240, The Ping-Pong Social Club Ltd, incorporated 27 March 1902.
62 *Table Tennis and Pastimes Pioneer*, 3 January 1902; *Games Gazette and Athletic Toys and Fancy Goods Record*, 8 February 1902.
63 *Ibid.*
64 Winstanley, *Shopkeeper's World*, 121; *Lawn Tennis and Croquet and Badminton*, 23 April 1902.
65 *Brighton Season* (1905–06), 'The croquet resurrection'; A. J. P. Taylor, *A Personal History* (1983), 1984 edition, 14.

66 E. T. Ayers, *Bowls, Bowling Greens, Bowl Playing* (1894), 33.
67 *Bowling*, January 1910.
68 *Bowling*, June 1908.
69 *Bowling*, July 1910.
70 *Bowling*, March 1910.
71 C. S. Hayward, *The Summer Playground* (1902), 286; G. T. Burrows, *All about Bowls* (1915), 39.
72 Burrows, *Bowls*, 14.
73 *C. B. Fry's Magazine*, 5(1906), 227.
74 Burrows, *Bowls*, 39.
75 Burrows, Bowls 14–17.
76 *Bowls*, 22 September 1909.
77 English Bowling Association, *Yearbooks*, 1907–1914.
78 *Bowling*, June 1911, April 1908.
79 Leeds Record Office, Headingley Bowling Club ('The Original Oak'), Minute Books.
80 West Sussex Record Office, Add. Ms 26769, Chichester Quoit and Bowling Club, Minutes, 1885–1911.
81 J. A. Manson, *The Complete Bowler* (1919), 72–3.
82 *Bowling*, March 1911.
83 J. M. Pretsell, *The Game of Bowls, Past and Present* (1908), 142–3.
84 Lincoln, *Reminiscences*, 183 ff.
85 Registrar of Companies, Retford Bowling Green Ltd, 24 June 1898; Worksop Bowling Club, 25 April 1910.
86 PRO, BT 31/2525, Co 13063, Ransworth Bowling Green Co. Ltd, 14 May 1879.
87 Sheffield Reference Library, Local Pamphlets, vol. 140, 13, *Articles of Agreement of the Nether Edge Bowling Club* (1868); PRO, BT 31/36032, Co. 120380, Castleford Bowling Club Ltd, February 1912; PRO, BT 31/33787, Co. 118103, Higher Broughton Bowling Club Buildings Co. Ltd, 18 October 1911.
88 *Bowling*, March 1911.
89 Winstanley, *Shopkeeper's World*, 121.
90 *Bowling*, March 1909.
91 *Bowling*, June 1909.
92 *Bowling*, June 1908.
93 *Bowling*, March 1909.
94 *Fortnightly Review*, LV(1894), 669.
95 *Fortnightly Review*, LV(1894), 679.
96 Wells, *Wheels of Chance*.
97 Bristol Reference Library, *Souvenir of the Bristol Bicycle and Tricycle Club* (1897); Northampton Reference Library, Miscellaneous Cuttings, Photographs and Miscellanea; Walthamstow Record Office, Add. Ms, Walthamstow Bicycle Club.
98 *Horse and Hound*, 29 March 1884.
99 *Amateur Sport* (Bristol), 24 April 1889.
100 *Northampton Daily Reporter*, 25 July 1891; *Clerk*, April 1890.
101 *Baily's Magazine*, 57 (1892), 307 ff.
102 S. H. Moxham, *Fifty Years of Road Racing, 1885–1935* (Bedford, 1935), 2.
103 *Ibid*.

104 *Nineteenth Century*, January 1885, 95.
105 Herschell, *Cycling*, 34.
106 Lincolnshire Record Office, J. R. Halkes of Lincoln.
107 *Badminton Magazine*, I(1895), 120 ff.; *Bexhill-on-Sea Illustrated Visitors' List*, 9 June 1896.
108 *Bexhill-on-Sea Illustrated Visitors' List*, 9 June 1896.
109 Bristol Reference Library, *Bristol Bicycle and Tricycle Club Gazette*, 1 January 1897.
110 Bristol Reference Library, *Bristol and Clifton Amusements*, 15 July 1901.
111 Rubinstein, 'Cycling in the 1890s', 47 ff.
112 R. Holt, 'The bicycle, the bourgeoisie and the discovery of rural France, 1880–1914', *British Journal of Sports History*, 2(1985), 127 ff.; G. A. Tobin, 'The bicycle boom of the 1890s', *Journal of Popular Culture*, 7 (1974), 838 ff.
113 *Fitzgibbon's Sporting Almanac* (1900), 117; B. E. C. Dugdale, *Arthur James Balfour*, I(1976), 195–6.
114 Cox, *M. R. James*, 55, 107–9, 168.
115 Russell, *For Better?*, 22.
116 J. T. Lightwood, *Romance of the C. T. C.* (1928).
117 *Truth*, 13 February, 3 April 1902, 13, 20 March 1907.
118 *Truth*, 28 August, 18 September 1907, 9 September 1908.
119 Earl Albemarle and G. Lacy Hillier, *Cycling* (1895), 256; *Cycling and Motoring*, 29 May 1905.

Chapter 5
Golf

Boom

More than any other sport, golf focused middle-class ambitions and anxieties in the later nineteenth century, enjoying the greatest 'boom' of any game. Neither invented nor in any real sense revived in England, it was imported, initially with little of the moral baggage of manliness. The extent to which it might be regarded as a sport was much canvassed. Certainly the broad figures of expansion are almost breathtaking. England boasted one ancient club, the Blackheath, at mid-century, possibly a dozen by the 1870s: but by 1914 there were almost 1,200 clubs playing over 1,000 courses.[1] The exact pattern and chronology of this spread are difficult to reconstruct because so many early clubs formed, waned or reformed, and the general directories of golf clubs do not always furnish accurate dates for each case.

The strength of growth in any given year is not easily explained, nor can geographical spread be established other than in the broadest terms. In the latter case local patterns are often more significant than national diffusion. The models offered by certain suburbs and resorts were important, not least in the gap between the genteel Westward Ho! Golf Club (founded in north Devon, in 1864) and the first, but equally genteel, flowerings of 'municipal socialism' in Bournemouth. In many cases, such as Eastbourne's, there was a ready interplay between urban middle-class interests and those of aristocrats striving for a readjusted weighting in the equipoise of local influence. There was a major rush of suburban foundations in the early years of this century, clubs marching across the heathland of Surrey and Hertfordshire. Much of this has been chronicled either briefly in the relevant, and nearly contemporary, volumes of the *Victoria County Histories* or exhaustively in a spate of local club hagiographies, but they only rarely hint at any wider context and do not explain golf's emergence in relatively isolated market towns such as Louth, Lincolnshire, in 1900. Much depended on the response of local oligarchies to 'fashion' as it worked through regional hierarchies. In some areas downward percolation can be partly identified, as in Brighton, where patronage of one club by a royal couple, the Duke and Duchess of Fife (enthusiastic but apparently indifferent players), was widely held to have been responsible for the mushrooming of other clubs in the town, or in those places where the Duke of Norfolk, equally keen, played as a 'democrat'. But aristocratic participation generally followed on the heels of established middle-class practice, and there are few examples in the sporting press of the period of the ascription of influence that was allowed to the fashionable elite in the bicycling boom.[2]

Much of golf's attraction lay in its origins. There are still widespread claims in popular golfing literature that it emerged as a game played on sheet ice by the medieval Dutch, but its importance in our context is that it was widespread among lowland Scots by the late eighteenth century. Its evangelising from that base has much of the mythical about it, following the spider's web of Caledonian *emigrés*. Missing their limited home comforts, they were credited widely with carrying it to England, Canada, New Zealand, the fringes of African deserts and St Petersburg when that city unfroze sufficiently for its Scottish merchant colony to play.

As important as this sense of mission was Scotland's role as a fashionable late Victorian holiday-making area in which upper middle-class forays followed on the building of Balmoral and the expansion of the deer forests. At their Scottish resorts Englishmen saw golf, and took it home with them, to develop it in ways frequently disapproved of by its early guardians. The relative wildness of Scottish links, the scrub and dunes of the eastern seaboard, was controlled and taken inland. It flowed south across and then inwards, from coast to heath and fields. One contemporary boast, that golf in Scotland was both cheap and absolutely 'democratic', seems to bear little weight when tested. If the poor played, then they did so as the servants or gleaners of an established, patronising and self-regarding Scottish *bourgeoisie*. Even so, the social net spread rather more widely than it did in England, where golf became *par excellence* a fine instrument of social differentiation.[3]

Appeal

So why did what was earlier derided as 'Scottish croquet' spread quite so rapidly south of the border? The American sporting writer Caspar Whitney was surprised in 1895 'that so many vigorous young and middle-aged men could find amusement in what appeared to me to be a melancholy and systematized "constitutional"'.[4] An observer in 1902 saw golf in moral terms. 'Certainly there is no other occupation in which the desire for self-improvement is so constantly present.'[5] He said this partly with tongue in cheek, since he went on to suggest that the golfer rarely ended up happy.

The attractions were both moral and practical. One obvious advantage was that the game could be played virtually all the year round; after a first few years of inland play on courses, such as Kettering, Northamptonshire, where the grass grew too long for summer games it ceased to be limited except by the most inclement weather.[6] The rubber technology which revolutionised ball production was also harnessed to provide rainproof playing wear. Such a level of use was in turn promoted by the amount of capital sunk into the game as its popularity spread. Hand-in-hand with this went a combination of modest physical exertion (a slow walk) with open-air activity, an idealised antidote for office-bound middle-class men. Many clubs owed a considerable impetus in their founding to local medical men, such as Dr W. F. Crosskey of Lewes, in Sussex, who championed the game's therapeutic value for middle-aged clients.[7] Its appeal was unlike that of many of the manly games in that it could be taken up in mid-life and practised as long as the modest physical fitness it was claimed to foster lasted, a value praised by one of its more influential addicts, the politician A. J. Balfour:

> Golf, while itself pre-eminently a game at which elasticity of muscle and lithesomeness of limb produce their natural and legitimate fruits, is a game at which the middle-aged and those who are past middle life can derive pleasure not less poignant, not less keen, than they did in the first flush of growth.[8]

Balfour, indolent by nature, despite his passion for cycling, took up the game himself in his mature years. But some Scots regarded this as less than desirable, arguing that English golf as a form of medicine represented a singular lack of serious commitment, turning it into 'simply the outcome of a disordered liver'.[9] In the Edwardian years it was often held to indicate national decline, but its proponents claimed virtues of personal growth:

> Golf, perhaps, gives us the best example [of noble competition], for there the player is playing against his opponent, against bogey, and against his former self. And it is a competition that need not beget despair or bitterness.[10]

In this secular puritanism the score card replaced the frequent moral self-evaluation which so many earlier evangelicals had recommended. Its demands could be softened, however, by 'comradeship in sport, the friendliness, the community of sentiment, the frankness of speech, the good-will, the "generosity in trifles"' of a new fellowship.[11] For many middle-class men the fact that this could be found in a *milieu* where they had a considerable degree of control undoubtedly made the golf club more palatable than their local church or chapel.

Yet there were *caveats*. Exertion and too much self-examination on the score cards could produce considerable unhappiness and anger, and the red-faced golfer on the edge of apoplexy became a stock figure for cartoonists and humorous writers. As Edward Lyttelton observed tartly, 'In the nineties, middle-aged cricketers taking to golf found themselves a prey to gusts of choler, novel in character, baffling in origin, and in potency not to be withstood.'[12] There is, as far as I know, no serious study of sport-induced illness and death during this period.

This risk, however lightly it was treated, demonstrated the seriousness now attached to a 'pastime'. Golf's movement along the recreational continuum could not go as far in terms of exertion as did some track events, but it did offer a wide range of acceptable levels of participation, from duffer to expert. It also provided a ladder of personal mobility, almost invariably upwards, both towards the more socially desirable clubs (measurement by external criteria) and in playing skills (the internalised rating against one's own past performance). Slower-moving and more time-demanding than lawn tennis, since an eighteen-hole round took rather more than three hours, the key lay in the interplay between the individual's assumptions, the objective factors of a course's layout and the difficulty of each hole, together with an abstract possibility of achieved perfection, 'bogey'. This individualist potential proved far more important in golf's popularisation than did its almost inevitable progression into a hierarchy of competition and trophies.

The social significance of golf was generally more important than skill and exercise factors. Yet the functional implications of the latter mattered in that, whilst it lacked the geriatric connotations of bowls, it had a far wider age-range appeal than did the racquet games. Its early solid attraction was to established professional and commercial men, especially over thirty-five years old, but it moved downwards both in potential age and in occupation ranges. For the young of the established middle classes it was obtainable virtually only as a holiday game, since their schools usually frowned on its perceived threat to manly collectivity.

The greatest attraction was to townsmen, as a game offering both physically and socially controlled exploitation of the open air. But it was also the most conspicuous game for flaunting social and economic success without wandering on to the fringes of the more traditional sports. Cost was a key factor, particularly as clubs burgeoned and their associated facilities grew in sophistication. One Edwardian writer on this, Mary E. L. Height, tried to claim a singular democracy for the game:

> One of the most noticeable points about golf is its levelling influence, while on the links a kind of universal brotherhood prevails, and class distinctions are, for the time being, cast into oblivion.[13]

This was very doubtful, in fact, and she went on herself to delimit this sporting Athenianism. She claimed that a 'working man' could play golf for £5 a year (some 10 per cent of one of Booth's or Rowntree's working-class family incomes), a middle-class man would expect to spend £30 a year and the 'rich' about £100.

The level of 'conspicuous consumption' in terms of expensive equipment ownership and sophisticated club facilities was reinforced, paradoxically, by the growing fashion for playing the game in shabby old clothes, the virtually universal Norfolk jacket and knickerbocker suit of the turn of the century. Expensive respectability that served the office or City street could be put behind with an increasing self-confidence in having earned the symbolic right to do so: it was this apparent informality, the wearing of soft collars, that deluded less perceptive observers into assuming a democracy of the links. The scarlet uniforms of earlier clubs, marking exclusivity and providing a hazard warning, disappeared except in the rarest instances such as Blackheath.[14] Golf allowed the flaunting of another acquisition as well, that of disposable time. The three hours or so needed for a round of eighteen holes, let alone the associated socialising, could certainly not be crammed into evenings. Growing popularity and the restricted opportunities of some middle-class occupations posed increased pressure on weekend time, particularly Sundays.

A study in 1913 of three 'typical' London clubs showed that, whilst Monday to Friday accounted for 36.3 per cent of games, Saturday and Sunday were occupied equally by the rest.[15] What is significant, though, is that over a third of games were played on weekdays and these could not all have been followed by the retired. It was not long, however, before a semi-guilty justification was found: golf became a mechanism of business negotiation, validated by extra-game purposes. The time span, the physical isolation of the players and intermittent demands on performing concentration made it more adaptable than most other sporting activities to this symbiosis. Of course, there is absolutely no way of testing the validity of these claims to business use.[16]

Golf became sufficiently widespread to function and be recognised as *the* elite game for the male urban middle classes. By 1900 membership of a club, and in larger towns of a *particular* club, marked an individual's social progress. But the theoretical openness of clubs to the financially qualified is deceptive. Golf refined the apparatus of snobbery for the clubable. The large cities and their suburbs created a club hierarchy, matched nationally and regionally. In this the Home Counties dominated, led by such clubs as St George's, near Weybridge in Surrey. At the other end of a restricted scale were small town clubs catering for a range of shopkeepers or the white-collar suburban clubs of the 1900s which carved out simple nine-hole courses. James Kenward recalled that his father and uncle as young clerks played 'point-to-point golf' across open fields until nine-hole clubs were founded whose modest subscriptions they could afford and which were prepared to accept them as members.[17] For many clerks of Streatham and Upper Norwood in south London, the Beulah Hill Golf Club, incorporated in 1913, offered reasonably cheap facilities.[18] They were lucky – in many other towns similar hopefuls were barred from playing, such as the '500 young men' claimed to be willing to pay £2 per annum to play in Harrogate in 1913.[19] It was from groups such as this that the pressure for municipal provision came.

There was often considerable tension between the claims made for golf club membership and the need in some areas for sufficiently broadly based recruitment to meet the burgeoning capital and management costs of some Edwardian clubs. Whilst Hurlingham and similar bodies in other sports could claim a nationally based membership, most golf clubs were more regionally focused, and claims of exclusivity for bodies with 400–500 members have to be viewed sceptically. There were areas where there was a certain validity to such posturings, and an Edwardian claim such as this lay on an uncertain divide between the socially realistic and the tongue-in-cheek:

> You must, of course, be a person of unimpeachable social status and moral respectability before you can secure the run of one or other of the courses available in Brighton. They are tolerably exclusive preserves, those of the golfing world, and it would never do to throw them open to Tom, Dick and Harry indiscriminately.[20]

The social fact was, perhaps, less important than the self-sustaining claims. In fact it is by no means easy to check the accuracy of many of the claims for membership. One possible source, the shareholder/membership lists of those clubs which took out limited liability status, does list occupation but with all the notorious vagueness of any such documents. Even the *rentier* catch-all 'gentleman' is suspect. When the Merton Park Golf Club was founded in 1912 its 212 members included 134 'gentlemen'. Their gift of social tone did not prevent its being wound up in 1915.[21] By comparison the very desirable Bramshot club counted seventy-three 'gents' among its 134 members. But it also included, alongside a building contractor and a diamond merchant on its committee, two manufacturers, one of whom was Burberry of the rainproof fame. It did survive. To join cost only five guineas a year, allowing access to one of the 'best courses' in the country, on Hampshire heathland.[22] But the election procedures, with the liberal use of 'blackballing', ensured that Bramshot and many clubs like it were well protected from over-ambitious interlopers.

Sizeable suburban clubs drew from a wider geographical range than their immediate locale, reflecting both the hunger for play and the growth of public transport networks. The Epping Forest Golf Club drew on the whole of north-east London, but also reached Dartford as well. It counted thirty-nine gentlemen, forty-six 'professionals' (including fourteen accountants) and fifty-six tradesmen, who included eight commercial travellers and seventy-six 'white-collar workers', of which the largest group was thirty-eight schoolteachers, followed by twenty-three clerks.[23] At this scale, face-to-face control of the membership was obviously limited, but the nomination and vetting procedures for entry did allow some notion of selection, presumably strong enough to deter the possibly unwelcome.

Away from London, club hierarchies were more easily recognised. In Eastbourne the Royal Eastbourne was opened in 1887 by two locals who had seen the game in Scotland and persuaded the two great local landowners, the Duke of Devonshire and Mr Davies Gilbert, to support them. The first captain was the Duke's heir, the Marquess of Hartington. 'Used by the aristocracy', the club represented the social peak of the acutely tone-conscious town, and attracted Horace Hutchinson, late Victorian golf's greatest apologist, when he moved to the resort with his father, a general. Shortly afterwards the Willingdon was founded for the lower professionals in Eastbourne, but there remained a substantial reserve of unfulfilled ambitions, among the tradesmen 'and artisans'. It was filled in 1908 by the Eastbourne Downs Golf Club, dominated by a dairyman, an ironmonger and a bookbinder.[24]

In the Leeds area social prestige, cost of membership and date of founding bore no strict relationship to each other, except that the spate of Edwardian openings represented a clear attempt to find facilities that the older clubs would not offer to a growing demand. Of the nine listed in table 4, two, the Headingley and the Leeds, stood far above the others in terms of social cachet, placed as they were on the edge of the city's most important suburbs. The earliest players at the former included the Revd. Cosmo Gordon Lang, the curate at Leeds Parish Church, who eventually became Archbishop of Canterbury.[25]

Another group played on farmland around the city's northern edges until it settled at Roundhay in 1896, sub-letting land from a farmer in difficulties. Gradually it took over more of his fields until the club and not the farmer became the tenant of the corporation. Its moving spirit was a Scot who imported tea, one Forbes. Despite taking limited liability cover in 1900 and providing an elegant clubhouse to reflect and maintain its social tone, the club existed on risky financial margins right up to the First World War.[26]

Its grandeur contrasted sharply with that of more rural clubs such as the Pickering and Thornton le Dale, which played from 1901 on Yorkshire pasture land, with 'natural hazards of ditches, trees and a fence-surrounded pond'.[27] And the Leeds club acquired, through its leasing arrangements, an early stability which was very different from the virtu-ally peripatetic nature of many suburban clubs: these usually stayed one jump ahead of the speculative builder until they could find enough financial muscle to put down roots. The Clapham golf club played from 1872 on common land, but lost out to other users. In 1888 it re-formed as the Tooting Bec club, only to be forced out of its playing space by walkers and excursionists. It then paid an annual rent of £455 for ground, until that fell to 'the onward march of the suburban builder' in 1906 and the club had to buy the freehold of 100 acres at Furzedown.[28]

Some clubs were rather less fortunate. In the Sussex market town of Battle a group of locals led by Dr Davison formed a golf club in December 1894 with the consent of the principal local landowner, the Duke of Cleveland. They played over farmland. The course was difficult, they were unable to find a suitable clubhouse and there were only eleven members at an extraordinary general meeting in 1899. The club struggled on, to be revived in 1903, when it counted forty members. But by 1905 support had waned considerably, and it was disbanded. Inadequate facilities and a very small likely membership base were important contributors to this, but there were other possible explanations as well. The town lay a few miles from Hastings, with grander facilities, easily reached by train, and the Battle club had had to admit a significant number of women on virtually equal terms (fourteen of the final forty) to reach even reasonable numbers.[29]

Much depended on the attitude of the ground landlord. The Duke of Cleveland had smiled on the Battle club but done nothing to strengthen it. The perennially hard-up De la Warr estate at Bexhill made land available to the town's club and also developed the rather

Table 4 **Leeds golf clubs**

Founding date	Club	Subscription (guineas)	Membership (1915)
1892	Fulneck	1½	95
1892	Headingley	5	430
1895	Leeds	5	380
1900	Howley Hall	2	102
1904	Woodhall Hills	2	120
1906	South Leeds	2	100
1907	Horsforth	3	250
1908	Alwoodley	6	300
1909	Moortown	2	380

Source: Golfer's Handbook, 1977.

more prestigious neighbouring Cooden Beach club. A long lease on a rising rental allowed the former club to use seventy-two acres near the new resort for some £7 an acre. But a need to raise cash in 1914 led the estate's trustees to offer to sell the land not to the club but to the town's corporation for £14,000, roughly twenty-eight years' purchase. The outbreak of war stopped this.[30] Had the deal gone through it would have added Bexhill to the small number of urban authorities that embraced golf as part of 'municipal socialism'. The corporation of the City of London maintained the course at Chingford in Essex at a charge of 1s a round, doubled before 1908 in order to pay a greenkeeper. In 1906 the income from this was £327, on some 6,540 rounds.[31] Municipal provision experienced a much higher normal level of use than many private clubs allowed.

Most of the resorts for which golf had now become a virtal attraction usually provided it in loose (i.e. financial) collaboration with local entrepreneurs or landlords. The town council of Great Yarmouth gave permission for the use of its North Denes, 'usually free from [fishermen's drying] nets' in 1882. Lord Scarborough laid out the golf links in Skegness at his own expense on the local sandhills in 1894.[32] In both these cases the actual investment was slight, since this generation of seaside clubs followed the hallowed Scottish practice of playing over sandy links which required little alteration. Bournemouth opened the first municipal links in England in 1890 and was taking £2,798 by 1907; in indirect terms the town's profits must have been much greater. Brighton followed in 1908 by converting the downland Iron Age hill fort on its northern edge to a nine-hole course at a cost of £1,050. The council's justification was the heavy pressure on established exclusive private courses.[33] But the important indications of further change came in Edwardian England when northern industrial cities began to consider municipal provision for their artisans. Nottingham provided good town links, and Sheffield followed suit, but it was the inter-war years which saw this development open up significantly.

Courses and play

Most of the course provision until the turn of the century centred on coastal links, sandy common or barely modified farm pastures, what a later writer called 'the heathland era'.[34] A more outspoken mid-twentieth-century writer, Sir Guy Campbell, dismissed the 1890s golf boom as 'jerry-building', claiming that it lacked charm or set patterns and, worst of all, had no relationship with Nature.[35] Where layout was attempted in these early days it was done largely by club professionals or greenkeepers, aiming to provide relatively low-cost facilities for very average players. The relationship with Nature that Campbell assumed as desirable was, in fact, in the sense of the eighteenth-century classically ordered landscape: playing golf should be an aesthetic as well as a sporting experience. Around the turn of the century there was a clear move towards this, and the grander golf clubs began to develop courses and associated facilities that had rather more links with the ideas of Capability Brown or Humphrey Repton than with sterner Scottish ideas on links. It could be seen in course layout, especially in the development of bunkers and the intertwining of fairways, rough and trees to combine an adequate golfing challenge with pleasing views. In this sense the very private world of the 'exclusive' golf clubs matched that of the similarly alienated formal-ised parks of the grander country houses. It was accompanied by a wholesale upgrading of clubhouses. As an occupation the 'golf course architect' was born; the *doyen* of this movement was H. S. Colt, also the paid secretary of the Sunningdale club.

The earliest clubhouses were often rented cottages, barely converted farm buildings or old railway carriages, such as the one the Goodwood Golf Club, near Chichester, paid £7 for in 1893 with a further £11 13s to erect and adapt it: they had an additional small shed as a urinal. When they moved, in 1904, to land owned by the Duke of Richmond and Gordon he kept the right to close the new club rooms, but not the links, for three weeks during Goodwood race meetings.[36] Prefabricated huts bought from such London firms as William Cooper's were a common source of clubhouses: East Brighton's provided 'a model of domestic sociability and *cameraderie*', and its continued appeal lay in its relative simplicity.[37] But aesthetic pressures mounted elsewhere, and *ab initio* developments such as Huntercombe, whose bars and kitchens were intended to rival grand hotels', or Alwoodley, whose clubhouse was laid out as a 'sun trap', provided the new markers. The older could survive if the social ambience was right: the New Zealand club at Byfleet, Surrey, boasted 'a romantic group which has grown up round an old farm building', and a bloody-minded masculine untidiness managed to preserve some clubs from the expense of great change.[38]

'The help art can give to nature for the purposes of golf', a tribute to Dr Mackenzie's layout of the new course at Alwoodley, became an increasing Edwardian concern, and 1908–09 were peak years for this.[39] Some felt that the new golf destroyed natural facilities ideal for the game. But they had little effect against the pressures from architects and developers. With clubs like Frinton paying £3,000 for a new clubhouse in 1904 or Formby, aiming to provide an imitation country house, the attractions of golf membership became much more clearly stated.[40] They often lay in the collaborative purchasing of a pseudo-gentry life style which individual members could not have afforded. In their bars, restaurants and vistas the Home Counties clubs in particular were significant complements to the scattered villas of Surrey or Metroland, particularly where the courses were linked in as an attraction by property speculators: 'Golf has done much to take the brain-worker to the country, and it is really amazing how cheaply one can fit out little cottage homes of picturesque design.'[41] A country house and park controlled by a committee of pseudo-yeomen who lived in the surroundings but whose use of the land was recreational rather than productive is not too fanciful a description.

There could be irony in this. The nearest that England probably got to the country club craze which surrounded United States golf was the opening of the Stoke Poges club in Buckinghamshire in 1908, designed by H. S. Colt: 'It is a spot to suggest rather the loved solitudes of the dryads but to Mr Colt it suggested also a very charming mashie shot.' After Colt, 'the vandal golfer', had cut down 2,000 trees to lay out his course the dryads seem to have migrated elsewhere; nor were they to be found near the club's four lawn tennis and four croquet courts.[42] When Colt designed the new Weybridge course in 1909 there was even less space for dryads: golf was augmented by a boathouse, bathing pool, tennis, croquet, cricket, archery, squash and clay pigeons. And the restaurant was managed by a professional firm, that of Signor Gilitto.[43] A new 'prestigious commodious [clubhouse] . . . built in an old-fashioned style', of mock Tudor, was provided at the Cooden Beach club in 1912, with the expectation that a 200 bedroom hotel would follow near by. 'Such is the confidence placed in southern English golf,' but it was increasingly a confidence in its social rather than its sporting role.[44]

That confidence reached its peak in the taking over of landed estates wholesale and the conversion of country houses for clubs rather than in providing pseudo-manors. There were a number of instances of this before 1914 but the most significant and best publicised was the conversion of Lord Eldon's mansion at Shirley Park, near Croydon, in

1913 by George Collins, an entrepreneur. It was a country club in the American sense and it was possible, if socially not so desirable, to hold separate membership for golf only. The Lord Mayor of London, attired as such, opened it just before the First World War broke out.[45] Whether in such splendour or in the smaller new houses on provincial courses the members were quite clear what they were now buying. As the *Yorkshire Post* commented on the new Leeds Golf Club's house in 1909, 'in this enchanted corner all signs of the dirt and disagreeable sides of the city's life are hidden from sight'.[46] Just as eighteenth-century grandees had moved unsightly villages outside their park walls, the new comfortable shifted the sources of their wealth metaphorically.

The fairways created for them may have been attractive but they were also, paradoxically, more demanding in terms of play. Sunningdale's new course was broken up by 'monstrous earthworks, resembling ancient fortifications': the *Field's* reporter felt that the new golf was losing its charm as a game.[47] In a sense it was because Edwardian playing was changed by significant developments in sporting technology. Much of the game's playing through the period was distinctly experimental. How-to-play manuals, with photographs of ideal stances, aimed at a style as formalised as rowing, but there were notable exceptions:

> No one has a more peculiar style than Mr. Horace Hutchinson. His is the style of bombastic freedom. The wrists are shaken about in the most war-like fashion, the ball trembles on the tee before the impending blow.[48]

Much depended on the implements. The basic tool was the hickory-shafted club, or rather the hundreds of them, wooden or forged iron, which came on the late Victorian market. One amateur golfer, H. E. Taylor of the Mid-Surrey club, owned 200 putters and almost 4,000 other clubs by 1914; they had cost him almost £1,000. Whether he used them or how they affected his play is unrecorded.[49]

It was not club design that changed golf significantly after the century's turn but ball manufacture. Until the 1850s the game was played with egg-shaped balls stuffed with feathers. These were hand-made at considerable physical effort: only four a day per maker, and they cost 4s–5s. From the 1840s they were steadily replaced by round balls stuffed with gutta percha which could be bought for a shilling, although half a crown was more common. These flew slowly and were well suited to the short distances most players could manage in the days of early popularisation. Major change came with an American import after 1900. With a core of tightly wound rubber strips, the Haskell ball was invented in 1898: it flew up to 20 per cent further than the gutta ball from the same stroke. Initially the Haskell balls were expensive, up to 30s apiece, but demand brought the price down to 2s 6d by 1902. Despite claims that 'one might just as well play the game with a catapult', that the athletic demands of the game would be destroyed, that the mediocre would strive solely after distance and that the cost would turn the game into a plutocratic preserve, they caught on.[50]

Haskell changed more than playing styles. The 20 per cent greater driving possibilities meant that virtually every existing course became obsolescent. Since longer fairways were essential, new courses could be designed to meet the new demands; all others had to be extended or even moved to find adequate space. Eighteen holes could be laid out on about seventy-five acres before 1902; thereafter they needed at least 100 acres, and golf's land hunger increased in voracity. It could well be claimed by a rather sad Yorkshireman in 1912 that 'today golf is a much more serious affair financially than it used to be'.[51] Even if it still paid lip service to Scottish links, its centre of gravity was now emphatically inland, in a thoroughly anti-social world:

> ... one famous course ... originally appeared as fifty-seven dreary little fields intersected with hedges and ditches. It now presents the appearance of an open heath, broken here and there with rough and irregular hillocks and hollows among which can be seen patches of white sand, and clumps of gorse and broom.[52]

The landscape proved rather more malleable than some other aspects of the game, not least its management. Golf's boom was almost breathless, its geographical distribution very variable, with a heavy weighting towards the south-east of England. Like cricket it had depended in its early days very much on local usages and informal competition, eventually developing country or regional organisations. Like cricket also it offered homage to one senior club as the arbiter of its sporting ethics and etiquette. But golf's was a Scottish model, and romanticism was often tempered by distrust. The other major sports used standard arenas: golf's great delight and problem was that no two courses matched each other. Balls and clubs were far from standardised, and it was a game with a large following which played in pairs or quartets. There was an urgent need for some standardisation, but very real differences appeared as to what level of regulation should be applied and as to which was the most suitable body. A number of English clubs formed county associations, such as the Yorkshire Golf Union of 1894, largely to arrange competitions within and outside its area. The following year it organised the first inter-county match in England when Yorkshire played Hampshire at Bembridge on the Isle of Wight: the southerners won.[53]

Arranging tournaments was one thing, controlling them, play and spectators another. Golf's *doyen* was the Royal and Ancient club of St Andrews. By the end of the century this singularly cosmetic body had 1,000 members, many of them English: before the First World War it even had its first English captain, the ubiquitous Horace G. Hutchinson. But it was designed to play golf, not necessarily to run the game internationally. It was a role it was forced into, one questioned repeatedly since. In 1885 the Royal Wimbledon approached the Royal and Ancient, asking it to provide a code of rules and to form an association of golf clubs. It balked at the latter but formed a Rules of Golf committee in 1890 which produced a new code in 1892. This committee has remained as the game's regulatory body ever since but essentially in terms of playing the game itself, the arbiter of disputes rather than the provider and regulator of all golf's activities.[54]

The English, however, found themselves with a burgeoning membership which was demanding all the competitive superstructures of other sports. The *Field* became exasperated with the conservatism of the Royal and Ancient, others complained at its laxity and inefficiency.[55] But they were really asking for something the Scottish club was not designed to do, and there was a sufficient current of sentiment for it among English members to prevent any significant change. *C. B. Fry's Magazine* deplored the possibility that golf would end up with a top-heavy bureacracy controlling licensing and national competitions such as had appeared in athletics or football.[56] One observer was clear in his abhorrence of the trend: 'The principle of democratic government in the political sphere does not hold in the sphere of golf.' The Scottish oligarchy remained preferable to an extended English one.[57]

Much of the problem underpinning the unsuccessful demand for greater regulation lay in fears that popularity was diluting the game's puritan virtues noticeably, and this was no longer just a Scottish lament over its adopted offspring. The use of the game for business, particularly by Stock Exchange members, was deplored: 'They introduce the atmosphere of the speculative jobber and broker to the club room. They constitute themselves the bookmakers of the golf course.'[58] Business, it was felt, should be confined to quiet chats on the tee. There were other worries. The growing luxury, the emergence of the nineteenth hole, were felt to be replacing playing golf with drinking and bridge; golf clubs had become for many middle-class men the equivalent of the working-class 'local', often with less decorum.[59] And spectators lowered the tone even further as swarms of them damaged the fairways to gaze on Hutchinson, Vardon and Ray, the new heroes.[60] *Truth*, which normally attacked the commercialisation of sport, argued strongly for gate money being levied at golf tournaments, solely to prevent a repetition of the disruption of play caused when 3,000 spectators turned up at Walton Heath.[61] These people, their betting and their passion for sweepstakes, now appeared as a 'canker' which no one could control. They fostered 'pot hunting' and the decline of amateurism. Paradoxically, it was felt that paid professionals had more concern for the ethics of the game.[62]

Golfing humour

There seems to be an inevitable point in a sport's growth when such risks are noticed, and this was a particular problem for one so closely identified with the English middle-class concern for social tone. That tone often appeared difficult to maintain in the face of ridicule but the attack was largely turned to the game's benefit. Victorian and Edwardian sport in general acquired a sizeable penumbra of humour, much of which was self-directed. Some later became satire but a great deal of it was controlled and absorbed by being taken up as part of the mystique of participation. Self-depreciation was an essential feature of the middling ranks of the game: it allowed the pretence that sport was not being taken too seriously, that it was only a recreation, and it fuelled some of the concern that we have already noted about the over-luxurious provision of facilities' debasing the game's initial simplicity.

Apart from general humorous magazines such as *Punch* there were scattered articles in most of the 'literary' journals and a growing number in specialist sporting periodicals. Cartoons in all of these found stock figures – weedy knickerbockered sportsmen, golf's version of Hoopdriver, apoplectic players in bunkers, and long-suffering caddies.[63] All these were bolstered by verbal eccentricities and improbable stories such as that of the Scottish clergyman visiting Egypt in the 1870s who used the Great Pyramid of Cheops as a tee and his umbrella as a club.[64] A. J. Balfour contributed to this:

> ... there appears to be something singularly inane and foolish about a game of golf. Two middle-aged gentlemen strolling across a links followed by two boys staggering under the burden of a dozen queer-shaped implements, each player hitting along his own ball for no apparent object, do not make up a specially impressive picture to those who see it for the first time.[65]

Like fishing, because of its fund of specialist language, golf could be seen as 'the renewal of an ancient and subtle religion', its Scots roots offering it 'a phraseology smacking of the Assembly of Divines'.[66]

Much of this material was collected together occasionally, and there was a steady trickle of books devoted solely to the game's humour, even more so than with fishing. The writers listed golf's diseases:

1. Stagnatio Vulgaris.
2. Mendacitis Anarathmetica.
3. Polyclubia Inanis.[67]

or they created imaginary notices for club boards:

> We cannot encourage the growing tendency among the members to treat the bunkers as a permanent residence. A club-house has already been erected at great expense.[68]

Love stories, of great banality, were written around the game, and it produced utopian fiction. The two best examples both use Rip Van Winkle figures to transport the reader a century forward. J. McCullough, the author of *Golf: practical hints and rules* (1899) also wrote *Golf in the Year 2000*, in which international televised tournaments have replaced war and all business is conducted by women so that men can indulge in the serious task of playing golf. The only post women may not hold is that of Prime Minister, since it is felt that they harbour personal grudges too much to be safe incumbents of that office.[69] One of the best players and golfing writers of the twentieth century, Bernard Darwin, wrote a short story for *Fry's Magazine*, 'Golf in 2009', in which he envisaged municipal socialism taken to its extreme with the wholesale nationalisation of the game.[70] Despite the put-down of another observer's comment that golf was 'somewhat like kissing your sister' humour did much to foster the game's popularity.[71]

Artisans

English and, by extension, Welsh golf was clearly regarded as largely a middle-class preserve. It has remained as a potent myth that this represented a major departure from the democratic ambience of its homeland, Scotland. At many levels the class elements with the English game were matters of personal encounter, of ambitions realised or frustrated in ways which defy historical reconstruction. Some items, however, did pass into narrative, others became institutionalised. *Truth* recounted an incident at an unnamed southern golf club which augmented its income by charging green fees in the hope it would attract suitable visitors. When the captain courteously approached a stranger and asked if he wanted a game, he reported the following encounter:

> 'What are you?' [Meaning handicap.] . . .
> [He replied] 'A 'at maker from 'Ammersmith. Wot are you?'
> Now I should like to know, by the rules and etiquette of the Royal and Ancient game, what was the captain to do? The green fees had been paid.[72]

The etiquette of play itself was more easily stated than the assumptions that 'gentlemen know how to behave' in terms of becoming members. Status in terms of occupation, purchasing power and even address was extremely fluid in the period of golf's rise to popularity. Hammersmith hatmakers were only a few of that lower middle-class fringe, the respectable artisans, who also felt attracted to the game. These aspirants frequently fell foul of a rarely concealed snobbery. 'Artisan golf' became one of the major discussions in golfing circles from the 1890s, not least in Scotland, where many working-class players now found themselves excluded as local arrangements were increasingly formalised in favour of commercial and professional men. For many Scots artisans it was more than a matter of pleasure; to be able to graduate from caddying to playing meant opening up possibilities of employment in England or the Dominions as a club professional.[73]

The job experience seems to have been less important to many English artisans than the attractions of play itself. Pressure often came when traditional common recreation grounds were annexed for golf. H. S. Colt was one developer who saw an instrumental value in encouraging some key artisans to play in order to defuse likely opposition when this happened. Some clubs, having taken to their pseudo-country parks, operated a limited form of paternalism by creating parallel and emphatically subservient artisans' clubs. Northam in Devon,

Westward Ho!, claimed the oldest club of this sort; Great Yarmouth inaugurated a Workmen's Golf Club in 1892 and provided a special badge to identify its members in 1901.[74] This would seem to have been rather redundant; surviving photographs show artisan players usually on course in their Sunday best clothes, a poignant contrast with the old clothes deliberately affected by their superiors. The Redhill, Surrey, club operated a threefold annual subscription scale: two guineas for 'full members', 15s for 'burgesses' and 4s for artisans.[75]

Occasionally artisan play was slotted on to the revived paternalism of more traditional landowners. In Northumberland the Bamburgh Castle Workmen's Golf Club was formed as a private one, 'open only to the employees on Lord Armstrong's estates'. He gave them the right (or rather 'privilege') of playing over the course of his tenant, the Bamburgh Castle Golf Club.[76] There was usually more than hostility to be bought off. When the Royal Ashdown Forest club founded an artisan body in 1897 it called it the Cantelupe, after the eldest son of the area's former most important landowner, Earl de La Warr. In return for very restricted access to play, at what would now be defined as 'unsocial hours', many artisan groups were expected to take part in general course maintenance, mowing and so on. It was cheaper than paying a regular large greenkeeping staff. The symbiosis was usually demonstrated by an annual tournament between the regular club and an artisan team, with trophies and a tea provided by the superior body. 'A lot of roughly attired men, come with nondescript bags of clubs' at Westward Ho! to play the men for whom they had formerly caddied.

In many such matches the artisans, for all their restricted chances of practice, won overwhelmingly: the Buxton and High Peak artisans beat their parent team thirteen and a half points to three and a half in July 1908. Very occasionally artisan teams broke out from their local ties and played each other; the Cantelupe played Walton Heath's artisans at Ashdown Forest in September 1910. *The Times* regarded this as sufficient of a 'novelty' to report it in terms so absolutely patronising that it clearly assumed that the players would not read the paper. It would never have reported the scores of middle-class players as it did those of the artisans, 'if we may use . . . freedom with their Christian names', a habit normally used in addressing lower servants.[77]

For all its reporting the move to formal artisan clubs was limited: there were probably fewer than a dozen such in existence by 1914. More hope was put in to the provision of municipal facilities, although these tended to be annexed rapidly by local middle-class groups. When a new course was provided at Hainault in Essex the local authority proposed a fee of 1s a round; it may have seemed cheap but it was estimated that, with other costs, it would cost £12 a year to play.[78] Sheffield was much more attuned to local artisan demands; when it opened its Woodseats municipal course in 1911 it kept green fees down to 3d and sold 10,000 in its first three weeks.[79] But these were small numbers in national terms and there is no way of knowing how many were taken up by the social grades above the artisans. For all that *Golf Monthly* could pretend 'advancing democracy' when A. Robinson, a Southport gas worker, won the Lancashire Union of Golf Clubs' championship in 1914, it just did not exist. It would have been too much of a threat.[80]

Land hunger

Golf was more land-hungry than any sport except game-shooting and it brought into the open tensions often expressed in class terms. Where courses were made out of redundant farms there was usually little problem, but a great deal of golf was played on former pasture or scrub land which had often offered other recreational opportunities for a wider public. The game's growth in many areas saw the systematic encroachment upon and alienation of open, often 'common', land from its customary uses. Golfers often flouted local wishes or exploited the very uncertain position of the law for their own purpose. These were a number of cases consequent on the revaluation of land after the 1910 Budget where clubs wriggled through loopholes by claiming dual use of land to their own advantage. In Sleaford, Lincolnshire, in 1912 the local assessment committee annulled a rating charge on the golf course on the ground that the course was already being rated for agricultural use and could not be double-charged.[81] But these problems appeared minor when compared with the clash between golfers' claims and local customary expectations about access to open space.

The spread of suburbia, the fencing off of shooting moors and land round the growing number of municipal reservoirs happened at a time when sub-Romantic 'Englishness' was emerging as a significant spur to protecting an apparently vanishing rural heritage. Golf offered protected enclaves and there were thousands who saw it as a process of enclosure, robbing them of their rights. In the early 1890s the annual reports of the Commons Preservation Society noticed the new game for the first time: 'golf clubs practically monopolise the commons'.[82] Flying balls and the large spaces needed were making it dangerous both to people and to established rights of way. The older clubs playing on Wimbledon or Blackheath had worn scarlet jackets and shouted 'Fore!' when driving off as a deliberate means of warning. Their successors in old tweeds were virtually camouflaged and seem to have assumed that non-players should have the sense to keep away. It set the scene for a number of conflicts throughout the country, some of very long duration.

Chorley Wood in Hertfordshire had a common of about 400 acres. A number of old Harrovians founded a golf club to play there in 1890 which grew rapidly to some 150 members of considerable social importance, including A. J. Balfour, Bishop Winnington-Ingram of London, the Marquess of Granby and Earl Wemyss. For over twenty years they fought ordinary common users: 'Unfortunately it was used indiscriminately by the public who ignored the course rules.' When Sunday play was allowed in 1910 golf threatened to take away the only opportunity for fresh air that many clerks and artisans had. The locals retaliated by driving cattle on to the fairways and 'furious commoners lie across the greens to bedevil the hard-pressed enthusiast'. Golf added to encroachments already made by a cricket club and subsequently by a football club. In 1910 the problem was partially resolved by traditional mechanisms. The lord of the manor, heartily sick of complaints from all sides, used his steward to adjudicate after a public meeting with commoners. The agreement restricted grazing, so the new sportsmen effectively won. Resentment rumbled on and it was only in the 1920s that the issue was finally regulated.[83]

This case indicated the complexity of the issues which were to be played out more fully elsewhere. Rights on common land went with property-holding, and use for commercial grazing had steadily increased over the centuries, so that graziers formed quite powerful lobbies. But behind their grievances, which made much of the disagreement essentially a debate between different middle-class groups, there lay deeper trans-class issues. Although their rights frequently had no binding sanction in written or customary law, many urban workers of all grades used such land for pleasure, and they often had no alternative if that use was curtailed or removed altogether.

On Rushmore Heath, outside Ipswich, a few local gentry founded a club in 1895 but were 'hampered by the refusal of the commoners to permit the furze to be sufficiently cut away'.[84] In Lincoln there was a much greater problem. A club was formed in 1891 with a 'small exclusive membership' to play on Carholme Common on a course laid out by Willie Park – on the whole it seems to have managed quite well, since the common in use was the town's racecourse, with a very large area. But in 1893 a club was formed to play on the city's other side, the South Common. It thrived, and its members wore red coats to warn people of their presence. In 1896 the Carholme Club gave up playing on the racecourse and joined them, putting much greater pressure on the much smaller South Common. Together with football and cricket it clashed both with ordinary strollers and with local graziers. In 1894 the city's freemen had formed a guild to protect their rights against commercial and professional middle-class pressures. Animals were driven on to the course during matches and the South Common players eventually moved back to the racecourse in 1901 and then some miles westward to Torksey, on the Trent, in 1904, exclusiveness now being physically bounded. Victory for commoners was, however, short-lived: the pressure for golf was too great. In 1906 a new Carholme Golf Club was founded to play on the racecourse and a Southcliffe Club was re-formed in 1912 to play on the South Common. Its justification was that it was largely for doctors, who needed to be near enough to the city if they were called out to patients whilst playing. That won them permission from the council. Once again the commoners lost.[85]

Some golfers achieved a rather better balance. The Royal Epping Forest club played over eighteen holes, picturesque and with natural hazards, maintained by the City corporation. This was the traditional playground of the working-class East Ender, so 'During July and August no play is allowed, owing to the crowds of holidaymakers who troop into the forest and overrun the links.'[86] The patronising tone remained but it allowed of some equipoise. Some clubs recognised this in other ways; the Goodwood Golf Club's rules of 1892 obliged players to wait until walkers on the public path across their links had moved on at their own pace. They were not to be hurried along with shouts of 'Fore'.[87]

Such courtesy appears to have been comparatively rare, and there were some sharp confrontations between players and walkers. In Weybridge the local club placed itself firmly across a public right of way in 1909. In response 1,000 people assembled on the Wey bridge, walked along the path, and used a hammer and chisel to open the padlocked and chained gate the club had erected before crossing a single plank over a ditch and marching over two newly made tees. All this occurred under the eyes of the police, but there was no illegal behaviour.[88] In the same year the owner of the North links in Skegness wanted to close two paths and open two others across the course but had to bow to the objections of local residents.[89] Alas for the romantically-minded historian, there is no record of any late Victorian successor to the Diggers attacking the soil of the St George's Hill club, which had laid out its palatial facilities on the ground of seventeenth century conflict.

The problem was sufficiently widespread by the end of the Edwardian period for one of the game's prime developers, H. S. Colt, to suggest advance conciliation where a new club was intended. It is worth printing his advice in full here, because it illustrates only too clearly the effective refusal to give way to local demands, the lack of understanding of some of the issues involved and the patronising manipulation that often exacerbated the situation:

> ... two difficulties exist – the commoners and the commonable beasts. The commoners need at times a lot of tact – the commonable beasts an even temper and considerable patience. Both are apt to resent interference in their rights; the former retaliate at times by digging up the best putting green with their spades, and the latter by destroying it with their hoofs. The best plan to get over both difficulties is to encourage the commoners to play golf themselves, and, if a club be started for them, and the ways and means provided for them to enjoy the game, the manners of the commonable beasts are apt also to improve. In time an annual match can be held between the parent club and the commoners' club, and during the subsequent convivial evening leave may be obtained for making a few more necessary bunkers, even at the expense of the commonable beast.[90]

Faced with that sort of approach, it is hardly surprising that what a contributor to the *Victoria County History* of Surrey in 1905 called 'contumacious members of the public [ready] to ferment a real or fancied grievance about the sacrifices which were being exacted from the people in order to minister to the privileged amusement of a small band of golfers' could be found.[91] It is surprising at first sight that the objections were not more widespread. The southern volumes of the *Victoria County History* seem to have been written by golf addicts, such was their level of support in the 'Sporting' sections, often sharply at odds with the measured distancing with which manorial histories were treated. The Surrey contributor saw a greater threat to common land from speculative builders who created working-class streets whose denizens assumed a natural right to play football and cricket on local open spaces. This forced the golfers farther afield and was exacerbated when local councils in Wimbledon, Clapham, Tooting and Streatham restricted golf to certain days or a few hours early on weekday mornings. He was quick to point out, in apparent contradiction of his deploring the march of working-class suburbia, that golf proved 'a substantial aid to local prosperity, for the game attracts well-to-do residents'.[92]

Similarly, the golf contributor to the Middlesex *Victoria County History* saw the golfer as saviour of rural England who had 'helped to preserve "open spaces" from the encroachments of the builder'.[93] He avoided the question as to who benefited and the commons were added to other places as battlegrounds for social tone.

Individual grievances surfaced from time to time. At different points in 1911 *The Times* reported cases from Wimbledon, Yeovil, where the urban population had virtually lost its common to golfers, and from Letchworth: a Wimbledon golfer was said to have driven a ball deliberately at a working-class family after cursing them.[94] This could not be validated but repeated instances like this added to the folklore of deprivation. In several instances the issue moved to litigation. Although common rights technically belonged only to lords of manors and tenants the inhabitants of the London area enjoyed extended rights of use for periods of recreation under various Metropolitan Commons Acts.[95] Where recourse to the lord of the manor failed, or people were just driven off, common use was widely lost. The golfers had the advantage of their own commercial or professional experience, with solicitor members as key figures. They also had a sense of sporting aggression and the collective power of clubs to reinforce their encroachments. Together they presented a formidable and often intimidating front which was difficult to challenge. Not surprisingly, there were relatively few cases of litigation against clubs; those that occurred were widely reported because they became a major part of the case law applied to commons, footpath and access rights. In the Isle of Wight County Court in June 1908 the Royal Isle of Wight Golf Club asked for an injunction to prevent locals taking their leisure on the Dover, a piece of land leased for golf since 1882. The jury upheld the golfers in their appeal against local claims to traditional rights and awarded them costs.[96] It was the risk of the latter that acted as a major deterrent to other commoners' protests.

In Redhill, Surrey, another dispute hovered outside the courts. There the common was regulated by conservators, who allowed the golf club to play: the club elected its members and maintained a club-house away from the common itself. In 1908 the conservators decided that anyone could play golf, that they could be 'burgess members', allowed to play but paying a smaller subscription and with no right to enter the clubhouse. Because the club, presumably anxious about its social tone, refused to elect a burgess the conservators withdrew permission to play. The club angrily pointed out that it spent some £400 a year in Redhill, excluding wages.[97] With pressure like that the problem was negotiated to a solution. It left in the air a debate as to how far the conservators' powers extended, whether they should be replaced by the county council. It also demonstrated the power a club as business could wield.

One instance of alienation dominated public attention for some two decades, becoming a classic case for golfers, common users and lawyers in the long debate over access to public land. It was on the fringes of suburban London, at Mitcham in Surrey, and, once again, it involved at some point A. J. Balfour. In 1892 Prince's Golf Club, with Balfour as president, was formed on Mitcham Common, with a lease of land for eighteen holes. Even with a ten-guinea entrance fee and a five-guinea subscription it soon acquired 700 members, and it bought up some of the manorial rights from the conservators of the common. In so doing it took away rights of pasture and extraction in an area that was then not much used for wider popular recreation. The club spent thousands of pounds developing the course and filling up gravel pits but within a couple of years began to encounter public opposition. There were complaints that the game was dangerous, that there had been a 'wholesale spoliation of public rights' and that the club was paying only £60 a year for its facilities. An initial attempt to fight a conservators' election in 1894 on a 'Golf or no golf' issue blew over.[98]

The issue came back, however, in the Edwardian years, and lengthy litigation ensued as a result of an apparently trivial incident. In August 1908 the golf club removed some notices erected by the local authority and did 4s worth of damage. By that time the conservators had extended the club's rights, and its rent to £250 a year. A public road ran across the common, and Croydon Rural District Council had erected four notice boards requesting golfers not to play across or on the roads. It was these which had been removed, on the grounds that they were a slander on the club's title to its lease.[99] When the council renewed them the case went to court and the magistrates upheld the golfers' case when it was claimed that the notices frightened people away from joining Prince's Club. The council appealed to the King's Bench, and in 1909 the judge ruled that the club's title was not infringed, so that the magistrates must retry the case.[100]

In the following year the conservators took three golfers to Croydon Police Court for contravening a local bye-law which allowed only Prince's Club members to play on the common. One player, Cox, had a permit from the club but was playing on a Saturday on its larger course without a caddie, in breach of the bye-law. What appeared to be a minor technical infringement in which conservators and club were acting together was made much more open when a King's Counsel claimed that the new regulations 'were made to exclude the poorer residents of Mitcham from the full benefit of the Common'.[101] The conservators lost but decided to appeal: the key to this appeared with the report in May 1910 that Mr H. Mallaby-Deeley, MP, of Prince's Golf Club, had been re-elected as chairman of the conservators.[102] When the case was heard in the High Court it was sent back, since the judges said that the locals had no right to play any game on the common at all.[103] When the case was reheard before the Croydon magistrates in January 1911 an extended claim was made for the benefits the club had brought and its right to exclusivity. Without golf's money, it was asserted, the common would have remained a bog until it would have eventually been turned into a 'great gravel pit'.[104]

The golf club won that case but the issue surfaced again early in 1912. Mallaby-Deeley and the club persuaded the conservators to pass a new bye-law forbidding non-members from playing between 9.30 a.m. and 11.30 a.m. and between 1.00 p.m. and 3.00 p.m. on Wednesdays and Saturdays from April to September, the club's principal playing days.[105] Strenuous local opposition was ignored. Resentment simmered until January 1914, when a local solicitor, A. O. Warren, applied to the Croydon bench for a summons against the Prince's caddie master as a test of the bye-law's validity. The club's defence was that by allowing play only by members accompanied by authorised caddies it was protecting the local public from risk. This time the bench favoured the plaintiff, with a 5s fine and 9s 6d costs against the club and the conservators. The club appealed to the High Court, and its appeal was allowed on the grounds that, having paid money to improve the common, it was entitled to some privileges. Although other members of the public could play on the common, there had to be restraint, and the club was allowed to reserve caddies and time for its members alone. Trouble rumbled on and it was a long time before amicable arrangements were made.[106]

The extended cases reveal the major problems of a sport and leisure-hungry society with limited time and space when rival claims within the middle classes and between middle-class and working-class expectations emerged. They also revealed in no uncertain terms the pressure that could be brought to bear by golfers in their own interests when collective wealth and overlapping political and professional oligarchies were placed at the service of a privileged sport with a voracious appetite for space.

Notes

1 Figures based on *Golf Monthly*, June 1912, 307; the founding dates given subsequently are from such annual directories as *Nisbet's Golf Directory*.
2 E. G. Holden, 'The East Brighton Golf Club, 1853–1954', *Sussex County Magazine*, 28 (1954), 71–4; Brighton Reference Library, *East Brighton Golf Club Official Handbook* (1914).
3 This will be treated more fully in my chapter, 'Golf', in G. Jarvie and G. Walker, *Scottish Sport in the Making of a Nation* (Leicester University Press, forthcoming, 1993).
4 Whitney, *Sporting Pilgrimage*, 337.
5 *Truth*, 8 February 1902.
6 Victoria County History, *Northamptonshire*, 2(1906), 387.
7 *Sussex Express*, 14 November 1896.
8 W. M. Short (ed.), *Arthur James Balfour as Philosopher and Thinker* (1912), 277.
9 *Baily's Magazine*, LXI (1894), 117–18.
10 E. Miles, *Let's Play the Game, or, The Anglo-Saxon Sportsmanlike Spirit* (1904), 11.
11 A. Haultain, *The Mystery of Golf* (New York, 1912), 244.
12 Lyttelton, *Memories*, 284.
13 Height, 'The expenses of golf', 58.
14 *The Times*, 26 April 1910.
15 Agenda Club, *The Rough and the Fairway* (1913), 22–3.
16 *Golf Monthly*, August 1912, 462.
17 J. Kenward, *The Suburban Child* (Cambridge, 1955), 28 ff.
18 PRO, BT 31/21440, Co. 128818, Beulah Hill Golf Club Ltd.
19 *Badminton Magazine*, 37(1913), 785.
20 'The craft of the niblick I, The Brighton and Hove Golf Club', *Brighton Season* (1904), n.p.
21 PRO, BT 31/13948, Co. 123411, Merton Park Golf Club Ltd.
22 PRO, BT 31/33789, Co. 122307, Bramshot Golf Club Ltd.
23 PRO, BT 31/22463, Co. 137396, Epping Forest Golf Club.
24 G. Campbell, *Golf in Eastbourne* (c. 1935); *Sussex Life*, August 1982, 30–1.

25 Leeds Golf Club, *Official Handbook* (n.d., 1930s).
26 *Yorkshire Post*, 28 July 1922; Leeds Golf Club, Minute Books.
27 Victoria County History, *Yorkshire*, 2(1912), 547.
28 Victoria County History, *Surrey*, 2(1905), 523–4; *Truth*, 3 June 1908.
29 East Sussex Record Office, Ac 2777, Battle Golf Club.
30 East Sussex Record Office, Ac 2777, 19, Accounts of Bexhill Golf Club; *Golf Monthly*, August 1914, 406–1.
31 *C. B. Fry's Magazine*, 9(1908), 190 ff.
32 *Yarmouth Mercury*, 20, 27 August, 3 September 1932; G. H. J. Dutton, *Ancient and Modern Skegness and District* (1922), 72 ff.
33 *C. B. Fry's Magazine*, 9(1908), 190 ff.; *Golf Illustrated*, 12 February 1909; *Times*, 12 September 1908.
34 G. S. Cornish and R. H. Whitten, *The Golf Course* (1981), 36 ff.
35 G. Campbell, 'Links and courses', in B. Darwin *et al.*, *A History of Golf in Britain* (1952), 102, 110.
36 West Sussex Record Office, Add. Ms 20,001, 20,002, Goodwood Golf Club, Minutes.
37 *Brighton Season, passim*.
38 H. S. Colt, 'Golf clubhouses', *C. B. Fry's Magazine*, 14, 130 ff.
39 J. H. Stainton, *The Golf Courses of Yorkshire* (Sheffield, 1912), 71.
40 Victoria County History, *Essex*, 2(1907), 593; *Builder*, July–December 1901, 214–15.
41 *Golf Monthly*, August 1914, 430.
42 *The Times*, 15 December 1908; Suburban and Provincial Development Association, *Gerrard's Cross, Beaconsfield and the Chalfonts* (1910–11), 18–19; *Golf Illustrated*, 9 July 1909.
43 *Golf Illustrated*, 16 July 1909.
44 *Golf Monthly*, August 1912, 40.
45 *Golf Monthly*, August 1914, 436.
46 *Yorkshire Post*, 4 October 1909.
47 *Field*, 25 January 1902.
48 J. L. Low, *Concerning Golf* (1903), 202.
49 *Golf Monthly*, May 1914, 220.
50 *Badminton Magazine*, XVI (1903), 403 ff.; Cornish and Whitten, *Golf Course*, 38; G. Campbell, 'The development of implements', in Darwin *et al.*, *History of Golf*, 83 ff; *Truth*, 15 February 1902.
51 Stainton, *Golf Courses of Yorkshire*, 5.
52 H. S. Colt and C. H. Alison, *Some Essays on Golf Course Architecture* (1920), 51.
53 Stainton, *Golf Courses of Yorkshire* 9 ff.
54 Darwin *et al.*, *History of Golf*, 21 ff.
55 *Truth*, 18 April 1906; *Badminton Magazine*, 36(1913), 19.
56 *C. B. Fry's Magazine*, 16 (1912), *passim*.
57 D. Hardie, 'The government of golf', *Golf Monthly*, February 1912,889.
58 *Truth*, 16 May 1906.
59 O. G. Thorne, 'Sport and drink', *C. B. Fry's Magazine*, June 1906, 198.
60 *Golf Illustrated*, 15 January 1909.
61 *Truth*, 28 November 1906.
62 *Truth*, 5 June 1907.
63 E.g. *Fry's Magazine*, vol. 12.

64 *Badminton Magazine,* 28(1909), 564–5.
65 Short, *Balfour,* 270.
66 *Baily's Magazine,* December 1905, 459; Haultain, *Mystery,* 16.
67 *Badminton Magazine,* X(1900), 626 ff.
68 E.M.B. and G.R.T., *Humours and Emotions of Golf* (1905), 73.
69 J. S. Murdoch, *The Library of Golf, 1743–1966* (Detroit, 1968), 121.
70 C. B. *Fry's Magazine,* Vol. 10, 549 ff.
71 N. Lytton, *The English Country Gentleman (c.* 1925), 55.
72 *Truth,* 25 December 1902.
73 J. P. Inglis, 'Rise and progress of artisan golf in Scotland', *Golf Monthly,* January 1912, 839.
74 *Golf Illustrated,* 26 November 1909; *Yarmouth Mercury,* 20, 27 August, 3 September 1932.
75 *Truth,* 25 November 1908.
76 *Nisbet's Golf Yearbook* (1906).
77 *Golf Illustrated,* 26 November 1909; *Times,* 21 July 1908, 6 September 1910.
78 *Golf Illustrated,* 8 January 1909.
79 *Bexhill Observer,* 1 August 1914.
80 *Golf Monthly,* August 1914, 414.
81 *The Times,* 6 June 1912.
82 Commons Preservation Society, Annual Reports (1893–96), 47.
83 G. E. Ray, *A History of Chorleywood* (Hoddesdon, 1969), 46. I am particularly indebted to Christopher Wrigley for this reference.
84 Victoria County History, *Suffolk,* 2 (1907), 383.
85 C. Moulson, 'The History of the South Cliffe and Canwick Golf Club Ltd' (1975), typescript, Lincoln City library; F. Hill, *Victorian Lincoln* (Cambridge, 1974), 222–3.
86 Victoria County History, *Essex,* 2(1907), 592.
87 West Sussex Record Office, Add. Ms 20,001, Goodwood Golf Club, Minutes, 1893.
88 *Golf Illustrated,* 10 September 1909.
89 *Golf Illustrated,* 8 October 1909.
90 H. S. Colt, 'The construction of new courses', in M. H. F. Sutton (ed.), *The Book of the Links* (1912), 1 ff.
91 Victoria County History, *Surrey,* 2 (1905), 522.
92 *Ibid.*
93 Victoria County History, *Middlesex,* 2(1911), 278–9.
94 *The Times,* 6, 9, 17 October 1911.
95 *Golf Illustrated,* 9 June 1905.
96 *The Times,* 8 June 1908.
97 *Truth,* 18 November 1908.
98 Victoria County History, *Surrey,* 2(1905), 524–5.
99 *The Times,* 12 October 1908.
100 *The Times,* 11 February 1909.
101 *The Times,* 30 April 1910.
102 *The Times,* 13 May 1910.
103 *The Times,* 17 December 1910.
104 *The Times,* 28 January 1911.
105 *The Times,* 28 March 1912.
106 *The Times,* 12, 29 January, 11 May 1914.

Chapter 6

Impurity or covetousness[1]

Codes of conduct

In January 1912 *The Times* reported a case from Kingston on Thames where two golf-playing students were charged with violent assault on a couple whose cottage adjoined a golf course. The defendants had broken down a fence to retrieve their balls from the couple's garden and a fight had broken out. In defence the students claimed successfully that they had been unaware of the customary practice of the greenkeeper's collecting lost balls from the cottage each evening and that the cottage owner had started the fight.[2] It is unlikely that this was an isolated incident. But few golf clubs, however aggressive they may have been corporately, would have welcomed such behaviour, since it departed from the gentlemanly codes to which they so anxiously aspired.

These mattered greatly to middle-class individuals and groups often very unsure of their social position, and sport contributed significantly to their development. Dunning and Sheard have claimed that ideals of 'purity' in sport among the new *bourgeois* arose largely from their being out of contact with traditional aristocratic and gentry values, so that they were able to develop unalloyed by older public school contamination.[3] This must surely be modified in the light of public school reforms, new foundations and their wider aping in the last decades of the Victorian period. Gentlemanliness was widely sought after even when shorn of its sub-Arthurian trappings. Unconscious caricature spelt out the ideal type:

> a born leader. There is power in his rugged, hard-set face. He has a stern, penetrating eye, and a stern, resonant voice ... There is strength and character in his every movement, in his every word.[4]

What later became the essential physical features of a hero from John Buchan or Sapper were ascribed in 1907 to the new president of the

Rugby Union, C. A. Crane; after public school at Cheltenham and a business career in Wolverhampton he was now a country gentleman, 'the life which suits him best'.

Both Mangan and Vance have outlined the instrumental and literary underpinnings of the cult of manliness, and it would be redundant to repeat them. The issue here is not so much the development and provision of the ideals as the tensions which emerged when they spread outside public schools. They were tested and modified in ways which their earlier proponents could not have foreseen, as props for either absolute or situation ethics as the occasion demanded. The secular theology of manliness could barely be coped with in the gathered elites of public school and universities; outside them its own evangelistic success proved its greatest difficulty. It should not be labouring the Pauline parallels too much to see sport in the later nineteenth century as experiencing problems similar to those of the early Church. In place of the apostle's Corinthian epistles we find the articles in literary and sporting periodicals lamenting the growth of unnatural practices: but these latter-day errors were more the worship of Mammon than sexual or liturgical deviations. Around two apparently simple words, 'amateur' and 'professional', there emerged an anguished ethical debate of considerable complexity.

The *amateur* was the absolute ideal:

> they run because the exercising of their bodies gives them delight and because, being Englishmen, they find it pleasant to have beaten an honest adversary in an honest competition.[5]

One key here is the nationalist ascription: these became xenophobic as well as class issues. But honesty was also at risk. In its strictest sense 'amateur', as the 'lover', the absolute enthusiast, achieved common currency not long before the sports boom began. It came to represent the peak of intention rather than performance, and it was never far from its derogatory extension, 'amateurish'. The greatest dilemmas arose when it was opposed diametrically to the sense of 'professional'.[6] Profound difficulties were caused because social classes which celebrated their own professional training and qualifications deplored their implications in recreation.

Across-the-board ideals proved impossible to enforce. In real terms relative levels of involvement across the continuum proved more important than total purity. The problem was made much more apparently intractable by questions raised by rising standards of sporting performance in which 'amateur' was often equated with 'less than competent' and by the problems experienced by those who moved from one sport to another.

The *locus* of purity was always in the individual and his conscience but it was often suggested that the safest way of preventing its corruption was by concentrating on the team. *The Field* claimed in 1902 that the rewarding of individuals by whatever means for their performance led inevitably to impurity.[7] Much depended on the nature of the prize; the purely honorary had no tradable value, except in terms of adulation, so it was 'pure'. The problems were compounded very early on by the costs of participation and the paying of expenses. Youth and its associated high levels of stamina and performance were rarely combined with the independence of means that allowed practice, travel and competition, all of which increased steadily with the institutionalisation of sports and their extension beyond local boundaries.

Baily's Magazine suggested in 1902 that 'the word amateur has only been imported into cricket since the payment of expenses became a somewhat burning proposition' – claims to ethical purity were shouted loudest when there was a perceived rather than actual decline in standards. The writer went on to encapsulate the issue squarely:

> *Prima facie* there is no reason why some person in a humble station in life should not be as good an amateur as a man in flourishing circumstances; but it has been found by experience that the amateur of good social position more nearly corresponds to what the ideal should be.[8]

By this time it was becoming only too apparent that few amateurs could match the levels of achievement of the much-practised and skilled professional.

There were some who could advance good instrumental reasons for the descent into payment, such as the Revd. F. H. Gillingham, who had kept his church going from cricket fees.[9] Others chose a much greater level of fudge. For some, honesty had to be a prime concern when choosing a game to play rather than its affordability or even availability.[10] There was a strong vein of enclave language. 'Gentleman are being gradually driven into private grounds for their sports,' when threatened with pot hunting, claimed a writer in the 1870s.[11] Yet the 'genuine' professional was admired, if only because he could easily be patronised as an employee: the difficulty came with the semi-professional or the 'shamateur'.[12] The American observer Caspar

Whitney saw a steady decline in *bona fide* amateurs by the 1890s.[13]

Much of this was crying wolf, questioned strongly by writers such as Aflalo, who said that realistic contact on open terms between amateur and professional could have only beneficial results, 'a higher standard of purity, of virile strength, and of freedom from the worst elements that can reflect national pastimes'.[14] Generally, however, reactions were much more pessimistic. It was widely held that the sharp drop-off in team game or athletic participation after school or university days was largely due to an amateur revulsion against the manipulation of rules for unethical purposes, namely winning at all cost.

Because sport was increasingly tied up with business, often by the individuals who cried loudest against professionalism, it was felt to lack risk and to have departed from its essential Englishness.[15] It had touched fundamentally nationalist activities, with the spread of tournament casting into fly fishing, 'exploitation by keen manufacturers who stick at nothing'.[16] This was blamed on American practice, a popular source to which to attribute decay. There remained throughout the period a suspicion of international competition as a likely cause of impurity in sport, which showed in the difficulties experienced when the organisers of the 1908 Olympics in London tried to harmonise various conflicting national definitions of amateurism.[17]

It also applied between different sports in which one individual might compete. Because he had played golf against a professional, A. J. Balfour would have been barred from rowing at Henley.[18] There were a few enclosures where the issues seem rarely to have been raised: neither croquet nor hockey had any professionals; the latter game avoided all prize competitions and agonised as to whether the publication of its results in the local press would encourage undesirable ambitions.[19] Very occasionally the complaints went the other way. 'The amateur has attempted to interfere with Physical Education, bringing it down to the level of "sport",' as distinct from a science.[20] And there were claims that sport maintained social anachronisms injurious to a developing society, preserving social distinctions unnecessarily.[21]

Henley rules

The most potent, the most widely discussed and among the least numerically significant of these distinctions occurred in rowing under the so-called 'Henley definition' of an amateur. The team game *par excellence*, rowing theoretically submerged the individual in the crew. Southern middle-class rowing saw the emergence of the most clearly class-specific definition of ethical standards and a singular refusal to adapt to rapid changes in the sport in the last decades of the nineteenth century. Long before gentlemen amateurs took to the sport, working watermen around the great ports and fishing towns had rowed in competition to demonstrate their skill and foster trade bonds. This was usually recognised when town regattas were held, as in Bristol in 1861, where separate competitions were organised of 'gentlemen' and 'watermen'.[22] The problems that emerged were twofold: the workers were usually physically stronger if less stylish (or stylised) and they usually rowed for a money stake, as did miners rowing in 'professional' races at Durham regattas.[23]

There were continued problems with organising either separate races by category or with races between crews from both groups and, especially, with crews made up of a socially mixed membership. An 1890s writer summed this up when discussing the 'disgraceful bad form' of professional oarsmen and 'their contaminating influences'.

> English professionals, owing to the manual labour with which most of them start life, became abnormally strong in the arms, and trust almost entirely to their muscles . . . nothing shows up their bad form in rowing so much as sandwiching a few pros. [*sic*] in a goodish amateur crew – 'by their style ye shall know them'.[24]

In fact it had become virtually impossible by then for such a sandwiching to take place.

The issue came to a head in the 1870s because the considerable popularity of Thames rowing since mid-century had extended the social constituency of the sport downwards. A number of clubs had appeared which were uneasily located somewhere between the professionals and the elite university and public school membership of bodies such as Leander and the London Rowing Club. Some of these had emerged as a result of the good work of university men; Thomas Hughes, of *Tom Brown's Schooldays*, who had rowed in the Oriel eight, had helped to form the Working Men's College Rowing Club in the 1850s.[25] Bodies like this assumed that they could compete at the Henley regattas, and it was there that the socially leading clubs decided to exclude them.

They did so in a way which assumed that all working men

were inevitably tainted by what a later writer called 'professional blackguardism'.[26] The Henley decisions of 1878 and 1879 were the logical outcome of a process which had begun some thirty years earlier when university and other crews had acted to remove both professional steersmen and coaches. Officials from the universities, Leander, London Rowing Club, Thames Rowing Club and Kingston Rowing Club met at Putney in 1878 and produced a definition of an amateur which is worth quoting here in full because it contains assumptions which influenced every other sport's treatment of the amateur/professional divide:

> An amateur oarsman or sculler must be an officer of her Majesty's Army, or Navy or Civil Service, a member of the Liberal professions, or of the Universities or Public Schools, or of any established boat or rowing club not containing mechanics or professionals; and must not have competed in any competition for either a stake, or money, or entrance fee, or with or against a professional for any prize; nor have ever taught, pursued, or assisted in the pursuit of athletic exercises of any kind as a means of livelihood, nor have ever been employed in or about boats, or in manual labour; nor be a mechanic, artisan, or labourer.[27]

It was amended slightly in 1879 to finish with the clause 'or engaged in any menial activity'.[28]

Quite clearly many forms of social mobility were banned and there were constant problems as to where 'menial activity' applied, as keenness on rowing extended downwards through white-collar workers. It is remarkable for the extent of its definition in negative terms. For nearly sixty years its apologists justified it as merely applying to sport the sort of distinctions which were normal in society, as providing 'our own sport among the more refined element'.[29]

The clubs which had drawn up the 1878 rules formed the Metropolitan Rowing Association in 1879, renaming it the Amateur Rowing Association in 1882, when the net of purity was given a national catchment. Into it came such bodies as the Warwick Boat Club, the Ironbridge Boat Club and the clubs of Birmingham, Leicester and Nottingham. A little later the Durham club joined, and so did imperial outposts in Dublin, Calcutta and Gibraltar.[30] By refusing the title 'amateur' it could kill a regatta and effectively ban a club from any competition if its membership was suspect. Throughout the 1880s the Windsor and Eton Amateur Regatta, founded in 1878, encountered criticism of its inclusiveness until, like many other clubs, it applied the ARA rules in blanket fashion.[31]

Trouble came in 1890 when a number of clubs rebelled openly against the Thames oligarchy, which was felt to be non-representative, incapable of change and far too exclusive to cope with changes in the middle-class constituency. The issue arose because part-time study at places such as the Regent Street Polytechnic opened up sporting possibilities to men normally debarred by the ARA's amateur definitions yet whose commitment to 'respectable' leisure was as firmly anti-professional as that of Leander.

The prime mover in this was the Chaucerian scholar F. J. Furnivall, who saw a profound inconsistency in sending university men out into settlements to help workers to improve themselves and then debarring them from expressing it by rowing.[32] After a series of London meetings a National Amateur Rowing Association was formed in opposition to the ARA. Furnivall was aided by a London clergyman, Prebendary Probert, and supported by Quintin Hogg, who eventually persuaded the Duke of Fife to become president of the new association.[33] The early days were enmeshed in acrimonious controversy, since Furnivall was a tireless and somewhat acerbic publicist who would not accept the claims of the *Cambridge Review* that artisans did not have the time to row and should not seek religious justification for their sport. He responded that the ARA was dominated by civil servants who despised the working men who paid their wages, in 'an exclusive caste spirit'.[34]

Furnivall encouraged pan-class activity as a means of ensuring the goodwill of the new educated workmen, a prophylactic against socialism. Despite royal patronage and a growing membership of clubs excluded from the ARA, the NARA stood virtually alone: the AAA refused to recognise it, and only the Amateur Boxing Association accepted it. Yet it survived and, with Bishop Winnington-Ingram as its president after 1901, provided a season of regattas which mirrored Henley in terms of performance if not of social glitter. And it was just as tight in its sanctions as its rival; it suspended Brighton Excelsior for taking part in a French competition with money prizes.[35]

A conference at Oxford between the two bodies in 1890 did nothing to heal the rift but it did bring pressure on the ARA to alter its rules.[36] This it did slightly in 1894, allowing some competition against mechanics if no money prizes were given, but maintaining Henley's purity. But there were further problems, because it was unclear about the amateur status of engineers who served apprenticeships involving some manual labour as part of their professional training, and it was another fourteen years before this could be partly resolved.[37] In fact there seems to have been some deliberate local fudging in the interpretation of the rules, since a significant body of the members liked neither the absolute exclusiveness of the 1878 clauses nor the 'heroics' of Furnivall and the 'brotherhood of man' view of sport.

There were almost farcical results. The Regent Street Polytechnic ended up with two rowing clubs, the Quinton (ARA) and the Poly-technic (NARA), which used the same boathouse but could not row against each other, and many individuals experienced difficulties.[38] Henry Blackstaffe of Vesta, an impeccably amateur body in ARA terms, won the Wingfield sculls from 1897 to 1908 and won the 1908 Olympic sculls at the age of forty, but he encountered problems in having his amateur status recognised, because he was a butcher.[39] It was not just an issue for the Thames. When Durham University clubs started to row against Armstrong College (the nucleus of the future University of Newcastle) there was uncertainty about the status of non-matriculated members of Armstrong and the college had to agree that only matriculated students would appear as members of crews against Durham.[40]

These difficulties in English terms multiplied significantly when rowing acquired an international dimension. It fitted well into some parts of the Dominions but their social fluidity gave rise to far greater tensions than even those apparent in England. In Australia only New South Wales, a home of Evangelicalism to this day, stayed Henley-pure: 'The other associations recognise men who would not pass muster at any regatta in the United Kingdom.'[41] Eventually reciprocal agreement on amateur definition was reached with Canada and the major European contributors to the sport, France, Germany, Holland and Belgium.[42] But *the* threat to rowing's purity came from the United States, whose university and civic crews appeared to threaten the amateur rules. Not merely did they lack a Grecian style, they won, and the return visits after the Princeton victories at Henley in the mid-1890s provoked major problems.

American clubs were held to use professional coaches, effectively dropped in England half a century earlier. Nor was it clear whether many of their crewmen would be debarred under English rules. The difficulty was exacerbated because no US organisation had the control that the ARA and its European equivalents exercised. So each American club that entered for Henley appeared as an uncertain element. In 1905 the Vesper Club of Philadelphia's eight was defeated by Leander amid suspicion that it was tainted by professionalism. It had come with assurances of purity from the National Association of Amateur Oarsmen of the United States, but that body was felt to be singularly lax in its standards.[43] The ARA usually demanded to see the membership lists, together with the occupations, of its affiliated clubs, and there were considerable difficulties in doing this for North Americans. In 1906 the Vesper was banned for taking money payments, but attempts to exclude all Americans on the grounds that they were automatically tainted had to be suppressed.[44] It had to be a very rich colonial or American who could afford to compete at Henley when even the payment of expenses was technically illegal, yet they continued to appear. One can only conclude that a certain amount of fudging or blind eye-turning went on until 1914, because the absolute standards proved ridiculously impossible to apply outside the very narrow circles for which they were first intended.

Pedestrian practices

The hard line taken by amateur rowing's management can be explained only if it is seen in the wider context of sports already established by the 1870s. Apart from the limited pan-class provision of cricket the only significant area where there had been much potential for inter-class competition was in track athletics. These suffered from the legacy of sponsored pedestrianism in mid-century. Shocked by the spectacle of collapsing walkers beaten by multi-day endurance events, the newly pure amateurs of the 1860s sought to contain track events within firmly defined limits of time and space which tested skill as much as stamina. Once again there was suspicion that the assumed muscularity of working-class men gave them an advantage in stamina that no middle-class competitor could rival. Paradoxically athletics were widely held to have come from middle-class attempts to emulate professional pedestrians: 'wherever there was an unusual galaxy of pedestrian ability the amateurs began to imitate them'.[45]

The founding of the Amateur Athletics Association in 1880 represented an attempt to create a 'ring-fence of gentleman amateurism' around a far larger series of events and clubs than rowing could ever have envisaged. Athletic competitions were an almost indispensable part of every mid and late Victorian charitable festival, town or village celebration and, at every level beyond Sunday school sports, were widely advertised for individual as well as club entries and offered prizes. The drive was to make the prizes purely honorary – cups, shields and medals – and the 'purer' events were often restricted to clubs, with their assumedly vetted membership. In an age devoted to individualism it was the individual entrant, difficult to vet and potentially corrupt, who seemed the greatest threat. But whole clubs could hover on the fringes of respectability, and the AAA's mental map was clearest in the London area. John Bale has remarked on the association's difficulties in recruiting in northern England before 1914, leaving amateur athletics emphatically southern in its focus. He has also demonstrated how 'professional' track events declined in the same period precisely because they lacked a comparable central organisation to that of other emergent professional sports.[46]

Nevertheless, amateur hegemony was hard won, and there were some embarrassing compromises. In 1873–75 the London Athletic Club found itself in turmoil because a regular competitor at its sports, and winner, was W. J. Morgan, who had links with commercial sport through his employment. He was widely regarded as a rather up-market professional pedestrian, and about half the club's members threatened to withdraw if his name continued to be included in programmes. Most were persuaded to remain, 'and in a year or two both the club and its entries gained in number what they lost in social standing'.[47] Morgan in person was never objected to; he was feared as 'the representative of a class'. The LAC dominated the capital's sport, and it eventually adopted the Henley definition, which excluded most northern entrants from running in London.

In retaliation the Northern Counties Athletic Association was formed, to allow working-class runners to appear as amateurs, provided only that they had never run for money. The resulting provincial tensions led to the meeting in Oxford in 1880 which founded the AAA. This soon regulated some 20,000 athletes, with a firmly negative prohibition of money, teaching the sport for income or competing against professionals.[48] At least it was far more open in class terms than the LAC's earlier use of Henley. There were many middle-class athletes who felt and expressed only too clearly a sense of betrayal in the subsequent decades. This surfaced in disputes with cycling organisations when athletic and cycling meetings overlapped but it was more openly stated when the implications of the widespread popularity of the track became apparent in the later 1880s and 1890s. 'Petty swindling, deceit and unfair play' came to be expected automatically because it was felt that working-class athletes had no reputations to lose.[49]

That many clubs in predominantly working-class sports such as coarse fishing had managed to impose 'respectability' through increasingly tight sanctions on their members was largely lost in these jeremiads:

> Nor . . . is it to be expected that the 'mechanic, artizan, and labourer' ranks will always have, when a valuable prize is at stake, as much sportsmanlike feeling and nice sense of fair play as one could rely on finding in the much-ridiculed 'gentleman amateur' of past days.[50]

This very class-specific attribution of ethics was repeated frequently in criticisms of athletics. When H. M. Oliver left the North London Spartans for Birmingham in the 1870s he took to organising crack teams of athletes, the Moseley Harriers and the Birchfield Harriers, whose repeated defeats of 'gentlemen' clubs fostered considerable resentment.[51]

The sporting press continued to claim an ethical decline. The *Sporting Mirror* claimed in 1882 that the advent of shopkeepers into 'the circle of Amateurism' was bringing pot hunting by 'athletic criminals'.[52] In many cases the old divides were reinforced, since it was Midlanders and northerners who could be blamed for 'a growth of "promoters" . . . which, in amateurdom, reproduces the gaffer of Sheffield handicaps'.[53] The same writer, in *Horse and Hound*, saw many clubs' honorary secretaries as the villains, since they made a substantial income from judging and arranging events as well as from writing for newspapers.

The southern response was to cut down as far as possible on 'open' competitions and, as in the case of the London Athletic Club, run only invitation events. In that way clubs' members were protected from contamination and could expect to compete only against people of their own kind; free from the 'great democracy' of profit-makers.[54] It is salutary to be reminded that the 'democratisation' of sport brought back some of the fears that had been raised in political circles against the extension of the suffrage.

The other risk that came with competition and, paradoxically, in the widespread reporting by an 'amateur' press (*vide Amateur Sport* or the *East Riding Athlete*) was the establishing of sporting records for standardised events. The inner direction of individual performance now moved into the realm of a wider standard of testing: the creation of a sense of the past in sport as a means of measuring the future took away much of the 'here and now' pleasure base which underpinned a great part of the amateur ethos. Athletics became another victim of the moral seriousness imposed on sport: the evangelising impulse found itself faced with a large number of individuals who proved singularly immune to being recalled to chivalry or to 'the competition of equally matched antagonists which brings out all the manly qualities of the Englishman'.[55] Only the wealthiest clubs could avoid the temptation to maintain their facilities through the year with gate money raised from opening a couple of annual events to a wider public. Spectators wanted to see performance and were bored by demonstrations of purity: so, one suspects, were a substantial number of athletes who, even when they were contented with unsullied honour, wanted it to be given for superior prowess. The diatribes continued loudest in London and university groups: the repeated plaints of the short-lived *Hull and East Riding Athlete* were a very lonely voice in much of the north.[56]

By the 1890s many observers could detect a sharp divide in middle-class athletics between the prestigious but relatively small clubs dominated by ex-public school and university men and the rest. They went on to decry the notion that mingling amateurs and semi-professionals could only raise the tone of the latter. Once again there appeared a major contradiction in the notion of sport as the moral agent *par excellence* being developed to assume that popularity meant inevitable corruption. When cross-country paper-chasing gave way in parts of the south to prize awards for running on the lines of established northern fell racing in the later 1890s the sense of *fin-de-siècle* in its most decadent form was invoked by a writer in the *Badminton Magazine*.[57] In these terms international events, unlike in rowing, could be welcomed in the hope that national partisanship would foster a purer patriotism to offset the decline: it would also cut down the hunt for novelty which was felt to be produced by gate-money hunger, so that competition would return to essentials.[58]

The London Athletic Club continued to provide an unsullied lead and extended the snobbery of participation when it introduced small gold shields for watch chains as prizes, attractive to 'even the most sordid pot hunter' if only because the traditional pots were not so portable.[59] The watch-chain medal took the record of personal success outside the home in a way which was deliberately restrained but only too clearly visible. Unlike silver cups, the increasing bane of amateur athletics, they could not be found in the pawnshops of Manchester, Liverpool and Birmingham; the contributor to *Baily's Magazine* who claimed this in 1908 assumed automatically that prizes never went into the hands of the capital's pawnbrokers.[60]

Unlike some other amateur regulating bodies, such as the Lawn Tennis Association, the AAA continued to object to competitors' expenses being met.[61] It was felt, however, to be starting to slip after the turn of the century. Claims of widespread 'shamateurism' were often based on a limited number of reported cases. In one of these in 1906 the South London Harriers' best amateur long-distance runner, Shrubb, was held to be paid for his sport by 'prominent members'. If true – and the Southern Counties AAA suspended him for it – this reflected the tensions within middle-class clubs over mutual aid for sporting and local social prestige.[62] The creation of this ladder of moral excellence was held also to be responsible for a general decline in amateur performance in that purity was anti-competitive in its ramifications and too 'narrow-minded'.[63] The Chavasse twins, sons of the bishop of Liverpool, were Edwardian Oxford's best track athletes but were generally not expected to run outside, not least because they might risk physical contamination from lesser beings. The two classes, it was held by *Baily's*, would never meet on the track until 'true deference is paid to the superior person in the way of making accommodation for him'.[64] Rarely was this physical as well as ethical abhorrence of contact made quite so clear but it remained a significant and not yet fully appreciated undercurrent of the moral debate.

The ethical tensions in athletics overlapped with and were often fuelled by parallel developments in competitive cycling. The new bureaucracies of both sports kept a very uneasy eye on each other. The National Cyclists' Union, founded in 1884, regarded itself as the appropriate licensing body for the amateur sport. Unlike athletics, cycling had a much wider purely recreational penumbra and also a much larger manufacturers' interest in view of the publicity given to ordinary road machines by track wins during the boom of the 1890s. Concern with record-keeping came early. The NCU provided a negative definition of amateurism in May 1878: a professional was one who had ridden in public for money (did people ride for reward in private?) or taught or helped cycling or any other athletic exercise for money, or raced against a professional.[65] There could be no mingling on the track, and amateur status could not be enjoyed in one sport alone. One issue that dogged many successful professional sportsmen until well into the twentieth century was their inability to enjoy amateur status in their recreation. The NCU was felt to be creating dilemmas: by taking sport so morally seriously the union seemed to be destroying its recreational functions and appeal as a pastime. When the NCU relaxed its harsher rules after protests in 1881 it provoked further difficulties. Restricting the professional definition to those who rode or taught for money, it caused problems for Coventry, with 'the numerous wealthy [cycle] manufacturers of the city being now entitled to rank on an equal footing with the half-starved clerks and counterjumpers who formerly constituted the bulk of "amateurs"'.[66] The double irony in this comment, of the rich as professionals and the socially despised as purists, is rare in late Victorian social comment on sport.

Cycling appears to have been bedevilled by a 'ring' of semi-sponsored competitors with regional or even national reputations for performance around whom a strong suspicion of fixing results hovered. It was clearly in conflict with the random-winner assumptions essential to amateurism and, although a cross-class element of disapproval was introduced in the debate, it was a major argument between overlapping sections of the middle classes. In the mid-1880s money prizes were to be discontinued, professionals were not to race against amateurs and prizes were not to be sold, not even 'yet another plated biscuit dish – an article of luxury which the secretaries of race meetings are popularly supposed to order by the gross'.[67] In real terms these measures proved ineffective and a writer of the 1890s could look back with nostalgia to a race of 1871 for the Amateur Bicycle Championship where seventeen of twenty entrants were disqualified solely on the grounds of being a mechanic, artisan or labourer, and a public schoolboy, M. P. Whiting won. The same Whiting had raced against the Hon. I. K. Falconer in 1875 before a large crowd of university men, in sharp contrast to what the writer thought he saw twenty years later.[68] The 'makers' amateur' now dominated the field, and he felt that only a Henley-type rule could save the NCU as professional foul practices were increasing.

Such complaints were endemic, but the NCU had few effective sanctions and was much more closely tied to the limited world of racing than to a wider cycling membership. It was estimated that only one per cent of cyclists actually participated in competitions but, as with motor racing later, the sport became a necessary prestige-bearer for manufacturers. The NCU had burnt its fingers in a row with the AAA over joint meetings in 1885 and had proved singularly unwilling to go very far down a purist road.[69]

The precise nature of manufacturers' involvement was widely hinted at but rarely clarified, and it was an exceptional case which revealed the complexity of the involvement. In late 1896 the Pneumatic Tyre Company applied for an injunction at Bow County Court against one James Green, to prevent his racing without using Dunlop tyres. The company had paid him 10s a week as an 'amateur' but had stopped doing so when the NCU made one of its occasional interventions and revoked his licence. So Green found another source of tyres. The judge refused the application and awarded costs to Green on the grounds that the company had known that he was effectively a professional and was therefore free to change if agreements were broken.[70]

Individuals reacted to the dilemma in different ways. In 1891 A. W. Harris was refused an amateur licence, so he joined the professional circuit. T. Gibbons-Brooks, who started cycling in 1892, won £300 worth of prizes over the next two years. In 1896 he fell foul of the NCU's current attempt to purify the sport and was refused an amateur licence, so, 'naturally not desiring to join the professional ranks, he has confined himself to the task of breaking records'.[71]

A rapid slackening of the bicycle boom around 1900 cut back manufacturers' involvement, and many fringe professionals without the usual middle-class employment resources found themselves in difficulty, supposedly reduced to delivering newspapers, 'mostly unfitted for other business by their mode of life and their past environment'.[72] Yet the shamateur hold continued, and attempts to cope with it were never more than sporadic. In 1908 the AAA and NCU met again at the Inns of Court to clarify joint meetings; the NCU agreed to follow AAA practice, and they set up a joint committee of six to oversee this.[73] But the problem lumbered on, and when the NCU selected three members of the long-established Road Racing Club for the Swedish Olympics in 1912 the club refused to let them go 'on account of the doubtful amateur status of some of the other nominees', let alone that of foreigners.[74]

Ethical conflicts also applied in two sports widely regarded as being on the fringes of athleticism. The Swimming Federation of Great Britain was founded in 1874 but eventually split over the usual difficulty of interpreting the word 'amateur': it was replaced by the much more explicit Amateur Swimming Association in 1886.[75] This latter body took the relatively unusual step of defining a professional in positive rather than negative terms when it began to issue an annual *Handbook* in 1899. Barred from amateur status or from competition with amateurs were people who swam for pecuniary gain, who sold prizes, worked as swimming bath attendants or – and this was comparatively rare in the contemporary debate – received expenses greater than those of a third-class train fare to competitions.[76] Even this was hedged about with qualifications that showed clear internal divisions reflecting the social grading of participants. Exempted from the ban were those who played professionals in club football matches, all schoolmasters and schoolteachers and – particularly sharp in view of the ban on attendants – baths managers and life-saving instructors.

Truth, examining this some time later, pointed yet again to some apparent absurdities and placed swimming firmly in the lower part of the sporting pantheon: 'as a body, swimmers are scarcely so well up the social scale as the leading tennis players. But social position covers a multitude of sins.'[77] The rules were occasionally bent: by 1905 Billington (once again the initials or Christian name were deliberately excluded) had become an amateur champion, but he was a bath attendant who, for *Truth*, could not be making an honest living. Yet the fit professional swimmer remained swimming's great attraction and an advertisement for participation which few other sports could match.[78]

The other sport where 'gentlemen amateurs' retreated into enclaves was boxing. As Stan Shipley has shown, middle-class withdrawal from participation in general terms was complete well before the end of the nineteenth century.[79] They could match neither the physical strength nor the stamina of most of their potential working-class opponents, so the sport remained largely confined in terms of middle-class direct involvement to the public schools and universities. And there was the ever-present revulsion of direct physical contact with the lower classes. In schools and universities it could be seen as a prophylactic, the 'best outlet for high spirits' – and how many headmasters assumed that the best answer to schoolboy arguments or bullying was a bout in the ring? It remained stained by the memories of paid pugilism, bare-knuckle fighting and other signs of decadence among aristocratic patrons. Yet it was a sport which earnest curates and settlement workers were happy to teach to slum boys as essential to the encouragement of self-reliance in their charges, and as the 'most British' sport it helped to counteract what many saw as the soft-hearted ultra-civilisation of too many Edwardian sensibilities.[80] Its real popularity, however, was as a working-class participant or spectator sport organised in clubs or bouts by small-scale entrepreneurs who were closer to their audiences rather than in any model of middle-class athletic assumption of ethical virtue. The Amateur Boxing Association, formed in 1880, did cover all classes but its large Edwardian membership was effectively stratified internally between a very small group of upper middle-class clubs, themselves breakaways from the aristocratic domination of the earlier sport, and the mass of working-class-run clubs which seem to have had very little contact with them.

Gentlemen and players

Such could not be claimed of cricket, apparently the most established of pan-class sports, in terms of participation. For local village matches or league friendlies this is perhaps justified, since the very nature of much rural cricket blurred any amateur–professional distinctions. Cricket's late Victorian problem was that it acquired a high national profile because of its identification with regional and national loyalties: it represented real fears over the erosion of the quintessential Englishness it was supposed quite wrongly to exemplify. At county and test level the tensions over pure sport revealed attributions of personality related to class that were not even clearly expressed in the Henley clauses.

The number of professionals involved was actually small but they occupied a key place in the game's competitive structure and they tended to be overshadowed in publicity by 'amateurs' whose probity was often doubtful.[81] Yet some observers at the turn of the century still claimed that cricket suffered least from the emergence of professionalism, with fewer 'tares among the good corn'.[82] If it did, it was not so much a question of limited numbers as of inherited patterns of deference within the organisation of teams. The professional cricketer could be subservient, usually a bowler for gentlemen batsmen, and a teacher of skills. Rather like a good butler or a regimental sergeant-major he trod a narrow line between the authority due to his experience and the fact that he was essentially a servant. And as with all servants his employers were quite clear that they knew what was best for him.

Lord Hawke, the organiser of many overseas tours, revealed only too clearly the patronising assumptions of most amateur cricketers when he wrote, 'When a professional gets £3,000 from a benefit, it is surely better that two-thirds should be invested for the recipient than that the whole should promptly be squandered to entertain friends.'[83] It would be a rarely fortunate professional who survived the game long enough to reach aged retainer status – most county managements were sharply instrumental in their employment patterns, leaving all but one of their staff to find their own way through the non-playing winter months.

Cricket was easily disguised as a game where individuals from different classes met on more or less equal terms, although the bowler/player distinction in many county teams effectively belied this. But the idea of a professional player actually demonstrating leadership seemed ludicrous:

> Amateurs always have made, and always will make, the best captains: and this is only natural. An educated mind, with the logical power of reasoning, will always treat every subject better than one comparatively untaught.[84]

The view expressed by A. G. Steel was reinforced by the Edward Lyttelton when he claimed that masters, not professionals, should teach cricket at (public) schools; otherwise:

> not only cricket, but many matters, some of them tinged with the associations of low life, will the boys look at through the professional's eyes and it seems undesirable that this functionary should be invested with an even larger influence than the possession of a peculiar gift, and of strong, though ill-balanced, opinions will inevitably secure for him.[85]

Heroes had to be pure: it is almost impossible to recover the reactions of professionals to the virtually automatic assumption that they were tainted with wickedness and incapable of mature decisions. Yet even Lyttelton had to recognise the dogged patience which the endless practice of his skills could give a bowler, 'so monotonous that no one who has not to live by it could endure it'.[86] More than any other, the cricket professional could be treated like a faithful carthorse lacking the chivalric breeding of his racing or hunting counterpart.

In general terms these would have been little different from any other later Victorian assumptions about the professional–amateur divide except, perhaps, that they were rather more kindly than most and there was a constant if artificial expectation of brotherhood rather than dependence. There were occasional eccentrics who moved at different stages of their career, often with overt support, between amateur and professional status in the sport. Richard Daft, an early amateur, played as a professional because he could not afford to do so otherwise, then returned as an amateur to the Nottingham Commercial club.[87] The later nineteenth century compounded this problem by producing a new brand of amateur whose marginal personal fortunes did not allow them to meet the costs of playing. Proposals that they should be salaried (note the acute difference from the waged professional) so that their cricketing skills could be developed were rejected by the MCC and county cricket committees made up of the wealthy.[88] What happened instead was a shamateurism which came only occasionally into the open. Despite naive claims that these new players received only expenses, it often became clear that the level of those far exceeded what was paid to professionals. When the *Field* pointed this out, *Truth* joined in on the grounds that 'it is the country gentleman's newspaper, so it ought to know'.[89] In the 1880s Northampton County Cricket Club paid Lowe, its leading professional bowler, £84 per annum, far less than many amateurs would receive in expenses that were rarely published in the accounts, and whose payments in certain cases revealed ambiguity that was not resolved before the First World War.[90]

The debate reached one peak in 1896 when five professionals threatened to strike on the eve of the Test match with the Australians at the Oval. Four of the players were from the Surrey club itself and had been chosen to play in the national team for an extra fee of £10 each, effectively a month's wages.[91] It became an issue when they realised that the level of expenses being paid to the team's key 'amateur', W. G. Grace, would far exceed their pay. Grace, whose personal unpleasantness has become clearer to a generation of historians less fuddled by earlier cricket hagiographies and the dissimulation of his own published reminiscences, was the outstanding example of a shamateur whose claims to personal probity were never effectively tested by a cricketing oligarchy which connived at his appearances and met his heavy financial demands for them. Whenever he played for Gloucestershire he was provided with a locum for his medical practice by the club. In 1879 the MCC opened a testimonial fund to buy him that practice and raised £1,458: the decision to call it a 'testimonial' rather than a 'benefit', such as an overtly professional player would have received, allowed the illusion of his being unpaid to remain, and Grace could be portrayed as an amateur hero for a whole generation which rarely wanted to see the other side. In his own writings he actually decried the professionalisation of the game, the slow decline of 'social cricket' represented by wandering players like I Zingari, and the regional division which gate-money league matches brought to the north.[92]

The 1896 threat of a strike was not the first in English cricket. Eric Midwinter has drawn attention to the 1881 'Nottinghamshire schism' when seven of the county's players struck for improved contracts, only to be dropped wholesale.[93] The Surrey club threatened to act similarly, because of 'the lack of gratitude shown by the professionals, towards some of whom they have behaved with lavish generosity'.[94] A reaction like this allowed charges of mercenary attitudes to be made whilst Grace's essential duplicity was glossed over. The professionals gave in, yet even *The Times* acknowledged the justice of their case when 46,000 people paid to watch the match. 'The Social Question' appeared in 'that home of harmony', cricket, and was bundled unceremoniously away, although wages at future Test matches were increased noticeably.[95] Grace slid out of it with loud protestations against 'initiating statements of an absolutely false character', continuing to demand and receive very large expenses for his appearances. To mention money in public, he maintained, did not befit a gentleman.[96] The irony was not lost on many observers, but it was some time before the deliberate naming of individual error quite common in other games was allowed to be applied to prominent cricketing shamateurs.

There was almost a sense of sacred space about the sport which fostered allusion to potential evil by the most roundabout of routes rather than directly. Grace's heir as an unlikely model of purity was C. B. Fry. Clive Ellis's biography of the latter has made the point that this singular pan-athlete was imprisoned into an apparent amateurism by his own social category. His cricket was paid for initially by his teaching and writing about it – effectively he was only one of a number of members of a sporting salariat, the authors and schoolmasters of the years around 1900 who could be given ample leave to play by extremely sympathetic employers. Fry received an £800 retainer for writing for Newnes, and he married Charles Hoare's cast-off mistress for a cash settlement which allowed him to give up teaching. He was resented by Sussex professionals for hogging the limelight and for receiving 'star' treatment, which did not make for good team relations. He was a good player and a great model for performance but, like Grace, Fry's attraction lay therein and not in his contributions as an amateur to good team management or *esprit de corps*. Although he became England's captain in 1912, he hardly fulfilled Lyttelton's assumption about an amateur in that role, and there were repeated criticisms of fund-raising suggestions on the ground that they would only be paying for his holidays in Australia.[97]

Yet the shamateur question occupied far less space in discussions of cricket's purity than it did in athletics. The issue always hovered more clearly about the place of full-blown professionals themselves and whether their growing number would corrupt the game and, therefore, England beyond redemption. Wray Vamplew has shown that a growing concern about employing professionals, and raising the necessary gate money to pay for them, did little to change performance ratings among county clubs increasingly concerned with their annual records.[98] Club oligarchies on the whole continued to move steadily towards a professionalised game whilst a host of sybils contributed prophecies of doom. If clubs could no longer be amateur, it could be claimed, then a leaven of amateurs should remain in each team, to provide moral and tactical leadership.[99] As with the army, there could still be an officer class, to maintain an English tone whilst the troops fought.

When Middlesex, Lancashire and Surrey took to employing Edwardian colonials as professionals *Truth* saw a real risk of decay but there were few suggestions as to how to stop the decline in the flow of true amateurs.[100] With unconscious irony it was Fry himself who referred to 'The Humbug of County Cricket', claiming that it was essentially professional by 1910, with the members of clubs being reduced to season ticket holders, spectators rather than players. Only MCC, Oxford and Cambridge could claim to be amateur.[101] But the amateur revival he hoped for would, had it really happened, have barred men like him from playing. His views on this became more rambling and confused as he aged, deploring the county championships which were the outcome of a rivalry he had done so much to foster.

Sir Home Gordon felt that first-class cricket was little more than a professional ladder, but effectively what was happening was an increasingly open showing of the payments to 'gentlemen' players that Grace and Fry had covered over in their own careers.[102] Lord Hawke decried this 'cancerous growth' but cricket was no longer just a game to be played for personal pleasure; the heavy moral loading placed on it in the 1880s and 1890s had given it a significance for spectators that was not foreseen then, and in the tension between purity and performance it was the latter which won.[103]

We have already noted the ambiguity over participant status when professionals in one sport tried to take up another for recreation, not least because they were frequently deemed to be incapable of keeping their own working attitudes from their play. In a wider sense this debate shadowed general middle-class fears about the extent to which any sport was suffering from the general importation into it of business practices. The playing professional suffered in this respect because he was much more identifiable as the symbol of a general malaise than the more anonymous run of golfing or cricketing stockbrokers. So quite small and apparently ludicrous incidents were used to focus tensions which reflected problems of far greater magnitude. In 1895 the Quaife brothers, well established professional cricketers for Warwickshire, applied for membership of the Birmingham Oriental Hockey Club as amateurs 'in the strictest sense of the word'. After a heated debate which spilled over into the press of other cities they were allowed in by a tiny majority. The absolute irony lay in the fact that the Oriental Club had asked W. G. Grace for an opinion on their suitability as amateurs: 'he sent an evasive letter'.[104]

Grace interfered as a high-handed amateur in another boom sport, bowls, until he was effectively elbowed out by its oligarchy. This booming game always recognised a clear amateur–professional divide, between crown and lawn, essentially between north and south. Because of the scale of the northern game and its strong working-class associations it furnishes one of the comparatively few examples where it is possible to get some idea of how professionals regarded amateurs rather than the other way about.

With the level of prizes available at major tournaments such as Blackpool, although they were open to amateurs as well as professionals, it was generally reckoned that no amateur could hope to win or even to afford practice time. Professionals who could make up to £800 a year disliked amateur participation intensely: amateurs slowed up the game, got in the way and were just not up to the highest standards of exhibition play.[105] Although many northern amateurs turned temporary professional for the Blackpool tournaments they were weeded out not on grounds of ambiguity but because of their general incompetence.[106] Although there were amateur clubs in northern middle-class suburbs, this particular ethical divide acquired a much greater regional emphasis than most, and many southerners realised only too clearly that the exclusion of professionals was a recognition of their own lower standards of play: 'An expert like this . . . introduced into a high-class suburban bowling club would be like a hawk set down in the midst of a family of house sparrows.'[107]

It was not quite so simple, however, and the crown green game divided along amateur/professional lines. A professional association was formed in 1905 and the British Crown Green County Amateur Association, the 'Jockey Club' of the game, in 1907.[108] The English Bowling Association, for the lawn game, remained strictly amateur but with very hazy definitions which repeated attempts to tighten did little to change, and it was claimed to have no northern members.[109] Northern bowls hovered much more ambivalently around class boundaries than did its southern neighbour and in many senses local divisions in industrial towns were clearer than the regional ones: 'The strict amateur there is of the middle class – i.e. the tradesman, clerk or publican predominating: the professional and semi-professional is the collier, the factory hand and other heavy-handed sons of toil.'[110]

To be amateur in this context was to be far closer to a self-ascribed sense of 'respectability' than that shown by frightened southern sparrows. The English Bowling Association from 1912 included a rule to combat professionalism but revealed the essential southern compromise that made for agonised continuity in ethical dilemmas: 'Makers of bowls and other articles used in the game, contractors of greens, and greenkeepers, or groundsmen, shall not be deemed professional on account of their calling.'[111] It was wrong to play for money but not to make money by making play possible.

This delicately drawn ethical line which was far from straight wandered most in those games which were almost exclusively middle-class in their following. Although even these difficulties appeared there, much less scope was available for wholesale class-based ascriptions of moral weakness, and the issues centred on the feeling that the side was being let down from within rather than attacked from without. Social tone was at greatest risk from those whose interest in the business of sport overlapped with their playing it, so what was at stake was the rectitude of the middle classes themselves.

It came into the open during a crisis fostered by the Edwardian revival in the popularity of lawn tennis. There was consistent harping in the sporting press on pot hunting and shamateurism, with a feeling that the great tournament round which peaked at Eastbourne and Wimbledon was actually attracting 'manufacturers' players', although these were not named. A Portuguese tour in 1901 by three women and four men players was attacked by *Truth* as little more than a 'cadging system': the complaint was never against honest professionalism but against paid players sheltering under an amateur umbrella.[112]

The ambivalence remained, but the veil of reticence was cut sharply in 1905 after the AELTC finals at Wimbledon. One of the referees, a Mr Eveleigh, resigned because he would not countenance the use of technically illegal balls at which the club generally connived. The balls were produced by Slazenger's, who had achieved a monopoly in the supply by donating all the balls used in the championship. What might normally have been covered up became public knowledge because the referee was a journalist and he leaked to friends in the sporting press the fact that he had been offered, as normal practice, an envelope containing £100 with a note from Slazenger's asking him to accept the gift. The issue was exacerbated because the AELTC's paid secretary, Archdale Palmer, was also Slazenger's manager.

Fry's, ironically, led a major attack on 'the thraldom of trade influence' both at Wimbledon and at Queen's. The MCC, it argued, would never have descended to finding its secretary in a City warehouse, and Palmer must have connived at the deliberate supply of wrongly sized balls.[113] There was a strand of personal animosity in the debates which followed but the powerful hold that Slazenger's had acquired on the game became even clearer when it became known that the firm also underwrote the Lawn Tennis Association's journal, which had been a financial failure before it intervened.[114] Yet it was the LTA which led the attack on Palmer. *Truth*, usually strong in its attacks on corruption, proved singularly ambivalent on this issue when it asked how else the facilities at Wimbledon could have reached such a high standard without trade help.[115] It also suggested that the ousted referee should not have gone to the press, a remarkable claim in view of its own consistent practice in seeking out scandal.[116] At stake, *inter alia*, was a continuing battle for domination of the game between Wimbledon and the LTA, and *Truth* repeatedly accused the latter of naivety and compromise when it suited it.[117]

The row staggered on for well over a year until in December 1906 the AELTC decided to pay for balls in future, using an open system of tender. 'The Smiths of Surbiton trimphed over the Palmers of

Wimbledon,' *Truth* said.[118] It was essentially a piece of London suburban in-fighting but it occurred at a time when probity in sport was being linked increasingly with arguments over national decline. Slazenger's, it was argued as the row petered out, had only done what its rival company Ayres had before it and was continuing to do in Bournemouth and Eastbourne.[119] But Palmer had to resign from the AELTC, although he could still play as an amateur, much to the disgust of the Surbiton amateur elite: 'They were fearfully shocked at the immorality of Wimbledon having a tradesman secretary of the club. It was naturally so upsetting to their sensitive suburban sensibilities that I quite sympathise with them'.[120]

Truth turned its attention to other, more sharply defined, questions of amateur ethics, but others saw the issue as symbolic of English decay. In *Wake up, England* P. A. Vaile claimed that the best lawn tennis players 'will go down to posterity as little, if anything, above tradesmen's touts'.[121]

Golf professionals played a more distinctive role and one which slowly changed from instruction to competition, although the former remained the experience of most. The professional golfer enjoyed something of the ambiguous position of his cricketing equivalent, 'as pleasant a life as can be spent by a man of that class, and . . . by no means the least profitable'.[122] The difference was in scale because of the near-universal employment after the earliest years of the boom of at least one professional by most golf clubs. The majority of these, often Scottish emigrants, could be treated with the condescension due to their class and race but this became more difficult even if they did not fulfil the claim of a 1913 investigation that 'The professional golfer of today is a man of good class and education who has mastered not only the practice but the theory of the game, and has a thorough knowledge of club-making and business generally.'[123] Professionals played amateurs regularly – it was essential for instruction, practice and to make up a pair or foursome when occasion demanded. But golf was never able to separate itself from many of the assumptions surrounding other sports even when it could be claimed that the professional might have greater sporting integrity than many amateurs.

The creation of a national championship, the British Open, in 1860 did not cause immediate problems. Instead it was played steadily for over twenty years, won repeatedly by Scottish professionals, until some separating-out occurred. Even when the English Amateur Championship was inaugurated at Hoylake in 1884/85 the Open remained just that, a place where amateur and professional could compete together. But it was 1890 before John Ball won the Open, both the first Englishman and the first amateur to do so. The creation of an English Amateur Championship was both a recognition of the greater skill of the best professionals, even though there had not by then emerged the subsequent distinction between tournament and club professionals, and golf's own reaction to the increasing ethical tensions of the 1880s. Yet the shadow of the trophy hunter and the shamateur hung over the game and there was a considerable ambivalence to professionals *per se*, particularly when a strike was threatened in 1899 if the Open's first prize money was not increased: despite splits over this among the professionals themselves, it was, to £50.[124] At that point money had been a significant issue only since a prize fund had been established in 1893 but it had intervened earlier. When the Amateur was established at Hoylake there was no golfing definition either of a professional or of an amateur, and there was a vague attempt to draw on the experience of other sports. In the event one entry, Douglas Rolland, was barred because he had once won a small money prize when playing against a professional. Horace Hutchinson resigned from the organising committee in protest.[125]

The Royal and Ancient formulated a singularly vague amateur definition in 1886 which caused problems for the next quarter-century. With its parallel competitive structure golf actually managed to hold this tension rather better than many sports but the wholesale business expansion of Edwardian England brought it into the open. Some club members had taken to buying balls wholesale and selling them to their fellows at prices which undercut the club professionals' small shops. This opened up a debate both on the issue of professionals' incomes depending on their selling abilities but also as to whether members who did this were shamateurs.[126]

It deepened when the widespread course redesign of the post-Haskell years brought large fees to golf architects. The question was raised as to whether golfing journalists and architects could really be regarded as *bona fide* amateurs.[127] Some pressure came from professionals who felt they were being undersold. The response was often similar to that of Alfred Lyttelton on cricket, that only the educated amateur had the tactical skill for a sufficient overview in course design. Responses that a real amateur would supervise professionals and not take the customary £20 fee were superciliously dismissed. H. S. Colt, widely regarded as the prime shamateur in this, rejoiced in the ambiguity of the Royal and Ancient's 1886 ruling. Whilst he happily pointed out that he would be regarded as a professional in some US clubs, he was fully prepared to be paid for 'perfectly clean, straightforward work' and to go on playing as an amateur.[128] Despite protests from the Professional Golfers' Association, formed in 1901, *Golf Illustrated* supported Colt on the grounds that 'The social distinctions have nothing to do with the amateur question, and they are already provided for by the ballot boxes of clubs.'[129] The argument left the professionals able to appear as the embodiment of purity.

Eventually the 1886 definition's inadequacies were recognised and effectively taken out of the hands of the Royal and Ancient. In June 1911 the Associated Golf Clubs, who dominated both the Open and Amateur championships, since they provided the venues, met at Prestwick and provided a new amateur definition. Unlike others it did allow for earlier corruption: up to the age of sixteen one could be paid for work or competition in the game itself. The young caddy could become an adult amateur. But it also banned the shamateur who received 'directly or indirectly from the promoters of any match or tournament any consideration for playing in such match or tournament'.[130] Defined it may have been, but the sporting press suggested that the rule had few teeth and debate continued.[131]

It was not in regulation alone that the social tensions of the ethical divide became apparent in golf. Despite a number of amateur victories in the Open there was some feeling that it should be recognised as what it was, a primarily professional competition, so that amateurs should be barred from it in the interests of their own purity. It was becoming increasingly difficult to demand from the top playing professionals the subservience their apparent status required, particularly where some had used the game as a clear avenue of personal social mobility. The secretary of Ashton on Mersey's club recognised this when he wrote, 'I think that if professionals were at their own clubs instead of being away most of the summer, it would be of decided benefit to the members of the clubs who engage them.'[132] Tournament play had, however, developed levels of investment which made this impossible, and a growing number of professionals, now men of middle-class tastes and income, used the fact to throw off what they regarded as the thraldom of petty local snobberies, so that one set of middle-class interests was used to offset the limitations imposed by another.

In 1912 Ben Sayers Junior resigned as the Royal Wimbledon's

professional to play professional golf full-time, on the grounds that his income would be far better.[133] The following year Abe Mitchell went the same way but published his reason in *Golf Monthly*. He had worked, when young, at the Cantelupe Club in Ashdown Forest, where 'My chief offence has been that I was born an artisan.' When he had played in the Amateur championship at Westward Ho! in 1912 he had felt the atmosphere charged with hostility, and he put his finger firmly on the main issue that the humbler amateur faced:

> Golf is the game of the classes in England, and my firm conviction is that the artisan golfer is unwanted in amateur circles, and that English amateurs consider that the artisan golfer's place is in the professional ranks.[134]

Mitchell claimed to be the victim of a general prejudice, but this was queried by some writers on northern golf because of 'the democratic opinions held by Yorkshire amateurs'. But it was really in the sense that service officers were occasionally 'democratic': 'nothing better can be seen than the sight of an Amateur, defeated badly, waiting upon his Professional opponent at lunch'.[135] The man who made this claim, Harry Fulford, was rather unusual among Edwardian golfers: intended as a youth for the Wesleyan ministry, he had instead become a golfing professional at Winchester, moving then to Wimbledon and Mid-Surrey, taking time off to study Egyptology before becoming a Bradford professional.[136]

For most of his kind the attempt to pretend that golf, like cricket, could exclude automatic distinction on the course had never really been effective. Like cricket it had to contain the professional within it to make serious play possible, but the prejudices of its participants and the divide within the middle classes over investment in the game restricted any significant *rapprochement*.

Schisms

The ambivalence over contamination in so many of the new pastimes of the middle classes has been less widely studied than more obvious difficulties in sports with a wider following. In the varieties of football, the amateur–professional divide has usually been shown as a mirror of that between middle and working classes. In terms of readiness to play it was often just that, but it was complicated further by an intra-middle-class debate on the extent to which play itself was affected by financial considerations. It is only too evident that the emergence of Rugby League and mass soccer could not have occurred without substantial entrepreneurial involvement – Korr has demonstrated the complexity of this for West Ham.[137] There was a substantial body of middle-class opinion which regarded the whole ethical debate in football as utterly misplaced, another group was quite happy to see professional and amateur exist in parallel but not in direct contact, and there were the powerful and oft-repeated voices of those who deplored the entire impact of professionalism.

For rugby this has been well rehearsed by Dunning and Sheard and, in its Welsh setting, by Smith and Williams. They have identified an overlap of regional and ethical schisms developing rapidly through the 1890s but also with distinct contrasts in the treatment of Rugby Union as a sport linked with national identity. Most Welshmen would have agreed with the claim of W. J. Lias in 1897 that the Rugby Union was suicidally isolated, looking after 'a few schools, the universities, and perhaps a dozen London clubs'.[138] Bodies like the Hull and District Rugby Football Union tried hard through the 1890s to hold off the illegality of professionalism, among whose qualifications they included anyone who transferred clubs annually.[139] The question of recompensing players for 'broken time', effectively paying wages for the game, led to the emergence of the essentially northern Rugby League, where affiliated clubs spent much time trying to poach players wholesale, particularly from South Wales.[140]

In many senses amateurism emerged, as Dunning and Sheard have claimed, as an attitude of purity against sin rather than as something resisting its own debasement: they also saw it as a social expression of self-indulgence, the exhibition through play of economic independence of the consequences of indulging in sport.[141] Whether Bale and others are justified in claiming that it was a north–south rather than an inter-class division is doubtful, if only because their case rests on the assumption that northern sporting society was more democratic, more open.[142] One is left wondering why sport alone of all northern social activities should have been isolated from the realities of stratification and snobbery in daily intercourse. A few perceptive, and usually reviled, commentators saw some of the ironies involved when it was possible for Rugby Unionists to decry the professional players' being found jobs in local industries whilst a Blue was one sure avenue to employment as a public school master. *Truth* was so alarmed by these 'illogical ... impertinent ... irrelevant ...

insolent' claims that it demanded 'a class definition' similar to that of the ARA.[143]

It was never able to get that but it went after the next best thing when the Association game found itself similarly split. Tony Mason has rightly pointed out that soccer's divisions were never simply on class lines, not least because of the extraordinary amount of middle-class investment in the game.[144] Yet as professionalism grew there appeared a deep schism in the ranks of players which in many ways is more important than the usually assumed class division between rugby and soccer. Occasionally there appear hints of other than ethical reasons for a broad class divide in Association Football: when a Corinthian (strictly amateur) footballer found himself on Millwall Athletic's ground on the Isle of Dogs he complained bitterly because, if he fell on the pitch, 'the smell wouldn't come off for weeks'.[145] The rarely articulated sub-agenda of sheer physical distaste for the working classes was a constant underpinning of many amateur attitudes well outside the Gentleman–Player divide at Lord's. The healthy sweat of a male middle-class body after a good game was very different in the context of late Victorian football from that of working-class men whose houses simply lacked baths.

Mason has reminded us that there was a complex interplay of notions about master–servant relationships in the debates over professionalism and amateur purity, exacerbated by sporting investment patterns from the 1880s. When the Football Association recognised professional players in July 1885 after an unsuccessful series of attempts to ban them it did not solve the problem. Instead it opened up a new level of debate in which amateurs were able to mount a moral high ground for several decades. It was headed symbolically by the Corinthian Football Club, founded in 1882 among ex-public school and university men to play touring friendly matches. It was quite happy to compete against professionals for some time, even if it was unable to match the rising standards of paid players. 'Corinthianism' became an amateur watchword, but it was one which increasingly meant fun rather than outstanding performance, pleasure rather than business. The high moral seriousness so often claimed for the amateur ethic was paradoxically used to support pleasure in an almost Manichaean assumption about the inevitable fallen state of the ordinary world of the mass game.[146]

The creeping threat of professionalism opened up regional debates again: it seemed to be spreading slowly from Lancashire and the north-east through the later 1880s and the 1890s. Despite the presence of professional clubs in London many southern players felt themselves to be encircled in a *laager* of purity. Yet it should not be seen entirely as a march of locusts – as Alan Metcalfe has pointed out, there were many in the north-east of England who saw the whole amateur ethos in negative terms, as 'a value system corrosive of traditional mining values'.[147] When Girouard portrayed the amateur sporting ethos in knightly terms he reiterated the essential isolation of its courtliness from the darker world which made its survival possible.[148]

Football's problem, unlike the other games we have examined, was not shamateurism by the 1890s but rather a full-blown divide which could be measured in incentives, popularity and performance. In the Badminton *Athletics and Football* (1889) Montague Shearman saw a regional as well as ethical split as inevitable, with no need to legislate for it.[149] The problem was that the amateur minority wanted protective legislation and, in particular, sharper regulation of referees' decisions and rules such as the offside rule which they argued made for aggressive and unfair play solely to secure goals. In some senses it was yet again an argument between style and performance. This worried general social observers like T. H. Escott, 'in view of the fashionable brutality not only of the players but the spectators', and Caspar Whitney: 'clubs of all sorts and kinds are constantly springing into existence, each a breeding den of strife, and every one trying, by bribery and by every other foul means, to outdo the other'.[150]

What was worse, for some, was that football was being 'democratised': it was the replacement of an ethical elite by a business one which upset them, not least because it had acquired virtual control of the Football Association.[151] This body acquired a very different role in its game from the parallel Royal and Ancient or MCC, let alone the lumbering AAA, if only because of the level of investment in large urban club facilities. One 1900 estimate put the number of professional players in the FA at around 6,000, whilst the amateurs numbered 250,000, but it was clearly the employers of the former who dominated the body. This was no longer the 'country house party' world of the Corinthians.[152]

The public school and university part of the game, with its post-education followers, fought back. H. H. Almond, the Loretto reformer of Mangan's pantheon of schoolmaster heroes, claimed in the *Nineteenth Century* in 1893 that football was a 'moral agent', but only if it remained amateur, although he begrudgingly allowed its possible value in keeping the urban working classes out of public houses on Saturday afternoons.[153] The following year there appeared demands for an amateur secession from the FA, on the grounds that 'there seems too much probability of these catechumens experiencing the customary fate of those who touch pitch'.[154]

This protest rumbled on until 1906, when an acute division opened up very rapidly. *Truth* began a series of attacks upon the leaders of the FA, claiming that they were seeking to drive amateurs out, that its president, Lord Kinnaird, was creating a Football Association Ltd.[155] An Amateur Football Defence Association emerged, forming the nucleus of an eventual break-away. John Lewis, a member of the FA council and vice-president of the Football League, founded in 1888, rejoined that it was a matter of standards which amateurs seemed unwilling to meet; it was not just a matter of play but of punctuality, of turning up on time or at all.[156] For him 'it was a revolt of the provinces and the transfer of power to the clubs outside the charmed circle', and professionals now expected higher standards of accommodation than most amateurs were prepared to provide.

The professional camp had all the values of the work ethic at its disposal; the amateurs turned it into a matter of honour, but one which preferred an unspoken code of conduct rather than the tighter rules the FA was demanding. In November 1906 the FA told the Amateur Defence League to disband. It did not, and, despite some misgivings, re-emerged in July 1907 as the Amateur Football Association. C. B. Fry accounted for the schism by claiming that 'sentiment counts for much in sport'.[157] For the AFA's leaders it was a natural reaction against the attempt of a northern-led FA to impose its immoral will upon southerners. It claimed 40,000 possible members, aimed for a county network on the lines of other amateur sports and sought to save sport as sport rather than business.[158] It found support from a new Odhams periodical, *Amateur Sports Illustrated*, which refused to report professional games and claimed that Lord Kinnaird of the FA, an old Etonian, had betrayed his class.[159]

The AFA had to decide what an amateur actually was. It deliberately avoided a class-based definition, since it hoped, rather vainly, to reach a working-class following. Instead it banned direct or indirect payment for play but did allow hotel and travelling expenses, for which receipts had to be produced. And only all-amateur clubs could affiliate.[160] Around the AFA grew another magazine, *Amateur*

Football, devoted entirely to the AFA, and it pointed to the wide support it drew from all classes, despite the weight of Old Etonians, including its secretary in its founding. It drew on the whole gamut of southern amateurism, the middle-class game represented by bodies like the Crouch End Vampires, but it trumpeted loudly the affiliation of 'working lads' when they came, as they did with the Rochester Free Church League.[161] By 1909 it had 500 affiliated clubs, representing 20,000 players – still only half its 1907 target.[162] In fact most of these were affiliated through country associations rather than direct, since it eschewed the FA's centralisation. And they were southern. By 1913 Nottinghamshire was the farthest north it could reach.[163] Many amateurs, or those in mixed clubs, especially farther north, stayed with the FA, and the latter body, through its representation on international bodies such as FIFA, was able to keep the AFA out of the symbolic peak of amateur appearance and performance, the 1908 and 1912 Olympics.[164]

The game remained split between amateur and amateur as well as between amateur and professional.

The protective walls stopped effectively at the Trent; north of them as well as outside them professional and amateur mingling went on as before. yet the A FA prompted hopes of a pale following when its values were applied to a new sport. Aeroplane racing was in its infancy by 1910 but already the manufacturers' shadow loomed, the airborne shamateur was appearing, and the AFA seemed to offer a model of wholeness and safety.[165] It was a forlorn hope, and the rate of technological advance as well as of business growth stopped aviation sport from retreating into the ethical sterility which so severely limited significant developments in those sports rigidified by clutching at an elusive purity.

Notes

1 The Bible (Revised Standard Version), Ephesians, chapter 5, verse 8.
2 *Times*, 1 January 1912.
3 Dunning and Sheard, *Barbarians*, 130.
4 *Baily's Magazine*, July 1907, 22.
5 Shearman, *Athletics*, 236.
6 B. J. Bledstein, *The Culture of Professionalism* (New York, 1976), 31.
7 *Field*, 28 June 1902.
8 *Baily's Magazine*, October 1903, 250–1.
9 *The Times*, 6 June 1912.
10 T. Claye Shaw, *Baily's Magazine*, September 1912, 67 ff.

11 *Baily's Magazine*, 1876, 274 ff.
12 *Hull and East Riding Athlete*, 19 March 1890.
13 C. Whitney, *Sporting Pilgrimage*, 14.
14 F. G. Aflalo (ed.), *Fifty Leaders of British Sport* (1904), 27.
15 Fagan *et al.*, *Football, Hockey and Lacrosse*, vii.
16 R. B. Marston, 'Angling', in Sportsman, *British Sports and Sportsmen*, 102.
17 T. A. Cook, *The Olympic Games* (1908), 175 ff.
18 *Baily's Magazine* (1908), 219.
19 *Croquet Annual* (1901–02), 83; Smith and Robinson, *Hockey*, 96.
20 *Physical Education*, March 1909.
21 C. B. Fry's *Magazine*, 7(1907), 490.
22 *Illustrated Bristol News*, July 1961, 34–5; the general issue is covered in E. Halliday, 'Of pride and prejudice: the amateur question in English nineteenth-century rowing', *International Journal of the History of Sport*, 4(1987), 39 ff.
23 Macfarlane-Grieve, *Durham Rowing*, 12.
24 Lehmann *et al.*, *Rowing*, 166.
25 Vance, *Sinews*, 138.
26 Crossland, *Pleasure and Leisure Boating*, 69.
27 Lehmann *et al.*, *Complete Oarsman*, 248 ff.; Whitney, *Sporting Pilgrimage*, 162–3.
28 *Ibid.*
29 Whitney, *Sporting Pilgrimage*, 166.
30 Lehmann *et al.*, *Complete Oarsman*, 346.
31 *Dickens's Dictionary of the Thames* (1894).
32 *Frederick James Furnivall*, lxxvii ff.
33 *Colebrooke Rowing Club Magazine*, 2(1891).
34 *Cambridge Review*, 5 March 1891.
35 Cleaver, *Rowing*, 122 ff., 140.
36 *Ibid.*
37 Lehmann *et al.*, *Rowing*, 325 ff.
38 *Truth*, 29 May 1907.
39 Cleaver, *Rowing*, 48.
40 Macfarlane-Grieve, *Durham Rowing*, 94.
41 Lehmann *et al.*, *Rowing*, 256.
42 *Truth*, 26 December 1906.
43 Dodd, *Henley*, 109.
44 *Yachting Monthly*, 2(1906–07), 217.
45 Shearman, *Athletics and Football*, 40–1.
46 Bale, *Sport and Place*, 111.
47 Shearman, *Athletics and Football*, 131–2.
48 Shearman, *Athletics and Football*, 271.
49 Shearman, *Athletics and Football*, 225.
50 Shearman, *Athletics and Football*, 227.
51 W. Rye, 'Paper-chasing and cross-country running', in Shearman, *Athletics and Football*, 376.
52 *Sporting Mirror*, 2(1882), 62–5.
53 *Horse and Hound*, 29 March 1884, 14.
54 *Amateur Sport* (Bristol), 19 June 1889.
55 Shearman, *Athletics and Football*, 212.

56 *Hull and East Riding Athlete*, 5 February, 19 March, 29 October 1890.
57 Conway, 'Cross-country running', 571.
58 Graham, *Athletics*, 135–6.
59 Graham, *Athletics*, 113, 115.
60 L., 'Are our athletes pothunters?', *Baily's Magazine*, May 1908, 395.
61 *Truth*, 26 December 1901.
62 *Truth*, 25 January 1906.
63 *Baily's Magazine*, August 1907, 120.
64 *Baily's Magazine*, May 1907, 362 ff.
65 Albemarle and Hillier, *Cycling*, 234.
66 *Sporting Mirror*, 2 (1881), 178.
67 *Nineteenth Century*, January 1885, 101.
68 H. H. Griffin, 'Cycling under three heads', *Baily's Magazine*, June 1892, 393 ff.
69 *Baily's Magazine*, May 1894, 325 ff.; Whitney, *Sporting Pilgrimage*, 310 ff.
70 *CTC Monthly Gazette*, November 1896.
71 *Sportfolio* (1896), No. 14, No. 88.
72 *Fitzgibbon's Sporting Almanac, 1900*, 119.
73 *Times*, 11 January 1908.
74 Moxham, *Fifty Years*, 77.
75 Bale, *Sport and Place*, 140.
76 Amateur Swimming Association, *Handbook* (1899), 27.
77 *Truth*, 6 February 1902.
78 *Truth*, 19, 26 October 1905.
79 Shipley, 'Boxing'.
80 J. G. B. Lynch, 'Amateur Boxing', *Baily's Magazine*, XCI (1909), 219 ff.
81 A. Briggs, 'The view from Badminton', in Briggs (ed.), *Essays in the History of Publishing . . . Longmans, 1724–1974* (1974), 196–7.
82 N. L. Jackson, 'Professionalism and sport', *Fortnightly Review*, LXVII (1900), 154.
83 Aflalo, *Fifty Leaders*, 75.
84 Steel and Lyttelton, *Cricket*, 192.
85 E. Lyttelton,' Cricket', in E. Bell (ed.), *Handbook of Athletic Sports*, I (1890), 2.
86 Lyttelton, 'Cricket', 29.
87 F.G., 'Greensward sermons I, The amateur cricketer', *Baily's Magazine*, May 1894, 297, 298.
88 F.G., 'Amateur cricketer', 296.
89 *Truth*, 6 November 1902.
90 Northampton Reference Library, Northamptonshire County Cricket Club, Annual Report, 1886.
91 *Sheffield Daily Telegraph*, 8 August 1896.
92 W. G. Grace, *Cricket*, 36.
93 Midwinter, *W. G. Grace*, 82, 129 ff.
94 *The Times*, 11 August 1896.
95 *The Times*, 3 September 1896.
96 W. G., *Cricketing Reminiscences* (1899), 1980 edition, 248–9, 260–1.
97 C. Ellis, *C. B.: the Life of Charles Burgess Fry* (1984), *passim*.
98 W. Vamplew, 'Profit or utility maximisation? An analysis of English county cricket before 1914', in Vamplew (ed.), *The Economic History*

of *Leisure: Papers Presented at the Eighth International Economic History Congress, Budapest, 1982*, 38 ff.
99 Spartan, 'The decadence of sport', 201.
100 *Truth*, 12 February 1908.
101 C. B. Fry, 'The humbug of county cricket', *C. B. Fry's Magazine*, 13 (1910), 289 ff.; 16 (1912), 123, 321, 460.
102 H. Gordon, 'Youth in cricket', *Fortnightly Review*, LXXXVII (1910), 980.
103 Club Cricketers' Charity Fund, *Official Handbook* (1913), 7, 15.
104 *Sheffield Telegraph*, 30 November 1895.
105 Burrows, *Bowls*, 48 ff.
106 *C. B. Fry's Magazine*, 5 (1906), 230.
107 *Bowling*, January 1910.
108 Burrows, *Bowls*, 35 ff.
109 *Bowling*, April 1908.
110 *Bowling*, June 1910.
111 English Bowling Association, *Yearbook* (1912), rule XI.
112 *Truth*, 12 December 1901.
113 *C. B. Fry's Magazine*, 7 (1907), 324 ff.
114 *C. B. Fry's Magazine*, 5 (1906), 79.
115 *Truth*, 30 November, 14, 21 December 1905, 15 February 1906.
116 *Truth*, 22 February 1906.
117 *Truth*, 7, 21 November 1906.
118 *Truth*, 26 December 1906.
119 *Truth*, 3 July 1907.
120 *Truth*, 3 December 1907, 30 January 1908.
121 P. A. Vaile, *Wake up, England* (1907), 99.
122 R. H. Lyttelton, *Outdoor Games – Cricket and Golf* (1901), 205.
123 Agenda Club, *The Rough and the Fairway* (1913), 37.
124 *Guinness Book of Golf Facts and Feats* (1982), 50 ff.
125 H. G. Hutchinson, *Fifty Years of Golf* (1919), 78.
126 *Golf Illustrated*, 27 November, 4 December 1908; *The Times*, 22 December 1908.
127 *Golf Illustrated*, 1 January 1909.
128 *Golf Illustrated*, 15 January 1909.
129 *The Times*, 19 January, 1 March, 2 April 1909; *Golf Illustrated*, 22 January 1909.
130 *The Times*, 1 January 1911.
131 *C. B. Fry's Magazine*, 16 (1912), 30.
132 *Baily's Magazine*, December 1910, 442.
133 *Golf Monthly*, November 1912, 702.
134 *Golf Monthly*, October 1913, 614.
135 Stainton, *Golf Courses of Yorkshire*, 40–1.
136 Stainton, *Golf Courses of Yorkshire*, 46.
137 C. Korr, *West Ham United: the Making of a Football Club* (1986).
138 W. J. Lias, 'The future of rugby football', *Badminton Magazine*, V (1897), 604 ff.
139 Hull and District Rugby Football Union, *Official Guide* (1895–96), 49.
140 E. M. Sigsworth,' Leeds and its industrial growth', *Leeds Journal*, May 1957, 149–50.
141 Dunning and Sheard, *Barbarians*, 147 ff.

142 Bale, *Sport and Place*, 55 ff.
143 *Truth*, 10 June 1908.
144 Mason, *Association Football* 69 ff., 240–1.
145 S. Inglis, *The Football Grounds of England and Wales* (1983), 238.
146 Mason, *Association Football*, 216.
147 A. Metcalfe, 'Organised sport in the mining communities of south Northumberland, 1800–89', *Victorian Studies*, 25 (1982), 495.
148 Girouard, *Camelot*, 24.
149 Shearman, *Athletics and Football*, 364 ff.
150 Escott, *Social Transformations*, 416; Whitney, *Sporting Pilgrimage*, 210.
151 Jackson, 'Professionalism and sport', 157 ff.
152 C. B. Fry, 'The story of the Corinthians', *C. B. Fry's Magazine*, 11(1904), 271; Jackson, 'Professionalism and sport, 158.
153 H. H. Almond,' Football as a moral agent', *Nineteenth Century*, December 1893, 902 ff.
154 *Fortnightly Review*, LV(1894), 35.
155 *Truth*, 3 October 1906.
156 *C. B. Fry's Magazine*, 6(1906–07), 264 ff.
157 *C. B. Fry's Magazine*, 8 (1907–08), 188.
158 Amateur Football Association, *Annual* (1907–08).
159 *Amateur Sports Illustrated*, 26 December 1907.
160 AFA *Annual* (1907–08), 24.
161 *Amateur Football*, 31 October, 28 November 1907.
162 *C. B. Fry's Magazine*, 10(1908–09), 175 ff.
163 AFA, *Annual* (1913–14).
164 *C. B. Fry's Magazine*, 16(1912), 300.
165 R. P. Hearne, 'The future of aeroplane racing', *Badminton Magazine*, XXX(1910), 195 ff.

Chapter 7
Lesser breeds

The later Victorian sports boom was middle-class in much of its temperament and aggressively masculine in most of its organisation and expression. But ambivalence and uncertainty emerged when the new sportsmen had to deal with those who, albeit on the fringes of their activities, were essential for sport to function both instrumentally and ideologically. They showed particularly in the case of two groups, employees and women. Recent fashion in historical writing has demanded that the latter usually be treated as a separate entity, and some very good studies, notably those of Dyhouse and McCrone, have resulted.[1] I choose not to seek hermetic isolation for women here, however, because the arguments over inferior ability and status were closely related to the masculine middle-class perception of other dependent groups and their supposedly inferior intelligence.

Masters and servants

Professional sea fishermen were regarded as mere 'hands' who would always need a 'head' to direct them.[2] Nor could freshwater river-keepers be trusted to carry out their work unless they were watched constantly by the honorary secretaries of game-fishing syndicates.[3] Sport's employees were generally as depersonified as factory labour. The fact that most sports workers worked alone or in very small groups in face-to-face contact with their employers rarely lessened this, although it did foster some paternalism. This mixed the common responses to the 'servant problem' as it was increasingly conceived in Edwardian middle-class society and modes of charitable relief adopted from the rather more established patterns of the better-run landed estates.

The rapid growth in field sports after 1880 demanded specialist labour. By 1912 there were some 800 hunt servants around the country, over 450 of them working for foxhound subscription packs. The established ones were generally more fortunate than many similar employees, at least if they fell on hard times.[4] The Hunt Servants' Benefit Society had been established by a group of masters in 1872, its income derived largely from subscriptions contributed by its 'honorary members', some 1,800 by 1899. The beneficiaries were the 420 'ordinary' members; hunt servants who would receive a weekly allowance of up to 15s if sick and an annuity of the same amount per week if they retired over the age of sixty. Their widows would receive block payments. The approach of the hunt members who supported it was both paternalistic and unashamedly Darwinistic: 'during the last century there has sprung up, as it were, a generation of hunt servants hired from a good stock, and like their hounds, carefully watched over by their masters'.[5] What is more, it was claimed that they were raised in tone considerably by their regular contact with people from good society.

Not quite so well treated but in even greater demand were game-keepers, whose numbers rose from some 9,000 in 1851 to about 23,000 in 1911.[6] Shooting, with the physical restriction of estates, and the buying-in annually of both game and syndicate members, kept them in isolation. Wages were high by labouring standards, low by skilled urban ones, usually around £1 a week.[7] There were usually tied but isolated cottages and the keeper was a classically marginal figure in rural England – note D. H. Lawrence's perceptive treatment of the character Annable in *The White Peacock*. Unlike the hunt servant the keeper had not only to provide good sport, enough birds for a day's bag, but also to police his territory in a social landscape where there was usually a strong inherited tradition of resentment against landlords' and syndicates' preservation of game. He was expected to be both deferential and aggressive, and to manage the assistants and beaters without whom even a small shoot could not manage.

Hardly surprisingly, there was a literature devoted to the problems of managing keepers and, through them, the locals: 'The working classes in the country, as a rule, esteem the present of a couple of rabbits very highly.'[8] Old clothes were also to be given to keepers and beaters as liberally as possible. Beaters became poachers if they were not both paid and compensated with such gifts, it was commonly argued, since they were often 'without a particle of true sportsmanlike feeling'.[9] To guide the 'new comfortable' at the butts there was usually strong advice on tipping: often but not too much.

Keeping was something to be expected of the lower classes, and there were frequent warnings against the younger sons of the wealthy taking to it to find romantic isolation. 'the chief stumbling-block of the gentleman-keeper is that he cannot forget his social status'.[10] What Lawrence later made a lynchpin of *Lady Chatterly's Lover* was a much-mouthed Edwardian fear: the *déclassé* would upset essential natural order.

The newer sports had other problems. Henley-ridden boat clubs still needed labour to move their craft and maintain them. Occasionally some of these men, realising that dependence, rather overplayed the crusty servant role. Morris (note the lack of any initials or Christian name), the Warwick Boat Club's boatman at the turn of the century, fell foul of the club secretary for his impertinence but when the latter tried to dismiss him a large number of members objected. The tension continued for several years until Morris resigned in September 1904. The club interviewed nineteen men without finding a successor and finally persuaded him to return in 1905 – at which the secretary resigned. Many an adroit employee manipulated this sense of being a tetchy lynchpin but it was no sinecure: Morris's assistant, Palmer, 'a civil and obliging servant', was drowned in July 1902. The members subscribed £114 to cover the funeral costs, some £7 10s, and to give his widow 10s a week till the fund ran out.[11]

The question of benefits was a constant issue in all sports. Usually it depended on local generosity, or lack of it, but there were other parallels to the hunting experience. The Cricketers' Fund Friendly Society was founded in 1857 and re-established in 1864: its members were wealthy individuals or clubs rather than the proposed beneficiaries themselves. By 1891 it had paid out £3,000 in various gifts. Its income depended less on subscriptions than on benefit matches: when MCC played Australia in 1890, £600 was paid into the funds. Even Grace, who profited from the sport rather better than most professional cricketers, supported them. Reticent about his own financial involvement in the game, he was, nonetheless, quite prepared to give details on the professionals, largely to show how generously he felt they were treated. Lord's engaged its bowlers for a sixteen-week season, where, Grace claimed, they could be paid up to £10 a week. For matches they were paid £3 10s for a victory, £3 for a loss. The common run of ground bowlers, i.e. men who gave the 'amateurs' batting practice, were paid 30s–50s a week, 'and they can always depend on handsome gratuities from the members'.[12]

The paid yachting hand earned slightly less but he would be allowed to keep his clothes, up to £7 worth, at the end of the season, 'besides his master's influence and good wishes during the winter if he has proved satisfactory'.[13] Exactly what that amounted to in terms of a domestic economy was rarely mentioned. Bowls, where play was limited to April–October, found another model. It was suggested that full wages should be paid for the season and half as a winter retainer: the greenkeeper was expected to make up the rest by jobbing gardening and serving at social functions. It would help if he learned a trade, as long as it did not interfere with his job. He could smoke about his duties, but should not be tipped.[14] Such treatment, however, was by no means common.

All these issues, as well as many peculiar to the game, were represented and possibly magnified because of the scale of the golf boom. The Scottish import needed professional staff as instructors and maintenance men. But it also used a vast army of casual labour, far more than any other sport, around which it created a supportive myth composed largely of caricatures. The majority of players seem to have regarded the disparities of employment practices as an integral part of a natural order: however close their occasional personal contact with their inferiors during games may have been, they needed major social barriers to be able to function at all.

Golf required three main groups of servants once any club was established; it treated them as an open hierarchy to be risen up by effort and merit whilst developing practices which made much of that impossible. What eventually emerged was a conflict between simplistic post-Darwinian assumptions and developing attempts to take paternalistic responsibilities seriously. The lowest rank was the caddie, whose numbers were so great and whose problems were so widespread that they attracted most debate. Next up were the various levels of professional, whose range of skills and influence was considerable. At the peak was the greenkeeper, often with his own specialist assistants, whose work was not only essential to maintain playing surfaces but of increasing aesthetic importance.

In the smaller clubs – by far the majority – professional and greenkeeper were often the same. These were the non commissioned officers, and apparently equal grades in different clubs were invested with all the differences in prestige to be found between cavalry, Guards and mere regiments of the line. The deference of a senior professional or groundsman was expected but was also invested with the disdain with which a regimental sergeant-major treats a subaltern, in this case represented by the average golfer. Golfing humour enshrined this, it made it desirable, and it could be more serious still. Horace G. Hutchinson saw the influence of the club professional as moral: 'Nature's gentlemen who never step out of their position, and yet never fail to make us feel that by right of courtesy they are equals with the best.' But that equality, he felt, should never extend to a member's buying the pro a drink, lest the moral leaven be infected.[15]

It was the face-to-face experience in the ordinary round of the game rather than the general ascriptions which mattered, however. This is rarely recoverable in detailed personal circumstances but surfaces occasionally in club records. There was considerable uncertainty in the early days of the sport's growth because there were so few extant models; what to expect and how to contain the greenkeeper and professional were major issues. When Leeds Golf Club was founded in 1896 it engaged W. B. Wilson as its professional on a three-month trial, although he could be given a week's notice. He was paid £1 a week, augmented by the right to sell clubs and balls and to charge 1s per round per member for teaching play. Five months later he was given notice with the alternative of being re-employed at 15s a week. There seems to have been no question of his competence, but he soon left after such treatment. His successor, Ferguson, was bought in at 10s a week. A couple of years later there was a new man, Cox, who was reprimanded for being unwilling to teach new members. When he replied that he could not do that and repair clubs as well he was told to do the latter at night, using the lamp they bought him for the purpose.[16]

It took club committees quite a long time to see how their growing demands could be reconciled in employees' time, and the matter was often resolved in the larger clubs only by employing more specialist staff. Hours were long – all those of daylight and beyond – and many early professionals were expected to maintain greens and buildings and organise caddies as well. Some, with their wives, were expected to run clubhouse facilities and provide meals as well. Goodwood's first professional, F. Goldsmith, was paid 12s a week on appointment in 1892: this was upped to fifteen shillings within two months but he was also made greenkeeper. It did not work, so he was sacked the following year, a part-time groundsman was appointed at 6s, and the club members taught each other. This could not last, but there were problems with successors. Just what was openly and covertly expected became clear when the club reprimanded its professional, Cox, in 1912:

> for not having kept the Ladies' Room in the Club House in a clean and tidy condition, for smoking while talking to a Member and [he] was forbidden to smoke at all in the Club House. He was also warned that when giving golf lessons he must pay more attention and display more keenness.[17]

As the bigger clubs moved into luxurious Edwardian premises, they encountered growing trouble with ancillary staff, the 'servant problem' spread from home and hotel. As Leeds noted in 1912, 'It is the opinion of this Committee that friction and unpleasantness would be avoided by increased and uniform civility on the part of the staff,' some two women, a cook, a boy and a charlady. Rarely was the incivility of members mentioned.[18]

The lore of servant management had only limited value when applied to golf, since the professional was being employed to do what the members could not rather than would not do. Most early professionals were Scottish artisans who combined playing skills with other crafts, ranging from club-making picked up at home in Scotland to carpentry, bricklaying and masonry. James Braid (1870–1950), who played a major role as an Edwardian course architect very different from the enlightened amateur approach of men like Colt, followed a route which was the stereotype of many. Born at Earlsferry, Fife, he claimed to have begun to play at the age of four. After caddying he became a carpenter at St Andrews, then moved at the age of twenty-six to be the professional at Romford in Essex. From there he moved in 1904 to the prestigious new club at Walton Heath, combining that with his designing career.[19] By that time the Scots were being equalled by younger Englishmen, and it was no longer axiomatic that virtually any well turned out Scottish artisan would make a suitable employee. Percy Hills, the Harrogate pro in 1912, was born in Sandwich, and learned his skills at Seaford in Sussex. Walter Toogood of Alwoodley was also born on the Isle, where he caddied before becoming a railway telegraph clerk: that bored him, so he returned to golf as a professional.[20]

Yorkshiremen claimed to treat their professionals as 'gents', at least in the years well after Leeds was founded, and there are occasional examples there and elsewhere of some regard being shown for the better-established staff. It was, however, rather more on the lines of their being well established butlers, golfing Admirable Crichtons rather than gentlemen in their own right. Anyone who combined sporting prowess with making a living from it could never easily cross a divide which was far more pervasive than ideas of ethical purity in themselves. When J. W. Walters, the pro at Brough Golf Club, married Emily Sayers of Hull the members subscribed for 'a purse of gold' and the groundsmen gave an inscribed salad bowl for this 'golf wedding'.[21] Esteem often needed these highly ritualised forms to express it, and there were similar transformed modes of coping with well regarded employees' problems. Despite claims that hundreds of professionals were making £300 or more a year from the game, it could be a harsh environment.[22] Professionals were usually expected to trade in sporting goods as well, with little capital, and we have already noted the threat to that when members bought balls in grosses. Most clubs used it as an excuse to keep wages down. Few followed Horace G. Hutchinson's warning that 'few professionals are good business men' who should be relieved of the uncertainties of trading and given a decent, permanent wage instead.[23]

Some pros suffered because of this and occasionally fell into serious difficulties. Alfred Laws, of Streatley Golf Club, Sutton Coldfield, went bankrupt in 1914, owing £212 4s 8d, against assets of £29. He lost his job and took to working for a golf ball maker at 30s a week. The club wrote him off, but not his debts, because of 'his inattention to business and losses by betting'.[24] The images of paternalism often revealed shallow roots in clubs whose businessmen members expected the same level of risk in their staff that they thought they faced themselves. It was an issue the Professional Golfers' Association, largely designed to act as a wholesaler protecting its members from further exploitation, could never deal with effectively.[25]

Yet there were occasional instances of paternalism's working. When Ramsay Hunter of the Mid-Kent club died he left his widow and family destitute. Only £9 was raised by the members after an appeal, so the committee made her stewardess and paid off her debts.[26] The professional at Prince's, Sandwich, D. Stephenson, was ill for eighteen months with an injured wrist which stopped him making clubs. A member lent him £90 for living and medical expenses, which Stephenson vowed to pay back. Such a 'deserving' case fulfilled the best expectations, and his place was kept open until he recovered. Sir George Riddell started a fund with £20 and *Golf Illustrated* gave two guineas and called for a public response. Individual cases like this could be dealt with by familiar mechanisms but golfers, when compared with hunting or cricket, proved generally unwilling to recognise the wider structural demands of organised paternalist benefits.[27]

This is well demonstrated in the case of the game's largest employee group, caddies, the one most readily caricatured. A composite would show a weedy, stunted and malnourished boy clad in dark rags with a cloth cap and poor boots, weighed down with a bag of clubs and staring with sheer amazement at a prosperous and incompetent golfer: it would have a caption in which the caddie would be muttering some biting home truth about the golfer, his inflated self-regard and his actual performance.[28] The very popularity of such a caddie myth drew a veil of virtual indifference between the majority of golfers and the implications of their employing youths as casual labour on a large scale.

The number of caddies is difficult to come by because of the very nature of the job, casual and sometimes only semi-legal. One 1912 survey showed twenty-nine clubs using 827 caddies, but it would be impossible to extrapolate the total national picture because of the considerable local variations. A conservative estimate, however, on the basis of ten per club would be 10,000 in England and Wales, and the actual number is likely to have been far higher. It is difficult to get past either idealised models or the jaundiced picture of some moralisers. The archetypal figure would come from a poor Scottish background, caddying in the school holidays and at weekends before taking it up full-time. He would use that period to practise golf surreptitiously with cast-off implements, graduate slowly to instruction, pick up another trade *en route* and then move to England as a full-time club professional. Such was the experience of Albert Edward MacTavish, the hero of Horace G. Hutchinson's Edwardian novel *Bert Edward the Golf Caddie*. Bert Edward not only follows the classical migrant path, to 'forty pounds a year, and a shop, and what you make by the sale of clubs and balls and your fee for teaching', he also wins the Open at Sandwich and marries happily.[29]

This career ladder offered a potent myth but, taking my conservative estimate above, only 10 per cent at the most could have expected to follow that route. For most, caddying was either an intermediate phase in a general life of casual labour or a 'dead end' in itself.

A caddie in full employment could possibly hope to accompany two rounds a day for six days in a week: at 6*d* a time the likely income was about 6s. As with casual agricultural labour, to which it bore a considerable resemblance, the importance lay in its being used to augment low unskilled family incomes. Yet the myth ascribed high levels of skill:

> The caddie may be, and very often is, a ragged member of what are known as the 'lower orders' – but on the golf course he brings right hon. gentlemen and noble lords to heel. They regard him with a deference greater than that displayed towards the working man at a time of general election – and he knows his power and rejoices in it.[30]

This masked a harsh reality. Many clubs accepted a waiting, shivering crowd of caddies touting for work under the vague eye of the professional, rather as they expected to see similar groups hanging about the larger railway stations. Some took early steps to organise this situation. The Royal and Ancient was asked to consider the issue in 1889 but decided that it could not set any general rules: employment lay outside the normative codes of play and course etiquette.[31] Its own practice was regulatory. It employed a caddie master who registered his charges, allowing them to charge 1s 6d for a first round and 1s for the second, noticeably higher than many English clubs. There was also a benefit club for deserving cases. Leeds in 1898 employed a caddie master, the Cox whose subsequent insubordination as professional we have already noted, and he was entitled to a penny fee from every golfer who employed a caddie.[32] The larger clubs assumed that using caddies was normal; it was only in poorer or more eccentric circumstances that golfers carried their own bags. Some clubs organised caddies' teams and treats on the lines of other employers: at Buxton, Derbyshire, 'the committee gives the boys a treat to the seaside every year, and in such ways as providing them with waterproof capes in wet weather, shows its interest in the lads and appreciation of their services.'[33]

Benevolence like this did little to stop a growing, if marginal, body of criticism. R. H. Lyttelton claimed that caddies were almost invariably loafers, many of them essentially school truants, and there was little doubt that many golfers effectively connived at this.[34] For some supporters of the work ethic golf was a significant contributor to economic stagnation: 'It is breeding a race of loafers all over the country. Walking round the links is easier than work.'[35]

There were other pointers to moral corruption in caddies, not least with the growing pressure for Sunday play. The Lord's Day

Observance Society monitored this fitfully. Some clubs tried to reduce criticism by playing without caddies on Sunday. Llandudno tried to buy off local Welsh outrage and its landlords, the Ecclesiastical Commissioners, who refused to renew its lease if Sunday play went ahead, also offering a rare exception to the usual run of caddie recruitment: 'They even offered to renounce their pernicious custom of employing girl caddies if allowed to play on Sunday.'[36] Most caddies seem to have welcomed the additional earnings likely to result from Sunday play but there were exceptions. On Sunday 21 May 1905 the caddies at Walton on the Hill struck against the practice. They attacked one player and his 'blackleg' caddies, but the golfer fought back and one of the protesters ended up in hospital. The Epsom police were called out and four of the caddies were bound over for six months.[37] A similar threat of a strike by the Zurich caddies was suppressed when the professionals spanked the culprits. Caddie protest at conditions was very rare indeed, since all the odds were against young casual labourers.[38]

From the mid-Edwardian period there emerged a small-scale attempt to cope with the accusations that golfers lacked social conscience, set in the context of New Liberalism, Fabianism and the growing concern to combat racial degeneracy. In July 1909 *The Times* published a special article on 'The problem of the caddie' in which it appealed to golfers' sense of duty and pointed to the lead being given by Sunningdale. There the club offered evening classes to fit the caddies for general employment outside golf. In Croydon the Education Committee, the polytechnic and Purley Downs Golf Club provided literacy, numeracy and painting, decorating and woodwork classes for caddies at a cost of 3s 6d per caddie for basic teaching. It soon appeared that Eastbourne, never to be outdone, had been doing as much also for some time.[39] The following year Middlesex County Council decided to give a grant of £25 towards caddie education at Fulwell Golf Club and £50 for those at Hanger Hill.[40] At Sunningdale its secretary, H. S. Colt, had been pressing for several years for proper working and training conditions, arguing against the philanthropy of free clothing and meals and for adequate wages; the latter he fixed at 10s–15s. He also wanted an upper age limit on caddying, on the grounds that men would loaf automatically: the latter, it was widely felt, were little more than 'scum'.[41] The Welsh club Llandrindod Wells brought in its labour from outside, some twenty-four 'Registered Street Trading Boys' from Newport in Monmouthshire. For their summer employment they lived under canvas, were fed and paid 5s a week, dressed in a uniform of scarlet jersey and 'Baden-Powell hats' and were drilled regularly by the caddie master, who had spent twenty-nine years as a colour sergeant in the army. If satisfactory, they were found work back home after the summer.[42]

Only a few clubs adopted such schemes, and the leading clubs tried to widen awareness. Fifty of them met in London in November 1911 to form a Caddies' Aid Association.[43] Pressure had come from influential individuals in the sport like Colt and the young Bernard Darwin but it also had the backing of a new quasi-Fabian body, the Agenda Club. In July 1910 'An open letter to English gentlemen' had been published in the *Hibbert Journal*, appealing to tradition, *noblesse oblige*, calling for the middle classes, as well as the gentry, to 'play the game' by the lower orders, find new outlets for chivalry and self-sacrifice, on the model, at least as Westerners saw it, of the Japanese samurai. It calculated that the United Kingdom now had 1.5 million rich, 3.5 million comfortably off and 38 million poor. In particular it pointed to the blind alley of golf caddying as exemplifying the latter. The Agenda Club, led by Sir Norman Lockyer, KCB, FRS, Sir William Ramsay, KCB, FRS, and the Hon. Sydney Holland, wrote also to the *Spectator* and the *Nation* in July 1910, outlining their proposals. Their target was to find support from men who would be repelled by the Charity Organisation Society or the British Institute of Social Science, to create an efficient and universal agency for social reform with funds to cover twenty-five years' work.

The club, emphatically New Liberal in tone, took caddying as its first problem both in actual social terms and as the object of a model empirical investigation expected to precede informed voluntary social reform. It borrowed the methods of enquiry of Booth, Rowntree and the Webbs to produce *The Rough and the Fairway* in 1912. The report was a mixture of general enquiry, limited local investigations and recommendation. It assumed that a major problem was that only one per cent of caddies would ever find work as professionals, that the job was actually a barrier to further employment and that only collective action by players rather than the state could solve it. Two-thirds of a caddie's time was likely to be spent hanging around, tips were demoralising because they encouraged cadging, and middle-class golfers who betted on each other were actually a bad example. It recommended that boys should be kept separate from men and that only pensioners should be employed as adult caddies. The job should end for most at the age of eighteen, by which time they would have been fitted for a career by compulsory training, preferably as market gardeners. During employment, wages and sickness benefit should be guaranteed. The market gardening emphasis may have developed from the structure of the enquiry: it was carried out by using a thirty-one-part questionnnaire sent to twenty-nine eighteen-hole clubs within a fifteen-mile radius of central London.

Yet its assumptions were that the problems were national, and it would be reasonable to assume that that was at least true in the case of the major provincial cities. Sunningdale provided a carpentry workshop. Birkdale taught boot-making. Hanger Hill ran a two-and-a-half-acre market garden with a staff gardener where the boys worked in their unpaid spare time. Sandridge offered its caddies allotments.

Provincial examples were fewer, but Sheringham offered seamanship and allotments, whilst Ipswich provided the latter. The general thinness of provision appalled the club, so did the weakness of voluntary take-up by the caddies. At Sandridge only eight boys had joined a scheme to open a Post Office Penny Savings Bank account. Yet the report saw these schemes, if made compulsory, as the only real way to cope with the problem. Uncertain whether its appeal to data would have any more impact than the usual round of social enquiries, it lapsed finally into moral appeal couched in sporting language: '... there are a lot of fellows who have a very cheap time and to whom life offers a succession of jolly rotten lies and unfair hazards between them and any sort of green ...'. It was emphatically not 'golf'.[44]

Golfers proved generally unwilling to 'play the game' as far as most of their employees were concerned. It may not be stretching things too far to suggest that the very assumptions built into the game's competitive patterns did not allow it to be coated as easily with transferred notions of chivalric and paternalistic responsibilities as were sports more obviously pan-class in their appeal and organisation. Individualistic and acquisitive, it could not respond easily to appeals based upon a sense of the team: large clubs were often little more than umbrella organisations for a playing membership rather than objects of affective, as distinct from socially instrumental, attachment. When the National Insurance Act was passed in 1911 it offered one solution to the employment of older caddies: because men over sixteen were subject to it there was an incentive to dismiss them.[45] In return it increased the pressure to make the most of younger, cheaper labour.

The Agenda Club and the Caddies' Aid Association were little heeded. *Golf Monthly* argued that they exaggerated the difficulty, that clubs should be left to assume responsibility.[46] Yet that was what both groups saw as the ideal solution. When the Agenda Club claimed that only twenty-five of a possible 1,800 clubs (in the United Kingdom) were making any systematic provision at all for their caddies *Golf Monthly* rejoined that it showed there was no wider need to be met.[47] There can be little doubt that the journal spoke for the majority of players. Nor did they respond happily to the suggestion of Sir George Riddell that the problem of employing youths could be solved by taking on former soldiers and sailors instead, men unlikely to turn out to be loafers. That would have raised the costs of play.[48] A trickle of clubs followed the improvers' example, such as Wallasey, which created a £200 fund in 1914 to train caddies in carpentry, market gardening and greenkeeping.[49] The majority continued to exploit without reserve, and to hedge about with romantic myth, what one contributor to *C. B. Fry's Magazine* called '. . . a sufficient supply of thoroughly qualified men and boys ready to earn a precarious living by parasitic labour, alternated with intervals of loafing'.[50]

Women

It was impossible for middle-class men to rely on the language of class separation when faced with demands from their own women. Eric Hobsbawm has characterised the emergence of women in sport in the late nineteenth century as a celebration of their public individuality, a separating off from their domestically focused subjection to men.[51] There is much to support this view, but it elides the way in which some sports became an extension of domestic restraint and the way in which debates over the sporting place of women were conducted at different levels of accessibility and suitability. As an area of conflict over gender roles sport was rarely treated either holistically or hermetically; it moved as a topic of discussion between widely placed poles of conflict. It covered issues of containment centring on fears of domestic disruption, a eugenic debate, arguments about physiological make-up, the extent to which codes of social etiquette would be modified and morals affected by a less restricted mingling of the sexes. Woven into this, far from tidily, were questions of the economic independence of women, the movements for intellectual and political enfranchisement and the matter of private and public gender identities. My purpose here is not to repeat some recent studies but to place some of the issues rather more centrally in the context of a male-dominated agenda of middle-class self-realisation. This is not, however, an unashamed reiteration of the hoary male arguments for exclusion or restriction; it is to recall dilemmas they caused for their proponents.

Michael Curtin has reminded us of the ambiguities in the Victorian sense of the 'lady', its use to incorporate some women selectively 'into the mainstream of sociability' and its function in denying them central places of power and prestige.[52] The key to this was the increasing sophistication of 'manners' and their use as a buffer against the crudities of economic life, denigrating 'work', so that middle-class women could move along 'something comparable to a career ladder' which was almost exclusively domestic in its operation. Within this framework sport could provide an additional point of contact, assimilation and differentiation, but it could also threaten the assumptions on which the models of behaviour were based. Recent American studies have shown this at its most extreme, 'The Lady as Jock'.[53]

Considerable tension emerged in late Victorian middle-class male attitudes between the essential subjection of women and their idealisation as potential domestic angels. Winning the game of courtship was widely held to involve a set of rules incompatible with male sporting codes. A woman in sport would play the wrong games. Pursuits fostering male purity were perceived as threatening the innocence of women who took them up. Yet this was an inevitable product of overlapping but diverse expectations of respectable behaviour. Conflict focused on the middle ground of intersection because, even more than with boundaries between different social classes, most men faced considerable female domestic influence. Some women colluded with this, often out of fear that their own relatively protected sphere would be impaired as well, with a consequent loss of domestic power.

Given their access to the press, it was usually men who articulated these fears publicly. Their negatives tended to be clouded in loose notions of what represented 'womanliness': a culture where the essence of manliness was disputed could not be expected easily to produce a clearly reasoned notion of the feminine. The diatribes were often wrapped in a discreet veil of reticence. If women were feared as potentially evil, corrupters of male purity or physiologically disbarred by the mysteries of menstruation, that was not stated as such. In fact some of the language is so opaque that it is difficult to read a code of hidden reference into it at all. The opponents of women's participation usually chose what they regarded as a safer ground on which to fight. 'Liberated' women were another means of debasing national greatness, and the example of the United States was one emphatically to be avoided: 'It will be a sorry day for England when her women forget their duty to God, their country and themselves. It will strike at the very root of our national life and character,' argued P. A. Vaile in 1905.[54] We shall later see this nationalist argument reversed to encourage sport for women but it usually reinforced fears that sport would both unsex them and and make men effeminate.[55] There was a largely unspoken assumption that sport was essentially anti-domestic, allowing men to get rid of tensions which might otherwise have threatened the home.

The counter-view was that the domestic sphere was now too civilised for either men or women, the latter increasingly 'susceptible to the evils that super-cultivation brings about'.[56] For this and its side effects of 'nerves', an unrestrained imagination, headaches or vapours, sport offered an ideal corrective. When Bishop Winnington-Ingram chaired a women's meeting on 'Proportion in life' at the Church Congress in Weymouth in 1905 the principal of Lady Margaret Hall, Oxford, warned of the risks of over-concentration on women's athletics but justified them nonetheless as helping 'to do away with foolish little social distinctions, and they give a chance to the stupid girl or the girls who may be handicapped in some other way'. Presumably she was referring not to her own students but rather to those some of them might have to teach or mother eventually.[57] The latter part of her statement might have been uttered equally happily by a male schoolmaster or don but it is unlikely that most men in middle-class sport would have welcomed the threat to the social markers they had worked so hard to develop.

The opponents of women in sport caricatured female inadequacies. 'That narrow-minded rivalry or jealousy . . . ingrained in the sex' which was held by some to make women's competition over-intense was linked with other views that women were incapable of systematic contest: 'even when they play among themselves, their games prove the evolutionary law, and show themselves to be refinements on primeval feminine occupations'.[58] The critics were rarely aware of the paradox in using diametrical opposites as justification for exclusion. The occasional dressing up with systematic rationality barely hid the strength of male fears. This is not to belittle the nature of some masculine resistance, since the proponents of change were equally paradoxical, nor should it be assumed that the irrational necessarily occupies a lower level of value historically than the logically systematic. Even partial supporters of women being allowed into such sports as *battue* shooting had reservations about chatter, a tendency among women to 'debase sport to the level of a picnic'.[59]

Women's performance levels, given different physical characteristics, frequently showed a singular seriousness that most men envied and feared. If women could be excluded from the harsher male contact sports there still existed the issues of complementarity in parallel provision or direct competition with rather than alongside men. Aflalo held that women should not box or wrestle but that they made first-rate fencers, not to duel with men or each other but to protect their virtue in city streets; the umbrella would keep the 'bully' at bay. He went on to justify their archery, golf and cycling in the strongest terms that could be employed by their supporters, those of eugenics, 'the athletic mothers of the coming race'.

He was supported by Lady Augusta Fane, who launched a swingeing attack on the majority of her contemporaries, women:

> who spend their lives in playing bridge, talking gossip and gambling in stocks [economic emancipation?]; eat four huge meals a day, sit up all night, and for exercise loll about in an electric landaulette ... Now I ask anybody, what sort of a son would a woman like that give to her country?[60]

But there were comparatively few who agreed with them. It was more common to meet arguments that a female obsession with sport was racially counter productive and actually the wrong way to develop healthy child-bearers.

When Dr James Cantlie argued in 1906 that it would take five children per family to keep the empire stocked he inveighed against the hockey boom as likely to develop the shoulders rather than the breeding parts of the anatomy, as well as 'a frame of mind at variance with womanly duties'.[61] He was repeating the arguments of a woman doctor, Arabella Kennealy, who deplored the growing emphasis on muscle tone: 'Womanhood is a beautiful achievement of evolution which it is a crime to deface'.[62] They both assumed that women with limited physical resources had to decide where to develop them: it paralleled uneasily critics of male athleticism and the debunking of 'flannelled fools'. If exclusion from all sport could not be justified for women, then the eugenicist position was one of extending conventional limits only partially, 'a good mediocrity, heightened now and then by a brilliant coruscation of startling excellence'.[63]

The most this view would allow a mildly athletic middle-class girl was that 'she is much more likely to get married and surrender the sporting capabilities to her husband'.[64] Sports that were held to give men grace were usually assumed to rob women of it automatically. Who wanted a wife with unnaturally large feet and hands? If women could not be excluded altogether, then there had to be restricted zones of participation, the games at the fringe of the manly cult rather than full-blown athleticism. On the edges of this debate was another one whose apparent frivolity actually demonstrated containment arguments splendidly. Cycling in the 1890s proved difficult for women who wore corsets, so many left them off. Unhappily Thorstein Veblen's dissertation on the corset in *The Leisure Class* was produced without being complicated by this paradox of luxury. Flab rather than muscularity was feared as a result. The undertones of the debate throughout the Edwardian years wrapped it in a simplistic symbolism.[65]

This contribution to the Edwardian physical fitness debate was limited emphatically to the middle classes, very largely because it took place in an arena of assumed options about leisure delimited by financial considerations. Whilst there was a base stratum of discussion about the role of games in many of the new girls' schools, this did not spill over into the codes of adult life in the same way that the manly sports arguments did for men. Post-school athleticism could be seen as a natural part of the maturing process for males but women were affected by the expectation that their usual prescribed roles were incompatible with continued participation in most games. Fitness for child-bearing was one thing, a consuming interest in sport appeared as a clear threat to rearing and the expected contentments of a domestic middle age. The assumed purpose of the latter was to be supportive to rather than competitive with men, and it was this that produced the repeated emphasis that, where women were allowed into club buildings, as distinct from grounds, their role was essentially an extension of the domestic.

In 1899 the ladies of the Warwick Boat Club were asked to form a committee to manage the club teas every Saturday.[66] Although the women lawn tennis members of the Rectory Manor Tennis and Bowling Club in Waltham outnumbered the men by thirty-four to twenty-three, the club was run by men; when a 'Ladies' Committee' was formed in 1906 it was to manage the teas.[67] There is little evidence that women used these committees as stepping stones to demands for greater participation in play and management. When clubs acquired grander accommodation there was usually some attempt at gender segregation, where women would remain in a supportive role and be content with exclusion both from major play areas and from the interchanges which attracted many men to club membership. Male language and relaxation after play would be seriously threatened by the public formality normally expected when women of the same social class were present. Occasionally it slipped. In 1910 the all-male committee of the Leeds Golf Club issued a reminder that lady members were not allowed into the smoking room, which they were using increasingly.[68]

The sports held safest for women to pursue had several major factors in common: they required delicate skill rather than strength, they flattered bodily appearance, were suitable zones for courtship, so that they actually strengthened the notion of the game as having a purpose outside its immediate pursuit, and they were initially restricted to private property. Archery, croquet and lawn tennis all grew out of this private world and remained largely within it even when they colonised semi-public space. They operated best at the overlap between gentry and upper middle classes, and allowed men and women to compete with each other because they were treated initially as games rather than sports. Performance was often secondary to other considerations. Archery had long declined from being a warlike skill to being a pleasant way of spending a country house morning with opportunities for mutual admiration and courtship. It did just that in Trollope's *Barchester Towers* and helped delineate genteel pretensions among upper middle-class families into this century. The numbers involved were small, the organisation was emphatically local, but reporting in the press gave archery a wider currency of values which passed into other sports. Twelve ladies competed for prizes of jewellery and ornaments in the gardens of Abington rectory, Northampton, in July 1861 with little value attached by the press.[69]

When the Brighton and Hove Archers appeared by the turn of the century the issues were much more explicit, the targets of these Dianas implicit in the descriptions:

> There is no violent exertion about it, no undue amount of exposure. You can stroll between the targets under your sunshade; and the correct attitudes for shooting are absolutely graceful and show off a good figure and a pretty frock in the most satisfactory way.

Archery was woman-dominated in Brighton; forty women and twenty men shot on four mornings a week and on Friday afternoons during the late spring and early summer. The shooting grounds were in the gardens of a private house, but local superiority was also maintained by regular shooting over the cricket ground in Preston Park, relatively recently opened to the public and designed as a lower middle and working-class breathing space.[70]

The croquet and subsequent lawn tennis booms reinforced this; we have already noticed the seasonal fillip given to places like Binbrook in the Lincolnshire Wolds. Although both games raised some issues about women's participation beyond the safe bounds of semi-domestic pastures, these rarely reached a very serious level because of their apparent gentleness. Their joint revival around 1900 coincided with much more general debate over the place of women. In croquet one issue was whether some acquisition of 'that sporting spirit which comes as second nature to men accustomed to give-and-take in games since boyhood' might lessen the temperamental viciousness of some women players.[71]

When Lily Gower, the 'Championess of England', wrote about the game she restricted herself strictly to technique, unlike another commentator who rather regretted that this emphasis on the outdoors was replacing pale complexions with 'Victorian khaki'.[72] An estimate that four-fifths of players were women caused problems because it opened up the possibility of their dominating play in 'that modern upstart jealousy between the sexes'.[73] Men might play against women instead of in the complementary dominant–submissive role to be found in mixed pairs. Women were frequently held to bring confusion to sport, playing 'for spectacular purposes' rather than within the rules themselves.[74] Yet female prowess on the lawn tennis court came to be recognised, if grudgingly, and the safe lawn ambience of croquet and tennis was held by some (usually female) Edwardian observers to be a useful means of replacing emotional outbursts with calm reflection.[75] The risk for reformers was that women would be limited to the 'pastime fringe', after-dinner billiards with its 'interests and excitement without fatigue' and 'delicacy of touch', or the briefly surgent table tennis where Constance Bantock, the daughter of a successful West End doctor, achieved brief fame as the winner of the 1902 Queen's Hall Ping-Pong Tournament.[76]

The attempts at marginalising implicit in such statements as 'the most violent opponent to women's sport could not take exception to bowls' were not so acceptable when women moved steadily and quite determinedly into outlets for aggressive masculinity. By the turn of the century an increasing number rode to hounds, although their strongest proponents regarded that as essentially an activity for the post-pubescent because of the risks to bodily development in early adolescence. For wealthier women it marked economic entry into subscription packs and a break away from watching the meet from carriages or ornamenting hunt balls. Yet the etiquette of hunting remained distinctly male; women were expected to stay at the back of the field; 'fast women' were dangerous in more senses than one.[77]

On the fringes of the hunting world women could acquire considerable prominence, usually bolstered with a large amount of eccentricity. The Crowhurst otter hounds in Sussex acquired a woman master in 1905 when Mrs Walter Cheesman took over from her husband, justifying her activity as a 'manly sport'. She claimed to have increased her ability to walk across country from three miles to almost twenty a day. Women who hunted, she felt, were much better at running their home. The society papers treated her with something of the amazement that *Reveille* would have given to a talking dog; she was unusual in her role but a useful mouthpiece for a limited freedom.[78]

In other field sports women were slowly admitted, very largely on the astute realisation that the numbers involved would be very limited. For middle-class game anglers there were royal models: Queen Victoria, Queen Alexandra and the Duchess of Fife all pursued some carefully ghillied fly fishing for salmon. On a wider scale it was argued that, if they could be persuaded to concentrate on angling rather than its social incidentals, women might 'be removed by fishing from those petty habits of gossip and little-mindedness which too often mar the character of home-keeping girls'. A few went further: Hermione Murphy-Grimshaw wrote about 'Tarpon fishing in Florida' for *Badminton Magazine* in 1897, but male use of angling as a key means of escape from the domestic restricted wider participation very effectively.[79]

Only a determined minority of strong-minded female individuals broke into 'manly sports', but very clearly on the edges. When the Revd. W. E. Durham went climbing, like most married members of the Alpine Club he left his wife and daughters to wander round the picturesque parts of Swiss valleys. Women, encumbered with long alpenstocks and safely roped to guides, were occasionally allowed on the safer glaciers, and very few went beyond that. A Mrs Jackson who undertook an expedition to the Bernese Oberland in January 1888 suffered severe frostbite and had several toes amputated. Miss Lucy Walker always left her village base in a crinoline which she removed to climb in a red petticoat: the first woman to ascend the Matterhorn, she firmly repudiated any idea of being a 'new woman'. It remained possible to treat women like this as eccentrics safely to be admired because there were so few of them and mountaineering pretended strongly to be non-competitive.[80]

Women who wished to row, however, were firmly excluded by both ARA and NARA. Punting was safe because, by emphasising the standing figure, it kept women firmly in the game whose rules they were supposed to follow, but sculling or eights seemed a real threat.[81] Only in one case was this breached. Not content with pushing the right of working men to row as amateurs Dr F. J. Furnivall founded the Hammersmith Sculling Club for Girls and Men in 1896 to overcome the 'pernicious exclusion' of the rowing world. Men were allowed in, not to row but to carry the boats to the river. He bought the clubhouse, and every winter Sunday morning until 1910 he coached a crew the fourteen miles to Richmond and back in language often barely polite. In 1904 he gave the club a converted eight shell bought from New College Boat Club: it was a major but limited step forward, since there were no other similar ones available. The girls could compete only with their own previous times except when, once a year, they rowed over two miles against the Polytechnic Boat Club. Yet the club survived, bolstered by garden parties and run by a members' committee dominated by women, to provide a firm base for women's rowing after the First World War.[82] Others were less fortunate; in 1913 those in Durham who applied for membership of its Amateur Rowing Club were kept out on the very basic grounds that the members' accommodation was unsuitable, a masculine last resort for a long time thereafter.[83]

Women were normally allowed on rivers only as fashionable accessories for pleasure-boating, but some wives were allowed to crew on the bohemian fringes of yacht cruising. The Falmouth Sailing Club allowed them to steer, crewed by men, in the novelty 'Ladies' Races' by 1898 and admitted them to membership in 1913 if they were *bona fide* yacht owners: they could not vote, or sit on the club committee, and were restricted to the ladies' sitting room and its appurtenances. The Humber Yawl Club expected that some of its members would be crewed by their wives and praised small boat designs such as that of *Cherub III* which had a separate women's cabin 'wherein might be kept those numerous and perplexing objects of attire and toilet affected by the gentler sex'. How widespread this was is virtually impossible to ascertain but Maude Speed, the author of *A Yachtswoman's Cruises*, offered the spartan virtues as eminently suitable to young wives. Her strongest justification was that sailing allowed the townswoman to return to natural and seasonal rhythms, the realities of weather and tide. She asserted the biologically determined living that much else in women's sport seemed concerned to deny.[84]

For all their supposed value as accessories to romance the lawn games were dismissed increasingly as the preserve of older women in the later years of the nineteenth century. Athleticism needed a greater expenditure of energy, its exercise opened up wholesale opportunities for ridicule and caricature. 'Surtout mes dames, point de zêle' was the horrified reaction of *The Clerk* to a report of the Lady Cricketers' Club's first London match in 1890, which attracted 2,000 spectators for the novelty value. In fact it was not the idea of female players *per se*, who might safely be contained in 'a quiet game among girls in a country village', just for the fun of the thing that was alarming but the prospect of women's sport being so public and even attracting gate money.[85] In amateurish frolics women cricketers could play each other or even men, but it should not be allowed beyond that. Limited athletic activity was patchily imported into the new girls' public and grammar schools and, when some young women went on to higher education, into firmly segregated student societies. Manchester University acquired a Women's Athletic Union in 1900.[86]

Both within that framework and in the middle-class young women's peripheries there emerged a need for a moderately athletic winter game, and it was well met by hockey. The game's high ethical purism in male circles as well as its limited social appeal made it much easier to transfer to women's play than most other sports. In theory, but rarely in practice, it was also free of bodily contact. Ida M. Webb has summarised its history crisply, as a fashionable holiday game, brought together in 1895 by the formation of the All England Women's Hockey Association under the presidency of Miss Lilian Faithful. She also has drawn out the ambivalence expressed over it by some leading proponents of women's education because its 'violent and unladylike' potential could do their cause as well as their charges harm.[87] Its growth was rapid: *Gamage's Hockey Annual* reckoned on 300 women's clubs and 10,000 players by 1911.[88] It spread outwards from the new women's colleges in the older universities but was firmly snubbed when affiliation with the men's Hockey Association was proposed: that body's spokesman, Stanley Christopherson, would not recognise women in the game at all.[89]

Women themselves were uncertain how far they should go in organising the sport. Royal Holloway College's club opposed reporting fixtures in *The Field* as 'tantamount to courting publicity'.[90] Some male doctors in particular felt that women would never achieve high standards in the game because they lacked discipline and were temperamentally unsuited to the real restrictions of team activities. But for its proponents hockey's value was that it removed both symbolic and actual bodily restrictions. 'For the time being the player is no longer a lady, whose social position is suitably expressed in her attire' was a social claim which accompanied a continued attack on stays and corsets. Yet this escape was temporary: the lure of the dressmaker remained but would have to be adapted to a new standard of feminine attraction, 'positively masculine length and litheness'. Tensions over bodily shape and function remained.[91] Like the men's game, it was usually played in friendly local fixtures with careful avoidance of potentially corrupting tournament structures. Although the Hockey Association remained aloof, it did not express its disapproval by disenfranchising men when they played occasionally against or even in mixed teams with women. The game's social cachet prevented a gender Henley rule from emerging.

Unlike men's athletic literature, that aimed at the late Victorian woman rarely used classical body models in the debate over function and form, yet there was continued conflict between ideals of the efficient and the voluptuous. Women's competitive swimming, which flourished mildly after 1900, was praised, by a man, as 'developing their figures and . . . obtaining the rounded curves and flowing form which go to the making of the modern artistic ideal'.[92]

The greatest problems emerged with sports involving greater public visibility and competition for usable and symbolic sporting space between both middle-class genders. It was the consciousness of this that led Lucille Eaton Hill, the director of physical training at the prestigious American women's college, Wellesley, to counsel against women playing into their opponents' hands by 'abuse'.[93] Such 'abuse' initially became most apparent in the international cycling boom of the mid-1890s. When society ladies moved on from accompanying their *beaux* at cycling lessons in Battersea Park and were followed wholesale by middle-class women throughout the provinces a number of issues opened up. The most obvious was that of physical safety, one which cannot have been helped by the spectacle of the first Mrs Thomas Hardy's having to be caught by alert passers-by every time she cycled down a sloping street because she did not understand how brakes worked.[94] There was also the question of safety to a woman's honour, simply because most younger women could easily outpace any older chaperone on wheels.

Almost inevitably there was a spate of medical discussion upon cycling's desirability in the 1890s, and this moved rapidly into what was probably the most persistent of the debates the activity produced, that of the relationship between health, safety, dignity and femininity in suitable cycling dress. David Rubinstein has dealt brilliantly with this issue, pointing out that the Rational Dress League, founded in 1898, was doomed not so much by the ridicule attached to cycling bloomers by jeering crowds as by the cost (£3 10s or more) of a suitable outfit. Even the patrons of improvement were divided: rational dress was widely regarded as an undesirable French importation.[95]

An article in the Cyclists' Touring Club's *Monthly Gazette* in 1896 claimed that the costume (bloomers with a long coat) might well be safe but it was 'excessively ungraceful'.[96] Plain feminine clothes were better. *Badminton* kept up a flow of articles on the need for activity to be subordinated to grace, on the lines that lawn tennis had produced freer but flowing clothing for movement.[97] Despite the traps offered by spokes and pedals it was the flowing cycling costume which triumphed. Some women's cycling clubs were formed, in Brighton and elsewhere; a London club, the Trafalgar, was the social pinnacle, with its 'charming homelike residence where tea and scandal were served daily through the season'.[98] It was there that the major issue of containing the sport within a protected female enclosure was developed by means of the 'musical rides' with their emphasis on restricted skill rather than athletic travel. Cycling could be transferred to large domestic lawns or local parks and kept there safely, holding the spectre of women's racing at bay.[99] There were some women racing cyclists – a touring French professional circus visited Sheffield – but it was firmly suppressed by both the male and the female cycling establishments.[100] Instead, cycling was seen as another accessory in the feminine game of male conquest. Wells's Hoopdriver played knight errant to one such, and Rose Macaulay, looking back in *Told by an Idiot*, placed the acceptable use of cycling to acquire health and enhance femininity firmly in context: 'The light wind sang in the pines and blew dark curls of hair from under Stanley's [a girl] sailor hat. Her bicycle basket was full of primroses.'[101]

Because of the sheer scale of its growth, golf provided the toughest arena. Athletic girls could be confined to sports at school or college in the hope that they would grow out of it, but golf had the same appeal for many slightly older women that it had for men. As 'Amazonae' or 'Bogeia' ('a life-sized female figure, with a countenance very arrogant and forbidding') women golfers faced widespread ridicule.[102] Despite jokey articles on 'Golf and matrimony' and some insipid stories and novelettes golf was expected by many men to be an extended escape from the domestic rather than a reinforcement of it, the links a refuge from the courting games.[103] There was a consistent resistance to women playing at all, on the usual grounds of a chattering inability to concentrate, but also because the advantages given to the display of a shapely figure that we have seen as justification of other women's sports were held to be a distraction to men.

Women were allowed on the fringes and penetrated steadily into the game with a determination and to an extent seen in virtually no other sport. Allowed to putt on separate greens at Westward Ho! after its foundation, they demanded more. In many cases where resistance proved difficult the debate became one not of exclusion but between integration into men's clubs and segregation either on to separate links or into limited areas and playing times on the men's facilities. A Ladies' Club emerged at St Andrews in the 1860s, with 500 members by the 1880s, but the English were much slower than the Scots to accept this innovation.[104] Women were preferred as clubhouse teamakers, a role they never lost even when they were allowed to play. When Kingsthorpe Golf Club, Northampton, held its annual meeting in 1914 women were noted in so far as the ladies' teas had made £16 profit the previous year.[105]

The proponents of women's golf were articulate members of the

more affluent parts of the middle classes. The relatively high participation cost made it a more challenging proposition than the other
activities we have discussed. Rarely did its propagandists use the
argument that it would ease away social restrictions: much of its
appeal to many women must have lain in the factors which made
it a valuable instrument of male social differentiation, namely that
it offered an extension of the circles of domestic exclusion operated
by the women themselves. There was an inevitable undercurrent
of tension in the women's case when they argued in favour of an
activity which offered an escape from domestic stuffiness but did so
within a framework which extended the tentacles of social power.
The Edwardian fashion for women's golf owed much to this but it
had its limits: one observer remarked of the Ladies' Championship
that it was initially run on the lines of a large house or garden party,
'until the large entries removed the intimacy'.[106]

Although many women players were spatially and temporarily
restricted to the margins of the masculine game, this probably
suited them, since it allowed greater social control of a restricted
sphere. Goodwood Golf Club, like most others, insisted that women
should give way to men when playing and limited the number of
its lady members, without protest, to seventy-five.[107] Where they
shared men's courses, women normally played over nine holes, were
limited to weekdays and were not allowed to play during the main
club tournaments. Yet *Golf Monthly* estimated their numbers at about
40,000 in the entire United Kingdom by 1912, some 20 per cent of the
total players.[108]

Much was owed to the early appearance of well publicised heroines
of phenomenal skill. The first, Lady Margaret Scott, whose father was
Lord Eldon, began to play at the age of seventeen, won the first
three ladies' championships in the 1890s and promptly retired.[109]
In 1904 Charlotte Dod, who became British Ladies' Champion, was
the absolute female pan-athlete; she was a Wimbledon ladies' singles
winner, an international hockey player, a champion skater, silver
archery medal winner at the 1908 Olympics, played billiards for
relaxation and was an Alpinist of note.[110] Yet for her there was
no career path, or need for one, such as developed out of sport for
C. B. Fry and Eustace Miles. On the eve of the First World War the
formidably 'masculine' Cecil(ia) Leitch, a doctor's daughter, began a
series of championship wins which lasted into the 1920s.

The masculinity of Miss Leitch represented a major dilemma for female players. A burgeoning number of 'ladies' golf' handbook writers placed particular emphasis on grace and style, especially in the swing. Power of drive was regarded as a major limitation, since few women could reach men's distances, however equally skilful their close play might be. The coming of the Haskell ball changed women's playing needs as much as men's.

When courses were relaid those shared by women provoked major management problems: the usual answer to the risk of very slow play was to provide separate teeing for women. The presence of an increased number of women pushed many Edwardian clubs towards their high-cost clubhouses and social facilities: we have already noted the arguments over segregation within them, although a few, like West Hove, bowed to insistent pressure and provided 'a sunny smoking lounge, which is shared by members of both sexes'.[111]

Some women preferred totally separate clubs and links. In Brighton, bored by 'gentle insipidity' at home and croquet, a group of health-conscious married women formed the separate Brighton and Hove Ladies' Golf Club, high on the Downs, in 1892 after the Brighton and Hove Club had declined to admit women. There was already a mixed club in the area, the East Brighton, but the demand to play was greater than it could cope with. Despite its name the new club admitted a limited number of men, some forty, as against the 150 women members.[112] Regrettably little is known of the attitudes and reactions of men who were prepared to form such minorities there or elsewhere, or of how they were regarded by those who would not join them. Such clubs were usually run by women of a local social position established by their husband's occupation, notably doctors, clergy and lawyers rather than middling tradesmen.

They offered local competitions, monthly tournaments and the honorary paraphernalia of sporting success. Fewer in number than men's clubs, they faced real difficulties in seeking wider competition, and there remained within women's golf the tensions over wider visibility, publicity and play that suffused both masculine and feminine hockey. Twenty women's clubs felt their isolation sufficiently strongly, however, to found the Ladies' Golf Union 1893, with strong backing from men in the Wimbledon club and four male vice-presidents. Thereafter they provided much of the bureaucratic institutionalism common to most sports by the century's end, although there remained a very broad base of limited-interest participants to the pyramid of sporting performance.

In the year of its foundation the union mounted its first championship, over nine holes at Lytham, for thirty-eight entrants and launched Lady Margaret Scott on her briefly visible career. It was followed in 1897 by the Midland Championship, and in 1901 the LGU established a tournament network involving fourteen counties.[113] In 1905 a Welsh Ladies' Union emerged. The last four years before the outbreak of war were matched by friction and schism when a rival National Alliance was formed over the issues of tournament play. It was a battle between a tiny minority.[114]

For most women, golf remained a local, emphatically amateur game played for health and social bonding rather than competition. There were few arenas for employment or professional play within the game; most instruction came from men employed jointly with neighbouring men's clubs or within mixed clubs. Mrs Gordon Robertson was employed by Prince's Ladies' Club on Mitcham Common before 1914 and Lily Freemantle, whose father was a professional, taught for Sunningdale Ladies' after 1911. One English lady amateur, Miss D. M. Smyth, turned pro for the Le Touquet ladies' club. But these were exceptions; there was no female tradition of caddying or artisan play to draw on, and few avenues to paid secretaryship, although such a path was mooted as desirable for 'a girl who is thrown on her own resources, without having any talent which is worth cultivating' by May Hazlet, the Ladies' Champion of 1899 and 1902.[115]

Women's golf, for all its extent, remained an area of considerable ambivalence, some conflict and continued symbolic if not always actual subjection. The younger unmarrieds were still open to active parental disapproval. Three Orr sisters competed in the women's championship in 1897 and one, Edith, won; their father refused them further permission to play when he discovered that there had been betting on the result.[116] There is little chance of recovering the substrata of familial exclusion from which that emerged to public notice. But there could be other tensions, particularly in a household where a keen and competent woman golfer used the game in a battle with a pliant or aggrieved husband. A. J. P. Taylor's mother played at Southport, and well, but she dragooned her very reluctant spouse to partner her until she became so exasperated that she found other sporting partners. That left the father happily free to go out with his young son again on Saturday mornings.[117]

By then golf provided a gender battleground on a much wider and more visible scale. Militant suffragettes found courses easy to attack; open greens and scattered sheds offered ready targets for vandalism. In 1907 the Edgware Club pleaded immunity, since 'At present all play over the same greens, and so the suffragettes are not likely to attack the place.'[118] When the militant wing erupted into action in 1913 it burned greens with vitriol, etching in messages such as 'No votes, no golf', and attacked Lloyd George's golf cottage at Walton Heath, which a later generation knows as his illicit love nest, an ironic symbol of exploitation.[119] Suggestions that greenkeepers should thrash the culprits met with little support; it proved impossible, anyway, since the attackers invariably got away. Behind the open protests and the engagement with male golfers on their own bureaucratic terms lay a level of domestic gender frustration which the caricatures of 'golf widows' in press and cartoon probably increased. Only rarely did it emerge openly, as when Mrs Edward Kennard produced her partly ironic *Sorrows of a Golfer's Wife*, resignedly accepting that it was less of a domestic risk than gambling or drinking, and admitting, 'For myself, I put up with it in the process of time, because I discovered that I *had* to do so.'[120]

Some wealthier women found other ways to freedom but in new activities of marginal significance. Motoring women were held to be free of headaches, likely to benefit from open-air adventure, although there was little discussion of technical skills in the articles advocating driving. The Ladies' Automobile Club of Great Britain was formed in 1904, housed on two floors of a wing of a London hotel, Claridge's. Its 325 members were essentially motor tourists; racing was usually regarded as distinctly unladylike. Lady balloonists were treated even more as privileged eccentrics. The Edwardian founding of a Women's Aerial League operated as a pressure group on men to foster their interest in aviation rather than direct participation.[121]

It was in another minor boom sport that a relatively small group became models after 1900 for the development of sporting women in the service of eugenics and the empire. By 1913 the National Rifle Association's *Proceedings* listed eleven separate ladies' clubs, with 292 members, and hinted at a number of other bodies' existing as branches of male clubs.[122] Twelve of these latter were listed with women honorary secretaries. The apostle of small-bore shooting generally was a millionaire, Walter Winans, who produced a handbook, *Shooting for Ladies*, in 1911. For women Winans saw the role of shooting as being jointly for amusement 'or for self-defence in uncivilised countries'. He was emphatic in his disapproval of women as game shots because he felt that it led to an unfeminine indifference to pain. Feminine biology would restrict shooting stances; the favoured male position for target shooting, lying prone or supine, would produce influenza and was indelicate. The woman with a rifle was expected to sit on a chair or stand, the 'prettiest and best position'.[123] Special guns would need to be developed to cope with busts, and there were repeated appeals by shooting's propagandists to its aesthetic appeal for women. Grace was an important prelude to performance. Winans also viewed women's participation as instrumental in developing male militarism; their shooting would shame men into emulation.

The clubs developed best where social cachet had highest value, largely in the Home Counties. Fifteen Surrey ladies' rifle clubs, led by Esher and Byfleet, formed a county association in February 1911. Byfleet had been the first ladies' club in the country and its members had started to shoot at Bisley, the national competition ground, in 1910. Baliol Scott of the Weybridge club was positive as to the value of shooting in calming nerves, training the eye and preparing young women for marriage to men who ran the colonies. Surrey was the fringe of a social focus which centred on women's joint membership of the Imperial Rifle Club in Cork Street, on the edge of Mayfair, 'a West End club which puts the cult of the rifle and revolver before everything else'.[124] Everything else, that was, apart from the attractions of membership of a body where half the 800 members were men. Few women shots, however, linked 'this feminine coquetry of the rifle' with any wider struggle for emancipation. The emphasis was largely on strengthening the gracious weapons of sexual conquest and of a subordinate partnership with men. The prospects of becoming Amazons was usually laughed at in women's own writing on the sport: for the small Brighton and Hove Ladies' Rifle Club, formed in 1901, shooting was 'a morning hobby only', giving way to bridge in the afternoon.[125] For all the wider claims of its place in protecting an empire under threat, it joined most other women's sports as a place of social containment, extending rather than challenging restrictive boundaries.

Notes

1 C. Dyhouse, *Girls Growing up in Late Victorian and Edwardian England* (1981); *Feminism and the Family in England, 1880–1939* (1989); K. McCrone, *Sport and the Physical Emancipation of English Women, 1817–1914* (1988).
2 Bickerdyke, *Sea Fishing*, 8.
3 C. G. Barrington, *Seventy Years' Fishing* (1906), 240–1.
4 *Baily's Hunting Directory, 1912–13*.
5 *Baily's Magazine*, 71 (1899), 5 ff.; *Baily's Hunting Directory, 1912–13*, 9 ff.
6 *Humanitarian*, November 1913.
7 Sargent, *Thoughts upon Sport*, 253.
8 Walker, *Shooting on a Small Income*, 103.
9 A. Stodart Walker and P. J. Mackie, *The Keeper's Book* (1904), 56.
10 F. W. Millard, 'The gamekeeper's profession as a career', *Badminton Magazine*, XXII (1906), 158.
11 Warwickshire Record Office, CR 1798/2, Warwick Boat Club, Minutes.
12 W. G. Grace, *Cricket*, 46, 210.
13 *Yachting Monthly*, XI (1911), 300.
14 J. A. Mason, *The Complete Bowler* (1912), 1919 edition, 148.
15 H. G. Hutchinson, *Golf* (1893), 282 ff., 298.
16 Leeds Golf Club, Minute Books.
17 West Sussex Record Office, Add. Ms 20,001–2, Goodwood Golf Club, Minutes.
18 Leeds Golf Club, Minute Books.
19 Cornish and Whitten, *Golf Course*, 167.
20 Stainton, *Golf Courses of Yorkshire*, 40 ff.
21 *Hull Daily Mail*, 12 June 1908.
22 *Golf Monthly*, August 1914, 461.
23 *Golf Monthly*, March 1913, 86.
24 *Golf Monthly*, July 1914.
25 *Golf Monthly*, January 1913, 828.
26 *Golf Illustrated*, 16 March, 2 July 1909.
27 *Golf Illustrated*, 22 October 1909.
28 Dr MacNamara, *The Gentle Golfer* (1905), 127 ff.
29 H. G. Hutchinson, *Bert Edward the Golf Caddie* (1903), 164.
30 *Golf Illustrated*, 26 May 1905.
31 *Golf*, 19 September 1890.
32 Leeds Golf Club, Minute Books.
33 *Golf Illustrated*, 11 August 1899.
34 R. H. Lyttelton, *Outdoor Games – Cricket and Golf* (1901), 199.
35 A. Shadwell, *Industrial Efficiency* (1905), 1913 edition, 500.
36 Lord's Day Observance Society, *Occasional Papers*, April 1906.
37 *Ibid.*, July 1905.
38 *Badminton Magazine*, XXX (1910), 63–4.
39 *The Times*, 27 July, 15 September, 18 December 1909.
40 *The Times*, 20 July 1910.
41 H. S. Colt, 'The caddie evil', *Golf Illustrated*, 30 July 1909; *Golf Illustrated*, 27 August 1909.
42 *Golf Illustrated*, 20 August 1909.
43 *The Times*, 17 November 1911.

44 Agenda Club, *An Open Letter to English Gentlemen*(1910); *Spectator*, 9 July 1910; *The Rough and the Fairway*(1912).
45 *Times*, 16 April 1912.
46 *Golf Monthly*, March 1913.
47 *Golf Monthly*, April 1913.
48 Sir G. Riddell, 'Caddies', in Sutton, *Book of the Links*, 99 ff.
49 *Golf Monthly*, March 1914.
50 *C. B. Fry's Magazine*, 16 (1912), 27.
51 Hobsbawm, 'Mass-producing traditions', 299.
52 M. Curtin, 'A question of manners', *Journal of Modern History*, 57 (1985), 418 ff.
53 S. Armitage, 'The Lady as Jock: a popular culture perspective on the woman athlete', *Journal of Popular Culture*, 10(1976), 122 ff.
54 *C. B. Fry's Magazine*, 5(1906–07), 177.
55 *Baily's Magazine*, June 1905, 437.
56 G. Cadogan Rothay, 'The outdoor life', *Sportswoman*, November 1908.
57 *Daily Telegraph*, 3 October 1905.
58 J.A.C.K., *Golf in the Year 2000* (1892), 99; Haultain, *Mystery*, 10.
59 F. G. Aflalo,' The sportswoman', *Fortnightly Review*, LXXVII (1905), 91.
60 Watson, *English Sports*, 45.
61 J. Cantlie, *Physical Efficiency* (1906), 203.
62 *Nineteenth Century*, April 1899, 643.
63 *Baily's Magazine*, June 1913, 405.
64 *Ibid*.
65 A. R. Haig-Brown, 'Women and sport', *Baily's Magazine*, January 1905, 25 ff.; An Oxford Blue, 'Are women approaching men in sport?', *C. B. Fry's Magazine*, 16(1912), 200 ff.; *Cycling: a Handbook*(1899), 72; *C. B. Fry's Magazine*, 1(1904), 110.
66 Warwickshire Record Office, CR 1798/2, Warwick Boat Club, Minutes, 31 July 1899.
67 Waltham Record Office, W37 3884 RM 8.
68 Leeds Golf Club, Minutes.
69 Northampton Reference Library, *Miscellaneous Cuttings*, 27 July 1861.
70 'Toxophilites of the twentieth century', *Brighton Season*, 1905–06.
71 Lillie, *Croquet*, 133.
72 Lillie, *Croquet*, 218.
73 Lillie, *Croquet*, 221 ff.
74 Osborn, *Lawn Tennis*, 30.
75 Mrs L. Chambers, *Lawn Tennis for Ladies* (1910), 2.
76 Watson, *English Sports*, 360–1; *Table Tennis and Pastimes Pioneer*, 18 January 1902.
77 Dale, *Riding, Driving*, 34 ff.
78 East Sussex Record Office, AMS 5788/3/1–3, Diary of the Crowhurst Otter Hounds, 1904–06; *Madame*, 16 September 1905.
79 *Angler*, 36 May 1894; E. Phillips, 'Angling as a sport for ladies', *Baily's Magazine*, July 1906, 62 ff.;*Badminton Magazine*, IV(1897), 313 ff.
80 W. E. Durham, *Summer Holidays in the Alps, 1898–1914* (1916), 162; Schuster, *Men, Women and Mountains*, 61 ff.
81 Rivington, *Punting*, 64.
82 *Frederick James Furnivall*.

83 Macfarlane-Grieve, *Durham Rowing*, 122.
84 Mead, *Royal Cornwall Yacht Club*, 108; Humber Yawl Club, *Yearbook* (Hull, 1911); Speed, *Yachtswomun's Cruises*.
85 *Clerk*, May 1890.
86 Fiddes, *Owens College*, 122.
87 I. M. Webb, 'Women's hockey in England', in R. Benson, P. P. de Mayer and M. Ostyn (eds.), *The History, the Evolution and Diffusion of Sports and Games in Different Cultures* (Brussels, 1976).
88 *Gamages Hockey Annual and Club Guide for 1911–12*.
89 Smith and Robinson, *Hockey*, 291 ff.
90 *Ibid.*
91 'Hockey's rise in Brighton', *Brighton Season*, 1905–06.
92 C. Holland, 'The ABC of swimming for ladies', *Badminton Magazine*, 17 (1903), 157 ff.
93 L. Eaton Hill (ed.), *Athletics and Outdoor Sports for Women* (New York, 1903), 415.
94 R. Gittings, *The Older Hardy* (1978), 84, 103.
95 W. H. Fenton, 'Cycling for ladies', *Nineteenth Century*, May 1896, 796 ff.; Rubinstein, 'Cycling in the 1890s', 64.
96 Cyclists' Touring Club, *Monthly Gazette*, October 1896.
97 W. H. Fea, 'Grace in cycling and how to attain it', *Badminton Magazine*, III(1896), 214.
98 Albemarle and Hillier, *Cycling*, 219; A. C. Pemberton *et al.*, *The Complete Cyclist* (1897), 56.
99 *Nineteenth Century*, September 1897, 447 ff.
100 *Sheffield Annual Record*, 2 March 1896.
101 R. Macaulay, *Told by an Idiot* (1923), 96.
102 B. Darwin, 'Golf in 2009', *C. B. Fry's Magazine*, 10, 552; Amy B. Pascoe, 'Ladies', in H. G. Hutchinson, *The Book of Golf* (1899), 223 ff.
103 H. Seton-Karr, 'Golf and matrimony', *Golf Monthly*, December 1912, 747 ff.
104 Enid Wilson, 'Women's golf', in Darwin *et al.*, History of Golf, 223.
105 *Northampton Independent*, 2 May 1914.
106 Wilson, 'Women's golf', 225.
107 West Sussex Record Office, Add. Ms 20,002.
108 *Golf Monthly*, February 1912, 932.
109 *Baily's Magazine*, May 1897, 367.
110 *The Guinness Book of Golf Facts and Feats* (1982), 237.
111 *Brighton Season*, 1905–06.
112 *Ibid.*
113 M. Hazlet, *Ladies' Golf* (1904).
114 Wilson, 'Women's golf', 226–9.
115 Mrs Gordon Robertson, *Hints to Lady Golfers*(1909); Hazlet, *Ladies' Golf*, 210.
116 *Guiness Book of Golf Facts and Feats*, 233.
117 Taylor, *Personal History*, 14–15.
118 *Truth*, 1907, 1339.
119 *Golf Monthly*, March 1913, 46.
120 Kennard, *Sorrows*, 295.
121 K. D'Esterre Hughes, 'Motoring for women', *Badminton Magazine*, 20(1905), 432 ff.; *C. B. Fry's Magazine*, 13 (1910), 285 ff.

122 National Rifle Association, *Proceedings* (1913).
123 W. Winans, *Shooting for Ladies*(1911), 11.
124 National Rifle Association, *Journal*, March, October 1911.
125 *Brighton Season*, 1905–06.

Chapter 8
Sport as business

Areas of investment

'Playing the game' was important, but for a substantial proportion of the middle classes it also produced a living; not from 'professionalism' but from their own 'secular' occupation. The money came from investment in and management of sport's material requirements. It matched some of the vicissitudes of the late Victorian economy but it also provided a partial counterbalance to the many claims of decline. In one piece of special pleading *Fry's Magazine* claimed in 1910 that the self-control that sport induced 'is of a marketable quality. It is of the greatest value in business and social life.'[1] Those qualities were expressed in the businesses that sport itself engendered.

The actual extent of the resulting economic activity is remarkably difficult to establish, although there were scattered 'guestimates'. One writer in 1895 reckoned on an annual British expenditure of £47 million and an overall investment of £46 million in sport which would have represented some 3 per cent of the gross national product.[2] By 1912 expenditure on golf alone was calculated at £7 million annually, of which some £600,000 went on buying the 7.2 million golf balls used each year.[3] An earlier Edwardian commentator claimed that the purchase of golf balls had come to exceed the annual import of bananas. If this were true some picture of the extent can be gauged, because detailed returns for some fruit imports were kept from 1900. In that year £548,956 worth of bananas came in; by 1910 the figure had risen to £1,698,556.[4] The actual bunch price fell in the period from some 8s to 5s 6d, just over twice the cost of a golf ball. Unfortunately there were no similar statistics for the balls. It was a fanciful comparison, weighing the value of two relatively new forms of middle-class consumption, complementaries rather than alternatives in the growth of pleasurable expenditure.

The American Price Collier offered another perspective when he set his estimate of a total sport expenditure of $223,887,725 against English export patterns. He reckoned the domestic exports of the United Kingdom in 1903 at $38 a head, as compared with $10 a head going on sport.[5] Unfortunately the nature of the data available means that only parts of the general sector's performance can be readily identified. *Chambers's Journal* argued in 1895 that the growth of manufacturing for golf and cycling had done a great deal to reverse the fortunes of areas suffering economic decline such as Coventry.[6] Official returns of exports of bicycles (which are not matched by any for the domestic market) were first kept in 1892, when some 915,856 machines went abroad. At the height of the cycling boom, in 1896, the figure had increased to 1,855,604. It dropped for some years after that, with 1905 a low point – some 307,592. Thereafter an oscillating recovery took place, to 609,482 in 1913.[7]

A sectoral share in gross national product of about 3 per cent hardly represented a major corrective to late Victorian claims of manufacturing decline. Much of the *matériel* used by British sportsmen was imported. But in some places and for some of the middle classes the new investment opportunities were considerable. They generated not only income and capital formation but also social prestige and opportunities for local influence, so that expected gains were not always expressed in economic terms.

A great deal of the money that flowed through sport at the turn of the century came from growing working-class marginal incomes, poured into angling or Association Football. But this was usually the purchasing of facilities on a limited personal scale. The investment that made the growth of mass football possible was essentially middle-class. As Tony Mason and Charles Korr have shown, this was both the seizure of new economic opportunities and the manipulation of complex local status networks by urban business and professional men. Mason identified a working-class presence as directors of only 8 per cent across a range of football clubs, with boards being dominated by wholesalers and retailers.[8] With minor local variations this pattern applied also to more exclusive facilities, where like met those they thought they might like, and to the growth of businesses whose markets were more impersonal. It is with them that this chapter is largely concerned.

Manufacturing: craft to factory

Between 1870 and 1914 existing manufacturing structures were adapted for sports goods products and modified by growing levels of consumer demand, some technological change and previously unavailable patterns of investment. What emerged was a continued tension between the small-scale, craft-orientated workshops that still accounted for so much of English employment and the tendency towards factories commonly associated with 'industrialisation'. The former proved singularly resilient in some areas, not least because of the growing snobbery associated with the possession of some of the implements of play, the tailored rather than the ready-made. There were, however, instances where both 'mass' production and the veneer of ancient craft quality were melded to profitable effect.

Traditional sports such as cricket or hunting had fostered manufacturing as a spin-off of existing leather or wood trades. Because of the nature of their raw material these were often regionally based. Hugh Barty-King has examined the growth of 'quilt winders and rod shavers', the cricket bat and ball manufacturers of Kent. There small local handicraft firms such as Duke's of Penshurst produced hand-sewn balls from the 1760s in small workshops until the level of demand obliged them to build a two-storey factory in the 1880s. They were essentially family-based firms, inherited across generations but fluid in the ways in which finance and partners came in through marriage or local influence patterns. Barty-King also demonstrated the growth of Warsop's, run from the 1870s as a family firm until it took on limited liability in 1900. Although Henry Luff came into it from Wisden's there were still five Warsops there. By 1907 they were supplying Harrod's, but the level of demand for the bats meant that they had difficulty finding supplies of raw materials.[9]

The best recorded example of all is Wisden's, located since the 1850s in London and Brighton, after starting up in Leamington, where John Wisden opened a new cricket ground in 1849. In 1855 he opened a cricket and cigar depot in London, initially in partnership with Lillywhite, who branched out into his own business, and shared that growth with his brother William in Brighton. They sold under their own brand goods which were made by others, including Duke's, a pattern which became increasingly common later in the century when the large London department stores such as Harrod's, Gamage's and the Army and Navy opened sports departments. John

Wisden died in 1884, and control passed effectively until 1910 into the hands of his manager, Henry Luff, who kept the established name. Luff owned it personally until incorporation in 1914 – after that his family still retained control. Long before that Wisden's had moved on from just retailing others' products. In 1896 they opened their first factory in Tonbridge, Kent, to produce cricket balls, within the traditional region of their manufacture, and opened another in West Ham some years later. They had also begun publishing the *Almanack*, a source of endless joy to the armchair cricketer.[10]

Not all small family firms became major ones: many were very ephemeral. When lawn tennis boomed in the later 1870s the leather and gut workers of the small Lincolnshire town of Horncastle turned to racquet-making, but their involvement had declined before the end of the century.[11] The capital formation necessary for these very small firms to take advantage of rapidly growing but distant markets was often difficult, and few grew considerably. There are, quite literally, a handful of key names, and their records are scarce.

One of these was John Jaques & Son, incorporated as a limited liability company in 1899. It was founded by Thomas Jaques in 1795 as a general wood and ivory manufacturer in London. The firm found a ready outlet for its ivory false teeth but had moved also to producing chessmen by the Napoleonic period. An heir, John Jaques the second, claimed to have introduced croquet to England, organising a display at the Great Exhibition of 1851. In 1864 he wrote the standard work on the game's regulations as a response to the steady growth in the market for family games and equipment into which the firm had moved. This John Jaques acquired the freedom of the City of London and played a prominent role in a livery company, the Turners. Innovation depended very much on continued family commitment; when John Jaques the third, a keen athlete, entered the business in 1884 he expanded the production of goods for team games, with 'improved' but unspecified manufacturing techniques. It was he who hyped 'Ping-Pong' in its early Edwardian rivalry, changing the name from its first one of 'Gossima'.

Jaques also responded to the bowls boom by installing new machinery for the faster production of cheaper woods. As a market leader the firm did much to move sports goods production away from its handicraft roots to cheaper machining. It also meant a decisive shift towards sports and away from the parlour games whose middle-class domestic appeal had underpinned the firm's mid-Victorian expansion. When the family decided on incorporation in 1899, presumably to protect its own liabilities in an expanding but fickle market, John the third took a salary of £400 a year for working 'full-time' in their Hatton Garden base in London. At that point the firm was valued at £35,000. When, in 1912, after John's death, continued growth was preserved by allowing in non-family shareholders, expansion was strictly limited to prevent loss of control by the family.[12]

Jaques's place in lawn games was more than matched by Hardy's in angling. Despite the general rule which assumed that prosperity would come to sports firms with factories located near the big industrial conurbations, Hardy's grew and stayed in the small Northumberland town of Alnwick, where several other smaller fishing tackle manufacturers were also located. The middle-class fashion for fly fishing prompted a level of demand which strained their joint production capacity. One estimate in 1894 claimed that the town's total output of fly rods in the mid-1880s was 800 a year, just over two per working day. By the mid-1890s the annual figure had risen to 3,500.[13] Craft production dominated, but rods were far from being the only part of the company's activities. Both collecting mania and the ability of fishermen to lose tackle ensured a steady market at this, the top end of the angling trade, something made clear in the 1880s by one retailer:

> We could never live by selling fishing tackle to gentlemen if they only took what they needed . . . our profit is made out of what gentlemen buy and pay for which they *don't* want, and which is no good to themselves, or any one else, and what *they lose in the grass*.[14]

Hardy's was begun by two brothers, William and John James, engineers, who turned to the fishing trade in 1871. Their skills were most clearly used in the design of finely engineered reels, including the Model Perfect, which has remained in production with only minor amendments for a century. The firm also developed rod production with the split cane technique, using bamboo segments glued together to give varying degrees of flexibility for the type of fishing undertaken. By 1905 the Hardy catalogue covered 400 pages, with most of the sport's requisites being manufactured on the premises.[15] The small shop the brothers had started in was replaced, until, after three moves, they opened in the late 1880s a four-storey 'Jacobean' factory (the North British Works) with a small retail outlet at the front. The machinery at different levels was belt-driven by a central gas cycle engine, and each floor produced different items.[16] In addition there was a fly-tying association which combined central management with out-work by Alnwick women. The products were exhibited regularly at international trade shows, where a collection of medals was acquired. This was the top end of the market, and the 'second and third sons of Britain's landed gentry became unofficial salesmen for Hardy Brothers' all over the world.[17]

These customers measured sporting possessions by their visibility. Although production grew and the brothers showed an astute ability to place their goods, they retained much of the small-workshop, craft-based ethos. They ran a benevolent factory whose annual outings to northern pleasure places by the whole work force were reported in the *Fishing Gazette*.[18] Seeking to expand further, they took limited liability status in 1907; the aim was to raise £10,000, but by debentures rather than public flotation. The directors included seven Hardys, and only members of the company were allowed to take out shares in a firm then valued at nearly £70,000. The range of employee involvement was considerable. Whilst William held 27,000 of the shares, the Alnwick foreman held 350, three rod finishers held twenty-five, twenty and ten, and Mary Mustard, one of the fly dressers, took ten.[19]

Hardy's success made Alnwick attractive to some of its rivals. In 1896 W. H. Dingley established the Climax Reel Works, producing the first mechanical spinning drums, and Walker Bampton's Northern Rod & Reel Works were opened in 1906. They posed little real threat to Hardy's social and sporting dominance, since what they offered were goods for that large part of the middle-class angling market which could not afford Hardy products.[20]

In Ashbourne, Derbyshire, Messrs D. & W. H. Foster occupied a similar, although less exalted, position to Hardy's. Founded in 1833, the firm specialised in the production and postal sale of flies and rods. Although it used split cane segments for the latter, it used a technique that Hardy's also came to employ: the rods were built round a thin steel core to give strength and resilience. The key to the success of many of these limited enterprises was the careful harnessing of new Victorian technologies to craft production.[21]

Much of the middle-class angling market overlapped with the huge contemporary increase in working-class fishing. To meet their needs a few large-scale manufacturers emerged, growing out of established industries. The wire-drawing and needle-making firms in Redditch, south of Birmingham, diversified into making fishing hooks. One concern, Allcock's, grew until it seems to have dominated the mass production of angling goods, with 600 'hands' by the mid-1880s. Its key figure until his death in 1910, aged eighty-one, was Samuel Allcock, a Wesleyan Sunday school superintendent, Guardian and Justice of the Peace, who built the firm up rapidly from the mid-Victorian years.[22] His Standard Works produced goods that won gold medals in international trade exhibitions in Paris and Berlin but kept to needle-making as well. The firm had branches in London, Paris and Toronto, and a silk gut factory for fishing lines in Murcia, in Spain; it marketed 200 different models of hook in up to thirty sizes.[23]

The rosy picture of Allcock's expansion, sedulously reported in the *Fishing Gazette*, had some hiccups. Samuel Allcock hinted that the market's growth by 1900 was being exceeded by overproduction, clearly by his competitors, when he spoke to the annual dinner of a local fishing club. He was worried by price-cutting, by the 'insensate cut-throat policy' of selling hooks at $8^1/2$ d per thousand wholesale instead of the £1 per thousand he preferred. He claimed it meant 'starvation wages for the work people'; his response was to suggest price-fixing by a combination of manufacturers.[24] There is little evidence that such a cartel ever emerged, but Allcock's survived without a substantial reduction in its prices. The angling press carried frequent reports of the firm's success and of its classic paternalism, annual outings, employees' dinners and so on. Samuel's death did not deprive the firm of family control, it passed laterally to his relatives. When his grandson, A. Courtney Williams, came of age in 1913 the firm's staff gave him the sort of dinner that the tenants of great landed estates had customarily afforded their lord's heir. Despite his preparatory school and Malvern College education this was one entrepreneur's scion who stayed with the firm that had paid for it – 'he had all the characteristics of a business gentleman'.[25]

With its rather smaller market the sporting gun trade depended equally on craft-centred production. At the 'best gun' end of the industry, this was linked specifically with retail outlets, since both shotguns and rifles were fitted like bespoke suits. Finish, with good wood and fine engraving, was as important as killing power. There were well known provincial firms, often providing for a wide range of shooting needs, such as Elderkin's of Spalding (founded in 1880), which still exists, but the greatest prestige attached to the West End of London's shops, providing for the grouse moor and pheasant covert and for the specialised big game hunting of a growing empire. The exemplar was and is James Purdey's. Combining carefully restrained innovation with tailored production, the firm moved from Oxford Street to South Audley Street in 1879.[26] Purdey shotguns were usually bought in matched pairs to allow for more rapid loading at the butts by their servants. The trade grew slightly in response to quality demand as qualified gunsmiths moved on after serving apprenticeships with established firms. Henry Atkin's of Jermyn Street (1878) and Frederick Beesley's (1880) were founded by men who had served initially with Purdey's. The number of these prestigious central firms was small; to those named can be added Boss, Churchill, Cogswell & Harrison and Holland & Holland. With a pair of their guns selling at around £120 and long queues of clients, they grew at a pace they could handle. The oak-pannelled West End premises, with frock-coated staff and discreet showcases, were supported by small factories in the suburbs, and by shooting grounds where the weapons could be tried out and anxious buyers taught to use them. Cogswell & Harrison opened one such near Harrow, Holland & Holland one in the Harrow Road.[27]

They could not have coped with the growing level of demand from rough shooters, clay-pigeon shots, farmers and gamekeepers. For them guns were mass-produced, with some minor alterations being made in their local gun shops. These 'reach me down' guns were made largely in Birmingham by big firms such as Greener or Westley Richards. The latter had a London outlet but relied on a much wider market; in the last decades of the nineteenth century the company sold some 10,000 hammerless ejector shotguns.[28] Many went through independent provincial retailers, still carrying the manufacturer's name, but were often relabelled by the retailer, especially in the sports departments of the big London stores. The fifty individual parts used in a shotgun were produced by specialist divided labour; barrels and stocks were machine-made and finished. The Birmingham trade's strength rested on military demand. Of the 12,000 or so employed in British gun-making by the 1870s some two-thirds were in Birmingham.[29]

When Westley Richards celebrated their centenary in 1912 they were offering some forty different models of shotgun, and 160 models of rifle, with a strong emphasis on overseas sport, in a 214 page catalogue.[30] But, unlike the 'best gun' firms in London, there were difficulties. Even their cheaper guns were being undercut by sharp foreign competition. Two of the Greener family examined this in a large book, *The Causes of Decay in a British Industry*, in 1907, claiming a steady decline since the 'zenith' of the 1870s. The number of London gunsmiths had shrunk from sixty-three in 1880 to twenty in 1906, and Eley's, the cartridge maker, had seen profits fall from 25 per cent in the 1880s to 5 per cent by 1904. They estimated that Birmingham's output had fallen by half. It was not just the growth of the big firms that had done this – they were unable to compete with overseas producers, particularly the Belgians, whose worker's output was at least a seventh greater than his British equivalent's. What has since become a familiar story, although it is Spanish gunmakers who have now replaced the Belgians, was blamed on outmoded English methods, the use of craft techniques for a low-quality, low-return market, and the gun licence tax, which restricted the sport's domestic growth.[31]

Big business

Manufacturing for the newer mass sports was generally more fortunate, although fashion and self-inflicted injury provided their own vicissitudes. Because of the novelty of their goods and their financial arrangements firms in this sector attracted rather more general attention than the smaller enterprises. Like sport itself, the new businesses, particularly where they were organised as limited companies, were often regarded as the epitome of both the opportunities and the ethical crises affecting English industry as the nineteenth century closed. S. F. Van Oss, writing in the *Nineteenth Century* in 1898, estimated that a tenth of all the nation's wealth was now so invested, leeched on by the 'modern company hatcher, the man who contrives to live, and live well, because he is able to extract profits from plausible theories'.[32]

It was cycling and its key ancillary, rubber manufacturing, that epitomised this moral crisis. In its early days the activity's slow growth was largely satisfied by craft production concentrated in the Midland metal trades, particularly round Coventry. A cycle could involve between 300 and 500 components whose production demanded some 3,000 workers employed by 145 bicycle and 140 tricycle manufacturers.[33] The average of around ten per manufacturer emphasises the scale of operation in small family firms. Some have survived until the present day but most were displaced rapidly by the technological changes and production patterns that emerged with the pneumatically tyred cycle of the later 1880s.

There had been a steady growth in the rubber industry after mid-century, based on domestic needs and on components provided for railway carriages. Eventually the demand for golf balls and contraception added new leisure requirements but it was John Boyd Dunlop's rediscovery of the pneumatic tyre in 1888 that prompted a rapid and singularly insecure expansion in the 1890s. W. Woodruff has examined this in the general context of rubber manufacturing; because of the new market, cycling came to rival footwear as the greatest customer for the trade whose workers, based largely in the Midlands, rose in number from 10,621 in 1891 to 18,516 ten years later.[34]

This growth saw investors mesmerised by some promoters. Dunlop formed a company in 1889 to find £25,000 as the start of his 'spectacular career'.[35] He and others were soon sucked into a speculative boom rivalled only by the Railway Mania of half a century before. The key figure in this, an apparent incarnation of Trollope's fictional Melmotte in *The Way we live Now (1875)*, was Ernest Terah Hooley, who eventually served two terms of imprisonment for fraud. He could claim with some justice in the 1920s:

I am the man who put cycling all over the world, not only because I was responsible for the flotation of practically all the big present-day companies, but because I put Dunlop on the market.[36]

He did this with financial legerdemain and corruption on a huge scale. He appeared on the market with a good reputation and £100,000 in 1895 and played on greed and gullibility, using the additional attraction of landed titles wherever he could suck their holders on to his boards as nominal directors. He purchased Dunlop for £3 million and floated it for £5 million almost immediately in 1896, spending £10,000 on advertising. In the next couple of years he promoted twenty-six companies, with a total nominal capital of £18.6 million – he managed to raise only some £5 million of that. Fifteen of the companies were cycle manufacturers, including Raleigh, which he floated for £200,000 in 1896, and the Singer Cycle Company, floated for £80,000. Between times he floated Schweppe's (for £1.25 million) and Bovril; he was a lateral thinker, associating the efforts of cycling with the need for respectable liquid refreshment.[37]

The bubble burst in 1898. Having lost £89,000, he was bankrupted, with 414 creditors. He had covered his tracks sufficiently well to go on living in luxury, spending an estimated £100,000 a year. He was then thirty-eight and had gone into voluntary liquidation to fend off a demand for £80,000 from Emerson Bainbridge, the MP for Gainsborough. At the peak of his City career he had given £15,000 worth of plate to St Paul's Cathedral to celebrate Victoria's Diamond Jubilee and been elected to the Carlton, Badminton and Royal Thames Yacht Clubs. The flotation of the Humber Cycle Company alone had netted him £365,000, but that, and much else of the money raised, had been diverted from its anticipated use in extending production. Long after his conviction he admitted, with consummate cheek, to being careless about his bookkeeping:

> When a man brings out two companies a week, as I sometimes did, it stands to reason that it would be utterly impossible for him to devote any particular time to detail.[38]

Public fury was not directed only against Hooley; the fraud was seen as another sign of the moral decay of the English middle classes. But it was the aristocracy involved who experienced steady erosion of their prestige. Hooley had had little difficulty in attracting 'peer guinea-pigs' for his boards. His most noted partner, Earl de la Warr, added support for Hooley to his other misplaced attempts to find a quick way out of the family's persistent financial decline. They included a one-mile cycle track, 'De la Warr Boulevard', on his faltering seaside development at Bexhill.[39] Hooley claimed to have offered the earl £10,000 to recruit a duke and £5,000 apiece 'for a couple of ordinary peers' for his boards. De la Warr's biggest catch was the Duke of Somerset.[40] When the collapse came it was Hooley who went down and the High Society which had courted him so assiduously for his bribes dropped him abruptly.

The collapse of the 1895–97 cycling boom was not just brought about by Hooley; he was the most spectacular symbol of misplaced confidence and poor reading of the long-term market. One cycling writer saw the recession as the embodiment of 'Darwin's law of the fittest', the outcome of malice in the tyre trade.[41] Another saw it as the failure of Dunlop's industrial czarism, the attempt to create 'a huge monopoly for their pecuniary benefit'.[42] But some companies survived to cope for the slimmed-down demand for cycles and their accessories. One that did so, albeit with continued difficulties, was F. Hopper & Co., located in the rather remote village of Barton on Humber in Lincolnshire. A. E. Harrison has analysed Hopper's problems in capital supply as its founder, technically brilliant but entrepreneurially inept, tried to keep going. Having begun in 1881 as a blacksmith assembling parts, he started frame production during the boom, and survived a buy-out and collapse, using his strong base of cheap Lincolnshire labour. He relied on bank overdrafts, an attempt at limited liability in 1907 proving a failure. It was the kindness of long-suffering local bank managers, or their appreciation of what would happen to Barton's economy if he went under, which enabled Hopper to remain as a respected name in the industry.[43] Others abandoned cycle-making and returned to their strengths. One such was William Cooper Ltd, of the Old Kent Road, in London. Cooper's had a well established business in horticultural supplies and prefabricated buildings, ranging from 'tin' mission churches to the clubhouses bought by so many bowls and golf clubs. For a short while they turned to cycle manufacture in the mid-1890s, claiming to produce a thousand a week, but by the turn of the century they had gone back to the safer world of the conservatory.[44]

The surviving English cycle makers operated on very tight margins, and the restricted turnover made capital formation for expansion unattractive to investors more cautious after the 1897 collapses. A *Badminton* contributor in 1900 reckoned that it cost £3 10s to produce an ordinary cycle and that the retail price of £4–£5 was insufficient to justify reasonable dividends.[45] He claimed that only nine of the twenty-three leading English makers had paid any dividend recently and that only two had reached the ten per cent he thought such speculation justified. But there were survivors. Thomas and Donnelly have shown that in Coventry the cycle trade had seen the first real establishment of modern factory production to replace the existing workshop base, acting as the bridge between a declining watchmaking trade and the establishment of motor vehicle manufacturing which came before the First World War. At one point in the 1890s the cycle makers had increased to seventy in number, buying-in parts from other Coventry makers and from Birmingham and Chelmsford accessory producers. Rudge Whitworth survived, to employ 2,700 workers who produced 75,000 cycles in 1906.[46] For such firms the 1890s remained as a warning. Others had cashed in on the peripheries briefly and gone elsewhere. Jaques acknowledged the boom with a board game, *Wheeling*, which offered tiny lead figures of male and female cyclists who started and finished at the Anchor inn in Ripley, facing obstacles formed by accidents, punctures and the police. It was indoor sport for bad weather.[47]

On the whole it was family firms, eventually protected as private limited liability companies, which proved the strongest sports manufacturers. H. S. Lunn, who later played a major role in the development of winter sports travel, originally spent the 1870s in lawn tennis retailing, selling racquets by post through *Exchange and Mart*. He was the son of a grocer in Horncastle, Lincolnshire, able to use his contacts with the town's leatherworkers, as we have already noted. When he decided to train as a Methodist missionary doctor in the 1880s he sold the business to his father for £1,000 and went off to India until illness redirected his energies into Swiss travel. In that, but with rather more rectitude than Hooley, he used 'hand-picked' aristocrats to whom he offered free tickets if they would introduce their friends to the firm. His father soon gave up the lawn tennis trade.[48]

There were many others prepared to fill the space. We have already noted the role of Jaques but very little can be reconstructed about T. M. Gardiner's Steam Tennis Works at Hoddesdon, Hertfordshire; the 'Steam' refers to the source of manufacturing power rather than the products.[49] In effect the heart of the game was increasingly dominated by two manufacturers. The first was F. H. Ayres, whose shop was in Aldersgate Street in the City of London. Ayres' provided a general range of services, such as installing removable grandstands for the Centre Court at Wimbledon, but the real money was to be found in selling balls as well as racquets. When Ayres' balls were used officially by the All England Club for the first time in 1881 it established the firm with a much wider market.[50] Ayres' adapted well to changes in fashion – when croquet began to boom gently again in the 1890s they sold 3,000 specimens of one mallet design alone in 1898 and as many again the following year.[51]

But one firm came to dominate public expectations of this trade – Slazenger's, who eventually claimed to be the world's largest manufacturer of tennis balls. Originating as a mid-Victorian producer of hand-made sporting goods, they moved rapidly into exploiting the demand for lawn tennis. By 1901 they claimed an annual profit of £26,867; it rose to £38,836 in 1910. To raise £110,000 for expansion Slazenger's went public in 1910. They succeeded – by 1913 profits had reached £49,226.[52] The success was based on the creation of a near-monopoly in supplying balls for English championships, centring strongly on Eastbourne and Wimbledon, with a strong Darwinian assumption about business life:

In this age of progress and the survival of the fittest, it is useless
attempting to cling to the sentiments of what is past.
The best of everything must assert its position.[53]

The architect of the firm's success was Archdale Palmer, 'Bland, but
decisive in manner, of first-class business capacity, sanguine but not
reckless, with many friends in and out of the City, a man of the
world with no known vices.'[54] At the time he was secretary of the All
England club he seems to have engineered a round-robin, signed by
all the leading players, requesting that Slazenger balls should replace
Ayres' in the championships. The committee preferred Ayres' but
gave in. Palmer joined Slazenger openly in 1905 whilst remaining at
Wimbledon, until scandal forced him out; thereafter the firm could
only benefit from his skills.[55]

Perhaps inevitably it was golf which claimed most attention in
terms of sustained economic development, although it never reached
the frenzied heights of the cycling craze. Henderson and Stirk have
calculated that there were about 160 club makers and seventy-four
golf-ball firms by 1914,[56] often small-scale. It was the golf ball itself
that attracted most business attention, partly because of its high loss
and damage rate but also because it became the symbol of new technologies in the rubber industry. The late Victorian game depended
on balls stuffed with gutta percha, either by hand or, increasingly,
by machine. Much changed in 1902 with the introduction to England
of the American Haskell ball, which had a core of tightly wound
rubber strips demanding machine production. It flew further but
was only really suited to large-scale production, and it was the big
rubber firms – Dunlop, North British, Rubastic and so on – which
dominated the market.

That dominance came about only after a series of legal cases arising
from the Haskell patent of 1898. The issue was whether Haskell really
had developed the method of production, or just patented it in the
hope of creaming off licence fees by blocking the use of similarly
produced balls already developed by others. In 1905 Haskell took
one such opponent, W. T. Henley's Telegraph Works Company, to
the High Court. The latter and other firms claimed that they had made
balls by a similar method since the 1870s, largely as children's toys.
Henley's claimed to have been making 700,000 balls a year before the
Haskell was introduced and had gone over to Haskell-type production
only because the new developments had virtually wiped out their

trade. Mr Justice Buckley ruled in their favour on the grounds that Haskell's patent was too vague and that Commander Stewart, RN, had made balls by a similar method in the 1870s. Haskell took the case to the Appeal Court the following year but it upheld the earlier judgement.[57] It was not a triumph for the continuation of gutta-percha; instead it allowed wholesale British manufacture without the additional costs of licensing.

In theory it should have led to a sharp fall in ball prices from the virtually universal half a crown, but, as *The Times* remarked, prices were more likely to increase, because the manufacturers were having to use more new rubber: not enough damaged balls were being returned for recycling.[58] By 1914, however, Spalding's were offering eleven different models, the cheapest, the 'Spalding Bob', at 1s.[59] The County Chemical Company of Birmingham offered its cheapest at 1s 6d. But most remained about the half-crown mark. It helped many rubber firms diversify, such as Wood-Milne of Preston, who mainly made rubber heels, but it was Dunlop who really dominated the market.[60]

On the verge of the First World War the boom was still attracting firms into new specialised production. The Rubastic Company opened new works at Southall, at an estimated cost of £650,000, to employ 5,000 in manufacturing a new seamless ball by a simplified moulding process.[61] Other events diverted its production, as they did that of the All British Boot Works in Northampton, which claimed a market in 1910 of some 250,000 golf shoes and brogues.[62] These were successful; others tried to move into the arena with insufficient funds and a poor reading of the demand. The Anglo-French Golf Ball Manufacturing Company of Bristol failed in 1912 when it stopped meeting mail orders. It had already received poor publicity; *Golf Monthly* had warned its readers to beware of its product.[63] Frank Johnson of Paternoster Row, London, failed in 1911 with £17,000 of debts on his golf implements business. He lacked capital; a flotation for £10,000 in 1909 had raised only £850. He had begun in 1900 with a borrowed £50 and opened branches in Glasgow and Liverpool when his profits reached £500 a year. But he was paying himself that amount a year as managing director.[64] The only way of surviving in the boom was either through the extended family networks that underpinned most capital formation for the smaller firms or through the diversified reserves of the market leaders.

By comparison with the crises to be found in golf-ball making, one

Edwardian boom sport, badminton, seemed surprisingly untroubled. Racquets could easily be made alongside those for tennis but the production of shuttlecocks remained a virtual French monopoly. In the days before plastics they were made by hand, and no English manufacturer could find labour ready to do it for as little as the French workers.[65]

Predators and protection

Manufacturing investment was only one aspect of capital formation and entrepreneurship. After the Hooley debacle speculators had a harder time, and a more substantial role was played by the provision of sites and services. In this the simpler assumptions of a direct investment/profit-seeking nexus prove an inadequate model for explaining what happened. As Vamplew has demonstrated in his studies of the capitalisation of professional cricket and football, the desired end results might have little to do with any financial return.[66] The hope of influence and the social prestige attendant on visible patronage could prove far stronger motives. There could be stranger twists. It is not uncommon to find evidence of clubs made up predominantly of the investing classes, using their own skills of capital mobilisation and management – and large gobbets of their disposable wealth – to create structures designed to prevent what they regarded as the predatory moves of their own kind, moves which often seem in other sectors to have provided them with the funds for it. The best example, the exploitation of land for sporting purposes, was replete with paradox.

Using syndicates to lease or buy attractive facilities was a well established practice before the late Victorian boom, but the emergence of such land-hungry activities as golf added a remarkable new dimension, and engendered ways of financing them which were often in tension or confusing. The title 'club', with its implicit assumptions about mutual association and regulation, was widely employed to mask direct speculative provision, on the lines of the late twentieth-century boom in 'exclusive' facilities for playing squash.

Mangan has shown how the cult of athleticism prompted some public schools to invest in sporting facilities. Harrow's fields grew from eight acres in 1849 to 146 by 1900, part of an expenditure of some £70,000. A similar rate of growth at Uppingham was financed largely by masters with private means.[67] That other great Victorian public institution, the seaside resort, played a more open role in a fierce competition for attracting respectable consumers and spenders. In 1914 a Littlehampton meeting was told that visitors to the town were likely to spend five times as much on its goods and services as they spent on golfing green fees. The assumption was that the latter would be the lure to profits from the former.[68]

The real issue was often not the provision itself but the means of investment. Bournemouth was convinced relatively early that providing for the demands of turn-of-the-century golfers would play a major role in any resort's ability to maintain its place in the hierarchy of social tone and profitability. The corporation laid out courses at its own expense on its commons in 1894 and, additionally, in 1903–05.[69] But, for most of its competitors, the encouragement of private investment was more acceptable than 'municipal socialism'. Scarborough relied on a limited company, formed in 1902, which dropped its initial joint intention of providing lawn tennis to concentrate on golf. When it opened its links in 1904 it found itself selling 3,000 visitors' tickets a year.[70] Farther south a Nottingham solicitor, Lawrence Kirk, bought a stretch of waste land outside Skegness and erected a 'miniature palace' of a clubhouse in the partly realised hope of persuading London golfers to spend Saturdays-to-Mondays there during the milder months.[71] The tiny inland resort of Woodhall Spa, in Lincolnshire, added golf and lawn tennis to its two grandiose hotels in the hope of luring suitable customers away from the seaside, again by private investment.[72]

Pressure in the resorts combined with that in players' home territory to add considerably to land values in some areas. One 1912 estimate reckoned that ground worth little more than 5s an acre in the late Victorian depression was by then fetching £20–£40 in ground rents.[73] Whilst there were often considerable regional variations in land use pressures, the desirability of local membership and the willingness of some landlords to lease or sell at lower prices for social reasons, there was generally a steep rise in golfing costs. The need to extend courses consequent on the adoption of the Haskell ball and the pressure for more grandiose social facilities added considerably to investment requirements and to the profit levels some speculators looked for. Some figures dominated golfing developments through their association with successfully marketed prestige proprietary clubs, although some of these were handed over to powerful oligarchies of directors when construction was complete.

W. Herbert Fowler, after an affluent youth spent playing cricket, took up golf at the age of thirty-five and laid out Walton Health in 1904 on land belonging to and financed by his brother-in-law. He went into partnership as a golf developer in 1910 with Thomas C. Simpson, a barrister from a wealthy Lancashire landed family, who gave up his practice to make money from the sport he had played at university.[74] The overlap between service and investment was most obvious in the career of H. S. Colt, another lawyer who had captained the Cambridge University club and gone on to be the paid secretary at Sunningdale, a post he combined with course design elsewhere whilst claiming to be the first non-professional to do so.[75]

These men responded readily to a growing market with schemes for which there were abundant models. The capitalisation of Association Football had been augmented by other proprietary patterns. In 1889 a Leeds businessman, William Howell, floated the Hyde Park Recreation Club, in a prestigious suburb, as a limited liability company; it offered lawn tennis, cycling, bowling and indoor social facilities for both sexes. In Newcastle upon Tyne a Cycling & Athletic Ground Company was formed in 1893 by local merchants and tradesmen to raise £3,000 for the twenty-one-year lease of eight acres of ground in Gosforth.[76]

The highest profile was that claimed where investment in playing facilities was used to help market 'exclusive' housing schemes. In what is now Dormans Park in south Surrey an old pheasant cover adjacent to the railway line to East Grinstead, a few miles away, was developed in the later 1880s by a Mr Barr with villas and verandahed bungalows as the Bellagio estate. It also offered a lawn tennis club with a small restaurant, and for twelve guineas a year the new inhabitants could fish for Loch Leven trout stocked in two lakes.[77] In this case the sport was virtually an afterthought, a meditative addition to pastoral calm. Elsewhere golf acquired a much more dominant role as a magnet for superior suburbs.

There is some irony in this. The golfer managed at the same time to appear as both the agent of uninhibited urban sprawl and as the preserver of open space against the developer. It led sometimes to less than subtle attempts to portray the game as a public benefactor, providing 'lungs that help in the operation of the suburb' whose development had removed yet more of rural England.[78] In the London area in particular a golf course as an integral part of a 'superior' development was regarded by the late 1890s as a singular inducement to investment and as an automatic enhancement of land values. In fact the results were varied. At Gidea Hall, on the outskirts of Romford in Essex, houses selling for £500 were built overlooking the new course. At Langley Park, Beckenham, an estate of almost 800 acres was turned into the 'new suburb of Park Langley', with large houses costing up to £600 surrounding a 160 acre course. Similarly, a development at Woodcote Park in Surrey provided 137 acres of golf amidst nearly 300 of houses.[79] The emphasis was virtually always on very low-density individual villas built in a revived vernacular style; the language that Ebenezer Howard had provided in his *Garden Cities of Tomorrow* (1902) found its way into the articles extolling these 'garden suburbs'. There was little perception among the advertisers of the irony in providing only the recreational side of Howard's vision, leaving the generation of wealth to the customary urban chaos.

Linking housing with play was not automatically successful. One such business, begun in 1896, dragged on hesitantly for nearly twenty years. In July that year a group of City businessmen, using money from the South African-based Estate Finance & Mining Corporation, floated a company to develop the 400 acre Canons Park estate at Edgware, then just beyond the northern limits of London's expansion. It had been laid out as a pleasant country retreat in the eighteenth century for the Duke of Chandos. They sought £50,000 in shares but had only partial success.[80] For the next decade or so they advertised in, or persuaded journalists to write for, the quality sporting journals with the message of a development growing in strength and attractiveness.

Willie Park laid out the course, spending £2,000 on draining 120 acres before its well delayed opening in 1907. But it was still difficult to get to. An article of that year expected that the Cricklewood tramline would soon be extended there, rather a come-down from the original grandiose claims of exclusivity, and taken even further by its being described as a 'jolly place'.[81] For those who rented houses, being built slowly, for between £32 and £130 a year there was preferential access to the course. The range of rents is instructive. This estate was far from being as 'exclusive' as originally intended, a point made further when the rail season tickets into the City were mentioned, since it made great play of the £10 *second-class* return. The development was piecemeal – those who rented villas in the late Edwardian eastern portion, for £45 a year, were offered tennis and bowling grounds as an inducement, a careful diversification into a less prestigious market. The company was liquidated voluntarily in 1913, leaving a golf club which had been successful in recruiting its 363 members from outside and a partially finished development that was filled in between the wars.[82]

There was often some doubt about how long such courses would survive if the building of houses proved more rewarding than course layout. Some critics saw the golf side as only a lure, and some clubs were forced to migrate when they lost their short lease to builders.[83] The trend encouraged some of the supporters of Lloyd George's land reform budgets to demand proper taxation of sporting land so that it could be released earlier for housing.

No such concern marred the development of what was probably the most self-regarding and snobbish of the linked flotations before the First World War, the St George's Hill estate at Weybridge in Surrey. In December 1912 a private partnership developing 'virgin forest' for golf and housing sold its assets for £19,250 to a syndicate with fifty nominal members as a form of mutual self-protection. H. S. Colt had designed the course, expected 'to rank amongst the finest inland courses in the world', for a membership limited to bond holders and residents, who had immediate nomination to it, and to the lawn tennis club which was also provided, with eight grass and four hard courts, as well as to the ancillary croquet and squash facilities. To the historian there is a pleasant irony of which the speculators were probably ignorant; the land is that on which the Diggers set up their short-lived egalitarian republic in defiance of Oliver Cromwell after the Civil War. Certainly the new development was a reassertion of the place of privacy and wealth, closer to Cromwell than to his critics. It succeeded largely because of the way in which the original development passed into the hands of a wealthy oligarchy determined to maintain its place by admitting only those whom it found suitable.[84]

The St George's scheme was unusual in its successful integration of a small expensive residential development with sport for a restricted clientele. By the time it opened many speculators had become wary of the possible drag of housing provision on the expected quick returns from sport and had turned to other models of proclaiming 'exclusivity' disguised as high-cost consumption with a wider numerical base. They found an attractive example, in the country clubs which had grown rapidly in the United States at the end of the nineteenth century.[85] These provided for a number of sports in an estate often modelled either on the eighteenth-century English pattern or on that of the deep south, with a central clubhouse on the scale of a major country seat. Hurlingham also offered an English template, and there were some attempts to emulate it before the First World War broke out. The English developers had an easier start than many of their American counterparts because of the trickle of landed estates and extant mansions which came on to the market in the aftermath of agricultural depression and family misfortune. It was often a matter of conversion rather than construction. The most prestigious was opened in 1914, when the Lord Mayor of London drove the first ball off the tee in the presence of the City sheriffs on the Shirley Park estate near Croydon. It was Lord Eldon's former country seat, bought by George Collins, the owner of a London hotel and of the Covered Courts (lawn tennis) Club, and W. Herbert Fowler, the developer of Walton Health. They employed H. S. Colt to lay out the fairways together with a separate putting course, boating lake and nine tennis courts. The house was advertised as a country club, separate membership of which could be available to non-golfers. Those who wished to play were given some self-determination as a club with a committee but members were expected to take out £100 debentures yielding 4 per cent as a means of joining. It was an expensive 'exclusiveness', limited to 400 members, yet the investors show a rather wider range than might be expected. They included six married women and a schoolmistress from King's Lynn who bought five preferential shares.[86]

Even grander was the Royal Automobile Club's scheme of 1913 to buy the Woodcote Park estate near Epsom, house and 338 acres for £50,000, for conversion into two eighteen-hole golf courses, with cricket, croquet, bowls, racquets, fives, and a gun club, shooting school, polo and archery grounds. These would add another £20,000 to the development costs, which it was hoped to meet by raising a 5 per cent debenture issue of up to £75,000 and by selling 100 acres of the land for building. The lure for this was the expectation of an eventual 250 per cent profit, based on the rise in property values observed in Surrey when Walton Heath was opened. The funds were raised readily, but war stopped the project.[87]

Success at this level was well advertised but limited in scope by a restricted market. Further down the scale a number of speculators overreached themselves during the Edwardian boom, and the failures prompted greater caution and a concern for self-protection among genuine clubs. Overemphasis on luxury was held to be the mark of the charlatan, but even some more widely respected individuals fell victim to overconfidence. Willie Park Junior, well established as a professional player, took to course planning in the 1890s. He eventually designed some seventy courses in North America but his English work was blighted by misreading the market. He became a major stockholder and promoter in Huntercombe, Oxfordshire, where he hoped to provide a challenging course as the centre of a housing development. The water tower erected in readiness loomed for a decade over its incompletion. Park also dealt in sporting goods in Cannon Street, in the City, but by 1911 he was preparing to retreat before strong established competition. The following year he was declared bankrupt in Edinburgh with an £11,507 deficit blamed entirely on the Huntercombe venture, on which the mortgages had been foreclosed. He managed to continue in course design, but Huntercombe had become a by-word for over-ambition, despite its survival as a fine course.[88]

A similar collapse attended a speculator far less well established as a public hero than Park. In July 1914 Arthur Henry Browne failed for £10,374 with assets of around £2,000. As Cross Browne & Co. he had developed three east coast seaside courses closely connected with speculative building. On Mablethorpe he lost £1,128; by contrast he made £2,064 on Felixstowe. But at Gorlestone he lost £3,430. He started business in 1910 with £250 – the Cross of the partnership was his wife. When he floated Gorlestone as a company in February 1912 he could not raise enough money to cover costs already incurred despite offering free plots of building land and life playing membership in return for £100 debentures. The housing part was grossly overvalued. He fainted at the hearing and vanished as quickly from the public eye as the company did from the registers.[89]

The instrument that most speculators used for development was the limited liability company. Designed essentially to prevent a repetition of the wholesale sufferings of the victims of Railway Mania in the 1840s, it was increasingly refined in the latter decades. With the creation of the private company in 1907, able to raise capital but not publicly quoted, it allowed family firms such as Hardy's to protect their place in the business and genuine clubs to meet their growing requirements without becoming victims of the land-hungry or of carpetbagging profiteers. The mechanism that had aided the career of Hooley was now used to protect other members of the middle classes from his ilk. Its adoption by many clubs represented a significant shift in their self-perception and in the level of their operations, and, in the majority of cases, a sense of successful establishment in the provision of their sport. Inevitably it was golf that was most affected by this, because of the scale of its needs.

Many clubs, particularly in the north, remained relatively low-cost, content with simple facilities and paying low rentals for their land. One such was Furness, begun in 1874, whose eventual extension of its seaside links to eighteen holes cost only £100. Even when it bought a new clubhouse in the early twentieth century it still needed no more than the £400 annual income from low subscriptions.[90] The question of risk capital did not arise. Many other clubs faced much greater difficulties, and raising large sums of money became an imperative either for survival or for prestige. Where in their early days clubs and landlords had often been content with simple annual agreements, the obvious success of golf led to growing demands for long leases or even for purchase. This became one avenue by which club committees protected their courses from encroachment by suburban builders. The Woking Golf Club took a long lease from the London Necropolis & National Mausoleum Company in 1901, the club at Olton, Warwickshire, a twenty-one-year lease of a former farm in 1903.[91] Some clubs were driven to purchase land to ensure their survival, and this made heavy demands. When it lost its lease at Furzedown to developers in 1905 Tooting Bec moved some two miles to the edge of Mitcham Common. It raised the £20,000 needed to buy and develop a former farm by taking out a £10,000 mortgage and issuing £100 debentures to those members willing to subscribe. Reading had to raise £3,900 to buy seventy-seven and a half acres in 1910, as well as leasing another forty-two. Sometimes clubs became speculators as well as protectors. The New Zealand Golf Club, founded in 1895, decided to acquire the 210 acres of land at Byfleet, Surrey, which it already leased, for £36,000; it would meet part of the cost by selling sixty acres for building to offset a £16,000 mortgage taken out for its development costs.[92]

Expanding courses in the post-Haskell world and landscaping for both aesthetic and playing purposes added strongly to clubs' problems. By 1909 it was estimated that they cost an average of £200 a hole, £3,600 for a full course – on a very different level from the £100 that its extension had cost Furness. To this expense could be added the provision of palatial clubhouses such as those Liverpool built for

£8,000 in the 1890s and Leeds for £3,500 in 1910. Walton Heath, opened at a cost of £30,000 in 1903, cost almost £3,000 a year to run, or £4 for each member – four times as much as Ilkley or Furness. But the big southern clubs with their high subscriptions were often able to cover capital or loan servicing costs out of their income; Walton Heath's was almost £5,000.[93] It was this level of operating surplus in many non-proprietorial clubs that allowed an easy floating of local bank loans or of debentures raised with confidence largely from their own membership. But even that needed protection, and the private limited liability company was ideal for the purpose.

The actual extent of take-up is difficult to establish, because incorporation was only rarely announced in golfing directories or periodicals. Discontinuity in clubs, company re-formation and the survivability and accessibility of records pose considerable restrictions upon an accurate reconstruction. Possibly some ten per cent followed this route before the First World War; some, such as Leeds, even did it twice. Because private companies were not required to provide annual returns of income and expenditure until 1978 it is often difficult to reconstruct what happened in individual cases.

The easiest type of private company to adopt was one limited by a guaranteed amount due from each member if the club folded with liabilities. Ravensworth, County Durham, was incorporated in 1912 with a personal limit of £1; £2–£3 was more common, but Ganton, Scarborough (1907), asked £5 from its 480 members, as did Erewash in Derbyshire (1910).[94] Leeds eventually settled on five guineas. Only rarely did the documents of incorporation list the actual capital requirements which prompted the move. Another popular form was the debenture issue, limited to club members, particularly among those clubs which incorporated on a private share basis, one member one share, usually with a nominal capital requirement divided into £1 units. The interest paid on debentures was usually solid but by no means attractive. Debentures both reiterated the social standing of the lenders and benefited clubs because of their low service costs and usual longevity. Many established middle-class people were clearly prepared to make wealth available for essentially non-profit-making purposes, almost a form of charity restricted largely to their own kind. Perhaps the complaint that sport was diverting the national energies had some limited foundation in this shifting of risk capital from industrial refurbishment. The nominal capital in these instances was a useful device for limiting club membership to a desired figure, since the process of changing it was complicated. When the companies were formed they usually took over the assets of the existing club in their entirety, but Halesowen provided an amusing exception on its incorporation in 1913, when its documents specifically excluded 'intoxicating liquors'. One is left wondering whether the new shareholders were dedicated teetotallers or whether they celebrated the transfer with a colossal binge.[95]

Only rarely is it possible to reconstruct detailed local cases. One such was Leeds Golf Club, formed in 1896 and incorporated in 1901, when it sought a nominal capital of £3,000. Two years later only £1,251 had been raised, even with the unusual step of offering 4 per cent interest, but it did allow the grazing land used for links to be improved and the clubhouse extended. The committee decided to reincorporate in 1908 to pay for a large new clubhouse; this time the shares would be replaced by a five-guinea guarantee per member to allow a loan of £2,400 to be raised from a local bank. The secretary, Joseph Watson, resigned, 'as he is not in sympathy with the new financial arrangements'. Some 150 of the members offered debentures of some £10 each. The club survived the change and managed to run with an overdraft of £1,500 for some years, presumably because of the strength of underpinning provided by incorporation; in 1912 it cut its interest payments on debentures altogether to reduce operating costs but the resulting loss of 8s per member seems to have produced little protest.[96]

For some clubs, incorporation included setting up a separate holding company or a trust for their land and assets. One such was the Royal Eastbourne, which founded the Eastbourne Links Company in 1913. Selby and Worplesdon also went this way, following the usual practice of leasing back from their own creation. But only a few went fully public, with its attendant risks. The New Zealand club sought to raise £20,000 this way, in £5 units, with a prospectus which gave as its chief assets 400 members and 'a very considerable waiting list'. It estimated that it would be able to pay a decently solid 5 per cent from an annual profit of £1,230, and this prospect was sufficiently attractive to pull in enough investors.[97]

Some new clubs used the process *ab initio*. Crowborough Beacon did in 1896, mainly to buy the large house it wanted as its centre.[98] Some of the clubs which did so, such as Mooortown, in Leeds, in 1909 and Harrogate in 1914, probably had to, because, as distinctly second-level associations in their local communities, they had fewer benefactors with large amounts of spare cash among their founders.[99] There could be a very direct appeal to local pride when this was done. When the Mid-Kent Club was formed at Gravesend in 1908 its prospectus kept well away from the strident claims of many commercial speculators: 'The Directors rely on the Members recommending the scheme to their friends and those interested in the welfare of Gravesend and the vicinity.' If these public-minded figures provided £100 they got two bonds in lieu of debentures, 4 per cent interest, free membership and a covering policy with the Royal Exchange Assurance, to be paid off on Lady Day 1929.[100]

Golf was not the only clubable sport to go this way. On a rather more limited scale others followed. Lawn tennis largely avoided it – probably only six or so of the 308 affiliated clubs of 1913 had made the change. One that did was Hull, which lost in 1901 the lease on ground it had held for twenty years. It raised £2,000 for a ten-court ground with a pavilion by issuing 500 £1 shares and taking up another £1,500 in £50 debentures from its members. These paid 4 per cent but, since they were paying it to themselves out of their own subscriptions, the idea of profit-driven investment needs substantial qualification in this and every similar case.[101] Bowls clubs seemed more ready, largely because of the need to buy greens close to town centres. Retford incorporated in 1898, with a predominantly lower middle-class membership. The needs of most such bodies were small, the capital requirements tiny by golfing standards. But incorporation also served as a means of reinforcing their perceived place in local hierarchies. When the bowling club in the retirement and resort town of Lytham St Anne's incorporated it built into the binding memorandum of association the right to disqualify a would-be shareholder/member by a one-in-four blackball on election; so did Worksop and Holbeck (Leeds) in their rather less salubrious surroundings.[102] Money alone was insufficient for acceptance in this model of capitalisation.

Not every proposal for taking up limited liability status was popular, however. The numbers that did are an indication of a distinct trend, but the majority did not go that way before 1914. There still existed a strong suspicion of the speculator's link with the company mechanism as well as a fear of being overstretched. The Leeds secretary was not alone in resigning in protest. When the Warwick Boat Club considered the move in 1902 members started to resign; after a close vote in favour of limited liability in 1910 fifty left.[103] Opposition of a slightly different kind, underpinning sentiments still widely held, appeared in a *Rucksack Club Journal* article in 1911. A joke prospectus was produced for the Rucksack Club Limited, 'to take over as a going concern the old-established business of producing walkers, climbers, etc.' It was to charge royalties on climbs, purchase and let out mountains and encourage the reading of *Gulliver's Travels* at evening classes.[104]

Printing money?

In 1904 an anonymous reviewer in the *Times Literary Supplement* wrote that:

> ... golf and all other popular games now support a race of literary parasites whose function, it would appear, is to flatter, and to flatter fulsomely, and indulge in an incredible excess of mock-enthusiasm.[105]

For a publishing industry already burgeoning with the spread of literacy, instructional and recreational reading, the various sports booms added another possibility of exploitation. Its reaction to it was as piecemeal and unevenly successful as some of the sports themselves. The range of titles can be recovered, but not the actual investment and profitability. In some cases existing press coverage was extended by the inclusion of regular sporting articles or features. *Truth* became one major source of pungent comment, but many other papers fitted far better the reviewer's strictures of 1904. In almost all cases there was a realisation that 'sport' had moved by the later 1870s well outside the usual journalistic limits of horse-racing and pugilism covered by *Bell's Life*, the oldest sporting paper, founded in 1822.

From the perspective of the later twentieth century it is the triumphant survivors that dominate the picture, nominally specialised magazines which actually built on the breadth of their coverage and an increased range of potential buyers. The healthiest had strong roots in traditional field sports, and their emergence indicated an extension of interest well beyond those for whom the activities were inherited rather than acquired. Socially the grandest, the *Field* appeared on New Year's Day 1853, costing 6*d* a week. It was edited by a barrister who later became a judge, William Cox, who bought it in 1854; his nephew, Horace, managed it from 1865 until 1912. Their strength owed much to the employment of specialist writers and assistant editors, the best of whom was Francis Francis, a civil engineer by training, who moved from being paid £2 a column for writing about angling to an annual salary of £200 for editing the fishing pages.[106] Slightly more utilitarian in approach and appearance were the *Shooting Times*, which first appeared in 1882, at a cost of 2*d* a week, and *Horse and Hound*, which emerged two years later at the same price and became the mouthpiece of hunting protectionism. It was not averse, however, to offering occasional articles on cycling, 'the iron steed', and football.

These and their many lesser Edwardian successors were packed with advertisements and were in small newspaper format. Aimed at a wider, and possibly even more self-selecting, readership were the 'cover all' magazines, with an approach closer to established literary periodicals and trying to endow sport with an intellectual respectability often belied by their contents. The very binding of their collected volumes was deliberately aimed at pretentious personal libraries.

Three of these journals in parallel mirrored, and helped create, the flow of sporting enthusiasms before the First World War, often to the extent of drawing on the same pool of freelance contributors. The solidest, *Baily's Magazine of Sports and Pastimes*, first appeared in 1860. Its early years were largely devoted to horses, hounds and occasional rowing; it was chatty, with little taxing of the reader's mind. But in the 1890s it diversified, both in its coverage and in the level of critical analysis in its articles, since it now faced competition. In 1895 the first issue of the *Badminton Magazine of Sports and Pastimes* (there was no copyright in titles) appeared, with a much wider range. Its first volume covered golf, cycling, cricket, hunting, athletics, fishing, football, racing, shooting, yachting, skating and pig-sticking, as well as providing miscellaneous notes.

In 1904 a new addition appeared, for once eschewing 'Pastime' for more serious purposes, *C. B. Fry's Magazine of Sports and Outdoor Life*. Until it ceased publication on the outbreak of war in 1914 *Fry's* tried to combine good writing with a high moral tone and an increasingly fervent patriotism. Its first issue dealt with G. F. Watts's statue 'Equestrian life' as a model of development; later ones offered repeated analyses of Japan's rise as a world power and the advantages of rifle-shooting as a national moral duty. It was identified, deliberately, with the model of manliness whose name it bore, Charles Burgess Fry. This pan-athlete, whom recent biographers have seen as rather less noble than his Edwardian image, had turned to journalism as an undergraduate to keep himself in the gentry life style he craved. By the time he was a Charterhouse master his earnings from writing were estimated at three times his salary. From 1902 he had had annual retainers from the publisher Newnes of £800 as a contributor to *Captain* and *Strand*, apart from writing for the new *Daily Express* as 'resident superstar' and numerous other papers. When Newnes decided to enter the sporting periodical market in 1904 Fry was an obvious choice, combining well known writing and editing skills with the draw of his name. Assisted by Wallis Myers, who wrote a popular biography of his hero in 1912, Fry wrote most of the early issues himself until enough good contributors could be attracted. In its early days the paper reached a circulation of around 100,000. But Fry's other activities turned his attention from it and its popularity suffered. When Sir George Newnes died in 1910 his successor had different ideas, and Fry's editorship ceased, although the paper still bore his name and he continued as a contributor. He was attempting a come-back to revive its flagging sales when war broke out.[107]

On a rather more restricted scale, individual sports generated their own specialist cover. *Land and Water* ran from 1866 until 1905, the *Fishing Gazette* appeared in 1877 and lasted until 1966, *Cycling* came out in 1891 and still appears monthly. Golf generated several contenders, each claiming unique coverage and quality; the strongest were *Golf*, which emerged in 1890, to be taken over by *Golf Illustrated* in 1899, and *Golf Monthly*, published from Fleet Street in 1911. This new generation of magazines differed from both the 'qualities' and their predecessors by their very heavy use of advertising and their absolute dependence on its income, and by a more overtly graphic layout made possible by the growing cheapness of block printing, which allowed plenty of action photographs. Heroes were no longer created solely from static poses, line drawings and flowery prose, although those still flourished. It was the modernity of games which was being sold.

These were the successful ones. Around and usually very much below them lay a stratum of failures, short-lived hopes which appeared at the wrong time, were badly marketed and insufficiently capitalised, largely because they failed to attract advertisers. Many of them had an Improving earnestness about them more fitted to earlier athleticism than increasingly sophisticated activities, and their producers seem to have expected that their survival could rest on that. At least twenty-nine failed cycling papers were published in London during the period, including *The Lady Cyclist*, which came out in 1895 and amalgamated in 1897 with *Wheelwoman* until that failed in 1899. The grandly named *All England Cricket and Football Journal and Athletic Review* was published from Sheffield in 1878–79; it had a London outlet, and its brief appeal lay in its sporting hagiographies illustrated with stuck-in photographs of heroes such as W. G. Grace in frozen poses. *The Youth's Sale and Exchange List and General Advertiser* appeared in January 1888, re-emerged as *Amateur Sport* in August, failed to build strong links with the Amateur Cricket Association through its fixture lists and died in 1889. The *Midland Athlete* of 1879 and the *Midland Cricket and Football Chronicle and Athletic Journal* of the following year had even shorter lives.

There was generally insufficient support to keep a regional sporting press alive. When the *Hull and East Riding Athlete*, 'the only athletic journal in the East Riding' – a place where even one comes as a surprise – appeared in November 1889 for 1*d*, it probably killed itself by writing only about purist amateur events in a city whose most public sporting expression was in Rugby League. Although it soon claimed 20,000 readers (*not* purchasers) and cut its price to $^1/2d$ it disappeared after October 1890. Other such papers fell foul of the seasonal emphasis of much of their coverage, as did *Amateur Sport*, which died in autumn 1889, six months after its first issue. Even in suburbia there was little local support for a dedicated press; the *Surrey Athlete*, produced by a small local printer in Reigate, lasted only one issue in 1893. Fixture lists of local clubs were insufficiently exciting to attract purchasers. The bowls boom added its own victims – *Bowls*, published by *Country Sport* (the erstwhile *Bell's Weekly Messenger*) in 1904, brought its parent journal down with it in September that year. The 2*d* monthly *Bowling* survived from 1908 to 1911. A press aimed at sportswomen, best represented by *Sportswoman*, 'The official organ of the Ladies' Kennel Association (Incorporated)', lasted on the whole just as briefly.[108]

It was in book production that the response to discerned markets proved most flexible and entertaining. Such is the thoroughness with which some sporting bibliographers attack their subject that it is possible to quantify output for the leading activities. During our period some 237 works dealing with guns and shooting appeared in England and Scotland, over half between 1890 and 1910.[109] Including a limited American cohort, golfers were offered some 260 between 1870 and 1914, ninety-eight of them in the first decade of this century.[110] It was fishing that generated the most significant output, thirty-five separate editions of one book between 1870 and 1902, and of growing cheapness. The book was Izaak Walton's *The Compleat Angler*, a majestic survival of High Anglican royalism from the 1650s. By the 1890s good copies of the original cost up to £150, as compared with the four guineas they had fetched in 1816, and most of those were selling to American collectors. The 'Made in Germany' scare of the decade was given a new twist when it turned out that good German photographic facsimiles were being sold as originals to the more gullible.[111]

The idea of a 'Sportsman's Library', covering the pursuits any would-be gentleman should follow, became part both of 1890s literary folklore and of publishers' lists. Grumbles that this would push out 'true literature' were discounted in the *Fortnightly Review* by one of the most prolific contributors to the genre, F. G. Aflalo. Born in 1870 and educated at Clifton College and Rostock University, Aflalo edited *The Cost of Sport* in 1899 as a guide to the money-conscious neophyte and wrote numerous articles for both sporting and general periodicals. With the Earl of Suffolk and Berkshire he produced *The Encyclopaedia of Sport* in two volumes in 1897, leaving the earl to produce a second edition in 1911 when aeronautics and clay-bird shooting were among the new sports covered. Aflalo's most splendid edition was *Fifty Leaders of British Sport* in 1904, for the Bodley Head, with potted adulation accompanying frozen poses taken by the leading Society photographers Elliott & Fry.[112]

The idea of a 'library' from one publisher was at its most sophisticated in the Badminton series, whose first volume emerged in 1885, to be added to by another twenty-nine over the next two decades. Asa Briggs has outlined this story brilliantly, recounting how a simple plan for seven or so volumes was overtaken by its own success, how the overall editing was done by the Duke of Beaufort (the series was named after his house), but the staff work by another Aflalo type, Alfred E. T. Watson. Analysis was sparse in the books, the emphasis being on literary skill, a naive humour and a snobbishness which undoubtedly added to the series' appeal and commercial success. The investment made in it by the publisher Longman's seems to have been well justified. Watson went on to edit the *Badminton Magazine*, the spin-off from the series' success. He claimed to have been paid a hundred guineas for one hour's advice to Aflalo's *Encyclopaedia*.[113]

Lesser publishers produced cheaper libraries. T. Fisher Unwin offered 'The Sports Library' for a half a crown a volume, beginning in 1899 with T. F. Daly's *Riding, Driving and Kindred Sports*. George Bell & Sons produced a four-volume *Handbook of Athletic Sports* from 1890 but also made it available in seventeen separate 1s parts for those whose enthusiasms and pocket were limited. They claimed deliberately to undercut Badminton, seen as appealing 'mostly to the veteran athlete and the monied class of readers'.[114] If Aflalo and Watson aimed at the gentry and the upper middle classes, these lesser libraries were pointed firmly at clerks and their ilk. Edward Lyttelton was quite happy to write for Bell, presumably out of a sense of sporting paternalism. Ward Lock entered the same market, making sport part of a world which included handbooks on etiquette and telling funny stories. Mills & Boon, already well established as the leading source of light romantic fiction, were in the field by the outbreak of war, covering golf, cricket and mountaineering.[115] They were well bolstered by a range of sporting annuals from various publishers aimed at a variety of readers; Gamage's put their name to one as an additional boost to their sports department.[116]

For many sportsmen anxious to spread their enthusiasms and to pay for them as well this was often a fruitful source of part or even full-time employment. Fry and Aflalo we have already noted. The golfer Horace Hutchinson produced numerous articles and thirteen books between 1896 and 1912, including his romance *Bert Edward the Golf Caddie* in 1903. The cricketer Gilbert L. Jessop was only one of the many, including Lyttelton, who pitched in.[117] For many of them writing became one lucrative form of sports-related income by which they avoided losing their amateur status; there were no Henley rules for brain workers. Others hid their talents behind initials. It is virtually impossible now to trace how many of the books notionally written by leading players without the benefit of higher education, such as Willie Parks's *The Game of Golf*, were ghosted. One assistant spirit was Arthur Ransome, who claimed to have produced a number of sporting autobiographies for their less than literate subjects. The first book to which he put his name, and one he never mentioned when he was famous, was *The A. B. C. of Physical Culture*.[118]

It was not just in instruction that the market grew. *Punch* widened its appeal with sporting humour, golf and other poetry poured out, and the romantic or comic novel added to the various mystiques. In M. A. Stobart's *Won at the Last Hole: a golfing romance* the bachelor hero wooed his wife by out-putting her. J.A.C.K.'s *Golf in the Year 2000* offered a utopia in which the game had replaced war and women did all the work whilst men played. Heavy melodrama, 341 pages, was offered by Mrs Edward Kennard in *The Golf Lunatic and his Cycling Wife*; semi-comic, it relied on the already hackneyed theme of mistaken identity to reconcile a spoilt, wealthy and self-indulgent couple for whom sport was a source of moral decay. Understandably, in such a market, it proved far less popular than what were perhaps the finest pieces of fiction produced during the booms, Wells's *Wheels of Chance* and Jerome's *Three Men on the Bummel*. They are virtually the only survivors of this late Victorian and Edwardian flood as books still published in their own right rather than as nostalgic facsimiles.

Notes

1 *C. B. Fry's Magazine*, 13 (1910), 383–4.
2 Sargent, *Thoughts upon Sport*, xv; B. R. Mitchell and P. Deane, *British Historical Statistics* (Cambridge, 1988), 828 ff.
3 *Golf Monthly*, January 1912, 858.
4 *Parliamentary Papers* (1914–16), LXXVI, Banana Imports.
5 P. Collier, *England and the English from an American Point of View* (New York, 1909), 234–5, 237.
6 *Chambers's Journal*, XII, 21 December 1895, 801 ff.
7 *Parliamentary Papers* (1900), XCVIII; 1914–16, LXXVI.
8 Mason, *Association Football*, 33–43; Korr, *West Ham*.
9 H. Barty-King, *Quilt Winders and Rod Shavers* (1979), 156.
10 J. Hartfield, *A Wisden Centenary, 1850–1950* (1950), 28–9; Barty-King, *Quilt Winders*, 61 ff.
11 N. R. Wright, *Lincolnshire Towns and Industry, 1700–1914* (Lincoln, 1982), 211–12.
12 *Jaques: 150th Anniversary*; PRO, BT 31/31693, Co. 61539, John Jaques & Son Ltd.
13 *Fortnightly Review*, LV (1894), 495.
14 F. Gale, *Modern English Sports* (1885), 87–8.
15 *Fishing Gazette*, 6 May 1905.
16 *Fishing Gazette*, 14 June 1890.
17 G. Stockwell, *Fly Reels of the House of Hardy* (1978), 4.
18 *Fishing Gazette*, 28 July 1900.
19 PRO, BT 31/18022, Co. 92373, Hardy Bros. (Alnwick) Ltd.
20 *Alnwick Official Handbook* (1934).
21 *Fishing Gazette*, 15 February 1890.
22 *Fishing Gazette*, 15 October 1910.
23 J.H. Keene, *Fishing Tackle: its Material and Manufacture* (1886), 10, 19, 21; *Fishing Gazette*, 17 January 1885, 12 January 1895.
24 *Fishing Gazette*, 17 November 1900.

25 *Fishing Gazette*, 15 February 1913.
26 *Shooting Times*, 25–31 October 1984, 24–5; R. Beaumont, *Purdey's: the Guns and the Family* (1984).
27 Teasdale-Buckell, *Experts on Guns*, 307, 310, 319, 342, 347, 396.
28 Teasdale-Buckell, *Experts on Guns*, 491.
29 G. P. Bevan (ed.), *British Manufacturing Industries* (1876), 1–26.
30 L. B. Taylor, *A Brief History of the Westley Richards Firm, 1812–1913*(Stratford upon Avon, 1913).
31 Artifex and Optifex, *The Causes of Decay in a British Industry* (1907).
32 S.F. Van Oss, 'The limited-company craze', *Nineteenth Century*, May 1898, 732.
33 *Nineteenth Century*, January 1885, 93.
34 W. Woodruff, *The Rise of the British Rubber Industry during the Nineteenth Century* (Liverpool, 1958).
35 Woodruff, *Rubber Industry*, 73.
36 E.T. Hooley, *Hooley's Confessions* (1924), 5.
37 *The Hooley Book* (1904), 15–16.
38 Hooley, *Confessions*, 35–6.
39 *Bexhill-on-Sea Illustrated Visitors' List*, 36 June, 28 July 1896.
40 Hooley, *Confessions*, 13.
41 Pemberton *et al.*, *Complete Cyclist*, 181.
42 J. Pennell, 'Cycles and cycling', *Fortnightly Review*, LXIII (1898), 67.
43 A.E. Harrison, 'F. Hopper & Co.: the problems of capital supply in the cycle manufacturing industry, 1891–1914', *Business History*, XXIV (1982), 3 ff.
44 Details on Mumbles Railway card, reproduction poster, MRP/240, History of Advertising Trust and Cooper's catalogue in author's possession.
45 F. P. Low, 'The cost of cycles', *Badminton Magazine*, X (1900), 516 ff.
46 D.W. Thomas and T. Donnelly, 'Coventry's industrial economy, 1880–1980', in B. Lancaster and T. Mason, *Life and Labour in a Twentieth Century City: the Experience of Coventry* (Coventry, 1989), 12–15.
47 A copy survives in Worthing Museum, West Sussex.
48 Lunn, *Come what May*, 17; *Memory to Memory*, 5–7.
49 Advertisements in Ayers, *Bowls*.
50 Hillyard, *First Class Lawn Tennis*, 32.
51 Lillie, *Croquet*, xvi.
52 Registrar of Companies, Co. 116000.
53 *Lawn Tennis and Croquet and Badminton*, 14 May 1902.
54 Hillyard, *First class Lawn Tennis*, 43.
55 *Ibid.*
56 I.T. Henderson and D.T.Stirk, *Golf in the Making* (Crawley, 1979), 73, 117 ff.
57 *Golf Illustrated*, 9 June 1905; *The Times*, 1 March 1906.
58 *The Times*, 22 January 1908.
59 *Golf Monthly*, April 1914.
60 *Golf Monthly*, April 1911.
61 *Golf Monthly*, January, March 1914.
62 *C. B. Fry's Magazine*, 13 (1910), 131.
63 *Golf Monthly*, February 1912.
64 *Golf Monthly*, December 1911.

65 *Badminton Magazine*, 24 (1907), 142.
66 Vamplew, 'Profit or utility maximisation?' 38 ff.
67 Mangan, *Athleticism*, 71, 100.
68 *Golf Monthly*, January 1914.
69 Roberts, 'Corporation as impresario'.
70 Stainton, *Golf Courses of Yorkshire*, 108.
71 *Badminton Magazine*, 36 (1913), 601.
72 *Official Guide to Woodhall Spa*, n.d., Lincoln Public Library.
73 Sutton, *Book of the Links*, 139.
74 Cornish and Whitten, *Golf Course*, 38–9, 213.
75 Cornish and Whitten, *Golf Course*, 38, 170.
76 Leeds Reference Library, *The Hyde Park Recreation Club Chronicle* (1897); PRO, BT 31/33762, Co. 38047, Newcastle-upon-Tyne Cycling and Athletic Ground Co. Ltd.
77 *Fishing Gazette*, 24 May 1890.
78 *C. B. Fry's Magazine*, 16, 88–9.
79 *Ibid.*
80 PRO, BT 31/6687, Co. 47012, Canons Park Estate Co. Ltd.
81 *Truth*, 1907, 1339.
82 *C. B. Fry's Magazine*, 16, 239, 723.
83 *Golf Illustrated*, 3 September 1909.
84 *Golf Monthly*, December 1912, 742, 746; *Nisbet's Golf Year Book 1913*, 265; *Official Guide to Weybridge* (1919), 34.
85 C.W. Whitney, 'Evolution of the country club', *Harper's New Monthly Magazine* (New York), XC (1894–95), 16 ff.
86 *Golf Monthly*, July 1913, 412; PRO, BT 31/21480, Co. 129177, Shirley Park Golf Estate Ltd.
87 Registrar of Companies, 127842, RAC Golf Club and Country House Ltd.
88 Cornish and Whitten, *Golf Course*, 36–8; *The Times*, 28 February 1911; *Golf Monthly*, May, September 1911; *The Times*, 26 April 1912.
89 *Golf Monthly*, June 1914, 310, July 1914, 388; PRO, BT 31/13818, Co. 120103, Gorleston Cliffs Golf Club Ltd.
90 'The cost of golf', *Baily's Magazine*, March 1909, 193 ff.
91 Registrar of Companies, 71601, Woking Golf Club Estates; 79014, Olton Golf Club.
92 Registrar of Companies, 110402, Reading Golf Club; 98139, New Zealand Golf Club.
93 Registrar of Companies, 71601, Working Golf Club Estates; 79014, Olton Golf Club.
94 Registrar of Companies, 121519, Ravensworth Golf Club; 93514, Ganton Golf Club; 111673, Erewash Valley Golf Club; 100386, Leeds Golf Club (1908).
95 Registrar of Companies, 127435, Halesowen Golf Club.
96 Records of Leeds Golf Club.
97 Registrar of Companies, 132651, Eastbourne Links Company; 129525, Selby Links Company; 136913, Worplesdon Estates Company; 98139, New Zealand Golf Club.
98 Registrar of Companies, 46833, Crowborough Beacon Golf Club.
99 Registrar of Companies, 101083, Moortown Golf Club; 136334, Oakdale Golf Club.

100 Registrar of Companies, 97391, Mid-Kent Golf Club.
101 *Hull News*, 23 November 1901.
102 Registrar of Companies, 57924, Retford Bowling Green; 83031, Lytham Bowling Club; 109201, Worksop Bowling Club; 132656, Holbeck Bowling Club.
103 Warwickshire Record Office, CR 1798/2, Warwick Boat Club, Minutes.
104 *Rucksack Club Journal*, 11 (1911–14), 160 ff.
105 *Times Literary Supplement*, 24 October 1907.
106 R.N. Rose, *The Field, 1853–1953* (1953).
107 C. Ellis, C.B., 149 ff., 161, 169; Fry, *Life*, 152 ff.; Myers, *C. B. Fry*.
108 Most of these periodicals are held by the British Library but some of the more ephemeral can be found only in local collections.
109 R. Riling, *Guns and Shooting: a Selected Chronological Bibliography* (New York, 1951).
110 Murdoch, *Library of Golf*.
111 R.Le Gallienne (ed.), *Izaak Walton, the Complete Angler* (1904), 401 ff.; R.B.Marston, *Walton and some Earlier Writers on Fish and Fishing* (1894).
112 F.G.Aflalo, 'The sportsman's library', *Fortnightly Review*, LXVI (1899), 968 ff.; Sportsman, *British Sports and Sportsmen*, 533.
113 Briggs, 'The view from Badminton', 189 ff.; A.E.T.Watson, *A Sporting and Dramatic Career* (1918), 161 ff., 245, 361.
114 Bell, *Handbook of Athletic Sports*, I, v.
115 See Burrows, *Bowls*.
116 S.Nowell-Smith, *The House of Cassell, 1848–1958* (1958), 116.
117 Murdoch, *Library of Golf*, 113 ff.; G.L.Jessop, *Outdoor Games* (1912).
118 R. Hart-Davis (ed.), *The Autobiography of Arthur Ransome* (1976), 85.

Chapter 9

Seeds of decay

A sense of crisis

The year 1912 was one of symbolic disasters for the English. The *Titanic* sank on her maiden voyage, Captain Scott and his companions perished in Antarctica and her athletes were far outshone at the Stockholm Olympics. All three resulted partly from over-optimism, arrogance and a singular level of amateurishness in which assumptions of national, racial and class superiority were shown to rest on thinly masked incompetence and inefficiency. Yet in each case the English press glorified defeat as victory. 'Tragedy is the opportunity for heroism', was *The Times's* judgement on the loss of the *Titanic*.[1] The beleaguered Captain Scott wrote, 'Englishmen can still die with a bold spirit, fighting it out to the end ... I think this will show that the spirit of pluck and power to endure has not passed out of our race.'[2] This vein is easily caricatured but it was part of a complex web of belief that found popular expression in the cheap prints of the 'last stand' paintings of Lady Elizabeth Butler and the poems of Henry Newbolt. There was an additional barb in Scott's final words; his foolhardiness arose partly out of a rejection of the notion of a country in decadence. It was trapped in another paradox, that the real glory came not from efficiently planned success but from failing with good intentions. 'Playing the game' had infiltrated the language of expectation to such an extent that it appeared to justify any risky action. It had become an integral part of the apparatus of jingoism, but not without some very hard questioning. Sport and its assumptions emerged as a battleground for questions of national identity, patriotic superiority and arguments over a perceived racial and spiritual decline which fuelled the preparations for war.

Scott's failure was not to miss the South Pole, nor to come second; it was to underestimate the risks and die unnecessarily. When he did not return there was an attempt to shift the focus of attention away from the assumption that he had lost a race towards an assertion of spiritual and imperial values. Roland Huntford's re-examination of this in the late 1970s revealed how sore the issues still were. He tried, with some considerable success, to dethrone Scott from the pantheon of sporting heroes by comparing his misuse of 'sporting' practices such as man-hauling sledges to the Pole with Amundsen's athletic instrumentalism in using skis.[3] It intersects with what has been characterised as 'the decline of the industrial spirit' or the 'weary Titan'.[4] My purpose here is to examine the debate primarily in its Edwardian and early Georgian context, relating to the middle classes in their role both as social exemplars and as actual or potential military leaders.

Sport became for many of its apologists both an instrument and a symbol of progress far transcending individual participation which 'made the nation stronger, manlier, cleaner and more sober than it was before the pursuit of athletics became a national characteristic'.[5] When Harvard gave the Cambridge oarsman John Lehmann an honorary MA for fostering 'wholesome sport' he was praised as 'typical of one very prominent feature of British civilisation', not least because the reward was honorary rather than material.[6] Ironically, the crew he had coached had been defeated decisively by Yale. This pursuit of self-satisfaction and national honour through sport remained paramount, and still seeped into writing for decades after the First World War. I. J. Pitman, writing in Ernest Barker's *The Character of England* in the 1940s, portrayed the values of sport in characteristically late Victorian English terms, 'to prefer skill to cleverness'.[7]

Like so much else reinforcing middle-class superiority, the athletic ideal was often portrayed as unitive both in class and in national terms. The Earl of Wilton valued sport as the foundation of national liberty in the later 1860s, particularly those pan-class games 'which bring together people of all grades, and thus for the time break down all class barriers'.[8] This temporary suspension of divisions in order to strengthen them flows repeatedly through the sport writings of the next forty years. As this developed the value of sport was portrayed as the natural outcome of enterprise: '. . . among the nations of Europe . . . those which are most vigorous in commerce and in intellectual culture, are those in which the most active recreations in mind and body are most prevalent'.[9] It also provided that fearlessness which had extended the empire, allowing it to develop as the playground for aspirant upper middle-class boys or the under-employed sons of the landed classes. Lauded in appalling doggerel and praised by bishops for fostering self-control, it formed a fitting preparation for life in the imperial wilderness, 'without suffering that mental, moral and physical deterioration which is so painfully apparent in men of Latin race'.[10]

Such racial stereotypes were useful in claiming superiority over southern Europeans but served less readily when the observers looked northwards or westwards. Virility and anti-intellectualism were significant components of their Englishness, occasionally reinforced by suggestions that athletics were the only way to escape the country's weather.[11] Complaints that the attention given to sport in schools and the press produced a singularly distorted impression of a sport-obsessed country often passed largely unheeded. The quirky Cambridge don A. C. Benson, a member of the Alpine Club, deplored the English assumption that 'a belief in games is a matter of faith and morals', but such views made little immediate headway against the neo-Pelagianism of churchmen such as bishop Winnington-Ingram or headmasters like Lyttelton.[12] The sporting racialists were sometimes excessively Darwinian in their sense of moral as well as physical struggle. When the Inspector of Military Gymnasia died in 1911 his British Israelite views on exercise were held to have produced a 'tremendous faith in the British AS A NATION, in the POTENTIAL strength of the race'.[13] Much of the ethical purity that some sporting bodies such as the AAA or ARA had sought to preserve with class-specific legislation could be held safe only if it continued within the total *hortus clausus* of restricted English participation. But racial superiority had to be claimed in practice as well as in assertion, and this became increasingly difficult for English middle-class sportsmen to manage.

The focus of much sporting *angst* was the United States, frequently so anglophile in its sporting practices yet so great a threat to them in terms of both its aggressive success and its persistent modification of ethical codes. The 'American, to whom the Englishman's comfortable way of conducting his business would of itself be recreation', posed major dilemmas of morals and morale for English observers after the mid-1890s.[14] English concern with sport tended to fall short of performance: the American middle-class attitude was regarded as both more serious and more thorough. The employment of professional athletic instructors, anathema in English field, track and river sports, became commonplace in American colleges and clubs, leaving English competitors floundering between views of sport as business or amusement. In terms of liberal ethics English middle-class sport remained firmly rooted in a voluntaryist mode whilst American activities had shifted firmly towards a directed professionalism of activity if not reward. Unease at consistent English under-performance in international events produced jibes that Americans were 'sporting men and not sportsmen', semantic distinctions serving to suggest wholesale corruption among opponents, a sense of envy and some rather loose eugenic thinking in articles such as that which F. A. M. Webster wrote for *Badminton* in 1914: 'Is the American more naturally adapted to athletics than the Englishman?'[15] There was also the consolation, if one was no longer the best, of having been the first, claiming the teacher's natural pride in being outshone by the good pupil.

This could just about be tolerated when it applied to Americans but if did little to assuage a growing sense of unease and of potential redundancy when the white parts of the empire demonstrated a similar superiority. Having used sport as a tool for staffing the colonies, the Edwardians found themselves faced with claims of atrophy – 'the Colonial is physically and mentally superior to the Englishman'.[16] New Zealanders began to defeat home teams at football, cricket and even lawn-tennis. Like the Americans they offered achievement with conscious and conspicuous effort; they were seen to take risks which paid off whilst the English plodded on safely. The actual number of international encounters was small, as were English defeats, but they attracted a growing amount of press dissection because of the symbolism attached to sport in terms of national self-respect.

Olympic encounters

After the 1908 London Olympics *Truth* demanded that 'In the interest of sport one must not place a burden upon it that it cannot bear.'[17] This ironic appeal was too late. The Olympic movement after its inception in 1896 provided a singularly fluctuating barometer for English nationalist emotions and fears. It is a truism that imperialism emerged out of perceived threats to a tenuous international supremacy, but that does not lessen its value for understanding the sense of racial upset which hovered around the early twentieth-century Olympics. Eugen Weber has characterised the obsessions of the movement's founder, Pierre de Coubertin, as 'the romantic elitism of a nineteenth-century autocrat fascinated by Darwin, by Taine, above all by Dr Arnold'.[18]

When de Coubertin explained his revival of the games in the *Fort-nightly Review* in 1908 he saw them as an extension to 'the whole civilised world . . . [of] Anglo-Saxon ideals' rather than the reintroduction of classical models as the agent of change.[19] But his choice of anglocentric values was highly selective; he rejected utilitarian individualism and over emphasis on personal performance. He was less ready than some of the movement's supporters to advance the view of sport as an agent of international peace-making, an issue that became particularly difficult when the adoption of national teams for the first time in 1908 shifted the games' symbolism significantly. He was happier to see sport as a loose agent of civilisation than to face what his offspring was rapidly becoming.

The first revived games in Athens had an air of amateurishness which offended even English observers. De Coubertin was more intent on using Anglo-Saxon ideals as a mode of improving continentals than in encouraging the English to flaunt their assumed athletic superiority in person. Only six Englishmen appeared, virtually as casual visitors who joined in for relaxation. The 'prehistoric condition' of European athletes drew down English disapproval, with claims that the tone of future events would be raised only if 'varsity men took the trouble to attend and provide real models of performance.[20] Subsequent games and the alternative Athenian series attracted growing English interest and uncertainty. The 1906 Athenian set saw Britain in second place, after the French, with ten wins in seventy-two events. It prompted one of the leading proponents of English participation, Theodore Andrea Cook, to reflect that a necessary cost of civilising Europe through sport was to accept the growing possibility of defeat by one's pupils.[21] But the pupils were prepared to learn only so much, and their attitude to financing their athletes' participation, paying properly the costs of attendance, was held to be both a model for English adoption and a growing threat to athletic integrity. As London prepared to host the 1908 games Cook went further and opened up the growing deep fears the series was engendering: 'It will . . . be a serious (I was about to say "a desperate") endeavour on our part to hold our own against all comers.'[22] Such could be done, he felt, only by a return to purity in sport.

That cause was already lost, because of internal English arguments about how best such purity could be maintained. All the other European teams that attended enjoyed some government support, but the English did not: even the New Liberalism of the post-1906 government would not step so far. Yet the English had already compromised in real terms. Most of the games were to be held at the new 'White City' stadium provided by the promoters of the 1908 Franco-British exhibition at a cost of £50,000. The gate money was to be shared with the promoters, who had already given the British Olympic committee £2,000 towards its expenses. This was not enough, and Cook's articles were part of an appeal for public donations, sponsorship for the general good rather than for individuals. It was a wobbly tightrope on which to walk.[23]

The dilemma was stated more openly by J. Astley Cooper, who claimed to be the founder of the Empire Day movement, in the *Nineteenth Century*. For him the games were only a sideshow to the exhibition, to be rescued by an understanding of their imperial significance. Co-operation and competition with foreigners were less important than emphasis on pan-Britannic sport, without which the empire could split. In no way could the Olympics compete with the bonding offered to the extended British interest by cricket.[24] *Truth* saw other threats. Rather than promoting understanding the games would reduce nations, particularly England, to the status of squalling city states in classical Greece. The Americans would welcome any opportunity to demonstrate how far they had emerged from colonial dependence, the marathon was little more than an excuse for 'a semi-circular tour of suburban London', and the whole business was a misguided attempt by the English to prove that the country was not degenerate.[25]

The overall results seemed to give the lie to that. The United Kingdom (not the English) led the performance lists, with 108 medals, forty-nine of them golds, as against the United States' second best score of forty-six. There was a very strong element of the 'home game' in this, and a number of writers saw it as a clear swan song of English athletics.[26] Particularly disappointing had been the native performance in longer track events, most notably the marathon, where the English came in behind an Italian, four Americans, a South African, four Canadians, a Swede and a Finn: the walk through the suburbs had proved painful rather than leisurely.

The English organisers had managed to impose, at least in appearance, their gentlemanly ethic of amateurism on the national teams, so a brief moral as well as performance success could be claimed. And there was great pride in the triumph of voluntarist material provision: a stadium for 80,000 people, £2,200 spent on medals, £4,400 on administration, everything provided for £80,000.[27] But doubts were growing, not helped by reports of postcards on sale in New York showing Uncle Sam twisting the British lion's tail. *Truth* claimed that 'the cad zone of sporting development' had crept in, led by the United States, as usual.[28] Figure skating on artificial ice, 'perhaps symbolic of the unnaturalness of the mammoth programme', seemed a very long way from manly athletics, whatever its beauty.[29] And there was a growing feeling that the games were fostering international tension. Sport had become a vehicle of the baser instincts rather than the agent of their reform, and the press agonising actually added to this. Essentially there was a profound tension between general views of sport as national symbol, usually held in tandem with a profound indifference to its actual development costs as such, and those which portrayed it as a moral imperative whilst keeping it back from corruption.

Expectations of English excellence and purity in the 1912 Olympics were trapped by this. Amateurism appeared to be degenerating into amateurishness, enterprise being strangled by the universities and the AAA. There were diatribes but no serious alternatives; the amateur ethical trap and its controlling oligarchies could not provide the £100,000 estimated as necessary to train a crack British (English?) team for 1912. T. A. Cook and Olympic supporters saw this as an index of the real decline of national athletics: that the English were not prepared to accept the logical consequences of their own developments.[30] It appeared as symptomatic of a wider shying away from entrepreneurial excellence, from risk-taking towards safety. But much of the general middle-class press, particularly the quality periodicals, preferred articles which questioned the whole Olympic movement as a symbol of moral degeneracy, replacing Greek vices with modern hypocrisy. True Hellenism would 'produce a kind of general-purpose athlete who can find health and *joie-de-vivre*' rather than the acrobatic freaks the Americans were held to be fielding.[31] A Lincolnshire hagiography of 1912, *Reminiscences of Sport in Grimsby*, whilst dismissing 'The Parrot Cry of Decadence' could also claim that American competitors were little more than machines, manufactured by dollar investment.[32]

British (essentially English) performance in the 1912 games more than justified these fears, revealing continued weakness in the track and field events that had been at the centre of the athletic stage of the previous thirty years. Whilst the United States managed a score of eighty-five, Britain only reached fifteen; that score was possible only because of a first in the mile and the 400m relay. Football, swimming and shooting saved the national face elsewhere in the games, but British assumptions about the Americans had to be modified by the impressive field performance of the much smaller Scandinavian countries.[33] 'An overwhelming measure of bad luck', with its emphasis on the apparently random, could be given some of the blame, but *The Times* saw a much greater source of malaise:

> The essential point is that we have failed ingloriously, and have failed not because we lack first-class material or have not good men individually, but because of our hopelessly incompetent management and lack of organisation.[34]

The same might have been claimed of the Scott expedition, but the games left no dead heroes at a vast distance around when noble myths could be built. And the fears of corruption by non-English models surfaced even more clearly. At a time of growing international tension the games exacerbated it even further by encouraging spectator loyalties. The 1908 events used national teams for the first time. In 1912 American supporters bought tickets *en bloc*, sat together, waved the stars-and-stripes and shouted nationalist slogans. British groups were seen to copy them. *The Times* felt that this should be forbidden by the organisers of the next games, due to be held in Berlin in 1916.[35] But by then other nationalist games were being played.

Apostasy

Worries over international performance were exceeded by greater anxieties over sport's identification with national moral decay. Activities which had been loosely charged with Victorian England's moral regeneration appeared as a potential threat to it by the turn of the century. The Pauline virtues of spiritual self-discipline which had been grafted on to competitive games wavered when play became a socially acceptable alternative to Sunday churchgoing for growing numbers of the middle classes. Not only were individual souls and the support of suburban churches now at risk, the example to social inferiors would be positively dangerous. At the extreme this concern offered a 'bread and circuses' argument, with evangelical clergymen comparing contemporary England with the declining years of the Roman Empire and other regimes. Canon F.

Meyrick, the rector of Blickling, in the diocese of Lincoln, claimed that 'the cry for *circenses* was an indication of a degraded Roman population and they were not a means of lifting it from its degradation' and 'the theatres were full during the orgies of the French Revolution'.[36] The Lord's Day Observance Society saw a considerable risk of moral infection, of the introduction of the continental Sunday and its Romish accessories, not least the Mass. Then, as now, strong concern over the secular exploitation by commercial interests of relatively defenceless workers was masked by a fundamentalist appeal to the demands of Old Testament scripture. The hegemony of official Christianity over social habits was revealed as tenuous indeed.

Yet this was not initially, nor even primarily, an open conflict between religion and a totally secular culture; the ethical and practical issues were far more closely intertwined than an oppositional explanation would suggest. Both religious and secular reformers had pressed for changes in attitudes to and the provision of Sunday recreation. It is worth remembering here that which they sought to alter; the 'Victorian Sunday'. Its best use was defined to the House of Lords' Select Committee on Sunday Observance in 1895 by the secretary of the Lord's Day Observance Society, the Revd. Francis Peake: 'Public instruction, public worship, the instruction of the young, the visiting of the sick, looking after people who are in trouble and difficulty, showing acts of kindness.'[37] That had to be set in the context of church or chapel attendance, preferably at least twice, for the accolade of Respectability to be earned. It was reinforced by overt appeals to Genesis and a hazy folk memory of the more amenable parts of seventeenth-century Puritanism. Attractive as it may have been in those terms, it was never as widespread as its defenders claimed, and there was a significant element of appealing for a return to a sabbatarian golden age.

What did cause deep concern was the way in which the assumedly automatic supporters of the observant position, the 'respectable' middle classes, now seemed to be turning away from it. In fact apostasy was numerically restricted and confined largely to the suburbs of the big cities, but it was accompanied by growing visibility as it spilled over into public spaces and competed for time with organised religion, particularly among men. The Churches' appeal was weighed against apparently equal choices by potential consumers. There was a certain element of irony in that many churches in the late nineteenth century had founded sports groups as an additional means of bonding the allegiance of their younger members.

In 1860, the year when *Essays and Reviews* opened up fierce controversy by bringing German ideas of historical criticism to English biblical scholarship, James Hessey, later to be Archdeacon of Middlesex, delivered the Bampton lectures in Oxford. Published under the title *Sunday*, they examined the scriptural base of sabbatarianism and argued for a revision of its demands appropriate to an urban industrial society:

> . . . the Clergy should, so it seems to me, not frown on those who consider Sunday to be, within certain limits, a day of cheerful relaxation, of family union, of social enjoyment, as well as of religious services. There is nothing in Scripture to forbid this, even though Sunday be (which it is not) identical with the Sabbath.[38]

Hessey still expected observance, those 'certain limits', but it was to be conventionally rather than legally enforced. Designed to help the poor find relaxation, his pragmatic arguments actually encouraged a justification of Sunday sport for the middle class. The argument spread along the lines of debate between Judaic pharisaism with its rigid sabbatarian legalism and the apparent liberalism of a Jesus prepared to bend the rules. It moved easily, but with little clerical help, to articulating opposition between repressive Judaeo-Christian claims and the expressive Hellenism that Matthew Arnold had supported in *Culture and Anarchy*.[39] Sunday came to be more attractive than the Sabbath in a case made up of historical claims for the practices of the early Church and the needs of the new cities.

A symposium of 1889, *Sunday Recreation*, included claims by its Anglican editor that strict sabbatarianism was doing little to encourage godliness. What was needed was more of an emphasis on Joy than on gloomy Duty. Archdeacon Hessey, one of the contributors, encouraged the Sunday use of railways for escape into the open air.[40] The Revd. Edgar Smith, vicar of All Saints, Highgate, wrote that he 'would not make it a sin that a young man, wearied with the work of "the city", should take his bicycle and go for a "spin" on Sunday afternoon'.[41] These views still assumed that there had been some religious observance in the morning; they were aimed at clerks confined to offices for most of the week. But when the clerks took to the roads on their bicycles their exemplars were less the concerned clergy than many of their own employers. Among the wealthier the growing cult of the 'weekend' alarmed the Broad and High Church Anglican proponents of Sunday, let alone the Evangelicals and the bulk of the Nonconformist clergy. For the latter the modest Tractarian seeking after a balance between observance and recreation was often the sign of a rapid downhill plunge into sin. Countless sermons were preached in local churches and chapels against Sunday sport. On a lighter level the myth built up that allowed a character in the much later novel by John Cowper Powys, *Wolf Solent*, to assert '. . . Bob says that High Church be a religion what lets a person play cricket on Sundays.'[42]

A slow trickle of apostasy in the 1860s grew rapidly as the century closed. In many senses younger middle-class men were only doing what a substantial proportion of manual workers had done for over a century, largely ignoring the Churches. It was the level of visibility which represented a threat to sabbatarians, plus the fact that they seemed to be losing those they regarded as naturally conditioned to join them. This was not a simple clash between Christians and secularists. Rather it locked into and was often determined by the emphasis on moral virtue which influential Englishmen (Evangelicals apart) often confuse with Christianity. Sport had been so far exalted as a moral examplar as to be used as a possible alternative in Christian teaching to the practices of the pulpit. It now offered itself instrumentally as a means of berating the claimed rigidity of ecclesiastical observance.

When Lieutenant-Colonel R. W. Osborn claimed in 1880 that 'there is no question that, as a moral discipline, lawn tennis on a Sunday afternoon is very superior to sermons' the issue had already moved beyond being tongue-in-cheek.[43] In parts of the sporting press the Churches were portrayed repeatedly as boring, with dim clergy and dull sermons. The *Fortnightly Review* in 1906 carried an article in a vein still familiar almost a century later:

> It is not, we submit, altogether the fault of the laity that London's churches are empty and its rivers, roads, and golf links crowded on Sundays . . . We need spirituality, not politics.[44]

Truth argued that 'Some day lawn tennis may be played on Sunday on the rectory lawn. That rector's church will not be empty.' More aggressively, an Edwardian proponent of 'the intellectual' values of sport reasserted the ethical virtues of play in terms almost strident in their opposition to organised religion:

There is more moral training for youth in the play of this game [Association Football] than there is in going to church, and listening to dull sermons, and in the monotonous repetition of dull formulae.[45]

Before examining the Churches' reaction it is necessary to assess how far Sunday sport had progressed in our period. In the field sports – hunting, shooting and fishing – there had been a traditional refusal to play on Sundays: the vast expansion of coarse fishing in the later nineteenth century still ran largely against a widespread popular non-church-attending sabbatarianism. Game-shooting on Sunday was illegal anyway, and when wildfowling for sport developed a number of the new county councils used their bye-laws to restrict it to weekdays.[46] But in many of the newer sports, particularly those which slid by the ban on commercial entertainment in the 1780 Lord's Day Observance Act, there was repeated tension between pressure for participation and expectations of self-regulation. After its foundation in 1907 the Amateur Football Association discouraged its members from Sunday play and the Essex county body took active steps in 1907 to ban its members from joining in Sunday friendly play in the Leytonstone area.[47] Paradoxically many of those who seem to have supported freer Sunday play for manual workers turned firmly against it for the middle classes.

What was often sharply at issue was the extent to which class-based privacy in sport allowed its Sunday concealment or exaggerated social tensions which were already present in the ways in which particular activities had developed and colonised space. To have played alongside workers in east London would have invited unwelcome publicity but to open up a golf course for Sunday play could cause even more public debate. Osbert Lancaster noted the finer points of social manoeuvring in his Edwardian childhood when he recalled that his grandfather had allowed home croquet instead of lawn tennis because the latter would be visible from the road, so risking leading 'the villagers into sin', whereas the croquet lawn was concealed behind trees.[48] What could cause problems at a domestic level became an acute issue when it involved larger space, whether private club premises or shared public territory.

Lawn tennis, bridging the two senses of space, proved a relatively minor area of conflict but one which could be more generally linked with accusations of growing middle-class selfishness. In 1888 the All England Lawn Tennis Club debated Sunday play. A general membership vote came down two-to-one in its favour, provided that ball boys were not employed. This compromise in dispensing with servants spread across the newer middle-class sports, allowing the pretence that there could be no resulting corruption of the working classes by example. The reaction of a number of Wimbledon people, however, was that Sunday play lowered local social tone. With its by now customary arrogance the club committee stayed firm, 'declining to sacrifice the convenience of the members to the Sabbatarian prejudices of adjoining occupiers'.[49]

It is virtually impossible to assess how widely the Wimbledon example was followed nationally because of the nature of lawn tennis club records, but there were critics even among the liberal clergy of the desecration of Sunday as distinct from its valid recreational use:

> I would condemn no one on this day to imprisonment within the four walls of his house, or to see nothing of his neighbour. Friendly intercourse is a real refreshment, and in no wise to be discouraged; but the great afternoon receptions and lawn tennis parties . . . are all of this world, and in no sense help to give that rest of mind and body which Sunday should promote according to God's ordinance, in addition to which they necessitate work on the part of others, and afford an example which others are not slow in following.[50]

Golf provoked the greatest arguments over organised desecration. It became an issue in the 1890s, although no English club admitted to being the first to allow Sunday play. Strays from Wimbledon, banned there because they were a risk to other Sunday users on the common, were playing on Epsom Downs in 1891.[51] The Lords committee of 1895 heard of its spread in the Old Deer Park in Richmond on Thames and of its corrupting influence there:

> . . . gentlemen are dressed in scarlet, with large bundles of sticks, and then from our Sunday schools . . . our lads are taken away to go into the park for the purpose of carrying the sticks, or to go after the balls. These lads are called 'caddies', and altogether we are in Richmond degenerating as a town.[52]

Degeneracy, threats to the social tone and corruption of the young and the poor were constant themes in the criticism of the spread of Sunday golf, supported also in many areas by the threat of further alienation of common land from other leisure users whose only day off this was. The golfers' arguments for relaxation included a wide mix: Sunday was often the only day when hard-working business and professional men could get in a convenient full daylight round, it was necessary to relieve the growing stresses of business life, on dedicated club land it was a use of private space which involved no spectators. In some areas these were bolstered by reasons not always made fully explicit; the heavy investment in improved facilities in the Edwardian years demanded maximum resource utilisation and the income derived from green fees; towns, resorts in particular, which did not cater for Sunday golfers would lose out in the fierce competition for quality trade.

Within the resorts themselves different middle-class groups found themselves in fierce debate over which path would make their towns most attractive. Hastings and St Leonards were held to have entered their long decline because Sunday golf was allowed.[53] Seaford's leading developer claimed in 1894 that 'a man who would play golf on a Sunday would not be very particular whether he paid his debts or not'.[54] In 1903 the Revd. the Earl of Chichester, vicar of Yarmouth, protested sharply against the game's spreading there. Leeds managed to overturn the ban on Sunday golf in its corporation lease in 1911 after a long debate held in secret to prevent the town's well known denominational frontiers from being hardened further.[55]

In the case of the new Sussex town of Bexhill, struggling to create a niche of profitable respectability in a crowded local market, the arguments illustrate the ethical confusion which could be generated. Early in the new century the local golf club started Sunday play, excluding caddies. This was changed by a proposal of February 1910, when the committee said it would employ caddies 'on a voluntary basis' if they were over fourteen years old. The rector, also the archdeacon, said that this would cause an inevitable 'deterioration of character', reinforcing caddying's dead-end as a job: but he avoided any wider denunciation of Sunday recreation. He found vocal, if eccentric, support from a local part-resident, Oscar Browning, the reforming fellow of King's College, Cambridge, who said that caddies should spend the day in church and Sunday school. An ironic and anonymous rejoinder to this followed:

> it's all very well for Professor Browning to sit in his easy chair on Sunday after lunch and think how lovely it is to go to church, but please remember he isn't half-starved and he isn't dependent on a round of golf for a meal.

Since the caddies did not usually go to church, and work, however poorly paid, was held to be of greater value than loafing, the club won its change quietly.[56]

At least in golf it is roughly possible to assess the extent to which Sunday play was introduced. Initially clubs were reticent to advertise their doing this – surprising, in view of the strident claims often advanced for its necessity – and the main mid-Edwardian golfing directory gives no instances.[57] Matters had changed by the eve of the First World War, when 436 of the 1,024 English courses advertised Sunday games, almost half with caddies. In greater London two-thirds of the clubs allowed Sunday play and almost a third of all matches were played on Sundays. But only eighteen of the eighty-three Welsh clubs did so, and they were all in areas of English middle-class colonisation. Scotland stayed much purer, with only eleven of over 400 clubs weakening the Sabbath.[58]

It was not in club and spatially limited sport, however, that the greatest shift took place, but rather on the public spaces of water and highway. From the 1880s the Thames grew rapidly in pleasure rather than competition boating, particularly among clerks and lesser tradesmen. Despite its associations with skill and athletic exercise, Sunday rowing could be dismissed by Bishop Mackerness of Oxford, a former college oar, in 1884 as showing that 'The idlers cannot omit one day in the week from their quest of pleasure.'[59] The scale was large and singularly visible: it contributed background flavour to Jerome's *Three Men in a Boat* in 1889, became an icon of pleasure in E. V. Gregory's painting 'Boulter's Lock on Sunday Afternoon, 1885' and over 1,000 boats and seventy launches passed through that limited space on the first Sunday in August 1900.[60] The prestigious ARA clubs continued to ban Sunday rowing, but some lesser bodies were competing by the mid-1900s, eccentrically augmented by F. J. Furnivall's Hammersmith Sculling Club for Girls.[61] On the whole it was an individual or small group rather than organised development.

Much greater in scale was the impact of the cycling boom. The AAA and NCU banned Sunday track racing but a great deal of unofficial 'scorching' took place. Cycling offered a dilemma because, although a mass phenomenon, it represented an essentially individualist response and the desperate need for open-air relaxation after confinement in offices. Individual it may have been, but it demanded growing local sub-industries, ranging from repair facilities to cream teas. And the pressure in spring and summer on these was considerable: in the road equivalent of Boulter's Lock, the Red Deer at Croydon, an LDOS observer noted 125 female and 1,797 male cyclists in a two-hour period on one Sunday in 1904; there were 125 cars as well.[62] Despite the society's pamphlet *To Cyclists – this hill is dangerous*, first produced in 1902, the decline went on.

These individual pursuits, however, opened up limited possibilities of religious compromise. Some people made their own arrangements. When J. R. Halkes, the Wesleyan architect of Lincoln, took his motor boat, the *Asp*, up Fosse Dyke to the Trent on Sunday 28 July 1907 he went to an evening service in Torksey, returning to the boat with friends, where 'a little part-singing was indulged in before retiring for the night'.[63] George F. Holmes, founder of the Humber Yawl Club, 'was deeply religious, and when away on a cruise on Sunday he invariably set off in the dinghy to the nearest Church, whether his crew accompanied him or not.'[64]

For some sportsmen churchgoing could be fitted in almost as an aesthetic accompaniment. When the Rucksack Club set off on its Easter Beckfoot climb in 1906:

Sunday saw most of the men off to the hills again, but, for those who wished to take it, a pleasant change was to be found in the bright Easter morning service by the little river.[65]

The important point here is that it was assumed that the majority of the club had more important things to do than go to church, even to commemorate the Resurrection.

Some churchmen tried to develop compromises. By the mid-1880s the vicar of Ripley, Surrey, provided Sunday afternoon services for cyclists. He was rewarded in 1889 when a group of them presented him with a work table and typewriter, in return for which he offered a Pauline sermon, 'So run the race that ye may obtain the prize.'[66] In a favoured spot in north Yorkshire, Giggleswick, the vicar invited cyclists to join services in cycling dress, even to leave before the sermon, reminding them that though Sunday cycling was not sinful, 'you do most certainly sin against God and wrong your neighbour if you neglect your clear duty, which is to publicly admire your Saviour, Jesus the Christ'.[67] Some cyclists combined sport with evangelism; twenty-five Congregationalists formed a 'Cyclists' Gospel Band' to cover north London and Epping Forest.[68] But generally cycling was one of the causes, rather than a symptom, of growing secularism in the eyes of many churchmen, part of the 'carelessness and athleticism' which the 'liberal' Bishop of Manchester saw as prompting moral decline.[69]

The national Church found itself tied in even further contortions on the issues of Sunday sport. The sporting Bishop of London, Winnington-Ingram, begged his City audience at the Guildhall to forswear Sunday golf in favour of churchgoing, but to little avail. 'The Sunday golfer is not a social backslider by any means; he is more the type of man who will morally elevate his associates'.[70] He went on to suggest the compromise of a short prayer service at the first tee on Sunday mornings, but there is little evidence of this happening. Non-evangelical Anglicans and the more progressive Congregationalists had effectively already ceded the position, with their revised theological and social teachings, and it was to escape some of the more disturbing of the latter that a growing number of prosperous men played sport on Sunday. Wesleyans, Primitives and Baptists generally kept to a harder sabbatarian line; the decline universally and ethically seems to have been largely Anglican.

The *Daily Telegraph* survey of suburban observance in 1905 identified particular areas of fall-off such as Penge, which 'has always shown a marked tendency towards the progressive idea as to how Sunday should be spent'.[71] Yet Charles Booth's much more systematic investigation of London's religious life ignored middle-class apostasy almost entirely.[72] What had become clear was that for many middle-class men, particularly in southern England, organised religion had become one of a number of possible ways of employing non-work time, that their ethical codes were reinforced less by specific theological teachings than by looser codes of sporting etiquette. Suburban support of churchgoing was becoming a matter for women, children and the elderly. Sunday sport represented an additional refuge from onerous domestic obligations, of which churchgoing was one. It was secularisation arising from social habits rather than theological convictions, and even protests against it had limits. The Lord's Day Observance Society refused repeated suggestions that it should oppose the golfing Prime Minister, Balfour, at the polls with a sabbatarian candidate on the pragmatic grounds that a non-golfing candidate might develop worse faults.[73] Sunday sport attracted opprobrium but the majority of men who escaped from worship probably just stayed at home.

Degeneracy

By the 1890s far more attention was being given to another area. It is a well worn truism that concepts of moral decadence were well mingled with sub-Darwinian notions of racial decay and thermodynamic laws of entropy by 1900. The warnings of H. G. Wells in *The Time Machine* and of a host of lesser writers were making it clear that the human race, or at least the English section of it, was on the way out. Luxury, 'over-civilisation', too great a degree of sensitivity, the rejection of hard work, were all widely held to contribute to a process that only a desperate effort could reverse, and sport was quoted repeatedly as a central phenomenon in this.[74] W. E. Henley encapsulated it in his epilogue to a hyper-nationalist extended poem, 'For England's sake':

> The nation, in a dream
> Of money and love and sport, hangs at the pap
> Of well-being, and so
> Goes fattening, mellowing, dozing, rotting down
> Into a rich deliquium of decay.[75]

But the issues surrounding 'sport' in these terms were complex. 'It had become such a catch-all word by 1900 that its very use was highly debatable and likely to produce both derision and a tightening of the boundaries of snobbery. The *Fortnightly Review* claimed in 1897 that:

> It is the introduction of easier pastimes which is wasting so much time that ought to be spent, if not at the desk, at least in taking stock of oneself, in associating with other minds, and bringing out one's latent powers.[76]

With presumably unconscious irony it went on to quote Walter Pater: 'Failure is to form habits.' It was near-daily indulgence in lawn tennis, golf or cycling which was under attack. More crudely, the *Race Builder* demanded a few years later that the British should 'give up our smoking and ping-pong playing' and seek to rival the Spartans.[77]

It is, however, too convenient an explanation of shifts to link the arguments over degeneracy solely with the turn of the century or, as Tim Jeal has done, with the popularity in England after the Wilde trial of Max Nordau's book *Degeneration*.[78] Twenty years earlier Charles Kingsley had warned of the risk of England's urban degeneration in *Health and Education*, suggesting that sport could prevent it.[79] In its first annual report in 1891 the London Playing Fields Committee had asked for support from 'all who detest the thought of national degeneracy, and abhor nervousness and effeminacy'.[80]

Thinking in this vein was sharpened considerably by two debacles of the Second Boer War, the time it took to win it and the wholesale medical rejection of volunteers to fight. It was refined in the subsequent report of the Interdepartmental Committee on Physical

Deterioration. Like Kingsley and the Playing Fields Committee, this assumed that it was the working classes who epitomised degeneracy, both physically and morally. In his evidence the London editor of the *Manchester Guardian*, J. B. Atkins, proposed the spread of games on the public school model: 'Directly a man begins to respect his body and want to get his colours, he hates anything which keeps back his bodily fitness.'[81] This repetition of words as likely to be used by Dr Warre of Eton or his equivalents could be found frequently in Edwardian England, but they presupposed a direct lead from the middle classes which was being questioned increasingly. Instead it was widely held in both the general and specialised press that addiction to sport was now sapping middle-class physical and moral fibre.

When the *New Review* asked in 1896, 'Are we an athletic people?', it questioned the 'pleasant fiction' that all Englishmen were sporting and drew a picture of the feeble clerk 'swelling with complacency over the athletic supremacy of the country he adorns'.[82] For the contributors to *The Athletic Sports* of 1898 it was even worse: they assumed an active participation rate of around one per cent, and this was under threat because of a growing tendency to see sport as an end in itself rather than as a means of preparation for higher purposes.[83] This view of potential decadence actually demanded a tougher attitude to sport and its greater popularisation: it was the restrictiveness of middle-class pursuits that was putting the nation at risk. That individuals might go overboard into a pathological obsession with sport, destroying their essential humanity, had an occasional rather alarming literary airing. Wilkie Collins's *Man and Wife* of 1873 is much quoted, as are the later Vachell and Waugh: for Collins, all sport did was release 'the barbarous hardness in his heart . . . the barbarous darkness in [the] mind' of his murderous subject.[84]

The debate was more obviously collective by the turn of the century, less prepared to rely on the possibility of an individual's perversion being sufficient to make the wide moral point. For some, Hellenism had been so successful that its outward athletic forms had been adopted without an adequate philosophical base, and the Judaeo-Christian elements of the Pauline emphasis had been ditched so that the essential moral purpose of sport had been lost. For A. C. Benson patriotism had been replaced by fanaticism, with its 'shameless glorification of athletic exercises'.[85] P. A. Vaile, concerned that even New Zealand could defeat England, saw the roots of decay in complacency, solidity, soporific cricket and snobbery; he quoted the case of a life member of a fashionable sporting club who had actually provided it with a mortgage yet was unable to enter the tea room because he was not a 'gentleman'.[86] In 1906 the Regius Profesor of Medicine at Cambridge complained in a speech at Leeds Grammar School that undergraduate enthusiasm for lawn tennis was a moral waste.[87] Several years later one of the leading proponents of moral athleticism, Lord Hawke, questioned the decay among the followers of his own teachings and called for a return to commonsense practices:

> I question whether anybody recognises the fact more clearly than those of us whose lives have been essentially athletic ones, a great tendency nowadays for sport and games to be overdone . . . a sensible level-headed moderation must govern the athlete.[88]

There remained, however, a current of writing which questioned this, clinging to individual evidences of sporting prowess as a denial of a movement towards decay and regarding criticism as unpatriotic. The sporting politician Balfour suggested in his Sidgwick memorial lecture of 1908 that England was a still rising society with a clear goal of progress.[89] More typical, perhaps, was R. C. Lehmann's earlier claim that the rowing man would have no time to be trapped in degeneracy:

> He will have trained himself to submit to discipline, to accept discomfort cheerfully, to keep a brave face in adverse circumstances; he will have developed to the full his strength and his powers of endurance, and will have learnt the necessity of unselfishness and patriotism. These are, after all, no mean results in a generation which is often accused of effeminate and debasing luxury.[90]

Such views would have been parroted cheerfully and uncritically by many a schoolmaster, and they were reinforced in 1897 by T. H. S. Escott. But it would have been difficult to say much otherwise in a book lauding the social changes at the second Jubilee.[91]

Defenders of sporting progress such as F. G. Aflalo questioned the *Fortnightly's* repeated assertions of decay by claiming that the early Edwardian Conservative Cabinet, although full of sportsmen, was too dedicated to its work to be led astray by pastimes.[92] This encouraged calls to patriotic duty. The president of the British Medical Association attacked fashionable 'claptrap' in 1907 by pointing out how far society had progressed since the poverty and disease of early Victorian England and by claiming that 'Athletic development has awakened the national mind to the need for physical culture and has taught people that the national strength is an important factor.'[93] The physical fitness movement, with its gymnastics and Indian clubs, was never more than a fringe cult, even among Edwardian sportsmen, let alone among the wider population, but it produced some loudly patriotic acclamations. A key figure was Eustace Miles, educated at Rugby and King's College, Cambridge, Amateur Tennis Champion from 1899 to 1903, who poured out a stream of books and pamphlets aimed particularly at non-athletic clerks. His object was to convert the 90 per cent who did not play at all.[94]

Essentially the debate centred on whether sport and fitness were actually compatible. The catch-all journal of the movement, *Physical Education*, doubted it, largely because sport had developed in ways, including wholesale spectatorship, that could cause 'an irretrievable national disaster in the near future'.[95]

Much of the debate on the critical side was conducted in this language of the abyss, and the self-proclaimed national hero, Baden-Powell, used it repeatedly to demand a return to the values of citizenship, service and the empire. He disliked both public school boys who preferred scholarship to games and working-class 'loafers' who puffed on cigarettes whilst watching football. He demanded a different bond for the threatened empire than games: 'Our forefathers did not depend upon games in building up the British Empire; neither have games kept it together, and certainly they will not in the future.'[96] To the founder of the Boy Scouts the new games were inadequate for fostering corporate spirit. The sports he had favoured when young, polo and pig-sticking, and the fly fishing of his older years demanded a contest with nature which a mass movement aimed at the working classes (and missing them singularly) could accommodate only by its artificial creation of camp-fire life. It was the middle-class young he captured, and what Jeal has characterised as his anti-intellectual anti-urbanism was well in the tradition of much of their fathers' sport.

Saving the young was one thing, with some limited long-term possibilities of success. The Edwardian prophets of decay, however, were much more urgent in their claims of the imminence of collapse. They were reinforced by foreign observers. The French writer Paul Adam saw a clear link between the decline of English performance in Olympic track events and the loss of markets to Americans and Germans: but he saw the pursuit of excellence in sport as being killed off by the inherent puritanism of the middle classes.[97] When the American Price Collier joined in he used the language of play to reinforce the sense of crisis:

Nothing but a tremendous, almost miraculous, wrench can turn our stout, red-cheeked, honest, sport-loving John Bull away from his habits of centuries, to compete with his virile body against the nervous intelligence of a scientific age . . . The nations are playing a new game now, and some of them seem to play it more brilliantly and successfully than he does.[98]

The issue was not so much one of performance in sport as of the extent to which amateurish play was symptomatic of a wider indolence that could be categorised as inefficiency for the sake of it. From there it was no great step to assuming that sport was not so much a symptom as a cause of the collapse in imperial and entrepreneurial ability.

We have already seen that sport itself contributed not insignificantly to sectoral shifts in the late Victorian economy, becoming a source of investment and entrepreneurship in itself. But this made little apparent impression on the large number of writers who pointed to a growing crisis in British industry. For them it was a question of accelerating decline, and there were relatively few who were prepared to argue as did Sidney Abrahams about English 'athletic bankruptcy' to an American, 'I was able to convince him that there had been no degeneracy in England but merely non-progression.'[99] Sport was now inseparably intertwined with the debate about national efficiency. This involved two strands of thought. On the one hand middle-class obsession with games was held to be deflecting energies from industrial management; entrepreneurs were failing. The other response was that the wrong sports were being pursued, for pleasure rather than for manly purpose, and that sections of the middle classes had made their pursuits so exclusive that the considerable potential of sport for moral and national regeneration was being lost. Twined round the two themes was that of amateurism: that love of sport for its own sake had reduced its instrumentality in promoting competitiveness and was sapping the will to win. Arnold White, whose *Efficiency and Empire* provided a primitive Darwinistic outlet for such views, saw the middle classes as the source of hope because they were caste-free, unlike the aristocracy and gentry. The paradox was that middle-class sport had created internal barriers open to achievement but beset by snobbery.[100]

In his comparative mid-Edwardian international study *Industrial Efficiency* Arthur Shadwell pointed to corruption by example from the middle classes. It was lawn tennis and golf, 'breeding a race of loafers all over the country', which bore the brunt of these attacks, as having become the daily obsession of commercial men.[101] Hence the somewhat feeble repeated claims of golf's popularisers that a great deal of confidential business was concluded on the links. Shadwell was unrepentant. 'The once enterprising manufacturer has grown slack, he has let the business take care of itself, while he is shooting grouse or yachting in the Mediterranean.'[102] For *Truth*, the iniquitous spread of professionalism was largely responsible for growing inefficiency:

> There is very little chance of the old country working up and maintaining a commercial supremacy as long as men of moderate means can make a livelihood out of sport.[103]

Yet quiet reiteration of the value of games remained and undoubtedly accounted for continued sporting growth. One author noted the possibility of decline but hoped that business would continue to be taken up by rugby players, 'training for the battle of life', and that 'hobbies' such as sport would encourage hard work because people would want the money to take part in them.[104] The proponents of this view were probably more successful than their detractors, but they shouted far less loudly. *C. B. Fry's Magazine*, like *Baily's*, provided a continued outlet for the latter, largely on the grounds that decline in sporting performance paralleled rather than caused economic decline: both were open to moral regeneration.[105] But their detractors had better access to the wider currency of the national press. In an article, 'Patball', in 1910 the *Saturday Review* saw the Liberal Cabinet as overwhelmed by its passion for golf, businessmen likewise, country houses dominated by bridge, and claimed that 'the Waterloo or Trafalgar of commerce' would be lost on the nation's playing fields.[106] The folk myth of a manly sporting past became also a mirror of potential decay: when Canon Newbolt preached against modern sport in St Paul's Cathedral in August 1912 he claimed, 'There are people who imitate Drake in playing bowls but who are not the least prepared to follow him in routing the Armada.'[107]

The Times offered a frequent outlet for similar views. Games undermined the psychological basis of entrepreneurial success because they emphasised the group rather than the individual: the intelligence and skill which had emerged from contests with nature or 'the undeveloped ball-game of an earlier period' were stifled by the concern for team spirit.[108] On the whole it preferred to blame the working classes for falls in national output, without questioning the entrepreneurship which provided the circuses of football in the first place.[109] On the eve of the First World War the paper moved slightly away from this stance when it encouraged a correspondence on golf as a time-waster which 'has crept up on the country like a destroying fungus', repeating the headmaster of Eton's attacks on it, but also noting an obsession with playing it among public school masters.[110]

National economic efficiency was attracting less attention by the later Edwardian years than national military weakness and sport's contribution to it. Darwinian casting about for species comparisons produced national models by which the British could be judged. *C. B. Fry's Magazine* ran repeated articles on the citizen army of the Swiss, with their apparent Athenian democracy underpinned by outdoor healthiness and Protestant virtue.[111] But it was the Japanese, with their rapid but selective westernisation, who attracted most attention, not least because they appeared to offer in the guise of the samurai a body closest to the Platonic image of the guardians as the masters of a modern economy. The ease with which these feudal freebooters were clothed by observers with the idealised nobility of a public school elite was remarkable.

Fry wrote articles idealising the Japanese army and the Agenda Club, whose concern for caddies we have noted, chose the samurai as the ideal it would prefer its socially committed Englishmen to follow. It all had slightly dotty undertones of Camelot: 'There is absent from the political ethos of today the spirit of chivalrous service and self-sacrifice.'[112] With such widespread adulation the views of Price Collier, who held that the best countries should have sportsmen as leaders, were a shock. He could not see the Japanese as transplanted public school men:

> Japan is a nation of athletes whose prowess has only lately been discovered, and they are the more dangerous accordingly. Indeed, it is an open question whether England's hypocritical and short-sighted alliance with these varnished savages has not done more to menace Saxon civilisation, both in Europe and in America, than any diplomatic step that has been taken for centuries.[113]

Attention shifted rapidly away from an idealised Pacific to the possibility of strife between Saxons for European dominance. As English paranoia about the possibility of a German invasion rose so did the claims that the decadent passion for luxurious sport would let the invaders in. The message that the gains won on the playing fields of Eton were likely to be squandered on the greens at Weybridge was passed from the earnestness of the *Fortnightly* or *Fry's* to ironic verse and story. In his 'Ruthless Rhymes' Harry Graham pointed to the breaches in the walls of 'The Englishman's Home':

> I was playing golf the day
> That the Germans landed;
> All our troops had run away,
> All our ships were stranded;
> And the thought of England's shame
> Altogether spoilt my game.[114]

At greater length 'Saki' offered the story 'When William came', on the eve of war in 1914. The narrator, returned from game shooting in the Mongolian wilds, finds England occupied without opposition and can easily see why:

> ... when it came to be a question of sport against soldiering, I don't know whether anyone has said it, but one might almost assert that the German victory was won on the golf-links of Britain.[115]

The game had destroyed the will of the 'leisured class' to fight more than any other sport, and the occupied went on playing it. In Saki's story the only hope of future resistance would come from the para-military Boy Scouts.

War games

This undercurrent of invasion fears sharpened discussion about the instrumentality of sport in military training, which also raised issues about middle-class ambivalence towards professionalism. With increasing expectations of occupational competence affecting the 'liberal' professions, preparation for war was drawn into the discussion. Army officerships in particular, with their messy location between the older gentry and the newer upper middle-class aspirants, served as a focus of much of this debate. The cult of honourable defeat which had grown out of conflicts between the small standing army and various dark-coloured foreigners proved less acceptable during the Second Boer War, and the multiple reverses in South Africa demonstrated the inadequacy of officer training among both the regulars and the growing number of amateur soldiers.

In the early 1900s sport as training or a pleasing diversion for officers became a matter of agonised concern as army and national authorities came very slowly to grips with some of the implications of modern warfare. Military and sporting honour were still felt to go hand-in-hand. The death of the golfer Freddie Tait in South Africa was portrayed not only as a major loss to that sport's growth but also as an iteration of the values which the game should inspire at its best.[116] So could the example of John Ball Junior, the 1890 Open Golf Champion, who 'When sterner work fell to his hand . . . was not backward, but went out to South Africa as a yeoman,' riding a horse given him by his employers, the Royal Liverpool Golf Club.[117] In this world-picture sport appeared to endow its younger players with military virtues almost automatically. Occasionally a word of warning crept in. In *The Brainside of Games, Sports and Pastimes* H. C. Donovan tried anxiously to dispel the image of the flannelled fool by claiming that cricket as 'a game' was the most demanding of all sports. But he also went on to reflect that it was preparation for an older mode of engagement, since no explosives were used during matches.[118]

The use of game language in war is well known; less clearly observed was a growing Edwardian tendency to reverse this by importing military terms into play. Price Collier, who saw the English as essentially unmilitaristic, also saw sport as a surrogate: 'merely artificial work, artificial adventure, artificial colonising, artificial war. It is shooting at a mark because there are no enemies to shoot at.'[119] Implicit criticism such as this usually broke more clearly into the open in fringe journals which questioned the symbiotic blood lust of playing and fighting. *Humanitarian* claimed that both war and sport were prehistoric, serving only as agents of English international greed.[120] R. B. Cunningham Graham used the journal to attack 'indecently bad riders and poor shots' in the Boer War, not to claim that sport was interfering with military efficiency but rather to demonstrate the impropriety of both.[121] But these were weak voices compared with those that wanted to improve both sport *and* warlike efficiency. It was a debate about whether team games stifled individual efficiency and initiative, and that had to be proclaimed loudly against claims like *Baily's* 'that it is sportsmen who have always been the best soldiers'.[122] Or against widespread doggerel:

For Roman, Anglo, Norman, Dane,
Have all infused their blood,
And none to Britain ever came,
Who did not cross the flood:

What they in deadly earnest dared,
Let us enjoy in sport,
And thus in pastime be prepared,
For games of sterner sort.[123]

That came from a yachting text; it was *Riddle of the Sands* senti-
mentality in a world where naval officers were presumed to be
professionals, and socially inferior as such, and where the arms
race was seen immediately in terms of Dreadnoughts. The creation
of a Royal Naval Volunteer Reserve after the Naval Forces Act of
1903 offered a cover, and a new set of uniforms, for large numbers
of yachtsmen.[124]

The racial virtues of Drake and Nelson were still extolled, despite
the fact that the Royal Navy had faced no serious opposition for
almost a century. But the crux of the Edwardian debate was about
the effectiveness of an army still recovering from the shocks of South
Africa. For all the invasion scares, it was preparation for a European
mainland war that now fuelled the discussion.

In fact the seeds of the debate were a decade older, part of the general unease about things 'made in Germany' and about decadence.[125]
When fox-hunting's future had seemed uncertain in the early 1890s
the Hon. F. Lindsay had justified the sport as a natural accessory of
'a stripling of good birth', much to be preferred as officer material,
particularly by his men, to a ranker promoted because he knew his
professional duties.[126] Even when competitive entrance to Sandhurst
seemed to be limiting the number of successful candidates, it was
felt that it could be taken for granted that they were experienced in
field sports: so physical training 'may safely be left to the various
influences which ever surround the young men of our nation'.[127] In a
world where military thinking was dominated by the drill and dash of
a cavalry elite, fox-hunting seemed to offer the necessary combination
of nerve, danger, decision and an eye for fast movement across
country. Its colonial extensions, pig-sticking and big game chasing,
offered similar advantages, with additional overtones. Colonel R. S.
S. Baden-Powell, the hero of Mafeking and founder of Scouting, seems
to have been at his happiest hunting down rebels: 'this manhunting
afforded us plenty of excitement and novel experience'.[128] In South
Africa it was the Boers who did much of the hunting.

As Tim Travers has shown, the issues that faced the Edwardian
officer were the tensions between the individualism of professional
competence and the pressures for corporate conformity which the

public schools and team games had inculcated.[129] At the turn of the century it was the latter which were praised, as producing 'the men, capable of any amount of endurance and unequalled for dogged determination, who are now giving the world an object lesson in South Africa'.[130] The unexpected defeats, however, prompted attacks on games and hunting. The Committee on Military Education which reported in 1902 suggested that sport could be more attractive to officers than fighting. The focus of most of this disapproval was polo, with its pressures to over-expenditure and gambling.[131] Out of the various analyses of failures on the veldt came suggestions that field skills such as scouting, and real physical exercise, should replace pseudo-aristocratic expense or undemanding team games.

The high incidence of disease among all the fighting men in South Africa prompted sharp doubts as to just how fit troops, particularly the volunteer officers, were. Sports which served as a safety valve for ordinary urban life were not necessarily suited to providing tough soldiers. Eustace Miles and his followers built a minor industry on this, but they seem to have made relatively little headway against the continued current of assumptions about public school sports, with 'the value of their athletic training for real warfare.'[132] The problem that reformers faced was that the British had eventually won in South Africa, thereby justifying the assumptions of Alfred Lyttelton and others that it was the capacity for endurance given by the public schools which had proved victorious.[133]

The principal shock of South Africa was that it had been seen by many of the English as a rehearsal for their part in an inevitable European land war. Despite the volunteer upsurge which accompanied turn-of-the-century patriotic fervour it dropped rapidly thereafter and considerable attention was paid to the implications of fighting the Germans. Latent anti-militarism, fostered publicly by leading Liberal politicians such as Sir Edward Grey, combined with a continued attachment to voluntaryism to resist significant expansion of the home-based standing army or the introduction of conscription on the European model. So the debate had little choice but to focus on the ways in which a 'citizen army' could be developed, harnessing civilian fears, patriotism and sporting practices with the minimum necessary cost. It led eventually to the emergence of a new military volunteer body, the Territorial Army, and its overlap with an established but rapidly growing sporting activity, rifle-shooting.[134] The first combined and reordered the existing part-time forces, yeomanry, militia and volunteers, as the basis of a mobile offensive as well as defensive entity: the other sought to foster local pride and give to a relatively sedentary activity the glamour of military necessity combined with 'scientifically' accurate musketry. Both were fostered in a way that sought to develop a natural flow between the activities and organisations of schools and universities and the pursuits of younger men at work. Given their gestation and costs, it was hardly surprising that their appeal was primarily to the slightly lowlier members of the middle classes.

The public figurehead of this was Lord Roberts, who had returned from South Africa in 1901 to become Commander-in-Chief. His concern about military training, including some well expressed doubts as to the value of fox-hunting and polo in producing professional officers, continued after his retirement, when he linked with the Liberal politician Haldane to foster the new Territorial Army, founded in 1907, and became president of the National Service League. The league had been founded in 1901, and largely favoured conscription, but ended up by giving wider support to voluntary movements: it boasted 115,000 members by 1911, largely in the London area.[135] Roberts had grave doubts as to how effective the Liberal compromise would be but he gave the accolade of military respectability to a movement which reflected much of the patriotic muddle of Edwardian England. Haldane encapsulated this in terms which showed little development from the assumptions of Lyttelton or Warre:

> If you leave our people alone, whether they belong to the working classes, the middle classes, or the upper classes, you will find a spirit shown among them which is perfectly ready of its own initiative to undertake in sufficient number the training that is necessary to make the act of war an art which is not unknown to them.[136]

Convoluted reasoning produced a convoluted response. On the whole it is hard to escape the conclusion that, apart from the pan-class battalions that emerged in parts of the countryside, the new force was largely a combination of solicitors, grocers and fervent clerks in uniform.

In 1906 C. B. Fry published a series of rousing articles in his *Magazine*. They assumed essentially that many middle-class games now lacked any national character:

> Great Britain enjoys amongst the European nations the supreme position of having within her borders a larger number of pure, selfish pleasure-

Sport and the English middle classes

seekers amongst the rich, and of idle, able-bodied tramps, loafers and hooligans amongst the poor, than any other European country.[137]

Yet he was as optimistic as Haldane that the response to this would be the rapid development of a spirit of national service led by ex-public school boys, which would concentrate on developing military skills, especially rifle shooting. This view was modified, however, by an emphasis on civilian rather than military virtues, as if it seemed necessary to sell an unacceptable idea to his readers by pretending that it was the pleasurable side of training which really mattered.

This was reinforced by an article that Lord Roberts published in *Fry's* two years later in which he accepted that the 'miniature' .22 rifle was more likely to find followers than the standard military weapon in local sporting use.[138] By that time the Society of Miniature Rifle Clubs had more than a thousand clubs affiliated to it. Roberts was echoing a remark made by Lord Methuen when he opened a miniature range at Haywards Heath in 1905, encouraging informal patriotism and friendly village competitions.[139] Both assumed, with Fry, that pleasant sport would develop almost inexorably into a serious national purpose. When the Territorial Army emerged it too offered an umbrella for games and the public displays of local elites. It overlapped with a boom in rifle shooting which attracted many civilians who wished to invest their spare-time sports with an air of seriousness but not with the military discipline Haldane's offspring required. Shooting could also be sold in terms of defensive readiness without the apparent capacity for aggression that the Territorials offered.

The National Rifle Association had grown out of the French invasion scare of 1859 which had prompted the formation of the Volunteers. Its headquarters were moved from Wimbledon to Bisley, Surrey, in 1890, where it provided the shooting grounds which still represent the national testing place of English competitive rifle shooting. During the Second Boer War it encouraged the formation of new rifle clubs: the ninety-two affiliated in 1901 grew to 328 the following year, and it was estimated to represent 30,000 members by the outbreak of the First World War. It provided a hierarchy of regional and national competitions, culminating in an annual fortnight at Bisley, and a structured series of qualifications, including 'skilled shot certificates', to be mounted and hung on suburban parlour walls.[140] Despite the rapid growth in shooting it drew down frequent criticisms: there could be little comparison between miniature and full-scale rifle

290

shooting, transfer would be difficult in times of crisis, and the restrained etiquette of the ranges, with leisurely shooting done largely prone, using sighting telescopes, was an inadequate preparation for the mobile, standing arena of the battlefield,

Yet the new clubs portrayed themselves as responding to national need. When the Leeds Rifle Club, whose forty vice-presidents included ten councillors and thirteen justices of the peace, was formed in 1900, it claimed 'generally to provide an efficient force to assist in the defence of the country in time of need'.[141] With a basic annual subscription of one guinea it was intended for a white-collar membership. In a number of areas firms such as Jaeger's and the London & County Bank added ranges to their company sports facilities.[142] The use of miniature rifles in indoor ranges offered year-round sport, free from the climate's exigencies, but it removed it even further from the sharp demands of military preparation.

Perhaps it was because of this that the movement grew. The NRA, War Office and philanthropy, including a gift of £10,000 from W. Astor, fostered growth at the rate of 17,000 new members a year, but the NRA felt that this was insufficient, an inadequate inroad into 'the degeneration from weapons to games' which the continued spread of golf and badminton represented.[143] The membership base seems to have been rather more limited than the gross figures suggest, because many Territorial soldiers were using the clubs as sporting and social extensions of their local companies. One crack shot, Private C. Wirgman of the London Scottish, belonged to four rifle clubs when not practising as a West End doctor; the NRA *Journal* regarded him as by no means untypical.[144] All the members were expected to develop range skills, which they did against conventional circular targets. When Lord Derby suggested in 1910 that these should be augmented or even replaced by figure targets if government aid was to be forthcoming the NRA dithered and postponed a decision. It feared a sharp public reaction against overt militarism.[145]

Although Bisley could be held up as a model, the number of competitors was falling by 1910. It was too expensive for most members to find the time, and it had come to bear as much relationship to ordinary shooting as Wimbledon or Eastbourne to recreational lawn tennis. It also found itself trapped in the tensions of its own middle-class membership, claiming in 1912 that ranges should be opened on Sundays because most junior clerks, the bulk of the Territorials, had very limited weekend leisure.[146] In areas where outdoor shooting competed for land with other sports it usually lost to the more powerful demands of golf, which the NRA could see only as prompting the end of empire. The rate of club growth had slowed down noticeably by 1913, with 1,529 altogether representing a rise of only sixteen over the previous year. Of the total, 728 were in London and the Home Counties, Yorkshire had 107, Lancashire sixty. The only sizeable non-industrial membership outside the south-east was in Lincolnshire, with thirty-two.[147]

To many it seemed that the justification of play by nationalism was to the detriment of both: in a leader in February 1914 *The Times* argued that patriotism was too serious a business for amusement, that proper separate spheres should be maintained, different purposes recognised.[148] But sport as an end in itself became increasingly difficult to justify, and the older assumptions of preparation and progression were only too clearly expressed in the enthusiasm with which many greeted the onset of the 'Greater Game' in August 1914. Norman Vance has suggested that war brought back a lost sense of purpose to the upper middle classes.[149] In her brilliant study *The Children of the Souls*, the Grenfells and their circle who moved with confident unease around the borders between the upper professional and aristocratic worlds, Jeanne Mackenzie has shown how rapidly the enthusiasm for war in Europe spread. The skills Julian Grenfell had acquired in pig-sticking would surely be transferred easily to chasing the Hun.[150] When the British Expeditionary Force went to France one of its officers could write back to *Horse and Hound* that:

> the individual superiority of the Briton over the Hun is due to our natural love for sports, and of all sports surely hunting is the finest for teaching self-confidence, quick action and cool-headedness.[151]

It certainly produced courage, but to little military advantage. The sportsmen left at home or not yet joined up were caught up in war fever. Attempts to smother past internecine differences with a blanket of patriotism had only limited success. Inevitably, perhaps, it was golfers who were accused of exploiting the crisis and hoarding. There were widespread rumours that a Sussex golf club had laid in £150 worth of dry goods.[152] In Bexhill on Sea, whilst the captain of the Tradesmen's Cricket Club demanded the suspension of the summer season in favour of action, dancing and golfing and motor-biking went on regardless. The master of the Southdown Hunt justified preparation for the coming season, despite the volunteering of many of his field, on the grounds that 'We are not going out for sport . . . it is a case of war against foxes.'[153]

With a short war expected, a strong case was advanced for sport's being maintained, although there was also a widely canvassed opinion in 1914 that the expected brevity of the conflict justified one season's suspension of sport. When Lord Roberts attacked golfers who continued their game as if nothing had changed *Golf Monthly* replied that it provided employment and killed time as well as having money-raising potential for war charities.[154] The same magazine looked forward confidently to an expected post-war spread of golf in imperial Russia, for which a new syndicate was trying to raise £30,000 in December 1914. When it celebrated the part played by 'the Niblick Brigade' in Kitchener's army it was noticeable that it was golf's professionals rather than amateurs who were mentioned.[155]

It took some time for the new pattern of warfare to emerge and longer for it to deaden some of the wilder language of play ascribed to it. *Badminton* expected cavalry breakthroughs as a justification of the number of horses being given to remount depots by huntsmen.[156] More perceptive was F. A. M. Webster's *Badminton* article suggesting that cyclists would replace cavalry.[157] Most sporting journals found writers in the early months ready to extol the contribution of each activity to the battlefield. It was not long before these turned into collections of obituaries as the 'lost generation' of sporting subalterns died. As the war progressed, some sports survived despite material shortages. Dunlop continued to produce golf balls in order to keep 2,000 women employed.[158] There was some considerable justification, since slightly demanding physical activity proved of considerable value in helping convalescent officers prepare to return to the trenches.

Clubs raised money for war work and provided tea and entertainment for troops at home; some, as at St George's Hill, offered their luxurious clubhouses as Red Cross hospitals.[159] Many on the east coast in particular found their links taken up with defences or ploughed up for cereal production. There were even new sports. In Sussex stoolball was revived as a game for officers convalescing in the Brighton pavilion: wearing episcopal gaiters and hat, but in shirtsleeves, Bishop Winnington-Ingram played in a match against a local team.[160]

The wholesale bloodshed of the western front and the aftermath of the Somme may have deadened some of the sporting enthusiasm which had taken the early sportsmen to Flanders, but they did little to check the continued importance of sporting metaphors among middle-class men. The jingoism of sporting competition proved stronger than the questioning. When the war ended the insistence that it had been English sporting virtues which had eventually defeated the Hun demonstrated just how far sport had become ingrained in male middle-class English life.[161]

Notes

1 *The Times*, 17 April 1912; Girouard, *Camelot*, 2 ff.
2 R. Huntford, *Scott and Amundsen* (1979), 243.
3 *Ibid.*
4 See Wiener, *English Culture*, and A. L. Friedberg, *The Weary Titan: Britain and the Experience of Relative Decline, 1895–1905* (Princeton, 1988).
5 Shearman, *Athletics*, 241.
6 Collier, *England and the English*, 233–4.
7 I. J. Pitman, 'Recreation and games', in E. Barker (ed.), *The Character of England* (Oxford, 1947), 446.
8 Earl of Wilton, *On the Sports and Pursuits of the English as bearing upon their National Character* (1867), 17.
9 J. Paget, 'Recreation', *Nineteenth Century*, December 1883, 939.
10 *Baily's Magazine* (1906), 346 ff.; *Sporting Celebrities*, January 1890, 1; Sargent, *Thoughts upon Sport*, 420; *The Barge* (Oxford, 1905).
11 Collier, *England and the English*, 246–7.
12 A. C. Benson, *From a College Window* (1908), 266.
13 *Physical Education*, March 1911.
14 Whitney, 'Evolution of the country club', 16.
15 *Truth*, 11 November 1908, 1144; *Badminton Magazine*, 39 (1914), 253 ff.
16 P. A. Vaile, 'Where John Bull fails', *C. B. Fry's Magazine* (1906), 535.
17 *Truth*, November 1908, 1080.
18 E. Weber, 'Pierre de Coubertin and the introduction of organised sport in France', *Journal of Contemporary History* (1970), 18.
19 P. de Coubertin, 'Why I revived the Olympic Games', *Fortnightly Review*, LXXXIV (1908), 110 ff.
20 *Fortnightly Review*, LIX (1896), 944.
21 T. A. Cook, 'The lesson of the Olympic Games', *Baily's Magazine*, July 1906, 35; R. Cohen, 'The forgotten Olympics', *Spectator*, 22 September 1988.
22 T. A. Cook, 'The Olympic Games in London', *Baily's Magazine*, February 1908, 116.
23 Cook, *Olympic Games*, 132 ff.
24 J. A. Cooper, 'Olympic Games', *Nineteenth Century*, June 1908.
25 *Truth*, 22 January 1908.
26 *Baily's Magazine*, September 1908, 215 ff.
27 British Olympic Council, *Official Report of the Fourth Olympiad* (1908); Victoria County History, *Middlesex*, 2 (1911), 295 ff.
28 *Truth*, 9 September 1908, 598.
29 *Truth*, 4 November 1908, 1080.

30 *Badminton Magazine*, 35 (1912), 507 ff.
31 E. B. Osborn, 'Olympic athletes', *Nineteenth Century*, July 1912, 204.
32 Lincoln, *Reminiscences*, 39.
33 *Baily's Magazine*, November 1913, 325 ff.
34 *The Times*, 20 July 1912.
35 *The Times*, 15 July 1912.
36 F. Meyrick, *Sunday Observance* (1902), 116; Lowerson, 'Sport and the Victorian Sunday'.
37 *Parliamentary Papers* (1895), HL 178, q. 1708.
38 J. A. Hessey, *Sunday: its Origin, History and Present Obligation* (1860), 333.
39 M. Arnold, *Culture and Anarchy* (1869), *passim*.
40 R. Linklater, *Sunday and Recreation: a Symposium* (1889), 43.
41 Linklater, *Sunday*, 81.
42 J. C. Powys, *Wolf Solent* (1929), 1964 edition, 77.
43 Osborn, *Lawn Tennis*, 12.
44 *Fortnightly Review*, LXXX (1906), 414.
45 *The Times*, 9 July 1913, 22 July 1914; *Truth*, 5 October 1905; Donovan, *Brain Side*, 77.
46 Lowerson, 'Brothers of the angle', 111; Duncan and Thorne, *Complete Wildfowler*, 55.
47 *Truth*, 16 September 1908; AFA, *Annual*, 1907–08.
48 O. Lancaster, *All done from Memory* (1953), 152.
49 Hillyard, *First Class Lawn Tennis*, 40.
50 Linklater, *Sunday and Recreation*, 76–7.
51 Lord's Day Observance Society (LDOS), *Occasional Papers*, January 1891.
52 *Parliamentary Papers* (1895), HL 178, q. 2588.
53 *Daily Telegraph*, 4 October 1905.
54 *Seaford and Newhaven Gazette*, 10 March 1894.
55 Leeds Golf Club, Minutes.
56 *Bexhill-on-Sea Observer*, 19, 26 February 1910.
57 *Nisbet's Golf Yearbook* (1906).
58 *Golfer's Handbook* (1913).
59 LDOS, *Occasional Papers*, February 1884.
60 Rivington, *Punting*, 45.
61 *Frederick James Furnivall*, 77 ff.
62 LDOS, *Occasional Papers*, October 1904.
63 Lincolnshire Record Office, Diary of J. R. Halkes.
64 Humber Yawl Club, *Yearbook* (Hull, 1940), 4.
65 *Rucksack Club Journal*, 1 (1907–10), 33.
66 *Hull and East Riding Athlete*, 4 December 1889.
67 *Daily Telegraph*, 11 October 1905.
68 Booth, *Life and Labour*, 167–8.
69 LDOS, *Occasional Papers*, October 1902.
70 R. B. Mathieson, 'Golf and the Church', *Golf Monthly*, January 1913, 820–1.
71 *Daily Telegraph*, 10 October 1905.
72 Booth, *Life and Labour*, 167–8.
73 LDOS, *Occasional Papers*, April 1906.
74 S. H. Jeyes, 'Our gentlemanly failures', *Fortnightly Review*, 61 (1897), 387 ff.
75 Quoted in J. H. Buckley, *The Triumph of Time* (Cambridge, Mass; 1967), 80.
76 Jeyes, 'Gentlemanly failures'.

77 *Race Builder* (1903), 276.
78 T. Jeal, *Baden-Powell* (1989), 358–9.
79 C. Kingsley, *Health and Education* (1874), 1 ff.
80 London Playing Fields Committee, *First Annual Report*, May 1891, 18.
81 *Parliamentary Papers* (1904), XXXII, 281.
82 *New Review*, XVI (1896), 42.
83 A. Sargent *et al.*, *The Athletic Sports* (1898), 4.
84 W. Collins, *Man and Wife* (1873 edition), 148.
85 Vance, *Sinews*, 189.
86 Vaile, *Wake up, England*, 49.
87 *Truth*, 8 August 1906.
88 Club Cricketers' Charity Fund, *Official Handbook* (1911), 55.
89 A. J. Balfour, *Essays, Speculative and Political* (1920), 1 ff.
90 Lehmann *et al.*, *Rowing*, 129–30.
91 Escott, *Social Transformations*, 414.
92 F. G. Aflalo, 'Statesmen who were sportsmen', *Fortnightly Review*, LXXV (1904), 864 ff.
93 *Truth*, 7 August 1907.
94 E. Miles, *An Alphabet of Athletics* (1904), 34.
95 *Physical Education*, September 1905.
96 *Physical Education*, May 1906.
97 P. Adam, *La Morale des sports* (Paris, 1907), 30–1.
98 Collier, *England and the English*, 271.
99 *Badminton Magazine*, 36 (1913), 65.
100 A. White, *Efficiency and Empire* (1901), 107.
101 Shadwell, *Industrial Efficiency*, 500; P. L. Payne, *British Entrepreneurship in the Nineteenth Century* (1974), 11.
102 Shadwell, *Industrial Efficiency*, 653.
103 *Truth*, 12 December 1901.
104 Morris, *Romance of Commerce*, 117 ff.
105 *C. B. Fry's Magazine*, 5 (1906–07), 172 ff.
106 *Saturday Review*, 2 April 1910, 424.
107 *Bexhill-on-Sea Observer*, 17 August 1912.
108 *The Times*, 29 December 1910.
109 *The Times*, 14 March 1914.
110 *The Times*, 2, 16 June 1914.
111 *C. B. Fry's Magazine*, V (1906), 3, 59.
112 *C. B. Fry's Magazine*, 3 (1905), 72; see G. R. Searle, *The Quest for National Efficiency: a Study in British Politics and Political Thought, 1899–91* (Oxford, 1961), 57.
113 Collier, *England and the English*, 243.
114 H. Graham, *Punch*, 25 August 1909, 136, also in his *Ruthless Rhymes for Heartless Homes* (1909); A. J. Morris, 'And is the Kaiser coming for tea?', *Moirae*, 5 (Ulster, 1980), 33 ff.
115 Saki, 'When William came', in *The Complete Works of Saki* (1976), 733.
116 Freddie Tait (1870–1900), see D. Steel, *The Guinness Book of Golf Facts and Feats* (1982), 238, H. G. Hutchinson, *Golf and Golfers* (1900), 143–9, and H. Vardon, *The Complete Golfer* (1905), 260.
117 Aflalo, *Fifty Leaders*, 18.
118 Donovan, *Brain Side*, 64.

119 Collier, *England and the English*, 243–4.
120 *Humanitarian*, February 1910.
121 *Humanitarian*, December 1904.
122 *Baily's Magazine*, March 1909, 249.
123 F. Cowper, *Yachting and Yacht Cruising for Amateurs* (1911), 5.
124 Humber Yawl Club Yearbook, *Yearbook* (1904).
125 E. E. Williams, *Made in Germany* (1896), 1973 edition.
126 *Baily's Magazine*, September 1894, 150.
127 *Baily's Magazine*, September 1897, 218–19.
128 *Badminton Magazine*, X (1900), 107 ff.; 7 (1898), 426.
129 T. Travers, 'The hidden army: structural problems in the British officer corps, 1900–18', *Journal of Contemporary History*, 17 (1982), 523 ff.
130 *Badminton Magazine*, X (1900), 91.
131 *Field*, 14 June 1902.
132 *Cassell's Book of Sports and Pastimes* (1907), preface.
133 *Ibid.*
134 P. Dennis, *The Territorial Army, 1906–40* (1987); H. Cunningham, *The Volunteer Force: a Social and Political history, 1859–1908* (1975).
135 Z. Steiner, 'Views of war', *Moirae*, 5 (1980), 14 ff.; G. Forrest, *The Life of Lord Roberts, KC, VC* (1914), 338.
136 Steiner, 'Views', 339.
137 *C. B. Fry's Magazine*, 6 (1906), 539.
138 Lord Roberts, 'Arms and the Spartan', *C. B. Fry's Magazine*, 9 (1908), 4–5.
139 Martin Cobbett, *Sporting Notions, of Present Days and Past* (Edinburgh, 1908), 322.
140 A. P. Humphrey and T. F. Freemantle, *History of the National Rifle Association during its First Fifty Years, 1859 to 1909* (Cambridge, 1914).
141 Leeds Reference Library, *Leeds Rifle Club Rules* (1900).
142 *C. B. Fry's Magazine*, 4 (1906), 299.
143 *National Rifle Association Journal*, July 1910.
144 *National Rifle Association Journal*, December 1910.
145 NRA, *Proceedings*, 1910.
146 *National Rifle Association Journal*, January 1912.
147 NRA, *Bulletin* (1913).
148 *The Times*, 13 February 1914.
149 Vance, *Sinews*, 201 ff.
150 J. Mackenzie, *The Children of the Souls* (1986).
151 Quoted in *Horse and Hound*, 30 March 1984.
152 *Bexhill-on-Sea Observer*, 8 August 1914.
153 *Bexhill-on-Sea Observer*, 8, 29 August 1914.
154 *Golf Monthly*, October 1914, 584.
155 *Ibid.*
156 *Badminton Magazine*, 40 (1914), 300, 305, 345.
157 *Badminton Magazine*, 307.
158 *Golf Monthly*, 9 May 1919.
159 *Golf Monthly*, September 1914, 490; 9 May 1919.
160 M. S. Russell-Goggs, 'Stoolball in Sussex', *Sussex County Magazine*, II (1928), 31 ff.; W. W. Grantham, *Stoolball and how to Play it* (1919).
161 *Fishing Gazette*, 16 August 1919; for the prevalence of language see also W. J. Reader, *At Duty's Call* (Manchester, 1988).

Index

Broxbourne, 117
Buchan, J., 154
Buckinghamshire, 10, 136
Buckley, Mr Justice, 239
Budleigh Salterton, 102
Burberry, 131
Burnham on Crouch, 51
 Yacht Club, 51
business, 225–57
Butler, Lady E., 261
butlers, 197
Byfleet, 135, 220, 247

Caddies, 150–1, 198–203, 218, 274–5, 284
Caddies Aid Association, 201–3
Caernarvon, 50
Calcutta, 159
Cambridge Reivew, 160
Cambridge University, 3, 4, 56, 70, 71, 73, 74, 84, 86, 90, 120, 174, 241, 262, 263, 274, 280, 281
Camelot, 68, 107, 284
Campbell, Sir G., 134
Canada, 25, 126, 161, 266
Cannadine, D., 23
Canons Park, 243–4
Cantile, Dr J., 206
capital formation, 226–51
Captain, 253
Carholme Golf Club, 146
Carlton Club, 235
Carr, R., 33
cars, 31, 86, 219
cartoons, 128, 140–1
Casting Club de France, 48
Cavalry, 37, 194, 287, 293
Cavendish Club, 110
CB Fry's Magazine, 91, 139, 141, 177, 203, 225, 252–3, 283, 284, 285, 289, 290
Central Council for Physical Recreation, 6
Chambers Journal, 226
Chandos, Duke of, 243
charity, 24, 162–80, 191–203, 248, 293
Charity Organisation Society, 201
Charnwood Forest, 102
Charterhouse, 253
Chavasse twins, 166
Cheesman, W., 35
 Mrs W., 35, 210
Chelmsford, 236
Cheltenham, 102, 155
Cheshire, 58
Chicago, 10
Chichester, 114, 135
Chichester, Earl of, 274
Childers, E., 51
Chiswick, 116
chivalry, 68, 107, 201
Chorley Wood Golf Club, 145
Christ, Jesus, 91, 270, 276

Christianity, 55, 64, 65, 74, 80, 86, 91, 269–77, 279
Christopherson, S., 213
Church Congress, 205
churches and chapels, 12, 15, 65, 109–10, 128, 132, 155, 268–77
Churchill guns, 232
City of London, 8, 31, 43, 45, 87–8, 129, 134, 146, 177, 228, 235, 237, 238, 243–6
civil engineers, 7
Civil War, 244
Clapham, 148
Clarendon Commission, 3
Claridge's Hotel, 219
Clarion cycling clubs, 116
claypigeon shooting, 40
clergy (Anglican), 7, 9, 10, 56, 64, 73, 80, 86, 87, 101, 132, 156, 160, 217, 268–77
Clerk, 135
clerks, 11, 13, 17, 30, 31, 54, 68, 79, 88, 90, 118, 130, 131, 176, 256, 279, 281, 289, 291
Cleveland, Duke of, 133
Clifton, 85, 102, 255
Climax Reel Works, 230
Climbers' Club, 58
climbing, *see* mountaineering
clothes, 24, 34–5, 41, 50, 59, 129, 214, 293
clubs, 9, 18, 21, 22, 23, 49, 52–9, 64, 68, 72–90, 95–121, 125–51, 166, 172–5, 182–3, 195–220, 240–51, 280, 291–2
Cobden family, 42
Cogswell and Harrison, 232
Collie J. N., 58
Collier, Price, 226, 281, 284, 286
Collins, G., 245
Collins, Wilkie, 279
Colt, H. S., 136, 142, 147, 179–80, 200–1, 242, 244, 245
commons, 144–51, 247, 273
Commons, House of, 70
Compleat Angler, 255
Complete Wildfowler, 41
Conan Doyle, A., 37
Congregationalism, 65, 276–7
Conservatives, 280
Cook, T. A., 265–7
Cooper, J. Astley, 266
Cooper, Wm, Ltd, 135, 236
Corinthian Football Club, 83, 183–4
Cornwall, 84–5
corset, 207
Cost of Sport, 15, 255
Coubertin, P. de, 264–5
country clubs, 97, 136, 244–5
Country Life, 25
Country Sport, 254
County Chemical Co, 239
Court
 Appeal, 239
 Chancery, 37

Index

Index

Index

Index

Sphairistike, 103
Sporting Mirror, 164
Sports Council, 6
squash, 104, 240, 244
staghounds, 32, 36
Stamford Bridge, 90
Stamp, J. C., 13
Stanley, A., 52
Stapley, T. K., 33
Steel, A. G., 78, 171
Stephen, L., 3, 19, 20, 55, 58, 73-4, 87
Stewart, Cdr., 239
Stobart, M. A., 256
Stockbridge, 45
  Fishery Association, 45
  Fishing Club, 45
stockbrokers, jobbers, 9, 51, 175
Stock Exchange, 9, 139
Stockholm, 261
Stoddart, A. E., 110
Stogden, J., 57
stoolball, 293
Strand, 253
Strange, A., 53
Streatham, 130, 148
Strong, H. A., 76
subscriptions, 32, 35, 42, 43, 44, 45, 57,
  77, 89, 107, 116, 133, 143, 149, 192, 193,
  240-51, 291
suburbs, 16, 22, 34-5, 81, 85, 97-121, 130,
  148-50, 176-8, 232, 242-51, 268-77, 290
Suffolk, 41, 54, 114
  and Berkshire, Earl of, 255
suffragettes, 219
Sunday, 40, 50, 86, 117, 130, 163, 119-200,
  268-77, 291
Sunningdale Golf Club, 137, 200, 242
Surbiton, 177-8
surgeons, 7, 52
Surrey, 10, 16, 71, 113, 125, 130, 135, 136, 137,
  143, 147, 149-51, 172-4, 220, 243, 244, 245,
  247, 276, 290
Surrey Athlete, 254
Sussex, 8, 10, 35, 71, 87, 102, 103, 108,
  112-13, 133, 173, 210, 274, 292, 293
Sweden, 168, 266
swimming, 90, 168-9, 213, 268
Swimming Federation of GB, 168-9
Switzerland, 55-7, 211, 237, 284
syndicates, 39, 46, 191-2, 240-51

table tennis, 25, 110-11
Table Tennis Association, 110-11
Tait, F., 286
tarpon fishing, 210
Tatler, 25
Taunton Commission, 3, 73
Taylor, A. J. P., 111, 218
teachers, 11, 13, 68, 131, 169
teams, 64-90, 172-5, 210-13, 228, 289

Teddington, 85
Territorial Army, 288-91
test matches, 71, 80, 172-3
Thames Rowing Club, 87, 159
Thomas, D. W., and T. Donnelly, 236
Thompson, E. P., 6
Thompson, F. M. L., 16
Thomson, J. M. A., 58
Thomson, E. A. C., 81
Three Men in a Boat, 54
Thring of Uppingham, 73
time, 15-16, 128, 129-30, 150, 273-4
Times, 143, 148, 154, 173, 200, 239, 261, 268,
  283, 292
Times Literary Supplement, 52, 251
Titanic, 261
tobogganing, 57
Tonbridge, 79, 228
Tooting, 148
Topham, H. W., 56
Torquay, 49
tradesmen, 73, 242
Trafalgar, 283
Trafalgar Club, 214
Travers, T., 287
Trent Bridge, 78
Trinity College, Cambridge, 71, 74
Trinity Hall, Cambridge, 73-4
Trollope, A., 4, 31, 208, 234
trophies, 23, 116, 162-80
trout, 43-8, 242
Truro, Bishop of, 86
Truth, 75, 86, 110, 140, 142, 169, 172, 174,
  177-8, 185-6, 251, 264, 266, 267, 283
Twickenham, 4, 16, 84

uniforms, 23, 34, 35, 100, 111, 117, 145, 201,
  287, 289
universities, 10, 56, 65, 67, 68, 71-7, 86-8,
  90, 100-1, 118, 157-9, 165, 169, 182-6, 212,
  267, 289
University College, London, 75-6
Unwin, T. Fisher, 256
Uppingham, 73, 240
utopias, 141, 257

Vachell, H. A., 79
Vaile, P. A., 178, 205, 279
Vamplew, W., 5, 31, 174, 240
Vance, N., 155, 292
Van Oss, S. F., 233
van Straubenzee, Revd. A. J., 52
Vardon, H., 140
Veblen, T., 207
Vesper Club, 161-2
Vesta Rowing Club, 161
Victoria, Queen, 210, 235
Victoria County Histories, 125, 147
Vitai Lampada, 4
voluntaryism, 21, 266

309